武士道

THE BUSHIDO OF BITCOIN

EDITED BY

JOHN CARTER

WRITTEN BY

ALEKSANDAR SVETSKI

FOREWORD BY

ROSS STEVENS

© Bushido book

All rights reserved.

Edited by JOHN CARTER

Typesetting by Josefina Alonso

Cover design by Clara Fai

ISBN 9798991756600 B&W Hardcover
        9798343790603 Paperback
        9798991756617 Color Hardcover

To my future sons and daughters.
May these words forever inspire you to live courageously and free.

"Aleksandar has created something that is truly hard to do today: a unique bitcoin book. It'll challenge you, and there will likely be things that you agree and disagree with, but you'll walk away from it having tested and probably updated your worldview. My favorite part was his contrarian analysis and elevation of beauty and the etymologies of multiple virtues"

Lyn Alden, Author of "Broken Money"

""The Bushido of Bitcoin" explores historical frameworks from governance, religion, and war to identify models that have successfully shaped societies. In order to achieve meaningful goals, we need clear objectives, an understanding of complex systems, and lessons from history. This book gives readers real historical examples and a framework for creating a peaceful and prosperous future. It serves as both a guide and challenge to those willing to apply these lessons in their own lives."

Mark Moss, Author and Host of the Mark Moss Show

"We live in a rapidly changing world where virtues like 'honour' and 'duty' have been sacrificed at the altar of expressive individualism and faux victimhood. 'The Bushido of Bitcoin' draws from ancient wisdom to offer insight on how to navigate our modern times."

Zuby, Rapper, Podcaster and Author

Acknowledgements

I'd like to thank John Carter for both his assistance in editing the book and the inspiration I took from his writings. I could not have written it to this level of quality without you. If you have not taken the opportunity to explore his work, this should be your next endeavor. Special thanks also to Louis Pomaret Cañadas for his last minute editorial assistance and making sure the language, etymology and definitions were on point. Also Eric Brown for helping me get the book across the line in the end, and John Goddard for some of the early inspiration on the Sovereign Cross story.

I want to thank Ross Stevens for not only writing an incredible foreword and the support he's given this book and my other projects, but more importantly, for being an example of the kind of man and leader this world needs more of. Thank you for everything Ross.

I'd like to also thank a series of incredible people who backed the crowdfund. Your contributions made this possible, and I hope the book does all of you justice. I am deeply grateful for the support.

Francisco Tomé Costa and Pierre Porthaux. You are at the top of the list. Thank you. Alan Lane, Rachel, J. Alexander, Noha Simsaa, Antonio Lombardo, The Brandon Cook Family, Christian, Benjamin J. Dion, Seth Long, oosplatoo, The Singer Family, Kevin A. Madsen, and Robin Choong. You are all not only forever memorialized in the book, but recipients of the special, leather edition. Only 21 people in the world will have a copy of that.

Travis Paul, Jason Fowler, Bruce Fenton, Michael B. Maxey, Josh Peters, Grayson and Lawson Niles, Nick Kryptr, Gary Swindale, Joseph Leon Echeverria, Simon-Benjamin Lariviere, Kim "Mo" Mahoney, Jacob Cottrill, Craig C Jonas, MD, Garth, Zachary Hollinshead, Hank Harris, John Montoya, Chuck R. Bell, and The Commoner. You are all modern Samurai, and I will forever honor your contribution by continuing to write and produce meaningful content.

I want to thank some of the thinkers, authors and content creators who inspired my work along the way, including Jash Dholani, Chad Crowley, Jerr, UberBoyo, Steven Pressfield and Dan Carlin. Of course, I must give thanks to the greats, including Inazo Nitobe, James Clavell, Ayn Rand, Friedrich Nietzsche, Oswald Spengler, Hans Hermann Hoppe, Thomas Sowell and many others who I've referenced throughout.

I'd like to give thanks to the great leaders and warriors throughout history whose lives inspired me, including; Alexander The Great of Macedon, Leonidas I of Sparta, Jesus Christ, Flavius Aetius of late Rome, Attila the Hun, Ieyasu Tokugawa, the great Shogun of Japan, Napoleon Bonaparte, Julius Caesar and many more who I've not the space to list. Also special thanks to Satoshi Nakamoto for being the kind of man who embodied through his actions and foresight, the virtues discussed in the book.

I want to thank my wife who continues to inspire me with her devotion, loyalty and patience. You are as wild as you are beautiful. Now that this is finished, I can pay you more attention.. *"Just for you know"* ;)

Finally, I'd like to thank all of you for taking the time to read this book. May it inspire you to live a life of greatness and virtue. May you and your descendants continue to build an inspiring, beautiful and ascendant world. And may the Warrior Spirit forever burn bright inside you.

Aleksandar Svetski
September, 2024

Contents

Appendix   **477**

About the Author   **481**

BONUS CHAPTER: Beauty Will Save the World   **487**

"Better to be a Warrior in a Garden, than to be a Gardener in a War."

Unknown

Foreword

By Ross Stevens

This is a book for heroes, unapologetic seekers of excellence, and those convinced their destiny is greatness.

All heroes begin life as ordinary people, but something changes along the way. Heroes turn their gaze upward, ignore probabilities, and summon courage.

Consider the incalculable bravery of those born-ordinary people who extraordinarily signed our nation's birth certificate, the *Declaration of Independence*. The document itself was a death warrant. Signing it was committing treason. If captured, any signer would be hanged. Some were, along with their families. The *Declaration*'s closing words – "we mutually pledge to each other our Lives, our Fortunes, and our sacred Honor" – were meant literally.

Every one of us underestimates the courage of the Founding Fathers. How can I be so sure? We know the outcome of the Revolution. The Founders did not. The great historian David McCulloch once said, "the hardest thing about writing history is getting people to forget they know how the story ends."

Ordinary blacksmiths, bookmakers, and farmers, the Founders did not know how the war would end – they were losing badly in 1776 – nor the sustainability of their revolutionary political philosophy. Yet *centuries* later, we still know the names of our blood-soaked, freedom-seeking heroes.

In spirit, *Bushido* picks up where the *Declaration* left off, honoring other legendary warrior cultures – Samurai, Knights, Spartans, others – by unearthing the specific virtues they had in common. Bushido teaches us that virtue implies *a way of being*, morality *in action*, not merely words flung without consequence from the safety of a keyboard or an ivory tower.

Studying the virtues of these warrior cultures (below), it is no wonder why – *millennia* later – we still know the names "Samurai" or "Spartan", and regularly re-hydrate their lives in books and movies.

Courage: not just know what is right, act upon it and bear the consequences

Compassion: suffer with those you love, with patience and humility see the world from the perspective of another

Respect: due regard for the fitness of things, respect for tradition, custom, and earned hierarchy

Justice: fair and righteous to uphold moral character

Veracity and Sincerity: without this politeness is farce, speech and deed must be one and the same

Honor: vivid consciousness of personal dignity and worth, honest with oneself

Loyalty: the glue that binds relationships of both love and respect, perform your duty even if it means you give your life

Self-control: the discipline to adhere to this code under all circumstances, whether it is hard or easy, in the presence of others or alone.

Responsibility: bear the consequences of your actions, fulfill your duties, own the impact of your decisions on yourself, others, and society

Excellence: separation from average, expands boundaries, the driving force behind progress and beauty

Enter Bitcoin, the most potent device ever invented for transferring wealth from the impatient to the patient. The soaring and inexorable socio-economic success Bitcoin delivers to its hodlers, however, merely provides the foundation for *Bushido*'s core message: **real wealth comes from the virtues we choose to live by.** Courage and cowardice are equally contagious. Choose wisely.

The Last Stand

Powered by ascendant values, **Bitcoiners represent the last stand against nihilism**, a battle we absolutely must not lose. To prepare, we must train,

train, and then train some more.

> *"There was a footrace held each year among the boys of Sparta. They had to run ten miles, barefoot, carrying a mouthful of water and weren't allowed to swallow the water, but instead had to spit it out at the end of the race."*
>
> The Bushido of Bitcoin

If we instituted this training today, I can already hear the "that's child abuse!"-screams emanating from a generation of soft-bodied helicopter parents, who never fought in war and have never even felt true physical danger in their entire lives. *Bushido*-trained Bitcoiners would counter, "what better way to teach self-control and restraint to the future warrior class?"

As anti-nihilists, how would *Bushido*-trained Bitcoiners teach that that actions have consequences?

> *"If a Spartan youth failed to show courage in battle, his fiancé would abandon him. The magistrate would not permit him to marry. If he was married, he and his wife were forbidden to have children. If the warrior has sisters of marriageable age, their suitors would be compelled to part from them. The man's whole family would be shunned."*
>
> Steven Pressfield, *The Warrior Ethos*

What do you pledge allegiance to? What is your duty or mission in life? Who and what do you love enough to go and fight for? What will you sacrifice when the time comes to pay the price for your beliefs?

Virtuous Warriors

Amidst socio-economic separation that will accelerate as the fiat money printer's decibel level brrr's louder and louder – as it must, driven by feeble, self-interested, "not on my watch" central bankers printing recklessly so the credit bubble bursts well after their time in office – *Bushido* reminds Bitcoiners that virtuous warriors are compassionate, treasure worthy adversaries, and never take advantage of the weak. How you win is just as important as that you win.

In the immediate, chaotic aftermath of the FTX implosion in November 2022, with million-dollar bills figuratively lying on the ground for those who knew where to kneel and reach, I wrote the following to my Stone Ridge colleagues under the header "What to expect":

> In times like these, character emerges. Unfortunately, for so many it won't be pretty. They will desperately cling to ephemeral notions of their (past) status, and lash out in various ways. As a form of psychological self-protection, you will see people be arrogant, aggressive, short tempered, and pinball from topic to topic. Their actions will create and exacerbate their own fragility.
>
> Professionally, it will be very easy to take financial advantage of these people. If you work at Stone Ridge, **you are forbidden from doing so**.

Bushido inspires Bitcoiners to adopt a similar mindset: once in power, do not double-down on the State's dishonorable maximization of the distance between its actions and the consequences those actions. Usher in a renaissance of responsibility. Lead from the front. As virtuous warriors, conquer – yes, absolutely conquer and take control – but conquer with compassion.

A student once asked the great anthropologist Marget Mead what she considered the earliest sign of civilization in a culture? Fish hooks? Clay bowls? Sharpened stones? Mead said:

> The first sign of civilization in an ancient culture is evidence of a person with a broken and healed femur. In the rest of the animal kingdom, if you break your leg, you die. You

cannot run from danger, go to the river to drink water, or hunt for food. You become fresh meat for predators. No animal survives a broken leg long enough for the bone to heal. A broken femur that healed is proof that someone took the time to stay with the one who fell, healed the wound, and cared for the person until they recovered. Helping somebody going through difficulties is the starting point of civilization.

No-coiners have broken femurs, for now. As tempting as it may be, resist frustration and anger at being slowed down by them, even though you are. *Bushido* inspires Bitcoin warriors to choose compassion and patience. Satoshi cleared the path, so we know the direction of travel. It will be worth it in the end.

When in the Course of Human Events

The *Declaration* taught us to reject unearned serfdom. *Bushido* teaches us to reject unearned guilt. In 1776, the Founders did not know the outcome of their war against the British, but they had a hunch. We Bitcoiners do not know the outcome of our war against fiat-induced nihilism, but we have a hunch.

Health warning: victory requires rejection and avoidance of the manufactured darkness flickering across our screens, competing for our precious attention. In reality, we live in a wondrous age. And with Bitcoin available to all, a self-evident truth, I am limitlessly optimistic.

In the *Declaration*, when Jefferson wrote "Life, Liberty and the Pursuit of Happiness", he inspirationally cautioned a nation against too timid a placement of the bar on our limits. In *Bushido*, Svetski roars that we Bitcoiners do ourselves a disservice by putting the bar anywhere.

Ross L. Stevens
Founder & CEO, Stone Ridge Holdings Group
September 2024

Why is this book necessary?

I was on a Twitter spaces a while back and someone asked: *"Another Bitcoin book? What the hell hasn't been written about Bitcoin yet"*?

Well… this is my response.

This book is not about the history of money, or even about Bitcoin *per se*. It's about the human spirit and what it will choose to do in a time of civilisational confusion and decline.

I'll make the assumption that Bitcoin is not only going to survive and 'win', but that its advent or discovery will be incredibly important on a civilisational scale. My goal is not to tell you how it will do this, why it's superior as money to fiat or other cryptocurrencies, nor will I dispel myths about its energy usage. If you're interested in that, the references section at the end of this book will point you in the right direction.

My goal with this book is to look for answers to bigger questions:

> *"What happens when we win?"*
>
> *"What does the world look like on a Bitcoin Standard?"*
>
> *"Does wealth make civilization soft, and thereby weaken it?"*
>
> *"Does power corrupt, or is weakness corruption?"*
>
> *"Can a weak man be a good man?"*
>
> *"Is a weak civilisation a moral one?"*
>
> *"… If not, how can an individual maintain morality and virtue in the face of immense wealth and material comfort?"*

If Bitcoin does win, it will no doubt have an incredible impact on humanity. The question that logically follows is: *"will those who hold the bulk of the bitcoin be virtuous or corruptible? Will they be builders or destroyers?"*

There is evidence that Bitcoin helps to lower people's time preference and encourages them to think more long-term, orienting them toward their full potential. But it's very early days: we're less than 15 years into the emergence of this global, technologically-driven socio-economic phenomenon, and decades from the realization of its full economic and social potential.

It's hard to predict how members of today's lower-middle class will behave when they're part of tomorrow's elite class: the obstacles along the road will only become apparent as we move forward.

I should note that irrespective of the 'risks' this path entails, it is of course still orders of magnitude better than having some parasitic class lord it over the rest of the world by virtue of owning a money printer and paying thugs to enforce their arbitrary decrees. The status quo is anti-life and parasitic. Instead of producing, it consumes, like a vortex into a black hole of nihilism. At the very least, Bitcoin is a game of strong, unbreakable rules and under such a standard we are more likely to orient ourselves toward excellence and to create a new, life-aligned status quo..

We all owe it to our descendants to consciously and actively become the best versions of ourselves - which goes for Bitcoiners in particular, and especially yours truly. I've created a bit of a reputation online as an asshole, and while at times I revel in the notoriety, I've come to realize that my behavior has been honest but immature at best, arrogant at worst.

The distance between my thoughts and the keyboard has oftentimes been short, and while I have pointed out injustices and truths, much of what I've written has been the ramblings of a young man angry about the state of the world, and in many ways frustrated by his inability to fix or change it.

This book is my attempt to challenge and hold myself to a higher standard of discourse and behavior, to contribute something of greater **quality** than just another Twitter tirade, as well as some inspiration for others to do the same. I will always remain someone who challenges the status quo but moving forward, with these words as my witness, I will aim to do it better, and embody the principles and virtues discussed in this book.

I hope you too will find value in the pages that follow. If the content resonates with you and you wish to spread the message, by all means take screenshots or quotes along the way and tag me on any social media so that I can amplify the message and together, we may build a stronger, more inspiring narrative for the future.

Who is this book for?

They say there are three kinds of people in this world: Those who make things happen, those who watch things happen, and those who wonder wtf happened.

This book is not for the latter.

I wrote this book first and foremost, for myself. I don't say that in a selfish or self-aggrandizing way, but from a place of genuine curiosity and interest. This is the book I wish someone else had written so I could read it myself, and since it wasn't, it's what I knew I would take pleasure in researching and writing because of how it would transform me as a person.

I wrote it because deep down I knew it was time for us to move on from pointing out what's wrong with the world, to actually doing something about it. As I went from draft to draft, I came to realize that the world is not going to hell, but is in fact ours to claim. The very act of writing pushed me from theory, into the paradigm of action.

The world did not end when Rome fell. Its demise spawned a new age, one that would integrate the Roman Apollonian-Martian spirit with the Christian soul and the warrior vitality of the Germanic, Nordic and Slavic tribes. What arose from the Roman ashes was a civilization ten thousand times more powerful.

Now, in the twilight of that civilization, something new is birthing. Something that, centuries from now will be ten thousand times more powerful again. This civilization will colonize space, in the same way our forefathers colonized the Earth. The same energy will course through the veins of our descendants, and they will do things on a scale that we can only dream of today.

I don't say this from a place of naive optimism. The pure optimist, à la Steven Pinker, is often a deer-in-the-headlights, happy-go-lucky kind of moron. I know the world has largely gone to shit. The first two drafts of this book were far more a longing for the past than this version you're reading is. But I realized along the way that the past is the past, and no amount of wishing it would "RVTURN" is going to bring it back. And even if we did, we'd end up back here again. The only way through hell is to keep on going, and if we're in a strange place today, it's not only because of "the evil people" but because the "good people" are not doing enough about it. Complaining never solved anything, it's merely the first stage. To be effective, you must be a "contrarian optimist." You need the energy and hope of an optimist, who alone can be gullible, mixed with the insight and intuition of a contrarian, who alone can be too pessimistic.

In my case, I don't like where the world is today, and my opinions are extremely unorthodox (as you'll find throughout the book), but I am very optimistic about the longer term future and our ability to influence it. If this speaks to you, and you too can sense that the future can be ten thousand times greater, not because some transhumanist weirdo said so, but because deep down, you know the human spirit is powerful enough to conquer the stupidity, ugliness, and corruption we're surrounded by today, *then this book is for you.*

> *"You're here because you know something. What you know you can't explain, but you feel it. You've felt it your entire life, that there's something wrong with the world. You don't know what it is, but it's there, like a splinter in your mind, driving you mad. It is this feeling that has brought you to me. Do you know what I'm talking about?"*
>
> Morpheus, *The Matrix*

If you can sense that you've been lied to about not only our recent history, but our ancestors and lineages; if you realize that it's not power that corrupts, but that the weak and corruptible hold power and keep you from it, *then this book is for you.*

If you're fed up with feeling helpless about the rot that has set into the world and with the ugliness it has brought forth; if you realize that beauty is so much deeper than what you've been led to believe, *then this book is for you.*

If you're sick of the HR nannies telling you that your safety is their priority, that we're all in this together, that you must ask permission to do this or that and that you should feel guilty about being an adult with a mind of your own, *then this book is for you.*

If you're done with the constant gaslighting by idiot bureaucrats telling you that black is white, that good is bad, that weak is strong, freedom is slavery, poverty is virtuous, that sickness is health, *then this book is for you.*

If you're ready to start acting, want to level up your psychology, and rekindle that fire within, *then this book is for you.*

I wrote this not for the sheep, or the NPC - for they can never be woken up - but for the lions. This is a book for those who want to lead, to build, to conquer and to produce. Warrior-leaders with the drive, energy and desire to claim space and make their dent in the universe.

Those content with living a life of average, playing the perpetual victim or the astute complainer - perhaps even all three at the same time - will likely be offended or triggered by this book. If that's you, feel free to take a pass. If equality, obedience, nihilism, compliance and complaining feed you, then by all means, keep doing what you're doing.

We are actually right where we're supposed to be at this point in civilization. The turning point that separates the lions from the sheep. It's time to make a choice, and I hope this book reinforces that choice - whatever it may be for you.

Prelude

*"Do not go gentle into that good night, Old age should burn
and rave at close of day; Rage, rage against the dying of the
light."*

Dylan Thomas, *The Poems of Dylan Thomas*

This book risks triggering some readers by weaving together ideas from
Christianity, Nietzsche, Rand, Austrian Economics, Anarcho-capitalism,
the new and old "Right", Bitcoin, Jordan Peterson, Warrior Cultures from
a pre-Christian West and of course, as the title implies, Bushido.

They will say that I am insane for trying to blend such apparently
disparate traditions because "they are at odds," because "war and freedom
don't mix," or that I am an "extremist" for quoting Evola and Spengler.

That's fine. We've all got opinions. My position is not swayed. I've
found a common thread in all of these sources and it's in their overlap
that I find truth and meaning.

I'm also aware of the fact that some of the people I quote may not have
lived up to their own ideals. Nietzsche is said to have been an incel that
wore a dress in his twilight, while Rand passed away in a public hospital.
Whether or not these claims are factual is irrelevant. The truth is that
life is hard, people are flawed, and when in the spotlight, it is easy for
spectators to point out your flaws, and ignore the rest of you. But, as
Roosevelt said, it's the "Man in the Arena" that matters - not the critic.

It takes a level of brilliance few can match to produce something like
Atlas Shrugged or *Thus Spoke Zarathustra*, especially at the time they were
written. I believe we can draw not only wisdom, but inspiration from
these people; and if not from their lives, then certainly from their work.
We can also have some compassion, because they tapped into such ideals
and truths that the juxtaposition of their lives, their life circumstances,
their environment or the age they were born in sent them mad! Imagine

having the foresight to prophesy the fall of man so vividly that you could write some of the most eloquent warnings about it, only to be cursed with having to live through and die in the age of the inevitable descent.

They may not have personally been 'the ideal', but they were able to point to it, so perhaps their grander purpose could be seen as inspiring others to embody and act out the roles of the noble hero, warrior and man-of-vitality they could only aspire to be. After all, Moses did not enter the promised land.

Our generation too will have to live not for ourselves, but fundamentally for our descendants. It's our job specifically to lay the foundation for what comes next, and something tells me that we are at a significant point in the journey of man; we inhabit an interregnum of sorts, where the age of fiat, materialist decadence, and Reddit-nihilism reaches its apogee, and simultaneously, the seeds of vitality and greatness are planted to sprout lineages that will span for centuries or more. True nobility awaits.

It's an incredible time to be alive, and as we trek the long road ahead we will have to come to terms ourselves with feelings Nietzsche and Rand had to grapple with. The interregnum will not be pretty, and we might find that the limited lifespans we each possess may not be long enough to carry us to the rainbow on the other end. What I called "Homo-Bitcoinicus", before I discovered Nietzsche's Ubermensch, is a possibility, only now that we cross a new chasm.

Do not allow your preconceived notions or opinions of the characters whose ideas I've drawn from distract you from the deeper truths in these pages.

Writing this book has been an incredible journey. It's caused me to inquire, to question, and to think. It's given me the opportunity to study human culture and psychology through a unique lens, to consider how we got here, where we might go, who we were, are, and might become, and what this deeper sense within all of us is: this sense of virtue and vitality. May it do the same for you.

A Moral Dimension to the Universe

Is there a moral dimension to the universe? Where does the soul reside? Why are we here? What is the meaning of life?

Are we here to have a physical experience, to develop a well-formed ego, to learn restraint, and do so within a moral context? Are we here to be vessels for life? Are we just spiritual beings experiencing something physical? Or are we meat for nature, nothing more than a carbon soup with trace elements?

Is this life a test to see if we can be virtuous in a realm where there exists the opportunity to do wrong, to hide, to cheat, to lie and to acquire unfair advantage? To see if we can be courageous when it is easier to be lazy, comfortable, weak and cowardly?

Might we actually be here to learn 'morality' because such a thing is not present from inside of the spirit realm? Could that be what's required for our soul to transcend the prior state into the next?

Or am I completely insane? Is this all a figment of my imagination?

Maybe.

I wish I had all the answers, but I don't. Instead I have my beliefs, first principles and a whole lot of questions - which at the very least are a pathway to better answers and approximations of what's true.

I spent most of my twenties as a raging atheist, but as I entered my thirties I began to slowly find my way back to a deeper appreciation for religion, because in whatever flavor it comes, it attempts to contend with many of these questions. Theology is a study of "what matters" and in a world so caught up in the "study of matter", it's arguably never been more important. Secularists thought we could transcend or ignore it, but instead we've found that the void left by religion would only be filled by something else which is often much uglier, shallower and less robust. It's why many atheists resemble that description (see Sam Harris).

Matthew Arnold, the Victorian poet, known for his reflections on education and critiques on a society becoming ever more secular, defined religion as "Morality touched by emotion." This is not only a beautiful description, but accurate in many ways. Religion is concerned with meaning, and much of meaning is an embodied phenomenon. It's something we feel, and without it, we find ourselves "feeling" less and less. In my opinion it's a big part of why we live in an era of unprecedented depression, nihilism and hedonism. Whatever your viewpoint on the definition or practice of religion, you cannot deny that there is an emptiness in its absence. Just go visit a church in Italy or walk through the streets built during the periods of high religion, then go find yourself a modern office or government building, and walk the streets of a new techno-city. See how each makes you feel.

I hope this book will give you a deeper appreciation and perspective of this ancient, sacred heritage of man. For those who are averse to the religious impulse, you might find that it is something we as humans cannot escape. Even atheists and scientists are religious!

> "We cannot get away from the spiritual no matter how much money we make or "stability" we acquire. At the end of the day, we search for poetry when we wish to eulogize the dead, we search for philosophy when life leaves us in quagmires of existential crises, we search for beauty when we walk from one place to the other, and we search for an ability to understand the narratives of history when we wish to make sense of the present. Man is not merely a material being with material needs. He is also a spiritual being with spiritual needs."

> Megha Lillywhite, Classical Ideals: What's the use of the Humanities in Society

For those who identify as religious, I hope you realize that it's not just about what you say you believe, what you've read, or what creed you belong to - but that religion is first and foremost a praxis, an *act*. The Samurai who embodies the virtues of Bushido may well be a better Christian than most Christians, and the Christian who embodies the cardinal virtues may well be a better Samurai than most Samurai. What you do is who you are. **Talk is cheap**.

> *"Few ethical systems are better entitled to the rank of religion than Bushido."*
>
> Inazo Nitobe, Bushido: The Soul of Japan

Something similar applies to Bitcoin. You're not a Bitcoiner because you bought some on Coinbase, or hold a fat stack and a Twitter avatar with laser eyes. There's more to it than just running a node and securing your keys. A life of meaning and wealth, deeper than just the material, requires greater aspirations.

I'm encouraged by what I've seen from the emergent behaviors and subcultures in the "cult of Bitcoin." There are strong tendencies toward homeschooling, health, nutrient-dense foods, localism, community, family, children, self-defense, self-sufficiency and other generally life-affirming ideals. These memes turn into micro-cults, and then become their own norms. It's a very interesting thing to behold - like watching a culture evolve in real time.

It's why I laugh at those who pejoratively label Bitcoiners as "religious zealots." They don't realize that the comment is actually a compliment. A movement like this must be as religious as it is technological and economic. Bitcoin is not just "science." It's so much more. Changing the world requires changing the behavior of the people that make it up. This starts with a narrative. It starts with the adherents to a new order believing in something not yet manifest, and acting accordingly.

So thank you for the compliment, and congratulations on the self-own :)

The Devolution Must Be Reversed

There's ample evidence of a lowering of time preference - which has a direct relationship to behavior - thanks to people's relationship to Bitcoin. This is very encouraging, but we are still swimming upstream.

Centuries of civilization coupled with centralisation and increasing material comforts have transformed men who once had honor and virtue into soft, weak, and ignoble creatures addicted to porn, Netflix, and Uber Eats. Of course this degradation is more complex and due to more than just those factors, but they are the thematic drivers alongside weak, easy money.

There have been similar periods in history. The following excerpt from the Samurai handbook, *Hagakure*, reminds us of this:

> "*That there are few men who are able to cut well in beheadings is further proof that men's courage has waned.* And when one comes to speak of kaishaku [the act of serving as a second in a ritual suicide, specifically to swiftly decapitate the person committing seppuku to ensure a quick and less painful death], *it has become an age of men who are prudent and clever at making excuses.* Forty or fifty years ago, when such things as matanuki [a practice where a Samurai would test the sharpness of a new sword by cutting through the bodies of condemned criminals or corpses] *were considered manly, a man wouldn't show an unscarred thigh to his fellows, so he would pierce it himself.*"

The good times that follow hard times soften the men so the door to bad times is opened, following which the hard men must rise up again and painfully recreate good times. So the cycle continues. Nietzsche most accurately predicted this with his description of the "Last Man", and he warned us that if we're not intentionally doing something to counter mediocrity, we could well dissolve in our own sludge.

> *"'We have invented happiness,' say the last men, and they blink. They have left the regions where it was hard to live, for one needs warmth. Another loves his neighbor and rubs against him, for one needs warmth. Turning ill and being distrustful, they consider sinful: they walk warily. He is a fool who still stumbles over stones or men! A little poison now and then: that makes for agreeable dreams. And much poison at the end, for an agreeable death. One still works, for work is a form of entertainment. But one is careful lest the entertainment be too harrowing. One no longer becomes poor or rich: both require too much exertion. Who still wants to rule? Who obey? Both require too much exertion. No shepherd and one herd! Everybody wants the same, everybody is the same: whoever feels different goes voluntarily into a madhouse."*

> *Friedrich Nietzsche, Thus Spoke Zarathustra*

He was right. We're at a unique time in human history where there's a chance we fail to continue the cycle because of our scientific prowess. There's a chance we're so technologically capable, materialistically obsessed, and morally ignorant that we obsolete ourselves in some attempt to beat life into submission. That would be a devastating result. The ultimate "own-goal" for humanity.

Disgust with this state of affairs, and to the contrary a love of life, is a big part of why I write. I am called to advocate the virtues in this book: Courage, Self-Control, Honour, Excellence, Compassion, Duty, Responsibility, Respect. They're like a magnet. They attract me, and when I see them lacking, I feel I have to say something to encourage myself and others to push through this stage of the cycle, like our ancestors did before us. We have to bear our own cross. It's our duty and responsibility to do better, to *be* better, and to turn this madness around.

> *"Courage is the willingness to face great danger. Since all animal pro-action presupposes such willingness, and since all pro-action is an expression of super-abundant vitality, courage is inseparable from super-abundant vitality in animals, including the human animal. In other words, courage is the foundational shape of vital potency in animals. All other shapes of animal pro-action pre-suppose courage. It is therefore not surprising that the warrior and the warrior's characteristic courage are always celebrated by noble morality."*

Lise Van Boxel, Warspeak

The upshot to all of this is that in the darkest, most despairing moments, the greatest *potential* exists. From a place of weakness, raw strength can be built. The greatest odds call upon the deepest courage.

This is our opportunity. To be the strong men of this generation. We can bring about good times, and then just as importantly, inculcate virtues into our children so that our descendants can carry humanity forward and hold it to a higher standard. The "Last Man" stage of history is the soil, rich in manure, where we plant the seeds of the *Ubermensch*. This is the trade-off. We may be both the luckiest and unluckiest generation ever to live. We get to be the founding fathers of a societal shift, possibly the largest and fastest humanity has ever experienced, but the price of admission is enduring - and overcoming - clown world.

Playing to Win

If winning is arguably the goal of all zero-sum games, then what Bitcoin does is not *"help you win the game,"* but instead set up the field so that winning requires a new set of behaviors, skills and orientations. A new "meta" so to speak. Put simply, Bitcoin changes the game in the literal sense (the hyperbolic too) such that winning by cheating is made far more difficult, and downstream of this is not just the effect on time preference, but also what I'd argue is the need for a new playbook.

The Bushido of Bitcoin is that playbook. As the world swings back toward more decentralization, fragmentation, and individual sovereignty, the need to embody these timeless virtues in order to win at the game of life will only increase.

You will still be able to cheat. You will still be able to play the parasite. Some will even still play the money-printing game through some sort of complex and abstracted rehypothecation - but the key difference will be (a) the speed of reckoning, (b) the magnitude of damage and (c) the extent of collateral damage or socialization of losses.

On a Bitcoin standard the speed of reckoning will increase, the magnitude of damage will decrease, and the consequences will be more localized. In other words: you get wrecked sooner, it doesn't damage the system, and **you** pay the price.

This is not some magical panacea that "fixes" all humans or their behavior. But it **is** a change of terrain, and those who adapt best, will win. We've adapted to a deranged fiat world. We can also adapt to a more praxeologically honest world.

This might seem like an impossible dream, but it always seems this way early on. The curious thing about movements is that when the winners begin to take the lead and move in a new direction, the rest follow.

This is how all trends work and this is how Bitcoin actually "fixes the world". The leaders and first movers who adopt this Silicon Age Bushido as their code, who live with it, lead with it, and win with it, will get ahead. People will watch, they will see, they will learn. As momentum toward this new orientation of behavior increases, the social drivers buried deep inside of us will subconsciously push us in this new direction.

The new Bushido doesn't need to be advertised. When people see that winning requires a new set of behaviors, they will memetically follow and emulate. FOMO kicks in. People change and they don't even consciously know why they're changing. It's an incredible thing to witness.

The key though, as with all movements, is having leadership with conviction. People who decide to lead and embody a new mode of being. It is YOU I've written this book for because you'll need all the help you can get. This new terrain will not be all sunshine and rainbows. It's going to be harsher in many ways, with less room for error, less welfare, less of a safety net, less government to take care of you, and ultimately less forgiveness when you make mistakes. A new world demands a new playbook for behavior, action, and virtue.

This might sound harsh. This is a tougher world, but it's also a more honest one. Without mommy-government to come bail you out, you're left with the support networks you've forged or been born with. So you better be a good human along the way: build a family, and create deep relationships with like-valued people. In such a world, it will not pay to be a Scrooge. Man is not an island, no matter how many AI agents he has at his disposal.

This "harshness" is the only way to strengthen civilization again. It's the only way to upgrade the structure of the house we call humanity. And this is necessary because we're not doing very well in the winter of this season of weak men. We got to the pathetic stage of hiding behind face diapers from friends and family for two years over a mild sneeze.

To turn it around, humans must become stronger again, not just just because they have to, but also because they want to. There must be both a carrot and a stick. All good systems have a reward function. You pay your dues and are accountable for what you've lost, but you also become richer in many dimensions. On this new terrain, the carrot is not just a material one, but a spiritual one. When winning is earned, victory is that much sweeter. When you've won by being excellent, you've done so by embodying virtues that the greatest of the greats throughout all of history have embodied. There is no feeling more powerful than being in sync with your ancestors and the progenitors of the world. You are aligned with a deep archetype. On a Bitcoin standard, those who find this alignment will be most rewarded.

This is the power of the Bushido of Bitcoin. It's neither an entirely new or old **way**, but a blend of old principles adapted to a new terrain. The tools have changed, the landscape and technologies are new, there is all sorts of noise, but how we play and win at the game of life will stem from how the greats have always done it. By being **better.**

I can't stress this point enough. To truly win is to win because you are better, not because you cheated. When cheating becomes the norm, the entire game changes. Instead of training to become the best boxer or football player, you instead work toward being the one who buys off the referees; when everyone begins to see that's the way to win, then they all consciously and subconsciously begin to orient that way too. At that point society splits into layers: you get the layer who makes friends with those who bought the referee, you get the layer that becomes hedonistic or numb, and you get the layer that just gives up. This is bad. This is where we are now.

The Interregnum

Coming out of this will not be easy. We'll have to endure this transition for a few generations. The next five to ten decades will be like a no-man's land as we transition off a fiat standard to a Bitcoin standard.

This "interregnum" will be the most dangerous time because it's the phase when two completely opposing value systems clash. Much like no-man's land in trench warfare, it's a zone where neither value system works well.

The following diagram might help to visualize this:

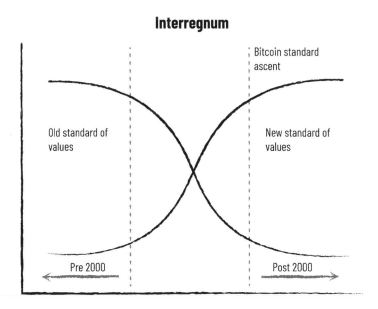

Getting through this will be the ultimate test. It's the cold turkey detox a heroin addict must go through to clean up his system. This is the most apt description of our modern civilization: a junkie desperate for another high, dreading the junk sickness of withdrawal, constantly chasing dopamine, constantly consuming, constantly mindlessly busy. Detached from nature and reality, ignorant, afraid, lost, and nihilistic. A sick society is a mirror of the sick individuals that make it up.

But just as the addict's body still has good in it, our society too still has good in it. There are people worth admiring and bright spots in all the darkness. This light is the source of hope for both the addicted individual and the junkie civilization to which he belongs. It's this light we must recognise. In many ways, this is what Satoshi represents. An individual came along, planted Bitcoin, and moved on, making room for it to do its thing. Fast forward a little more than a decade and it's cleansing the heroin from the system by virtue of making it less and less potent, until one day, we find ourselves free of the drug.

The key thing then will be to build new habits, because like an addict, unless we take on a new set of behaviors, we may well just go back to the old drugs, or find new ones. Bitcoin sets fire to the money-printing heroin but it also leaves us with the need to find something else to do.

Hence the Bushido of Bitcoin. If we don't cultivate these virtues, then we may find ourselves seeking to fill the heroin void with another drug. Transhumanism, the metaverse, or some other stupidity. We have to cultivate these new behaviors and codes. Starting now.

Equality: The Great Evil

"Equality belongs essentially to decline: the chasm between man & man, class & class, the multiplicity of types, the will to be oneself, to stand out – that which I call pathos of distance – characterizes every strong age."

Friedrich Nietzsche, *Twilight of the Idols*

Equality is the great evil of our time. It stands against not only freedom, but even more insidiously opposes excellence, each of which make the flourishing of life possible. Equality and quality are mutually exclusive.

Quality is the central theme of culture and civilization. It runs back through all of human history and forms the basis for tradition, nobility, distinction, and achievement. Every great figure in ancient literature, from the *Iliad* to the Epic of Gilgamesh, embodied the **qualities** and virtues listed throughout this book, and as such they became intrinsic to all great civilizations, Western civilization being the soaring pinnacle. They came to infuse hereditary nobility, cultural traditions, and governance systems; they became the North Star for the pursuit of excellence in war, physical fitness, family, business, and religion.

Equalitiarian ideologies, be they Communist, Socialist, Democratic, Anti-racist, or any other leftist variation, are a modern invention. They came about after wealth and stability were developed as a function of this qualitative foundation. They are the beneficiaries of a structure they had no part in building, and in their ignorance, are attempting to tear down, for a vision that is fundamentally anti-life.

This is the fundamental distinction between life-affirming and death cult philosophies. The former prioritize quality, while the latter demand equality.

Leftism in its many forms is a peculiar and artificial death-cult ideology that deviates from the historical norm. Its core tenet, that *"all men are created equal"* has taken root and gained an almost divine, cult-like status. People on both sides of the political spectrum pay homage to this idea, despite the fact that it is not only metaphysically impossible, but is clearly disproven by just looking around and observing human differences. We are not all equal. We are **different**. Ignoring reality doesn't change that fact. It only leads to the suppression of quality where it matters, and worse to Streisand-Frankenstein effects where stupidities such as 'intersectionality' rise to fill the 'diversity-void' left in the wake of this blind pursuit. Necessary discrimination and discernment in human affairs (e.g., differences in pay) come to be seen as malicious, while equality is made sacrosanct and homogenizes everybody and everything it comes into contact with (e.g., the woke movement).

Freedom is counter to equality. As soon as you are free, you begin to **de-equalize.** The only way to equalize nature or humanity is to force it, or in other words, to get equality, you must eradicate freedom. Believing you can have both is a form of schizoid delusion that people who operate purely from the left hemispheric brain can remain oblivious to - especially once it's been pointed out; it takes some professional level mental gymnastics to reconcile the two.

If you want excellence, freedom, quality, or vitality, you must accept the truth about equality. You must deprogram yourself and understand it for the anti-life lie that it is. These are strong words, yes. And they may hurt. They might call into question parts of your identity. That's a good thing. It means you're learning. The truth often burns in this way. It is an acid to both lies and stupidity.

Resist Mediocrity!

A culture that embraces homogenization is signing its own death warrant. A culture that ignores its unique DNA and works to consciously or unconsciously dismantle the hierarchies and structures that hold it together will fall apart. A culture that rejects myth, theology, spirit, and a moral dimension to existence, will soon find that nothing is sacred. From this point, relativism, nihilism, and debauchery follow.

If any of this sounds familiar, it's because it is exactly how we got here. Jash Dholani - the old books guy on X - reminds us that while *"Reason is a useful tool, it can't become the sole yardstick for judging ALL of life."* We as a civilisation (especially in the West) are suffering not only from irrationality but also from *over*-rationality.

"The modern tragedy is not the tragedy of reason defeated but of reason triumphant."

Nicolás Gómez Dávila, Scholia to an Implicit Text

Myth and tradition both deal with deep and timeless questions. To discard them is to be left with trivialities that harbor only a rational dimension. This is a shallow existence and one we're experiencing today. Dávila said that: *"The enemies of myth are not the friends of reality but of triviality."*

The opposite of mediocrity is greatness and nobility, in the same way that the opposite of shallowness is depth. Mediocrity is shallow. It has roots like astro-turf. It's the plant in the pot, the nomad with no territory. Nobility runs deep. It has roots like an ancient Oak Tree. Its territory is its line, extending back through time. A society that has no reverence for the noble will ultimately find itself shallow and mired in mediocrity.

> *"Those who proclaim that the noble is despicable end up by proclaiming that the despicable is noble."*
>
> *Nicolás Gómez Dávila, Scholia to an Implicit Text*

It's no wonder the people telling you to untether yourself from your ancestors by convincing you they were savages are the same ones telling you to ignore your body, and the same people who want you to eat the bugs, to feed you tumors and fake meat, to block out the sun, to print unlimited money, and to make you a helpless dependent. They are the same people who will slander the Napoleons, Achilles, Caesars and Alexanders of history by calling them tyrants, homosexuals, dictators and "short power-hungry men." Such people cannot appreciate beauty, because they are ugly inside. Instead of seeking to climb to the level of those better than them, they choose to tear them down. Nietzsche said that resentment was the most vile of emotions and drives. He could not have been more accurate. **It's not that power corrupts, but that power corrupts the weak and resentful.** The noble use power to reach higher. The weak use it to tear things down. They revere nothing. They are not the same.

Ayn Rand echoed this when she said: *"Kill reverence and you've killed the hero in man."* While she was a materialist, she had a deep appreciation for beauty. She knew that virtues such as excellence, integrity and honor are sacred. She did not frame them as guilt-laden, altruistic facades, but as what they truly are - acts of nobility. They were something of a higher order. She had many more layers than the midwits can notice.

> *"Don't let anything remain sacred in a man's soul— and his soul won't be sacred to him."*

Ayn Rand, The Fountainhead

Her master works put these virtues on display. Her heroes were not just businessmen; they were **noble**men. They acted "first hand" - as she would call it. Her villains were the opposite. She drew a deliberate contrast with the hero, depicting her villains not as 'dark evil characters' but as ignorant, jealous and mediocre people fueled by resentment, who lived what she called "second-hand" lives. In her words, people who *"don't want to be great, but to be thought great,"* who *"don't want to build, but to be admired as a builder,"* and who put the *"the impression of doing"* over the act itself.

This class of resentful parasites has been despised by every great and noble culture since the dawn of time, from the ancient Macedonians to the Samurai. They are Nietzsche's slaves and Last Men, and BAP's bugmen. They were illustrated in Rand's books, and today we deal with them in real life, as the moochers, the looters and the mediocre globohomo class. The ones who, too lazy or inept to create, are all too ready to take, leech and destroy.

We must resist this at all costs, for in Rand's words: *"Enshrine mediocrity—and the shrines are razed."*

A Call to Vitality & Heroism

"I welcome all signs that a more virile, warlike age is about to begin, which will restore honor to courage above all. For this age shall prepare the way for one yet higher, and it shall gather the strength that this higher age will require some day—the age that will carry heroism into the search for knowledge and that will wage wars for the sake of ideas and their consequences."

Friedrich Nietzsche, *The Joyous Science*

I want to close this prelude with a call to greatness. This is our time. A new energy is rising. His timing was a little off, but Nietzsche called it. This can be forgiven because one can guess what not when, or when not what, but rarely both when and what. Or perhaps his reference to "about" was on a genealogical timescale that meant a century or two. In which case, he may be spot on. Either way, his point stands.

The noble type, the **hero of the future** will have the capacity to bring together in a life-promoting manner the ferocious courage that creates and bends the external realm to his will, along with the self-conscious intellect necessary to command his inner world. This tension between opposites, that draws tight the bow (*Tonos* in Ancient Greek) is the same tension that makes life possible.

This is the true meaning of "the will to power." It is the vitality that constitutes what we typically recognize as life itself, and its highest manifestation is the hero and warrior who can direct it. How better to express and experience this vitality than through acts of heroism and the practice of the virtues listed in this book? Our modern enemy may be well-funded, they may have the institutions, but they do not have the will or the *pothos* (an ancient Greek term meaning a yearning, longing and desire for something higher) that we do. Time is on our side, and coupled with a deep-seated desire for greatness and some good tooling, we can shift the course of history.

Will it be easy? Of course not. But ease is not the goal. *Excellence* is.

You cannot LARP your way into greatness. Not only because other people will notice, but because you yourself will *know this*. The higher you reach, the greater your own conquests, the more you will understand not only with your mind but with your blood the vitality of the heroes that came before you, and the more their acts of courage and virtue will inspire you. You will feel their stories in your bones, and this will fuel your own desire.

> *"He who has not experienced greater & more exalted things*
> *than others won't know how to interpret the great & exalted*
> *things of the past. When the past speaks it always speaks as*
> *an oracle: only if you are an architect of the future and know*
> *the present will you understand it."*

> Friedrich Nietzsche, On the Use and Abuse of History for Life

It's not enough to read about great men and become a Reddit historian. You must go out and walk the walk. At age 32, Julius Caesar broke down and wept at the foot of Alexander's statue, because by that same age Alexander had conquered the known world. It was a decade later, when visiting his tomb in Alexandria, that Caesar was able to finally feel worthy in his presence. He too had now conquered the world, and could appreciate what it meant to be great.

That is an example of excellence walking in the footsteps of excellence. And it's not the only one. Every great ruler, hero, and conqueror modeled themselves on Alexander, from the time of his death, through Rome, the Middle Ages, the Napoleonic era, and all the way to the modern day, when General Schwarzkopf quoted the battle of Gaugamela as the blueprint for a perfect battle. Alexander too modeled and drew inspiration from Cyrus and Achilles, in the end exceeding them both.

These men of history were all men of vitality. Learn from them. They were less interested in the minutiae, in the dry facts and figures of history, but in history's grand deeds, lessons and stories. They used them to cultivate a superior will. This is the key, and it's a constant work in progress.

I sit here writing this on a train through Germany, not as some 'sage' who's achieved mastery, or a conqueror like Alexander. I pale in comparison to him and every one of the greats I've quoted throughout - but nevertheless I am inspired by all of them. I am someone on a journey with a lot of work to do across every one of these dimensions, but each day, I venture forth, keeping in mind that true understanding is ultimately physiological. I remind myself that courage, honor, compassion and self-control are something we must *do* on a consistent basis, and only become more important when they become hard. I write this as much for you as I do myself. It's my personal reminder. It's a way to put myself on the line and hold myself to a higher standard.

> *"If a man wishes to become a hero, then the serpent must first become a dragon: otherwise he lacks his proper enemy."*
>
> Friedrich Nietzsche, *Thus Spoke Zarathustra*

Only by such acts can we induce the practice of these virtues until they become a part of our behavior. Only when we employ our physical faculties toward their pursuit *unconsciously*, can we truly say that we've achieved any level of mastery - and even then, new peaks can be sought. We are all apprentices in training.

The key is selecting the North Star that calls us to greater vitality and heroism, because it's only by following this light that we'll move in the direction of greatness.

This transition to a better world is a multi-generational project. Whatever greatness we might achieve in our own lives, we will not live to see this new peak of humanity become a reality. But it's our duty to lay the foundations. Like the medieval cathedrals commenced by those who would never see their completion, we today embark on something similar, but more enduring.

I hope the words on these pages, and the many quotes I've sprinkled throughout, inspire you the way they've done me. That they spark something inside of you that is great and noble.

The heights of our heroism will be found in the establishment of a sound order that reaches back in time, drawing wisdom and stability from the traditions of the past, and projects forward into a new age. One when we look upwards, toward a brighter and more desirable future. An age in which we once again explore and expand our territories, coming face-to-face with new frontiers: the way we are compelled to when life is pulsating through us.

This is what I want to show you, in the pages that follow.

A playbook, for a new world, on a Bitcoin Standard.

The Bushido of Bitcoin.

"Be not afraid of greatness. Some are born great, some achieve greatness, and others have greatness thrust upon them."

William Shakespeare, Twelfth Night

PART I

Origins

Introduction

I've always felt as though I was born in the wrong era. My wife tells me this on a regular basis and I am consistently drawn to stories from a time for which only an echo remains. An age of heroism, honor, valor, and hand-to-hand warfare.

There is something deeply inspiring about the feats of courage performed by our ancestors. The fact that we made it this far, without things like toilets, sanitation, electricity, refrigerators, supermarkets, and the like is mind-boggling if you think about it. Men crossed hundreds of miles on foot, with no Nikes or special military footwear, carrying armor, weapons, and supplies on their backs, over mountains, valleys, and rivers, to challenge each other, to fight hand-to-hand, smelling the very sweat, bile, blood and excrement of their enemy, and in the process, getting stabbed, slashed and wounded; but still, somehow, surviving. Overcoming all of that, they went on to build the monumental foundations of the civilisation we live in today.

Humanity when viewed through such a lens is truly awe-inspiring, and it's unfortunate that most people don't appreciate this.

Much of the corpus of modern anthropo-historic study suggests that the story of humanity is a progressive one. The general view is that humanity evolved from savagery to barbarism, and from there into civilization. In fact, if you ask Francis Fukuyama, in the last few decades we reached the end of history! We finally transcended our savage roots and are now more representative of... civilized (domesticated?) humans? Obedient little pets? Who knows.

Others such as Friedrich Nietzsche, Oswald Spengler, Julius Evola and, more recently, Bronze Age Pervert have pushed back on the notion of 'progress', and made a case for history being cyclical. In their view, ancient man was closer to "the gods", while modern man is but a husk of his ancestral greatness, who over the centuries has exchanged his honor and virtue for the material comforts of a soft civilisation.

I used to be in the naive camp of the former, believing that the story of humanity has, besides a few troughs along the way, been one of *"progress"*; but I've come to reconsider this and cede mental territory to the latter arguments. While there has certainly been a general undercurrent of technological progress, the social, structural and moral fabric that binds us is undoubtedly more cyclical. Sure, we live in a technological golden age, but we also live in a moral, intellectual, emotional, and physiological dark age - a perspective that more people are beginning to agree with, not least because of the growing amount of supporting evidence.

Obesity rates in the most materially affluent countries have skyrocketed in the last fifty years, as have rates of anxiety, depression, drug addiction, autoimmune diseases, autism, sexual confusion, loneliness, and childlessness. Birth rates are floundering and the nuclear family is being actively attacked in an attempt to dissolve it. We're told that "we live longer on average", but this is primarily due to lower infant mortality. The actual human lifespan has not changed that much at all - but we are fatter, sicker and uglier than we've ever been, and there's no averaging that can hide it.

Number of people with depressive disorders, by region

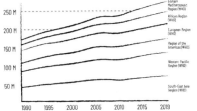

Data source: IMHE, Global Burden of Disease (2019)

Obesity in adults 1975 to 2016

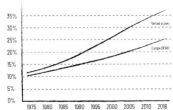

Data source: WHO, Global Health Observatory (2022).

Testosterone levels in the USA

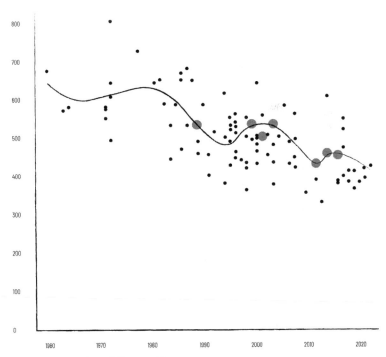

Data source: Hundreds of studies across the US, testosteronedecline.com

The rise of one-person households

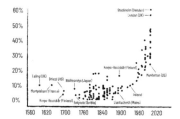

Data source: Snell (2017). The rise of living alone and loneliness in history.

Total fertility rate in the United Kingdom from 1800 to 2000

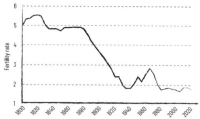

Various sources; UN DESA; Gapminder

Divorce Parties

3.5 K
Mo Volume

43%
Yr Growth

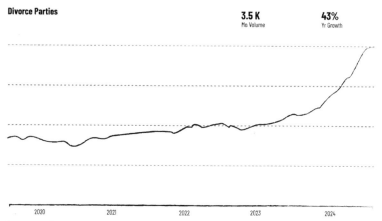

Data source: meetglimpse.com

Our nihilistic age is characterized by a pervasive, nebulous sense of hopelessness and creeping disquiet. We are trapped in a longhouse of our own making, managed by an administrative class to whom we've ceded ever more power. The world has become one giant HR department run by crazy cat ladies and a never-ending horde of bureaucrats.

It's no wonder we have a populace gripped by endless hysterias of every kind. Be it the fear-mongering by climate catastrophists who've been predicting the end of the world "next decade" for the past century, the more recent mass lockdowns and paranoia over flu variants, or the current panic over AI. Add to that the never-ending stream of nonsense coming out of mainstream media, Hollywood, Netflix, reality TV, celebrity tantrums, and social media meltdowns, and you'll get a sense for what I mean.

We used to have hand-to-hand wars involving real warriors. Now we have either invisible wars, or "Hollywood Wars" involving actors, mainstream media, and Time Magazine. Some of it is so clearly ridiculous that you don't know if it's made up or the result of a confluence of mass stupidity and LARPing. Either way, it has led us into the Golden Age of Scamming, both visible and invisible. While you work, these bureaucrats literally scam you through inflation and taxation to fight bigotry, inequality, terrorism, drugs, Russians, North Koreans, and whatever the new flavor of boogeyman is this week. Then, to add insult to injury, people like Sam Bankman-Fried who, instead of being held to account by those he robbed, are actually protected and praised by the media, and allowed to fly first class in time for Christmas with the family.

I'm not sure we've seen a time in human history so strange and absurd. There are even multiple accounts on social media dedicated to ridiculing this "Clown World" - for it truly is.

But despite all of this... there are glimmers of hope. There are cracks in the facade, where rays of light can enter the darkness. People are thinking and talking about Rome again. They are hungry for beauty. The Hopf cycle and midwit memes have become commonplace in online discourse. There is of course Bitcoin, and the promise it brings - and most important of all, is the reawakening of the human spirit and the rekindling of its highest and most valiant expression: the warrior archetype. It is this energy I will speak to throughout and do my best to inspire in you, because this is most representative of life-*force*.

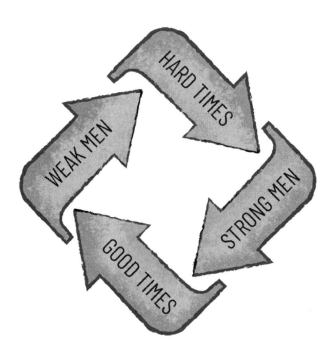

Whether you subscribe to the progressive theory of history, or the rise and fall theory, you cannot deny that it is made up of seasons and cycles, which encompasses both. While history may not exactly repeat, it certainly rhymes, but it also spirals upwards. The parallels between the modern West and the Roman empire are inescapable, and if you have the courage to truly open your eyes and look around, you'll get the inner sense that we're both "at the end of an era" and that "we've been here before." It's an eerie mix of feelings that many people are experiencing and searching for a way to understand. Hence the growing desire to read from 'taboo' authors such as Evola and Spengler. But as much as this should concern you, it should also give you hope, because we made it then - and if we are intentional, we will make it through again.

This book will help you make sense of these feelings, understand what's happening today, why it is happening, what happened to the great civilisations whose shoulders we stand upon but have lost touch with, and ultimately come to terms with the fact that winning requires competing. You can't complain your way to victory. With that, my goal is to inspire you to become a better person through better thought, action and an ascendant attitude.

We all have battles to fight, both externally and internally. There will be times you want to take the easy way out of a situation, but your inner voice, the one which taps into the greater truth of your higher self, will tell you you're not on the right path. You are sinning, or "off the mark" in the original sense of the word. Listen to this one. The inner battle to do what's right, even when it's hard, will call upon the better parts of you. It is for these battles that the virtues discussed hereafter will be most useful.

History and its stories are incredible teachers - and if you decide to be a receptive pupil, there is much to learn. You will know you've found truth when it shakes you to your core, moving you viscerally and emotionally. This is your soul speaking to you. Inviting you to be and do more.

My goal is to open the door for moments like this when you read the words that follow.

A Warrior in a Garden

A warrior is he who brings order and peace through the application of disciplined violence, when it is necessary. The Chinese ideogram for warrior 武 (wǔ) is in fact a blend of the symbols for "weapon" and "stop".

The top part 戈 (gē) represents a "weapon" or "spear," underscoring the martial aspect of the warrior, and the readiness to engage in combat or to defend. The bottom part 止 (zhǐ) means "to stop" or "foot," symbolizing both cessation—of bringing conflicts to an end—and the mobility or groundedness of a warrior.

It reminds me of an Internet legend, that the word 'meek' is poorly translated into English from the Bible's original Greek word "*praus*", and that the true meaning is something more like "those who have swords, and know how to use them, but choose to keep them sheathed". Whether or not this is accurate, the analogy is a powerful one. Those who shall inherit the Earth, are the ones who are prepared. They are "The Remnant". It of course also echoes the Latin: *Si vis pacem, para bellum* (if you want peace, you had best prepare for war).

These are but a few of the profound parallels between East and West that I discovered while doing research for the book. Seeing how principles and virtues overlapped in cultures that had no contact, and evolved independently, tells me that there are truths here. Truths we will explore as we progress.

The opening quote of the book is:

"It's better to be a warrior in a garden than a gardener in a war."

This is one of those maxims that sticks with you. It encapsulates the soundness of preparation, the quiet readiness of one who's mastered his craft, and the approach to a life of continual development. These attributes make the warrior the quintessential archetype of man.

No domain exists where the stakes are higher than war. It is why we are naturally drawn to history and, in particular, historic warfare. *It moves us*. In fact, if we really think about it, what is history if not a compilation of the stories of war and of conflict? Of one man's will and frame against another? Of battles and their triumphs and tragedies?

Our greatest stories are the battles of Gaugamela, Thermopylae, Waterloo, and Sekigahara. They are Edmond Dantes' fight for freedom or Tristan and Isolde's fight for love. These contests always involve some level of violence, because violence is part of our psycho-biological make up. It moves us, and unlocks a deep, primal element in our being. We feel most alive when we are faced with violence. Conflict plays a central role in life and the greatest battles are thus remembered because they call upon the deepest part of us to stand up for what we believe.

Aversion to war and conflict is a major blind spot for libertarians. While I understand why, their disdain for war, violence and conflict may actually be the reason why it is subconsciously unappealing to so many. Growth is conflict in action, and operating from a continually defensive philosophical framework is defeatist. It's why they are and always will be the number one losers.

"I'll sleep when I'm dead" may be the calling card of the young and stupid, but there is truth in this statement. There is the promise of adventure and conflict. There is life and vitality in it. Peace is a weak state because it ignores both the necessity for war, **and** the virtues which warriors must embody.

Peace is at best, the period between conflict, and is ultimately what we experience *after life*, i.e., in death. In fact, I've come to believe that without war, peace is meaningless. For that matter, without peace, so too is war. They are forever entwined, like Yin and Yang. Life, chemistry, physics all require tension and polarity to exist.

Life itself is in a constant flux and battle. It's a struggle to get out of bed in the morning, to ensure your kids are fed, that your home is orderly, that your career is on the right track, that you're building wealth, that you're having an impact. The Lion struggles to catch the deer and the deer struggles to flee. The food on your plate had to struggle to get there. Billions of sperm had to be discarded and lose the battle of individuation in order for one to win and create you. All of life involves conflict and, at times, there are real battles. We must recognise this. To ignore it is to ignore reality - which only leads to weakness, emptiness and death.

This is why it's better to be a warrior in a garden and, paradoxically, why only those who are prepared for war deserve peace.

Si vis pacem, para bellum

War finds us, whoever and wherever we are, so **if you want peace, you had best prepare for war.**

War strengthens us, and if we do not face it, we are relegated to the dustbin of history. We have the choice to literally or metaphorically roll over and die, or to stand up and fight.

Over the millennia, the great and noble cultures have all found their roots in war. Whether Macedonians, Romans, Huns, Mongols, Spaniards, Japanese or Americans, these cultures cultivated nobility and character through hardship. This reality is lost on moderns, and as a result, the culture we are left with is lacking something.

The Samurai understood warriorhood as a 'unified character' both cultural and martial, much like Yin and Yang are the differentiated yet inseparable poles of the one force of the universe: the Tao.

> *"The sensitivity and efficacy of human nature are a single quality with distinctions of cultural and martial."*
>
> Thomas Cleary, Training the Samurai Mind

The Samurai handbook *Hagakure* states that *"Warriorhood without culture is not true warriorhood; culture without warriorhood is not true culture"*. Just like Yin is the root of Yang, and Yang the root of Yin, warriorhood is based in culture, and culture is based in warriorhood.

Has modern culture degraded because we've forgotten the martial element? Has virtue been lost due to a false peace that we've been conditioned to believe is "civil"? Have we tricked ourselves into believing that by abolishing the warrior culture and replacing it with a comfortable, peacetime culture we would no longer have war? Has this in fact made us weak, and thus more susceptible to serfdom, and worse, to less noble forms of war?

These are important questions.

Modern warfare is increasingly becoming the domain of video-game players operating drones from a distance, while taking orders from bureaucrats siphoning money from the people they 'represent'. Notwithstanding the hard infantryman who is willing to slog through the mud and do what a machine or drone cannot, the ancient glory of the battlefield hero no longer exists. Achilles or Alexander, leading from the front, is no longer a practical reality.

Modern warfare is far from noble, and to that extent, I can certainly sympathize with libertarians. To be against such acts of cheap and despicable carnage is correct, and because much of modern war has devolved into this state, it makes sense to oppose it by default.

Perhaps we are living in an age where ancient, or Bushido-like degrees of warlike nobility are not practical in the purely physical sense. If so, the question then becomes, how can we still cultivate this warrior ethos in other ways? Where can we find conflict that pushes us to dig deep inside and make contact with the vital? Can we develop this warrior ethos elsewhere and apply it to other endeavors? We'll explore this and more throughout the book.

The warrior archetype

"Under conditions of peace, the warlike man attacks himself."

Friedrich Nietzsche, Twilight of the Idols

Carl Jung, the foremost student of Freud and one of the founding fathers of modern psychology, termed the *"stored wisdom of the human race"* as *the collective unconscious.* He believed that we as a species accumulate and store the knowledge of every generation into this collective unconscious, and it becomes the software we're all born with. Steven Pressfield, ex US Marine Corp and military author, calls it *"our package of instincts and preverbal knowledge".*

Jung described these instinctual packages as "archetypes": larger-than-life or mythic personifications of the stages of maturation we all journey through. These archetypes guide us as we develop, with a new one coming into play at each stage of life to make it feel more natural and appropriate.

You might be familiar with some of them. The Youth, the Lover, the Wanderer, the Joker, the King or Queen, Prince or Princess, the Wise man, the Mystic, the Monster, and of course, the Warrior.

> *"The Warrior Archetype is not the be-all and end-all of life. It is only one identity, one stage on the path to maturity. But it is the greatest stage—and the most powerful. It is the foundation upon which all succeeding stages are laid."*

> Steven Pressfield, The Warrior Ethos

Archetypes tie back into narrative. Stories are how we're wired to learn, hence why legendary tales like those of King Arthur and the Knights of the Round Table, the 300 Spartans of Thermopylae, Alexander the Great's conquest of the world, and Japan's 47 Ronin, regardless of how much is fact or not, are all subconsciously relatable to us. We each have a warrior within.

If we can cultivate this energy, we can become individuals with the weapons needed to bring order and stand strong in the face of tyranny and ugliness. This is the duty of the warrior, whether in the garden, the ring, the battlefield, the home or the workplace. This is the duty of those who shall inherit the Earth.

Origins of Bushido

Bushido was the name given to the unwritten "moral code" that evolved in feudal Japan and came to reflect the virtues the Samurai class would aspire to embody. The earliest known use of the term "bushido" dates back to the Edo period (1603-1868); however, its principles have much older roots.

During the Heian period (794-1185), the Samurai began to emerge as a distinct social class in Japan. Similar to knights in medieval Europe, the Samurai were warriors who served the nobles of the ruling class, and they followed a set of ethical principles - which came to be known as bushido, the 'the way of the warrior' - that guided their behavior.

Bushido was formally codified during the Edo period as the warrior class found themselves without a war to fight. Their noble rank in the feudal hierarchy of the time meant that they needed to move beyond just 'fighting', and begin to think about how to apply these principles to other areas of life.

They sought to develop and embody a set of core virtues that would inspire those beneath them, while simultaneously earning them status amongst their contemporaries. According to Inazo Nitobe, the 19th century Japanese scholar, there were eight of them:

1. **Justice,**

2. **Courage,**

3. **Benevolence,**

4. **Politeness,**

5. **Sincerity,**

6. **Honor,**

7. **Loyalty, and**

8. **Self-control.**

Like the Magna Carta in Britain or the US Constitution, bushido is said to comprise the essence of Japanese cultural beliefs, and it continues to influence the structure and incredible efficiency and efficacy Japan is known for, despite the 'fiatisation' of modern society.

> *"Chivalry is a flower no less indigenous to the soil of Japan than its emblem, the cherry blossom; nor is it a dried-up specimen of an antique virtue preserved in the herbarium of our history. It is still a living object of power and beauty among us; and if it assumes no tangible shape or form, it not the less scents the moral atmosphere, and makes us aware that we are still under its potent spell."*
>
> *Inazo Nitobe, Bushido: The Soul of Japan*

In true Japanese warrior style, Bushido was a code handed down primarily by word of mouth in the form of short maxims, in some cases penned by a warrior-savant, the most well known being Miyamoto Musashi. The code was expressed in the deeds of those who embodied the highest ideals of the Samurai.

There is a strong parallel here between the complex, emergent roots of Bushido and Bitcoin. Bushido was an organic, emergent growth of centuries of military conflict; much like Bitcoin, it was not the creation of "one brain", nor was it modeled on the life of a single personage. While we do have Satoshi and the Genesis Block to point to as 'starting points' for Bitcoin, it too has a more complex history. Much had to come beforehand, technologically, philosophically and economically. I'm not sure we'd have Bitcoin, for example, without the works of great thinkers like Mises or Hayek.

We know that Bushido 'attains consciousness' after centuries of warfare, in the same way Bitcoin attains consciousness in the age of Quantitative Easing. Both feudalism and the new heroic age we now embark on are the springs that come after the winter wars.

Bushido and chivalry are no longer practiced explicitly, but it's my hope that Bitcoin invigorates humanity enough to once more integrate the values and virtues inherent to these warrior codes, but, unlike those of the past, resisting their fading into a new age of madness and moral relativity.

The etymology of the word

The closest English comparison to the Japanese word Bushido is Chivalry. Both were a sort of 'precept of knighthood' the warrior class sought to embody, and which demonstrated their *noblesse*. While their etymologies are a bit different - for example, Chivalry finds its roots in horsemanship - at their root, both are more expressive.

The actual word "**bushido**" is composed of three Japanese characters: 武 (bu) and 士 (shi) which together mean "warrior," and 道 (do) which means "way." The word "do" can also be translated as "path," "principle," or "teaching," depending on the context. Therefore, the word "bushido" can be translated as "the way of the warrior," "the warrior's path," or "the warrior's principles."

Bu-shi-do can also, and more literally, translate to Military-Knight-Way, which was the manner in which fighting nobles should engage in daily life as well as their vocation.

If we look at the Chinese Pictograms that make up the word, we find the following:

Bu-shi-do 武 士 道

武 (Bu), meaning 'war' as well as 'military,' is composed etymologically of the two radicals for "stop" and "spear". Bu was that which would subdue the weapon and therefore stop the spear. Note the similarity between the definition of 'meek' (or *praus*) in Biblical terms.

"Shi" refers to a person of great ability or someone of an official capacity. It often referred to a nobleman of some literary prestige, but also referenced those who were well-armed. In China, "Shi" were *the men who kept the peace.* In other words, the warriors.

"Do", also known as "Dao" in Chinese, is composed of the radicals for "movement" and "head" which indicates intelligent action, or *movement governed by intelligence.* As mentioned earlier, "Do" is used in reference to "The Way" or "The Path". You see it not only in Bushido, but also in the naming of practices such as Aiki**do** (way of the adapting spirit), Ken**do** (way of the sword) or **Dao**ism (way of life), or in Japanese **Do**kyo 道教.

"A Samurai was essentially a man of action."

Inazo Nitobe, Bushido: The Soul Of Japan

Together this deeper etymology of Bushido echoes what is more commonly referenced when defining it. Bushido speaks to the way of the nobleman - the practitioner of the arts, both martial and literary. The way of the man of action, who is both a man of the mind and of the body.

War, struggle, bloodshed and bushido

"In Japan as in Italy 'the rude manners of the Middle Ages' made of man a superb animal, 'wholly militant and wholly resistant."

Inazo Nitobe, Bushido: The Soul of Japan

The knightly code of Bushido emerged and evolved during a millennium of constant struggle and war. Imagine an era of feuding warlords and clashing Samurai, where the air was thick with the tension of impending battles. Lands were fragmented under the rule of powerful daimyos, each vying for dominance over the other. Villages fortified themselves while the clash of steel rang out on the battlefields. Samurai, bound by a duty to their lineage and a loyalty to their lords, fought with a ferocity rarely matched by any other warrior class. In this world where the line between life and death was as thin as the edge of a katana, the principles of Bushido emerged. These essential principles were few and simple but helped bring structure and a sense of stability to one of the most unsettled periods in Japan's history.

And much like Chivalry did in medieval Europe, this warring states period saw feudal structures emerge alongside codes of virtue in Japan. If Bushido was the spirit, feudalism was the body in which it would reside.

"The light of chivalry, which was a child of feudalism, still illuminates our moral path, surviving its mother institution."

Inazo Nitobe, Bushido: The Soul of Japan

The warrior class in Japan, from whose character came the inspiration and force behind Bushido, were known as the Samurai. We will explore their origins in the next chapter.

The emergence of similar codes of noble ethics and warrior conduct from parallel eras of chaos and bloodshed in two regions with absolutely no contact - medieval Europe and feudal Japan - is a fascinating phenomenon. In fact, it can be argued both codes have been a kind of virtuous or moral peak for human civilization.

Which leads me to a contentious, at least in Bitcoin and libertarian circles, idea.

The virtues & morality of war

"War is the foundation of all the arts, I mean also that it is the foundation of all the high virtues and faculties of men."

Inazo Nitobe, Bushido: The Soul of Japan

War is a tricky subject. As I mentioned earlier, modern warfare is something which scarcely carries with it the traditional spirit of valor or dignity. There is a distance and therefore detachment to war in the digital age that makes it different to classical warfare, similar to the difference between buying your packaged and sanitized meat at a brightly lit, air-conditioned Costco, versus hunting an alert and fleet-footed deer in the freezing darkness of a winter forest, with nothing more than stone-tipped arrows shot from a bow made of tendon and wood.

There is a visceral connection between man and beast that lends the relationship a sense of profundity during and even after the hunt. This process remains a deep, spiritual rite of passage for warrior tribes today, albeit far more rare. The popularity of hunting among the rural communities that provide America's warrior class is one such example. There is a different appreciation of life and death when you have to take life with your bare hands. Buying the same, pre-packaged meat at the supermarket carries with it none of this reverie.

The same goes for battle. Two warriors who are dueling to the death within spitting range of one another inhabit an entirely different plane of existence than the drone operator dropping bombs on the pixels they see scurrying about on a computer screen.

I think this is why blood sports like boxing and UFC are so viscerally popular. They stimulate something primal inside of us. When it's real and raw, it is more alluring.

Steven Pressfield wrote "The Virtues of War" almost two decades ago, and it remains one of the most important books I've read.[1] It helped me see warfare as something that can not only **be** virtuous, but in its noblest and most honorable forms, **is** where the highest virtues are found.

There is a brilliant quote from Inazo Nitobe that echoes this same point:

> *"Fair play in fight! What fertile germs of morality lie in this primitive sense of savagery and childhood. Is it not the root of all military and civic virtue? We smile (as if we had outgrown it!) at the boyish desire of the small Britisher, Tom Brown, "to leave behind him the name of a fellow who never bullied a little boy or turned his back on a big one." And yet, who does not know that this desire is the cornerstone on which moral structures of mighty dimensions can be reared."*

> *Inazo Nitobe, Bushido: The Soul of Japan*

For me, this idea of fair play in the heat of battle, of courtesy and respect toward your enemy, of duty and a sense of honor in the moment of bloodlust, is the cornerstone of all true virtue - which is upstream of all morality.

---

1   I will quote extensively from this book throughout. Despite the many passages 'in the voice of Alexander' not being factual, since we have no written words from the great man himself, they do echo anecdotes found in early historians such as Diodorus, Arrian and Plutarch. More importantly for the purpose of this book, Pressfield's renditions convey deep truths, the kind that is felt deep within.

Without virtue, we would not be here today. We would have savaged each other into oblivion, or, lacking a higher purpose, would not have been the kind of species that could endure through millennia of significant hardships.

There's something about a fair contest that, even when the intent is to kill, calls upon the better, nobler part of us. Contrast this to the frameworks of modernity, designed to detach us from our adversaries and distance us from the consequences of our actions and whom they impact. The latter results in a series of battles that are fundamentally **unfair**, bringing out the worst in us. We have slowly but surely shrugged off the virtues that originated in noble warfare, and in the process left behind the notion of fair play. We've been desensitized and led to believe that winning alone is the goal, while forgetting that **how** you win actually matters more.

The bureaucrats who run the institutions that are waging modern wars don't care about integrity, honor, or justice. They just want the points on the scoreboard, and since they don't have to pay for it in money, blood or land, they'll have it, whatever the price. Because they don't believe in the sacred, or something 'higher,' they are conceited enough to think there is no such thing as a spiritual cost. They don't play by a code of honor or virtue, so the spirit of the contest is ignored. In their mind, winning is winning, the intangible consequences be damned.

The broader social result of this is nihilism, because deep down, nobody really wants to play an unfair game. Those who are disadvantaged give up, and those who are cunning or advantaged enough to compete, simply lose themselves in the process and become soul-selling humans. They no longer become better by winning virtuous battles. They instead become weaker and uglier, desperate to hang onto their ill-gotten gains, knowing that beneath the facade is an empty cavern of deceit. They didn't win because they deserved it, they won because they cheated. So they become **bitter** instead of better. This all makes for a vicious cycle, and the 2020s have thus far been the clearest example of nihilism and widespread meaninglessness we could possibly have asked for.

Fairness in both war and play is critical. To win because you're better, not because you cheated, is noble. And if you lose, it should drive you to improve and try again, knowing that winning is possible. Only in this environment can the noblest of virtues arise.

Hence why those who become the new financial, entrepreneurial and social elite must begin today to think deeply about who we are to become, and what sort of a world we want to build.

What a failure it would ultimately be for Bitcoin to win the economic game, only for those who hold all the bitcoin to become like the very parasites they deposed.

Religious roots

In Japan, there was a unique merging of two schools of spiritual and religious tradition, unlike almost anything else in the world.

Buddhism, founded over 2,500 years ago by Siddhartha Gautama in ancient India, spread across Asia and found its way to Japan in the 6th century AD through Chinese and Korean monks. To this day, its practitioners aim to attain liberation from suffering and enlightenment through the Four Noble Truths (*Suffering, Cause of Suffering, Cessation of Suffering and the Path to the Cessation of Suffering*) and the Eightfold Path (*Right Understanding, Intent, Speech, Action, Livelihood, Effort, Mindfulness and Concentration*).

Shinto, on the other hand, was uniquely Japanese. Unlike Buddhism, there is no founder or specific body of scripture, but instead a deep respect for nature, ancestors and tradition. Its name means *"the way of the guardians or gods"* and it focuses on the worship of *'kami'*, or deities who are believed to inhabit natural phenomena such as trees, rocks and mountains. In fact, Shinto posits that everything has a spirit, no matter how humble, which includes man made objects.

Zen was a unique Japanese blend of Buddhism and Shintoism that produced an extraordinarily contemplative spiritual practice that had a major influence on the moral underpinnings of martial behavior; and therefore, in time, Bushido. Its influence lives on to this day.

> *"What Buddhism failed to give, Shintoism offered in*
> *abundance."*

Inazo Nitobe, Bushido: The Soul of Japan

Without getting into the specifics, for it is out of the scope of this book, Zen can be thought of as the Japanese equivalent for the Buddhist *Dhyâna*, which represents the human effort to reach, through meditation, zones of thought beyond the range of verbal expression.

The Zen method itself is a contemplation of the absolute for the purpose of placing oneself in harmony with it. The following from Nitobe will give you a better mental image:

> *"Shinto shrines are conspicuously devoid of objects and*
> *instruments of worship. A plain mirror hung in the*
> *sanctuary forms the essential part of its furnishing. When*
> *you stand in front of the shrine to worship, you see your own*
> *image reflected on its shining surface, and the act of worship*
> *is tantamount to the old Delphic injunction, "Know Thyself."*
> *But self-knowledge does not imply, either in the Greek or*
> *Japanese teaching, knowledge of the physical part of man,*
> *not his anatomy or his psychophysics; knowledge was to be*
> *of a moral kind, the introspection of our moral nature."*

Inazo Nitobe, Bushido: The Soul of Japan

Unlike Christianity, Shinto theology is without the notion of original sin. In fact, the central doctrine is that of the innate goodness and purity of the human soul. Despite this fundamental difference, a very similar moral framework, and duty to something higher, was found in both Japanese bushido and Christian chivalry. Each code had a similar effect on its respective feudal society. I believe it has something to do with the kinds of virtues extolled by each creed, and points to this idea of a golden thread for virtue and behavior, a way of being that is life-affirming. We'll come back to this concept throughout the book.

Confucian inspiration

"The calm, benignant and worldly-wise character of his [Confucius] politico-ethical precepts was particularly well suited to the Samurai, who formed the ruling class. His aristocratic and conservative tone was well adapted to the requirements of these warrior statesmen."

Inazo Nitobe, Bushido: The Soul of Japan

While Zen and Shinto influenced Bushido in a spiritual dimension, it was the philosophy, ethical doctrines and the teachings of Confucius that were the most prolific source of inspiration for Bushido.

Shinto doctrines, more than any other creed, had already inculcated a deep loyalty to the sovereign, a reverence for ancestral memory and an extreme filial piety into the very fabric of early Japanese culture. There was an upward flowing respect and a condescending love that came naturally to the Japanese, and the Confucian enunciation of the five moral relations found fertile soil in the hearts and minds of the Japanese noble class. These relations had embedded within them a notion of hierarchy and order, outlined in the relationship between:

1. Master and servant (the governing and the governed)

2. Father and son

3. Husband and wife

4. Older and younger brother

5. Friend and friend

Confucianism is mostly known for its emphasis on order and hierarchy. In later chapters on Respect and Duty, you will come to learn why relations were organized as such, and how they bring order and stability to a culture. But beyond filial piety (respect for one's parents and ancestors), it also advocated that individuals should strive to cultivate virtues such as righteousness, loyalty and benevolence, and that these virtues should guide their behavior and relationships with others.

Reading, understanding and, most importantly, embodying these Confucian ideals became a part of the way of the warrior in Japan. Which brings me to my final point for this chapter, and what will be a central theme throughout the book.

Embodied knowledge

The Samurai believed in **doing**, not saying. Action and behavior demonstrated their faith, knowledge and values, more than words ever could. This will be a recurring theme in the book.

Inazo Nitobe has a great passage in his book:

> *"A mere acquaintance with the classics of these two sages [Confucius and Mencius] was held, however, in no high esteem. A common proverb ridicules one who has only an intellectual knowledge of Confucius, as a man ever studious but ignorant of Analects. A typical Samurai calls a literary savant a book-smelling sot."*

In other words, to just read Confucius is meaningless. One must 'do Confucius' if he is to really show that he understands anything at all. Nitobe continues:

> *"...knowledge becomes reality only when it is assimilated in the mind of the learner and shows in his character. An intellectual specialist was considered a machine. Intellect itself was considered subordinate to ethical emotion. Man and the universe were conceived to be alike spiritual and ethical."*

In Samurai culture, knowledge was not pursued as an end in itself, but as a means to the attainment of wisdom, which was defined as knowledge in action, or the *'doing of the right thing at the right time'*.

Therefore, he who stopped short of this end was regarded *"no higher than a convenient machine, which could turn out poems and maxims at bidding."* -*Inazo Nitobe*.

This idea of embodied knowledge was encapsulated by the Chinese philosopher Wan Yang Ming in the following quote: ***"To know and to act are one and the same."***

Toward the end of the book, I will explore the training of the Samurai and how action is in fact the purest representation of character. In it we will come to understand 'embodiment' as the true measure of wisdom.

For now, let us move onto the Warriors themselves, the men of action, who were considered the living, breathing examples of Bushido: *the Samurai.*

The Samurai

The word Samurai roughly translates to "those who serve." The Kanji for "Samurai" is 侍. Breaking it down into its components helps us better understand its meaning and etymology.

The left part of the Kanji, 亻 (ren), is a radical that signifies "person" or "human." This radical is commonly used in characters that pertain to human actions or roles. The right part, 寺 (sì in Chinese, tera in Japanese readings), historically means "temple." In the context of this character, it also relates to its original Chinese meaning of "to attend" or "to serve," derived from the duties associated with maintaining and serving in a temple.

The combination of these components reflects someone who serves or attends to another, particularly in a personal or protective capacity. Service is central. Over time, 侍 came to be specifically associated with those who served and protected their lords and their lands with martial prowess—thus, the Samurai.

The history of the Samurai can be traced back to sometime in eighth century Japan. The early proto-Samurai, also known as Buké or Bushi (Fighting Knights), were armed and militant supporters of landowners; similar to the proto-knight of the early European Middle Ages, for example the Thegns of Saxon England, who were landholding freemen and nobles, expected to contribute to the common defense.

As feudalism was formally inaugurated, these warriors became a more distinct class in the social hierarchy, much like the European *cniht* (knecht, knight), the Roman "*soldurii*" and the "*comitati*", who attended the Germanic chiefs. They were all a rough **breed** of men, who made fighting their vocation.

"This class was naturally recruited, in a long period of constant warfare, from the manliest and the most adventurous, and all the while the process of elimination went on, the timid and the feeble being sorted out, and only "a rude race, all masculine, with brutish strength," to borrow Emerson's phrase, surviving to form families and the ranks of the Samurai."

Inazo Nitobe, Bushido: The Soul of Japan

It took a number of centuries for this group of warriors to emerge as a specific, distinct class but, by the end of the 12th century, the Kamakura Shogunate (literally 'military government'), was established, and large-scale landholders (the closest Western equivalents were the counts) popularized the use of Samurai and formally codified their privileged status in the feudal hierarchy of Japan.

What's interesting to note from Thomas Cleary's work is that this Samurai class was an *offshoot or specialization of the already prevailing aristocracy*. The upper classes produced more children than could be absorbed at the same level of society; because the rule of primogeniture meant that only one son inherited the full privileges of his father, social pressures created differentiation in the patterns of livelihood of those within these upper classes.

> *"In Japan, as in Europe and elsewhere, those sons of aristocratic fathers who did not inherit their paternal estate commonly became warriors or monastics. In Japan both of these specializations were originally conceived for the protection of the state; the ancient warriors were first called "Samurai" or "attendants" because they formed the armed guard of the aristocracy. When the Samurai eventually took the reins of government from the aristocracy, as an independent class, one way in which they manifested their new status and dignity was to distance themselves from the "attendant" Samurai label and call themselves bushi, "warriors" or "knights.""*

> Thomas Cleary, Code of the Samurai

Following the failed Mongol invasion of the 14th century, the Kamakura Shogunate was destabilized and Japan ostensibly fractured once more into rival fiefdoms, each warring for dominance. What followed was almost two centuries of intense fighting culminating in a re-unification of Japan which started with Oda Nobunaga, one of the country's most well known and ruthless warrior Samurai. Upon Nobunaga's betrayal and death, Toyotomi Hideyoshi, a prior peasant-class warrior, took on the mantle. He too was defeated and, ultimately, the most patient and strategic of them all, Tokugawa Ieyasu, succeeded in formally unifying Japan as supreme Shogun (military leader).

It was in this *sengoku jidai* or "warring states period" that the Samurai would truly come into their own as the warrior elite. Ironically, immediately following this peak stage of warriorhood, they would find themselves without a war to fight, and in need of a new identity.

During the reign of Tokugawa Ieyasu and the subsequent Tokugawa Shogunate that he founded, there was a long period of peace and prosperity. The Samurai were no longer required to provide military force; instead, they were expected to lead civil governance. Their role slowly transitioned from being warrior knights that fought in battle, full of vitality and blood lust, to encompassing the responsibilities of teachers, scholars, physicians, artists and government officials.

There had to be an outlet, and it was in this same period that martial skills developed into more elaborate systems of philosophical, intellectual and moral training, known as 'the martial arts'. It was in the clash of these two periods, i.e., peak war, where the spirit of Bushido emerged, and peak peace, where the more formal code of Bushido developed and took root in Japanese culture.

Nietzsche reminds us that, in the absence of war, the warlike man turns on himself. This spirit, this vitality, this energy must be channeled. It cannot be quelled or turned off. Older cultures knew this far better than we do today, with all our talk about "toxic masculinity" or bioengineering ways to remove aggression. This kind of thinking is anti-life, and can only weaken a culture.

The Samurai had behind them a thousand years of training in the laws of honor, obedience, duty, and self-sacrifice. As such, they were the ideal candidates for leadership in this new era, and took it upon themselves to develop a moral code by which to live. They had to. The elder Samurai perceived, and rightly so, that the end of warfare, an increase in material prosperity and the decline of knighthood would weaken the warrior spirit, and threaten both moral and social order. The traditional and practical philosophies of the Samurai elite thus became the basis for this new moral code.

"Coming to profess great honor and great privileges, and correspondingly great responsibilities, they soon felt the need of a common standard of behavior, especially as they were always on a belligerent footing and belonged to different clans. Just as physicians limit competition among themselves by professional courtesy, just as lawyers sit in courts of honor in cases of violated etiquette; so must also warriors possess some resort for final judgment on their misdemeanors."

Inazo Nitobe, *Bushido: The Soul of Japan*

The ensuing centuries saw the Bushido of the Samurai class exert decisive formative influence on the whole of Japanese society - the echoes of which are still heard today.

In fact, neither 'religion' or 'morality' were taught in pre-19th century Japanese schools, because Bushido was the vehicle through which the essence of Japanese culture and virtues (and therefore morality) was conveyed. It wasn't until the late 1800s and early 1900s that Americans and British traveling to Japan brought with them 'modern' schooling, which 'modernized' Japan, both for better and for worse. It helped make the country more technologically powerful, but also distanced it from its historical roots, which had a weakening effect on its culture. For that matter, systemised schooling is a large part of what killed the relationship to feudalism, hierarchy and, in my opinion, eroded excellence all throughout the world. As the socio-organizational pendulum swung toward ever-greater extremes of centralisation and standardization, the focus of schooling became indoctrination, not education - which of course, only breeds compliant serfs. But that's for another discussion, or another book.

I'll end this chapter with a quote that drives home the importance of a warlike code of virtue, and its impact on culture.

"As a process of many hundreds of years' duration, this element of Japanese civilization acquired extraordinary momentum and force, both politically and psychologically. Even today the conventional Japanese culture and mentality cannot be understood without recognizing the residual influence of those Samurai centuries."

Thomas Cleary, Code of the Samurai

Parallels

For many of you, this book will be your first real exposure to the Japanese tradition of Bushido. You're probably more familiar with Austrian Economics, or Christianity. Before we get into the main course of the book, I'd like to explore some parallels between them - some of which might surprise you.

For starters, in my reading of Inazo Nitobe's *Bushido: The Soul of Japan* (written in 1900) I came across quotes from Western philosophical, free market and conservative pioneers, such as Thomas Carlyle, Edmund Burke and a gentleman I'd not heard of before, named William Hurrel Mallock. After doing a little research I discovered Mallock was one of the early voices of reason in the resistance to socialism and democracy. He was basically a proto-Austrian! His early work *The Limits of Pure Democracy* critiqued the socialist and utilitarian ideologies of his time, and advocated for a conservative, hierarchical society bolstered by Christian moral values. He was one of the early thinkers that questioned the effectiveness of democracy and socialism in addressing the complexities of human nature and society. Interestingly, if you search for his books on Amazon, you'll find none other than Murray Rothbard in the "similar authors" section.

Inazo references Mallock when describing the influence Bushido had on the culture in Japan, and how the same 'essence of aristocracy and greatness' influenced the development of all great civilisations, whether Roman, Graeco-Macedonian or the Renaissance European West, whose social order was inspired by the knights and their own warrior-code: chivalry.

Chivalry

"Chivalry is the Christian form of the Military Profession.
The Knight is the Christian Soldier."

Leon Gautier, La Chevalerie

The word "Chivalry" first appeared in the English language somewhere around the 14th century and referred to the code of conduct followed by knights in medieval Europe. The word comes from the Old French word *chevalerie*, which means "knighthood" or "the qualities of a knight". It is derived from the Latin word *caballus*, which means "horse," and *caballarius*, which means "cavalier" or "knight".

Much like Bushido, its core virtues were not a formalized list but an implicit collection that constituted a moral code of the noble knight. Those virtues generally included courage, martial prowess, courtesy, honor, generosity, loyalty, and faith.

> *"It is indeed striking how closely the code of knightly honor of one country coincides with that of others; in other words, how the much-abused oriental ideas of morals find their counterparts in the noblest maxims of European literature. If the well-known lines*
> **Hae tibi erunt artes—pacisque imponere morem,**
> **Parcere subjectis, et debellare superbos,**
> *were shown a Japanese gentleman, he might readily accuse the Mantuan bard of plagiarizing from the literature of his own country."*
>
> Inazo Nitobe, Bushido: The Soul of Japan

These well known lines are from Virgil's *Aeneid*: O Romans, **"these shall be your arts, to set forth the law of peace, to spare the conquered, and to subdue the proud,"** and they point to something more noble, in the character of a lost age. Contrast that with the modern view of chivalry as 'an outdated and patriarchal concept' that is no longer relevant for society.

The average university-indoctrinated midwit will argue that the ideals of chivalry, such as leadership by men, honor, respect and brotherhood, reinforce "gender stereotypes" and are not in line with modern ideas of equality. Funnily enough they're both right and wrong: right because chivalry is not in line with the ridiculous modern ideal of equality; wrong because it's neither irrelevant, nor is there something wrong with this model of the world or kind of behavior.

Like Bushido, I can't think of a time in which such a set of virtues or such a code is more needed. The rhetoric against it, and those it comes from, is only further proof.

Historical context

Like bushido, chivalry evolved over time. In the early to middle medieval period, knights were a critical part of European society and its class structure. They were men selected for their strength and valor, trained in the art of warfare and expected to defend their lord's lands - akin to the duty a Samurai had to his lord. Also like the Samurai, these European knights came to be a class and force of their own. They became defenders of kingdoms and leaders of crusades. They formed their own creeds, their own codes and their own set of ethical principles that guided their behavior in all aspects of life. Like Bushido, this code came to bear its own name (chivalry) and also centered on virtues like honor, loyalty, and courage. The major difference in Europe was of course the emphasis placed on the importance of faith in Christ.

In time, as the social fabric of Europe became more complex, and the need for a knight as the "defender-of-law" or the "warrior-leader" diminished, Chivalry, like Bushido, evolved. It found its way into broader European culture and became the behavioral North Star of the nobility.

Notice that both the "Chivalric Code" and "Bushido" emerged in feudal societies and became a way of life for the warrior class. Both knights and the Samurai prized similar virtues, and their respective codes became the bedrock of nobility in their respective civilisations. This all occurred during roughly the same period in history, but in completely different parts of the world that had *no direct interaction*. For those who think feudalism was backward, think again. The social structure is part of the soil from which culture springs. Feudalism was clearly unique and profound in this way.

The virtues of chivalry

Like Bushido, there are varying accounts of what the exact Chivalric virtues are. Most sources include between six to eight core virtues. I've drawn seven from the works of G.K. Chesterton, the prolific English writer, philosopher, and theologian. Many of his essays were a tribute to the values and ideals of the knightly class, and a reflection on the enduring importance of their moral code - which he felt was dissolving into oblivion over a century ago. What a shock he'd have if he could see how far society has fallen since then. Keep this list in mind as we explore the Japanese virtues later, and progress through the virtues in this book.

Courage was the willingness to face danger or death in order to defend what is right.

Loyalty involved being faithful and true to one's lord, one's country, and one's friends.

Generosity was a willingness to share one's wealth and resources with others, and to act with kindness and compassion.

Honor was the intangible currency of reputation, and the measure of a man's word and name. It was the most notable virtue of Chivalry and central to the nobility of all great ancient and feudal societies.

Temperance involves controlling one's passions and desires, and not being controlled by them. Temperance means moderation, which is a form of self-control and restraint.

Chastity referred to a purity in thought and deed, and, in a Christian sense, being faithful to one's future or current spouse, in the eyes of God.

Humility is very similar to politeness. It involves being modest and recognizing one's own limitations and faults.

Note that like Bushido, this wasn't just an abstract 'code' for knights, but fundamentally a way of life that shaped their behavior. Practicing these virtues was the definition of being a knight, as much as being born into that class. This way of life was so significant to that era that it inspired entire legends. The Arthurian mythos has its roots here, as do love stories we're familiar with 1000 years later, such as those of Tristan and Isolde or Gwynevere and Lancelot.

Misconceptions

It's worth noting that the knight-in-shining-armor holding a rose for his beloved aspect of chivalry is probably the single factor that most distinguishes its legacy from Bushido. I'm not sure if this was originally a symbolic representation of spiritual devotion to a higher ideal - or if it was really a thing among knights - but it certainly did evolve into a range of strange pathologies.

The modern 'simp' and 'white-knight' are two such examples: people who've confused protecting and providing (which are leadership roles) with pleasing (a follower role). You could also make the case that, over time, it was this pathological distortion that opened the door for women's suffrage - quite possibly the greatest political mistake the West ever made. Instead of bearing responsibility and leading, men of the West, confused by this chivalric distortion, bent the knee and put the burden of political and economic responsibility onto women's shoulders. In the process, they mixed emotion into the rational world, and changed the time preference of politics (the feminine has a biologically higher time preference than the masculine). We're dealing with the ramifications of these issues today.

Beyond that, a second more pertinent and more relevant-to-our-discussion misconception is the rift between European paganism and Christianity. There is much misplaced opposition here that needs to be smoothed out. The truth is, early chivalry, and the original knights and nobles who embodied it, were both Christian and Pagan - or, more accurately, Nietzschean. They lived by ancient values infused with Christian morality. Contrary to popular belief, the medieval period was not a rejection of positive classical and pagan values, but an evolution of them - led by this noble-warrior class. This warrior-aristocracy maintained a patriarchy and competitiveness in all they did, particularly in their dedication to combat, conquest and the legacy they sought to leave. They represented both the pinnacle of Christian faith and a relentless will to power. Contrast them with the peasants of the period, who often had a folk-type understanding of the Bible along with many pagan holdovers, and lived a much more communitarian, collectivist, and matriarchal existence.

These classical ideals did not merely die with the surge of Christianity, but in fact lived on among Christians for many centuries, especially in the most noble classes and warrior castes who would become Spengler's original "Faustian Man." They set the stage for the West's conquest of the world - a drive that would manifest in everything from soaring Gothic cathedrals to ships that crossed the Atlantic, to splitting the atom and the modern exploration of space. The knight was a warrior and explorer, driven by an internal desire to discover and claim, to bend the arc of history. The eternal quests for the Holy Grail, El Dorado and the Crusades were not just stories - they were acts in which thousands of men, led by the nobility themselves, crossed mind-boggling distances on foot, horse or wooden boat to fight wars, place themselves in great peril, away from family - for the glory, the discovery and the mission. These 'Homeric' tendencies were not a coincidence, but a familiarity with their ancient pagan roots (whether Roman, Greek, Germanic, Slavic, Saxon or otherwise). The knight, who literally dedicated his life to these endeavors, was the genesis of this period and his 'Faustian Spirit' brought forth the glory of high medieval Europe and shaped the world for the next 1000 years.

I hope this speaks to you, whether you're a Christian or Nietzschean. We have far more in common than not, and in my view, healthy Christianity can only thrive atop a culture of powerful warrior-ideals. Speaking of which...

Christianity

"One remarkable difference between the experience of Europe and of Japan is, that whereas in Europe, when chivalry was weaned from feudalism and was adopted by the Church, it obtained a fresh lease of life, in Japan no religion was large enough to nourish it."

Inazo Nitobe, Bushido: The Soul of Japan

This is not a book on Christianity. I suggest you pick up the Bible if you want that. I'm not here to convert or convince you otherwise. That's a journey you'll need to undertake yourself. That being said, I find the similarities between it and Bushido fascinating.

Take for instance, the four cardinal virtues of Christianity (*virtutes cardinales*) which are considered the most important worldly virtues for Christians to cultivate, next to the divine virtues of hope, faith and charity. They are:

Prudence: The virtue of practical wisdom and good judgment. It involves being able to discern what is right and wrong in a given situation, and acting accordingly.

Justice: The virtue of fairness and righteousness. It is the treating of others with fairness and respect, and the willingness to stand up for what is right.

Fortitude: The virtue of courage and strength. It is the ability to endure difficult situations and challenges without giving in to fear or despair.

Temperance: The virtue of moderation and self-control. It is being able to control one's passions and desires, and not being controlled by them.

Now, not only will you recognise these, or elements of them, because they're found in many other philosophical, ethical and theological traditions; but these four were in fact adopted from the ancient Greek (pagan) philosophers, most notably Plato, who discussed them at length in many of his works, particularly in *The Republic*. These virtues were associated with the ideal state and well-being of the soul, both necessary for individual excellence and societal harmony. Aristotle, Plato's most famous student, further elaborated on them, especially in his work *Nicomachean Ethics*.

The early Christian thinkers, most notably Saint Augustine, clearly found great value in these virtues. They saw them as not only compatible with Christian teachings but also as foundational for a moral life that complements faith. They adapted and added to them the divine virtues of hope, faith and love (or charity) to create the "seven heavenly virtues."

What I like about this example, and in large part why I chose to write a book focused on virtues, is their ability to transcend religion and creed. While beliefs can vary, timeless virtues are often universal.

Where religion is most powerful is in creating a cohesive narrative and framework for these select virtues. It's why I've come to admire and respect Christianity so much. Like bushido, chivalry, and feudalism, what it stands for is so much deeper than what we're being conditioned to believe. Christianity established the moral fabric for the civilization we still depend upon - despite all its problems. It's wise not to throw the baby out with the bathwater, but instead look beneath the surface for what's most consistently true. I say this to my ardent atheist friends. I was a determined atheist in my twenties, angry with the hypocrisy I saw, conceited enough to think I was above it all, dumb enough to think I would discover 'Truth' on my own, and blind enough to ignore what had been thought of and discussed for centuries before I was alive. Life experience has a way of humbling you, and I hope you look deeper here, lest you wind up like Sam Harris.

Feudalism

While not really a parallel to Bushido - it is more accurately the era, age, and social structure from which it emerged - I felt it necessary to include feudalism here with a challenge and question:

If codes as powerful and profound as chivalry and bushido came from feudalism, then could its framing as "bad" or "backwards" by modern politics and educational systems be a farce? What about the beautiful art, architecture and literature produced during that age? Could this have been created in an age of spiritual and social retardation? I think not.

Japan was the last great nation to formally and finally abandon feudalism, in 1900. Despite this, the virtues of the Samurai class, *their bushido*, continued to permeate the social structure that came to replace it. Its echo is part of what makes the country such a unique place today, despite the negative effects of central banking and government-enforced equalitarianism. I often wonder how much more interesting and authentic it would be had the Tokugawa Shogunate remained strong enough to keep Japan closed to foreigners. The same goes for Europe.

Alas this is something we will never know - and cannot dwell on. Feudalism in its medieval state was conquered. What replaced it was economically superior, but a few centuries on, we've found it is morally inferior. We got rich, but soft. We went from having warrior cultures to victim cultures; from the Olympics of conquest, to the 'oppression Olympics'.

We cannot go backwards, only forward; so the question is, how do we revive the best of the old moral fabric, and blend it with the best of our modern technological and economic prowess? I believe virtues are the answer. I've dedicated the final section of the book to this examination. But before we get to that, we must venture into the Ten Virtues of the Bushido of Bitcoin.

PART II

The Virtues

The Virtues

The original subtitle of this book was: *"A moral code for Bitcoiners"*. I chose to move away from the word "moral" because of how much baggage it carries, and how easily it can be weaponized. I chose instead to focus on **virtue**, which is more universal, and is arguably upstream of morality.

Virtue is more action-oriented. It implies a way of being. Virtues transcend cultural interpretations, and avoid the "holier than thou" brow-beating that often comes along with proselytizing about "morality". Nobody likes to be *moralized* at, but virtues - these are things we can all aspire toward.

Think about courage for example. It is valued cross-culturally, all throughout history, not because it is divinely ordained or because it's written in ancient texts, but because it inspires something inside of us all. Courage is fundamentally life-affirming and ascendant. It doesn't need to be explained or analyzed or described; it is something we can intuitively see and feel. The same goes for love, compassion, loyalty, respect and the other virtues we'll explore in this book. They are actions and ways of being which make up the framework for 'morality'.

As will be common in this book, I'd like to begin by exploring the etymology of the word virtue.

The Japanese term for "virtue" is 徳 (Toku). The kanji is made up of four key radicals, each with their own associations. 彳 (Chì), the radical on the left side is often associated with movement or the path one takes. It suggests progression or the journey of life. 士 (Shì), positioned at the top right, can mean "gentleman" or "scholar." Historically, it referred to individuals of a certain social class who were educated or possessed qualities associated with leadership and responsibility - both virtues. 寸 (Cùn), which is found beneath 士, means "inch" or "a small measurement." It often symbolizes taking care of the details and control or precision of actions - themes very common in Japanese culture. Finally, 心 (Xīn) at the very bottom, is the heart radical representing the heart, mind, or the emotional and moral core of a person. It's central to many characters that deal with feelings, thoughts, or spiritual aspects.

The composition of 德 suggests that virtue is not static but involves active cultivation and practice. It implies that virtue is something developed over time, through deliberate actions (彳), guided by wisdom and ethical principles (十), with attention to detail and control (丁), and rooted in the heart and mind (心).

The etymology reflects ancient Chinese and, by extension, Japanese philosophical concepts that virtue and excellence are achieved through continuous effort and action. This maps tightly onto the etymological roots of the word in English.

Virtue comes by way of Old (10th century) French *vertu*, which meant "force, strength, vigor; moral strength; qualities, abilities". *Vertu* derives from the Latin *virtus*, which carried the meanings of "strength, high character, goodness, manliness." The word *virtus* is in turn derived from *"vir"*, the Latin word for "man", echoing a similar meaning of the Proto-Indo-European root *wi-ro*.

In its original context, virtue was less about 'moral goodness' in the modern fluffy sense, and more about the qualities that defined the ideal Roman male, and implied courage and excellence - particularly in the context of action and war. In its deepest sense virtue was synonymous with manhood. It still fundamentally is because it carries a masculine charge, and implies leadership - something we will get deeply acquainted with in this book.

The same was true in Classical Greece. Virtue most closely translated as *arete* "ἀρετή", which meant to be "the best" and referred to excellence in specific activities, most notably warfare.

The meaning of "virtue" has evolved over time. In the twilight of the Classical Greek era, Plato came to characterize virtue as behavior that fosters human flourishing or *eudaimonia*.

Something similar happened after the fall of Rome. With the rise of Christianity virtue took on a moral connotation and began slowly to move away from the Classical Roman ideal of strength, excellence and valor.

The seven heavenly virtues for example, are made up of the four cardinal virtues (prudence, justice, fortitude and temperance, originally derived from ancient Greek philosophy) and the three theological virtues (faith, hope and charity, stemming directly from God).

The evolution of the word continues across multiple cultural shifts. Phrases like "by virtue of" echo an alternative Middle English sense of "efficacy." The 14th-century Wycliffe Bible, for instance, uses virtue in places where the King James Version uses power. From the late 1500s, Virtue also began to apply to women, coming to signify "chastity" and "purity."

Today, virtue has become confused. It's come to encompass a broader range of moral and ethical qualities, which is both good, because all things must evolve, and bad, because we've lost touch with the essence of the word. Its over-moralising has led to what is called "virtue signaling" - a fake attempt to convey or display one's (mostly empty) morality.

This is why we must never forget the root of the words we use. Words carry a charge, and their origin will always matter.

With that in mind, in this book, I use "virtue" less in the moralizing sense, and more in the action-oriented, behavioral sense. Of course, I can't and don't want to completely avoid the moral element - this is now a part of its meaning - but I strive to stay as true as possible to its raw essence: excellence and valor.

In the chapters that follow, we will explore the virtues I believe are the most excellent, vital, and important for leaders to develop within themselves, and inculcate in their children.

It will take multiple generations for us to turn the tide and set sail on a new course. We, as stewards, should spend that time working on ourselves so we can lead by example. We are the only legitimate teachers and role models for our children, and they are likewise the only legitimate role models for theirs - not the government, Hollywood, Netflix, Social Media, their "peers" and certainly not some disembodied virtue-signaling global organization that thinks it knows best.

Let us start this section by exploring the virtues of feudal Japan and their elaboration in the code of Bushido - where the inspiration for this book came from - and then proceed to the Bushido for a new age: *The Bushido of Bitcoin.*

The Bushido of Bitcoin

Ten Virtues for a new, heroic age.

Much of Part Two of the book is indebted to Inazo Nitobe's *Bushido, The Soul of Japan*. This Japanese scholar from the Meiji period had a unique perspective because he wrote as his country was undergoing radical modernisation, and therefore before modernists revised all our history.

As such, his book captured a kind of truth regarding the long tradition of "bushido", that would be impossible to find today. It is one of those special books, written in the age before political correctness had infected culture, which shows us how much things have changed since then.

The following is a definition of each virtue in bushido, in the same order Nitobe used, along with my interpretation of what each means, supported by quotes from Nitobe (in italic), and both the Japanese word and kanji for reference.

1. Rectitude or Justice (義, gi): *"the first virtue of the Samurai"*. Justice is a reflection on what is fair and righteous for the purpose of upholding a moral character.

2. Courage (勇, yū): *"the spirit of daring & bearing"*. Courage is faith in action. It is the inner strength to not just know what is righteous and just, but to act upon it. It's the ability to face fear, and act despite it.

3. Benevolence (仁, jin): Japanese tradition considered benevolence, compassion, magnanimity and affection for others as *"the highest attributes of the human soul"*. Compassion is the ability to suffer with those you love and requires the patience and humility to see the world from the perspective of another.

4. Politeness (礼, rei): *"the outward manifestation of a sympathetic regard for the feelings of others."* My focus on respect deals with the broader regard for not just the experiences and feelings of others, but the fitness of things, tradition, hierarchy and order.

5. Veracity & Sincerity (誠, makoto): *"Without veracity and sincerity, politeness is farce and a show".* Sincerity, integrity and honesty fundamentally represent a wholeness of congruence of character. In feudal Japan, the word of the Samurai was his reputation. The expectation was that speech and deed were one and the same.

6. Honor (名誉, meiyo): Nitobe tells us that honor implies a *"vivid consciousness of personal dignity and worth".* The Samurai lived by the highest code of conduct, and it was this honesty, first and foremost with oneself, that defined honor. Honor is the immortal part of oneself, that which lives on after one's physical body has passed on.

7. The Duty of Loyalty (忠義, chūgi): Loyalty is the glue that binds relationships of both love and respect. In feudal Japan, loyalty and duty to one's lord or compatriot were distinctive features. Loyalty means you keep your word and perform your duty, even if it means you must give your life.

8. Self-control (自制, jisei): Along with courage, this is the quintessential virtue of the warrior: *"the discipline of fortitude".* Self-control in Bushido meant the discipline to adhere to this code under all circumstances, especially when it is hard, whether in the presence of others or alone.

In addition to the eight listed above, which I've adapted to make more current, I included two more. Together, they complete the ten core virtues of The Bushido of Bitcoin:

9. Responsibility: (責任, *sekinin*): If courage is the ability to act, responsibility is the obligation to bear the consequences of one's

actions and the fulfillment of one's duties. It's about owning your decisions and their impact on yourself, others and society.

10. Excellence: (優秀, *yūshū*): Excellence is the genesis of virtue, psychologically, emotionally and etymologically. It is the separation from average and the energy of vitality. Excellence pushes boundaries, establishes new standards and is the driving force of progress and beauty.

In the chapters that follow, I will explore each virtue etymologically, historically, philosophically and psychologically to establish their importance, how they helped shape the characters of those who built civilization and, hopefully, to inspire you to pursue each in your own life.

As a homage to Inazo Nitobe's work, we will begin with the skeleton that forms the structure: ***Justice.***

Justice / Righteousness
(seigi)

Courage
(yūki)

Compassion / Love
(jin / ai)

Honor
(meiyo)

Honesty / Integrity
(seijitsu)

Responsibility
(sekinin)

Excellence
(yūshū)

Respect
(sonkei)

Duty / Loyalty
(chūgi)

Restraint / Self Control
(jisei)

Justice / Righteousness

(seigi)

Justice / Righteousness

義

正

The virtue of justice can be defined as the power of resolution or decision. To decide literally means to *cut off* other alternatives. To exercise judgment is to discriminate. Inazo Nitobe quotes an unnamed Samurai: *"Rectitude is the power of deciding upon a certain course of conduct in accordance with reason, without wavering—to die when it is right to die, to strike when to strike is right."*

The ancient Confucian philosopher Mencius, called righteousness a man's path, and justice the *"straight and narrow path which a man ought to take to regain the lost paradise."*

The Japanese word for "Justice" is Seigi, which is made up of two kanji: "正義", although Gi is most commonly used alone.

The first kanji, 正 (Sei), is composed of two elements. The top part resembles a "lid" or a "cover," and the bottom is the character for "one" (✕). Originally, 正 depicted a tool used for making things straight or correct, symbolizing correctness, rightness, or propriety.

The second kanji, 義 (Gi), is more complex. It's formed by combining the elements 羊 (sheep) and 我 (self or ego). The original meaning stemmed from the idea of a sacrificial sheep, a significant motif in ancient societal rituals. This kanji evolved to symbolize things done for a higher purpose or duty beyond oneself, encompassing meanings like "righteousness," "duty," and "obligation."

Together, 正義 (Seigi) combines these concepts of correctness and duty to convey the idea of "justice" in Japanese, implying that it is "the tool for achieving correctness through sacrifice."

The English etymologies of both justice and righteousness tell us similar stories.

Just (from the Old French *juste*) refers to one's being "morally upright, righteous in the eyes of God" and comes directly from the Latin *iustus* meaning "upright, equitable, lawful, true, proper, perfect, complete".

Righteous is an alteration of the older word, rightwise, which is from Old English *rihtwis* (*riht* + *wis*). In Old English *riht*, from Proto-Indo-European (PIE) root reg, meant "to move in a straight line," or "to rule, to lead straight, to put right". It described actions as "just, proper, in conformity with moral law" and more literally as "straight, direct, erect." Note the similarity with the first kanji of *seigi*.

Moderns have an allergic reaction to the word "rule" when in fact it refers to straightness. The tool you use to draw a straight line is a 'Rule' or a "Ruler".

Wis has its roots in Proto-Germanic *wison* meaning "appearance, form or manner", which evolved into Old Saxon *wisa*, Old Frisian *wis*, Danish *vis*, and Middle Dutch and Old English *wise* meaning "way of proceeding, manner,"

Thus, *rihtwis* described actions "characterized by justice, morally right," and persons who are "just, upright; sinless, conforming to divine law".

We see this recurring theme of straightness, morality and fitness, and it reminds me of another Bushido definition of this virtue:

> *"Rectitude is the bone that gives firmness and stature. As without bones the head cannot rest on the top of the spine, nor hands move nor feet stand, so without rectitude neither talent nor learning can make of a human frame a Samurai. With it the lack of accomplishments is as nothing."*

> *Unkown Author, Feudal Japanese text on Rectitude*

Moral symmetry

"Nothing is more loathsome to [the Samurai] than underhand dealings and crooked undertakings."

Inazo Nitobe, Bushido: The Soul of Japan

In the feudal age, duels were seen as a way to resolve disputes and uphold the virtues of justice, honor, and rectitude. If a Samurai believed that his honor had been challenged or that an injustice had been committed, it was his duty to challenge the offending party to a duel as a way to right the wrong and restore *balance*.

The duel itself was usually a one-on-one fight, often to the death, where the winner was expected to show mercy to the loser. The goal of the duel was not necessarily to kill, but rather to restore honor and balance, a concept known as "satisfaction". If the challenger felt that his honor had been satisfied, he would often spare the life of his opponent.

Dueling and similar rights of restitution were central to all great cultures and civilisations, from Hammurabi's Law, which institutionalized the principle of Lex Talionis ("an eye for an eye, a tooth for a tooth") through to the Germanic Wergild (blood money), which mandated monetary compensation as a means to restore peace without further bloodshed. These codified and ritualized rights of restitution not only helped reestablish 'moral symmetry' and restore honor or dignity to the injured party, but they also acted as deterrents. Much like firearm ownership does today.

While dueling is seen by most as a barbaric remnant of a more violent and dangerous past, there was something profound about two rivals facing each other one-on-one to settle their differences or to reclaim justice, each staking their own life. The knowledge that you'd be called to account, or the inverse, that you must call someone to account, made for a different caliber of man. Much of this has been outsourced to the state in the modern era, and as such I fear we have not only *less justice*, but in many cases, *inverted justice*.

We are all drawn to a 'cosmic balance' of sorts, much like we are drawn to symmetrical structures and faces: symmetry creates a feeling of rightness or completeness. Whether it's the Count of Monte Cristo, Braveheart, The Equalizer or John Wick, some of the greatest stories are those in which the protagonist is unjustly wronged, inspiring the unfolding drama of the hero's search for restitution through a balancing of the "moral ledger". What initially seems like 'revenge' is in fact the restoration of 'moral symmetry to the universe.'

One of the best known examples in Japanese history is that of the 47 Ronin - the group of Samurai who sought to avenge the death of their lord in the 18th century. The story has become an enduring symbol of loyalty, sacrifice, and the importance of justice in Japanese culture.

It begins with a Samurai named Asano Naganori, the lord of a small domain in Japan. Naganori was provoked into attacking court official Kira Yoshinaka, and as a result, he was ordered to commit *seppuku* - ritual suicide via self-evisceration. Naganori's retainers - his Samurai - thereby became 'ronin' - leaderless Samurai.

The 47 ronin, led by Oishi Kuranosuke, believed the provocation was ill-intentioned, and as such decided to avenge Naganori's death by killing Yoshiaka. They spent two years carefully planning their attack and gathering support. Finally, in December 1702, they attacked Yoshiaka's mansion and killed him.

After achieving their goal and restoring 'moral symmetry', the 47 ronin turned themselves in. They were sentenced to death for their act, but as a show of leniency and a sign that the Shogun understood their commitment to the virtue of rectitude, they were allowed to commit *seppuku*, thereby retaining their honor into death.

To date, their loyalty and sacrifice are celebrated as an example of the highest ideals of Bushido. Books, plays and movies have been made that still captivate us because of the "moral of the story."

Righteousness beyond reason

There are of course many instances when the virtue of justice can transform into something more sinister. Examples of this are plenty in the modern world where injustice masquerades as "justice" because it was so decreed. A good way to describe this is "fiat justice".

This was known in the time of the Samurai. Gi-Ri (Right Reason) could over time devolve into dogmatic customs, especially in classes of Japanese culture that did not temper or practice other virtues alongside it. For example, Inazo Nitobe tells us that:

"Carried beyond or below Right Reason, Gi-Ri became a monstrous misnomer. It harbored under its wings every sort of sophistry and hypocrisy. It would have been easily turned into a nest of cowardice, if Bushido had not a keen and correct sense of courage, the spirit of daring and bearing."

This is why it is so important to weave virtues together in a more holistic tapestry. The Japanese Bushido had eight core virtues, the Bushido of Bitcoin has ten so they may act like counter-forces along spiritual, psychological and emotional lines. A constellation of virtues creates a healthy tension, *tonos*, to counterbalance the extremes, ensuring that no singular virtue is over-indexed for, or deformed, thus becoming a shadow or a vice.

A skeleton without muscle, mind or spirit is just dry, dead bones. In many ways, that's all the state is: a lifeless, faceless, disembodied skeleton whose role is to serve justice, but whose limbs are easily co opted by those who lack courage and self restraint, that the apparatus becomes an unjust tool of mindless homogenisation and oppression. In such cases, rule ceases to become a rule in the true sense of the word. It becomes crooked, and Justice is its true victim, along with all those who support it.

Three modern examples of this, incidentally very close to the hearts and minds of Bitcoiners, are Edward Snowden, Julian Assange and the Samourai team. These men literally put their lives on the line to expose truth but, as befits a world in which justice has been inverted, they are exiled, locked up and tortured instead of being celebrated. How many others have, like them, sacrificed everything for Justice, only to be repaid with Injustice?

For example, in order to temper Justice and ensure it does not go awry, one must practice and embody the virtues of compassion, courage (which we shall explore next), and most importantly, self-restraint (which we will explore at the end).

Justice is about balance and moral symmetry, not enforcement.

Bitcoin & Justice

"Money is a measure of fucks given."

Devon Eriksen on X.com

Recall justice and righteousness are concerned with "straight lines," "rules" and "directness". Many have called Bitcoin a money of "rules, not rulers": a money that transcends opinion, that is more akin to a physical law, than to anything that came before it. Bitcoin resembles justice and directness in many ways.

Fixed rules, visible to everyone, make for a fair and therefore just game.

Furthermore, Bitcoin is both voluntary and open, meaning anyone can play, and continue to play, so long as they play by the rules everyone else is playing.

Instead of requiring layers of bureaucracy, banking, central banking, payment processors, merchant facilities, judicial systems, and a military industrial complex to secure the promise of buying a coffee with a tap of a card on a terminal, Bitcoin converts energy (via raw compute) into a global, always on, monetary unit & network. There is no more direct form of money.

Bitcoin has no rewind button. Like real life, it is in continual forward motion. This means that mistakes cannot be reversed and that the consequences for poor action and behavior are real. In other words, on a Bitcoin standard, you cannot rob Peter to pay Paul. In the absence of a central controller, there is no redistribution. This can be harsh, yes. But it is just and fair.

What does this do to our behavior? Can it encourage us to be more just in the way we live? I hope so. The no-rewind or -bailout function of Bitcoin is incredibly important here. Money talks, and bullshit walks. In other words: don't tell me what you believe, show me your bank account and I'll tell you what you believe. When people, businesses, institutions and governments know that there is no bailout coming, when there does not exist a mechanism to paper over losses, or print your way out of stupidity while someone else unknowingly foots the bill, you quickly wise up, or cease to exist. Reciprocally, Bitcoin is more just than central bank debt money from the perspective of those who are no longer made to pay for the debts of others via the stealth tax of inflation.

This "reality" is a forcing function for behavior, and as humans have done since the beginning of time, they will adapt and orient themselves around it. There is ample evidence that Bitcoin has this effect on people (for the first time in decades we have a culture of savers, known as Hodlers). I'll explore this further in the chapter on responsibility.

Courage
(yūki)

Courage

勇
気

"Hope has two beautiful daughters; their names are Anger and Courage. Anger at the way things are, and Courage to see that they do not remain as they are."

St. Augustine

Courage is faith in action. It requires venturing forth into the unknown: the zone of uncertainty. It is not absence of fear, but a quality of mind and spirit that enables one to meet danger, *in spite of fear.* I'm convinced it is the alpha virtue, and where virtue itself originates. Courage animates life and is the progenitor of action. Without it, we could not exist.

If justice is the "frame", then courage is the "soul" of Bushido.

The Japanese word for courage is yū 勇 or more fully, yūki, which represents the deeper meaning of the word and is made up of two kanjis: 勇気.

Yū (勇), consists of two primary elements. The bottom radical is 力 (riki or chikara, depending on the reading), which means strength, force or power. The top radical resembles ✕, a character not commonly used on its own in modern Japanese, but which means 'a road with walls on both sides' or a narrow path. Together these could be interpreted as "power confined to a path", a rather vivid image of courage, like throwing yourself into an unavoidable battle.

The second kanji, 気 (ki), expresses the concept of energy, spirit, or mood. It represents steam rising from rice, the staple food of the East, as it cooks, conveying the idea of a vital force or the energy inherent in living beings.

Together, 勇気 (yūki) combines the notions of bravery and vital energy to express the idea of "courage" in Japanese. It implies not just the *act* of being brave, but also the *spirit* or *energy* that drives one to face challenges boldly.

The word "courage" in English comes from Middle English and Old French *corage*, which translates to "seat of emotions" or "spirit, temperament, state or heart of man". *Corage* in turn derives from Latin *cor*, meaning "heart", whose Greek equivalent is *kardia*, via the Proto-Indo-European (PIE) root *kerd* - which also meant heart.

We see its use in terms like "encourage", the modern form of the Old French *encoragier* meaning to "make strong" or to "hearten". There is also a relationship to the concept of "will", as in the Middle English *fre corage*, meaning "free will".

I've always held courage as the *cardinal virtue of greatness*. In any great story, true or fiction, it is courage that stands out to me as the defining characteristic of the protagonist. It is the inner substance that inspires the hero to action, and as a result, causes the audience to search within themselves.

I know not of a virtue more profound.

Confucius, in his Analects, defines courage via negativa: *"Perceiving what is right, and doing it not, argues lack of courage."* Which, turned into a positive statement, says: *"Courage is doing what is right."* I'd go further by adding; **Courage is doing what is right, despite the consequences.**

Indeed, Nitobe tells us that in Samurai culture, *"Courage was scarcely deemed worthy to be counted among virtues, unless it was exercised in the cause of Righteousness".*

Doing what's right when it's easy is not courageous. It is simply "Just". Doing what's right when it is hard or risky, or when your fear and desire for self-preservation threaten to overcome you - that is courage.

The foremost warrior virtue

"I shall find a way, or make one."

Hannibal

We explored archetypes earlier in Part 1. Courage is the defining virtue of the warrior and hero archetypes. When we think of what animates the warrior, it is this inner spirit or force of the soul. When we think of what 'defines' the warrior, it is this 'stalwartness in the face of death'.

Steven Pressfield therefore considers it the "foremost warrior virtue". He offers the example of the Spartan king Agesilaus, who was once asked what was the supreme warrior virtue, from which all other virtues derived. He replied: ***"Contempt for death."***

The Sacred Band of Thebes, similarly, were known to advance to the cadence of the flute, and had no call for retreat. Their code was simply ***Stand and Die.***

In warrior cultures, including that of the Spartans, failure to show courage in battle would result in severe consequences for the individual and their family. Courage is the backbone of the warrior code and without it, all other virtues fall apart. In a warrior's world, it is the one virtue that cannot be compromised, and is the one that earned a warrior respect, glory and status.

> *"If a Spartan youth failed to show courage in battle, his fiancée would abandon him. The magistrates would not permit him to marry or, if he was married already, he and his wife were forbidden to have children. If the warrior had sisters of marriageable age, their suitors would be compelled to part from them. The man's whole family would be shunned."*

> *Steven Pressfield, The Warrior Ethos*

Fighting fear

Courage is the waging of war against the invisible foe known as fear. There is no adversary that threatens a greater number of men and women, and when we fight, it is fear we must overcome first. External enemies come second.

This passage from Pressfield, in the voice of Alexander, captured me like few others have:

> *"Those who do not understand war believe it to be contention between armies, friend against foe. No. Rather friend and foe duel as one against an unseen antagonist, whose name is Fear, and seek, even entwined in death, to mount to that promontory whose ensign is honor. What drives the soldier is cardia, "heart," and dynamis, "the will to fight." Nothing else matters in war. Not weapons or tactics, philosophy or patriotism, not fear of the gods themselves. Only this love of glory, which is the seminal imperative of mortal blood, as ineradicable within man as in a wolf or a lion, and without which we are nothing."*

We see *kardia* used here, Greek for **heart**. Courage is the virtue of the valiant because it employs something more than the rational intellect to vanquish fear: it employs the heart and soul.

Fear dissolves in the presence of courage, and it is in such moments that miraculous things happen: light defeats dark, truth prevails, the underdog wins, righteousness defeats the crooked.

Winning against the odds is a function of courage. It always has and always will be. Losing with dignity and honor also requires courage. The knowledge that one might **not** win, and their willingness to fight on regardless, is a defining aspect of courage.

This is why a last stand, or a charge by an enemy, even in the face of annihilation, are such powerful things. When your back is against the ropes, and you have nothing to lose, you drop all pretense of fear, and something primal, visceral and savage comes out of you.

Courage is also composure. If courage means doing what is right even when it is hazardous, then it benefits from calm in the presence of danger. This spiritual, peaceful form of courage is how someone who has faced fear on many occasions, comes to fight it. It is best summed up in the following passage by Nitobe:

> "The spiritual aspect of valor is evidenced by composure—calm presence of mind. Tranquillity is courage in repose. It is a statical manifestation of valor, as daring deeds are a dynamical. A truly brave man is ever serene; he is never taken by surprise; nothing ruffles the equanimity of his spirit. In the heat of battle he remains cool; in the midst of catastrophes he keeps level his mind. Earthquakes do not shake him, he laughs at storms. We admire him as truly great, who, in the menacing presence of danger or death, retains his self-possession; who, for instance, can compose a poem under impending peril, or hum a strain in the face of death. Such indulgence betraying no tremor in the writing or in the voice is taken as an infallible index of a large nature—of what we call a capacious mind (yoyu), which, far from being pressed or crowded, has always room for something more."

Courage is leading from the front

In the battles of the Granicus River, Issus, and Gaugamela, Alexander the Great employed a specific battle formation, with allied horse on the left flank, the infantry phalanx in the center, the "Silver Shields" (distinguished group of highly experienced infantrymen known for their silver-plated shields) to the right, and the elite Companion Cavalry at the far right.

Alexander would always personally lead his detachment, riding at the front on his horse Bucephalus, and wearing a distinctive double-plumed helmet that was visible to all soldiers. He was always known for being the first to engage the enemy in leading the charge, and would thus inspire such courage in his men as no other commander in history ever has.

He was the pinnacle of *leading by example* and also embodied the ancient precept that killing the enemy is not honorable unless the warrior places himself equally in harm's way — and gives the enemy an equal chance to kill him.

Alexander bore all of his scars on the front. In ancient times, this was a physical sign of courage. It was bad form and considered dishonorable not only to strike someone from behind, but also to be struck from behind. To strike from behind implied treachery unbecoming a warrior to be struck from behind was evidence that one had fled from the enemy. True warriors prefer death to dishonor.

> *"The Samurai code of Bushido forbade the warrior from approaching an enemy by stealth. Honor commanded that he show himself plainly and permit the foe a fighting chance to defend himself."*

> Steven Pressfield, *The Warrior Ethos*

This ideal was tied into the ancients' more empowering understanding of fate, as a sort of predestination. It wasn't "determinism" as thought of by the modern atheists or nihilists, but more an understanding that your death was "written in the sky", and as such there was no point in being afraid of it.

The Confederate general Stonewall Jackson was known for his belief in this kind of predestination. For Jackson, *"God has chosen the day of your death, so you must go out and live your life to the fullest."* With such an outlook, he embarrassed the Union and beat them in every encounter, despite being ridiculously outnumbered and under equipped.

You should ponder this. What can you do to lead from the front? Is there a way to do this without becoming an unnecessary martyr to the machine? Can we inculcate the essence of this leadership from the front, and this courage to face danger into our kin?

Let's explore how warrior cultures did this.

Developing courage

"Courage is modeled for the youth by fathers and older brothers, by mentors and elders. It is inculcated, in almost all cultures, by a regimen of training and discipline. This discipline frequently culminates in an ordeal of initiation. The Spartan youth receives his shield, the paratrooper is awarded his wings, the Afghan boy is handed his AK-47."

Steve Pressfield, *The Warrior Ethos*

Throughout the ages warrior cultures sought to inspire courage in the younger generation by way of initiation rites. The point of these ordeals was for the youth to face both fear and death, and conquer them.

The Samurai expression *"bears hurl their cubs down the gorge"* meant that the sons of the Samurai were made to undergo severe trials and hardships, spurred into ordeals such as deprivation of food or exposure to cold, as methods of inuring them to discomfort and inculcating endurance.

"Stories of military exploits were repeated almost before boys left their mother's breast. Does a little booby cry for any ache? The mother scolds him in this fashion: "What a coward to cry for a trifling pain! What will you do when your arm is cut off in battle? What when you are called upon to commit hara-kiri?"

Inazo Nitobe, *Bushido: The Soul of Japan*

As these youths grew up, they would seek to ingrain courage into their 'play'. They would venture into graveyards or execution grounds and come face to face with the demons of their imagination. They would re-enact the stories told by their mothers and grandparents, and seek to embody the courage and character of their forefathers and the great warrior leaders of legend.

It was the same in the Classical era, the most famous example being the Spartan Agoge, which many of us came to know via the movie *300*. The Agoge was a rite of passage for Spartan boys, designed to transform them into the most feared warriors in Greece. Boys from the age of seven would be taken from their mothers to undergo a grueling education that emphasized endurance, willpower, and the willingness to defend Sparta at any cost. Through rigorous physical and mental training, these boys would learn courage and discipline 'in the body' and were transformed into not just "soldiers" but into "***Spartans***".

A key element of rites of courage is adversity. Facing it is the key to developing courage.

Adversity

> *"The bravest sight in the world is to see a great man struggling against adversity."*

> *Seneca, Letters From a Stoic*

We will see the theme of adversity come up again and again throughout this book. Rites of passage themselves are a form of spiritual awakening, spurred or unlocked through extreme physical, psychological and emotional adversity.

Adversity is the *tool* of the rite of passage, and it leaves the traveler of this world marked for life. The very first rite of passage was the kicking, screaming and gasping for air as you exit the comfortable, warm water-world of the womb, to enter the harsh world of oxygen and light.

Light, air and sound all shock you from a state of comfort and safety into **life**. In this moment you went from embryo to baby. Adversity transformed you, forever.

This is precisely what the warrior seeks, and in fact, what any living 'being of growth' seeks. There is no growth without resistance. Life itself is a battle against entropy. It is the force that brings order to chaos by counteracting the tendency to decay.

All great philosophies and traditions have recognised this. Nietzsche famously said:

"That which does not kill us, makes us stronger."

He believed that by facing and overcoming difficult challenges and obstacles, individuals can develop resilience, self-reliance and self-overcoming.

Heraclitus said the same thing 2700 years ago: *"Always having what we want may not be the best fortune. Health seems sweetest after sickness, food in hunger, goodness in the wake of evil, and at the end of daylong labor sleep."* In other words, the pain of loss and suffering not only inures you against future pain, but it enhances pleasure via contrast. It's why food tastes so good after fasting, or sex feels so good after a period of abstinence.

Modernity teaches and encourages us to do the opposite: to avoid suffering, to avoid all pain and to seek only pleasure and comfort. This is ultimately the path to weakness and is the principal spiritual danger of peace. Francis Bacon, the famous philosopher and strategist had three rules. First: Remove Bias, Second: Advance learning and knowledge, and third: *"Be proactive and make moves."* This last one is relevant here, and for it he advocated not just waiting for adverse occasions to happen, but to *"challenge and induce them."* The path to strength and power is *through* challenge, not in its avoidance.

Finally, to clarify, none of what I'm saying suggests that one should blindly make his life harder than it needs to be. That isn't courage, but stupidity. Adversity always exists. The question is: are you leaning into it and becoming stronger, or avoiding it in fear, and thus becoming weaker?

> *"Do you always want to have an easy life? Then always stay with the herd, and lose yourself in the herd."*
>
> Friedrich Nietzsche, *The Joyous Science*

Courage or stupidity

Like justice, it's important we separate light from shadow or, in this case, courage from stupidity. In the East, the distinction between "Great Valor" and "Valor of the Villain" was embedded in stories and even rights of passage for children raised in Samurai families.

> *"To run all kinds of hazards, to jeopardize one's self, to rush into the jaws of death—these are too often identified with Valor, and in the profession of arms such rashness of conduct - what Shakespeare calls "valor misbegot"- is unjustly applauded; but not so in the Precepts of Knighthood. Death for a cause unworthy of dying for, was called a "dog's death."*

> *Inazo Nitobe, Bushido: The Soul of Japan*

Knowing the line is hard, and perhaps impossible to describe in words. The Prince of Mito said; *"To rush into the thick of battle and to be slain is easy enough, and the merest churl is equal to the task; but it is true courage to live when it is right to live, and to die only when it is right to die."*

There are genuine times in which fear is valid - for example leaning over the edge of a precipice. Doing so has no deeper meaning or purpose. Plato said that courage is *"the knowledge of things that a man should fear and that he should not fear."*

Courage is like Love in that sense. It's one of these things we know and feel when we see or experience it. It moves something inside of our soul, and stirs our emotions. It is especially powerful when facing the greatest of enemies: death. Courage comes to mind when I think of the Spartans and their final charge at Thermopylae, the unwillingness of William Wallace to yield on the torture rack, and of course the quintessential Christ bearing his cross.

There must be a purpose or righteousness underlying courage, else it is wasted. Alexander leading his detachment from the front had a distinct purpose, as did the dignity with which each of those listed above faced their deaths.

Life and death

"The real question is not whether life exists after death. The real question is whether you are alive before death."

Rajneesh Osho

Courage is the antidote to both great fears of man: the fear of dying and the fear of living. The fear of dying is self-explanatory, but it's the fear of living that is more prevalent in modern society. You might ask, why should someone be fearful of life, and who are these people? I'd tell you to look around. The majority of people are content with living a life of quiet conformity and servitude in order to not place themselves at the risk of failure. They are afraid to engage their own spark of life, of what it might mean to fail at an endeavor they commit themselves to.

This is why slavery has and will always exist. Enslavement allows a man to exist, if not really to live, by giving him guaranteed food and shelter. It consoles a man from the fear of living because if he fails, he no longer needs to take responsibility for it. Living with the knowledge of unfulfilled potential, to know that one could have done better but didn't, is the greatest, soul-crushing burden, so to protect his psyche he self-selects his way into subtle forms of servitude, outsourcing responsibility for the greater, more meaningful things in life.

The modern 'citizen' tells himself that he is freer than his predecessors, because his society has crafted an illusion of freedom by offering choices in inconsequential matters, like what airline you can book a flight on, which brand of car you can buy, and even what flavor of cabal you can vote for at the polling booths on election day. But in critical matters, such as how you educate your children, how much and to whom you pay taxes, what you're able to use as the means by which you store and exchange the product of your labor - these matters are all decided for you. If you have a dissenting opinion about such matters, you are reminded of your 'freedoms' with a 'carrot' such as historical propaganda about *"how hard life was for the serfs"* and the fact that *"you have a toilet and a fridge in your home."* If that doesn't work, you can also be reminded that you do not carry the big stick, and in an increasingly individualized society, who are you to speak out? Why take the risk? We're all independent right? Maybe this modern slavery thing is an exaggeration? Conforming doesn't sound so bad after all...

But this cheap slavery of the mind and soul does not offer true, noble answers to a man's deepest desires: to be useful and capable in his life; to exert his will upon the world; to ignite his spark. The path of slavery comes with its own price, to be paid on one's deathbed and once more on judgment day. Every man who is enslaved knows deep down that he did not conquer his fear of life, and in failing to do so, he remained a husk of what he could've been. His 900 months on this planet were squandered.

This is why courage is so central. It is **the** life-affirming virtue. It is vitality and the will to power in action. It **is** the spark of life. It's why I have such respect for warrior cultures, and the men who make them up. While it's true that a warrior might die in battle, he lives more in those hours than most men do in a lifetime. Alexander the Great may have died at the age of 32, but he lived many lifetimes, and his legacy lives on today.

The point of courage is to channel life through oneself. We are all vessels for life. It runs through us, uses us up, then replaces us with the next living, breathing vessel. This is the beauty and tragedy of life. Death, despite what the Peter Pans and nerds want to believe, is not a disease. It is a process. We will defeat neither death nor life. The best we can do is live with courage and when the time comes, face death with courage, eyes forward the whole time. Staring in the rearview is an injustice to this gift. It is a form of cowardice. Choose life, by choosing courage. Death is the most worthy adversary you will ever face, precisely because it is unconquerable.

The enemy

The Brave know the brave. A great enemy should inspire you.

> *"Indeed, valor and honor alike required that we should own as enemies in war only such as prove worthy of being friends in peace."*
>
> Inazo Nitobe, Bushido: The Soul of Japan

Warrior cultures have not only bred courage into their own, but have respected and modeled the courage in their adversaries. Nietzsche once said, *"You are to be proud of your enemy; then the success of your enemy is your success also."*

The greatest adversaries had the greatest respect for each other. The legendary Attila the Hun, who united the tribes of the steppes to bring Rome to its knees, was not just the general Aetius's enemy, but was his spiritual, psychological and mortal peer. By contrast, the weak Roman senators and aristocrats continually tried to buy Attila off. He would then take their money, use it to procure more mercenaries and attack once again, because he disdained such cowardice. He refused to trade courage for coinage. In the end, it was only the courage of Aetius, who stood up and faced Attila, that was able to halt the Huns' advance. Ironically, today we remember Aetius through Attila, because the cowardly "leaders" of a dwindling Rome ultimately killed him out of envy and spite. Alas for them, the great and honorable have the last laugh, for the final emperors of Rome are remembered not for their valor or courage, but for their weakness and pusillanimity.

Examples abound throughout history of similar reciprocal admiration and respect for the bravery of one's foe. In an earlier, more noble Rome, it is said that Caesar was enraged at the execution of his rival Pompey, and that both Antony and Octavius were overtaken with sorrow at the death of Brutus. In Japan, Kenshin, who fought for fourteen years with Shingen, wept aloud at the loss of "the best of enemies" when he heard of the latter's death. The idea of a "worthy adversary" and the honor of "dying a good death" at the hands of such an adversary were sacred in a warrior culture, and could not be more foreign to a weak, civilian culture.

One of the greatest examples is the scene of the day before the battle of Chaeronea. Alexander and one of his generals, Black Cleitus, are said to have crossed the battlefield to speak with the Thebans. During their exchange, a Theban general of the sacred band introduced Alexander to his son. Alexander, in admiration of those who the next morning would likely fight to the death, offered the young man his gem-encrusted dagger, worth an entire talent of gold, who in turn is said to have replied: *"Only, if you will take this,"* giving Alexander the lion's crest of his breastplate — a fine item made of cobalt and ivory, inlaid with gold.

It's such a powerful scene, and one we could barely imagine today. We see it at times with good sportsmanship, and it brings tears to our eyes. Why? Because it's part of a greater ancient archetype that's within those of us who are moved by such a gesture. To those with ears to hear, it calls to something greater within us.

Consider the clash between Alexander and Tigranes, a champion and one of the most revered horsemen of Persia, during the battle of Issus. Tigranes, dressed in a brilliant, noble Persian kit, led a line of Kingsman cavalry that crashed into the Macedonian center line, aiming for Alexander. The following is an excerpt from Pressfield's master work again (*Alexander speaking*):

> *"Iskander!"*
>
> *Tigranes cries my name in Persian, claiming me as his own. His Meteor plows into Bucephalus like a trireme on the ram. The press swallows all. The heat sucks the breath out of you. The animals' necks, straining against each other, burn like surfaces of flame. "Meteor's jaw is so close to my face that my cheek piece catches against his bit chain. His eye is wild as a monster in the sea. The horses lock up chest-to-chest, fighting their own equine war, while my antagonist and I clash like fencers, shaft against shaft, dueling for an opening.*

Tigranes could plunge his lance into Bucephalus's gorge as easily as I can sever Meteor's windpipe with my own. But he will not, nor will I.

"I am Tigranes!" my rival cries in Greek. I love the man. Here is a warrior! Here is a champion!"

Where is this level of love and respect for the enemy? And the courage required in order to behave as such? Does it not exist any longer? And if not, how can we bring it back? It is my hope that, one day, it shall return. But for that to happen, it's up to us to inspire the next generations to live with valor once more, like the ancient warriors did. Your adversary exists to make you better, but it's up to you to direct the outcome of this clash. The noble outcome doesn't just happen. It is made to happen. These are the lessons we can learn from the Alexanders, the Attilas and the Caesars of history. I will close this chapter with one final quote from Pressfield, in the voice of Alexander.

"I love even those who call themselves my enemies. Alone meanness and malice I despise. But the foe who stands with gallantry, him I draw to my breast, dear as a brother."

Steven Pressfield, Virtues of War

Bitcoin & Courage

Bitcoin is new. People who project a technological adoption curve on it, don't understand it. Bitcoin is just a baby. 15 years is barely the beginning, for something that is designed to last for centuries, or perhaps even millennia.

It took thousands of years for gold to monetise and embed itself into the fabric of our civilisation. Gold is still fundamental to everything you see around you - we've just abstracted so far away from it that we've forgotten. Bitcoin is the first real money we've had since gold, and because of how it's engineered, we may not see another step change until we reach the next level on the Kardashev scale.

As such, it takes a degree of courage and faith to put your wealth into it and to transact with it. If you make a mistake, either in opting for this new form of money, or in using it, it's gone. It takes more of that courage to make that call when Bitcoin is young, and even more so in proportion to how much of your net worth you put into it. A few basis points? Not bad. Bitcoin is the only thing you hold? That takes courage - although by the time people reach that point, they've likely come to understand that it's the only way forward.

Still, it takes courage to back the greatest lever for a more just and responsible society, while everyone is against it, ridicules it, or is too busy gambling on shitcoins.

It takes courage, too, to avoid the allure of quick riches that come at you from all sides once you've been proven prophetic. I know many who have sold their soul and reputation just because the money was easier elsewhere. I also know a few who have been Bitcoin-only from the beginning and were not willing to lie to others or themselves. These people I have respect for. At this point in Bitcoin's lifecycle, you can certainly make more money (in the short term) from an up and coming shitcoin, but doing so does very little for moving civilization toward freedom and responsibility. It's similar to Wall Street traders who commoditize everything and anything they can get their hands on, so they can "speculate" and "trade" their way to more money, for the sake of nothing but more money.

In a world devoid of substance, where everything has become cheap, inflated and meaningless, it takes courage to work on something meaningful, to build something beautiful, to generate real value and create wealth. Bitcoin makes that possible, because it makes savings great again.

Bitcoin makes it so that the world rewards the courageous: those who produce something of value, because they work on something of substance and meaning. They can set aside the excess product of their labor, and instead of consoooming into the abyss, or gambling their way into staying afloat - they can live ... and who knows - maybe even create something beautiful.

Compassion / Love
(jin / ai)

Compassion & Love

仁
愛

Justice is richer when coupled with courage, because you're combining mind and spirit. But so too are both courage and justice made richer when tempered with compassion. This is part of why Christ was such a profound and powerful figure.

A tapestry of virtues is the path to depth, wholeness, and well roundedness, and like all good fractals, each virtue is itself a combination of all other virtues. Nitobe outlines this beautifully in relation to Courage in its compassionate form:

> *"Fortunately mercy was not so rare as it was beautiful, for it is universally true that "The bravest are the tenderest, the loving and the daring." "Bushi no nasaké" - the tenderness of a warrior - had a sound which appealed at once to whatever was noble in us; not that the mercy of a Samurai was generically different from the mercy of any other being, but because it implied mercy where mercy was not a blind impulse, but where it recognized due regard to justice, and where mercy did not remain merely a certain state of mind, but where it was backed with power to save or kill."*

Which brings us to the third virtue: Love and Compassion - both which condescend and "come from above."

In modern Japanese, "Ai" is the word for love. Represented by the kanji 愛, it is composed of a few interesting elements. The upper radical of the character is a form of the kanji 爪 (tsume), meaning "claw" or "nail," which surrounds the inner part. The middle radical consists of 心 (kokoro), meaning "heart," or "spirit" and symbolizes emotion and feeling. Below it is 夊 (sui), a character that suggests walking slowly or trailing behind, often used to convey the idea of following or pursuit. Altogether, these elements convey love as an enduring commitment of the heart. They symbolize the careful and nurturing attention one would give to something precious or cherished.

There was no such concept in feudal Japan, where words like "duty", "affection", "compassion", "magnanimity" and "benevolence", each pertaining to a kind of relationship between giver and receiver, were instead used.

Jin, which is represented by the kanji 仁, is the one most referenced in the context of warrior or cultural virtues. It is composed of two elements. The right-hand radical is 二 (ni), which means "two." The left-hand radical is 人 (hito), which means "person" or "human." This is one of the most fundamental kanji in the Japanese language and is often used to denote human-related concepts. In the context of this kanji, it symbolizes the idea of two people or the relationship between people. It's a representation of interaction or connection between individuals.

Together, they represented the idea of a human relationship or interaction characterized by benevolence, kindness, or humaneness. Over time, *Jin* has come to represent the broader concepts of compassion, empathy, and humanity. It's not just the feeling of compassion but also the idea of ethical and benevolent action towards others.

In English, the word "Love" has somewhat clearer roots, but has also evolved with time. The modern word derives from Old English *lufu* which refers to "affection or friendliness". It has roots in the Proto-Germanic *lubo* which means "to desire," which itself derives from the PIE root *leubh*, "to care, desire, or feel for."

Love itself has many flavors. The Greeks recognised this, and they defined love as a threefold force or energy: *eros*, *agape*, and *philia*.

Eros was romantic or passionate love, related to physical attraction and desire. Named after the Greek god of love, it was characterized by strong emotional feelings of desire and longing and was usually associated with sexuality and the pursuit of pleasure.

Philia was the love of friendship and companionship. It was characterized by loyalty, mutual respect, and shared interests. It was the bond between two individuals who share common values and goals, who've shared experiences and ordeals and it is the kind of love found in close friendships, partnerships and true unions between man and woman.

Agape was the selfless, unconditional form of love that transcended personal gain or benefit. It was the spiritual, religious and transcendent form of love, found in kindness, compassion, and forgiveness. It was a love that is freely given without expecting anything in return.

Each of these forms of love are unique, and inseparable at the same time. They're flavors of the same core substance that we are aware of and feel in our bones, across both space and time.

The word "compassion" on the other hand, comes from Latin *compati* which means "to suffer with". It is a combination of *com-* meaning "together with" and *pati* meaning "to suffer". While love is a feeling, compassion is more of a verb.

I've called this virtue '*love and compassion*' because the essence of what I am trying to get at is a blend of two things. First, the desire for something or someone, and second, the feeling of togetherness or a 'cosmic fabric' that binds us, akin to the way the 2014 Christoper Nolan movie *Interstellar* portrays love as a force or dimension that connects us in a way that transcends time and space.

The yin of justice

Compassion, sympathy and affection for others were recognized to be supreme virtues of the Samurai and the highest of attributes of the human soul. The combination of compassion and benevolence was deemed necessary for nobility of spirit and of profession.

What makes this virtue so important is that it is the soft *Yin* to the harsh *Yang* of Justice, the yielding and nurturing feminine that balances the rigid and disciplined masculine. Compassion does have a feminine charge and its inclusion is another example of the tapestry I described earlier, which Nitobe again eloquently describes:

> *"We knew benevolence was a tender virtue and mother-like. If upright Rectitude and stern Justice were peculiarly masculine, Mercy had the gentleness and the persuasiveness of a feminine nature. We were warned against indulging in indiscriminate charity, without seasoning it with justice and rectitude."*

Relatedly there is also *mercy*, which can be considered the masculine form of this virtue. Mercy is quite prevalent in Christianity and warrior cultures. It is the gift of compassion bestowed upon the subject by the arbiter of justice, and carries with it a different kind of charge. It comes from a place of power, strength and privilege. Lord Masamuné was one of the most powerful and influential figures of the Sengoku period in Medieval Japan (1467 - 1615). Despite being best known as a warrior, he was also a poet, and described the relationship between compassion, mercy and strength as follows:

> *"Rectitude carried to excess hardens into stiffness; benevolence indulged beyond measure sinks into weakness."*

In Bushido, compassion and mercy were considered key components of being a Samurai, because they implied strength and magnanimity. Both carrying the burden with another, and bestowing gifts in the moment of justice, were considered acts of real strength. This was common in all of the great warrior cultures, not only feudal Japan.

Magnanimity: love in leadership

The word "benevolence" comes from the Latin *benevolentia*, which literally translates as "good" (*bene*) "will" (*volentia*). Benevolence is the quality of being kind and generous, and is associated with actions that are done to help others. In the context of Bushido, a Samurai who acted with benevolence was seen as noble and virtuous.

In fact, there was a specific form or flavor of benevolence that was expected from nobility, and this was not only seen in Japan, but in warrior cultures all throughout history.

Magnanimity.

Nobody loves or respects a miser. Frugality may be useful in some contexts, but as a general rule there is nothing expansive, noble or magnanimous about it. It's not for nothing that Jupiter, ruler of the planets, is associated with generosity and good fortune in astrology.

Something wealth and love share is that they both flow, and in doing so, multiply. The greatest leaders in history have been those who treated their acolytes, their followers or their people at large, with great compassion and care.

Contrary to what some may think, magnanimity was highly prized in warrior cultures, not only toward allies, but also, as discussed in the prior chapter, toward enemies.

Alexander, for example, would learn thirty to forty of his soldier's names every day, and more importantly, remember them. He would furlough those soldiers who married locally, allowing them to go home for winter to bear an heir in the spring. He repeatedly paid off his soldiers' personal debts, and more importantly, he would write personal notes for those who displayed bravery or valor to pass onto their families. Such an honor, bestowed upon a common soldier directly from a king, was unheard of - and speaks volumes as to why Alexander was so successful in motivating his men to accompany him on his unprecedented conquests.

This kind of behavior is a truly noble form of love, and like all great virtues, it must come from a place of truth, not deceit. True magnanimity and generosity can be felt. One of the best illustrations is a Macedonian assembly called by Alexander, prior to his march on Persia. I'll quote Pressfield again, whose words I believe channel this moment best:

> *When all the army had assembled, Alexander began giving away everything he owned. To his generals he gave great country estates (all properties of the crown); he gave timberlands to his colonels, fishing grounds, mining concessions and hunting preserves to his midrank officers. Every sergeant got a farm; even privates received cottages and pasturelands and cattle. By the climax of this extraordinary evening, his soldiers were begging their king to stop. "What," one of his friends asked, "will you keep for yourself?"* ***"My hopes,"*** *said Alexander.*

Love of family and of tribe

Love of family requires no explanation, so there is little to discuss here, other than reinforcing the importance of such an institution. Family is not only the most important bond, but also the core unit of civilization and the smallest, most functional form of "government".

> *"The abolition of family ties particularly in the past fifty years has led to an incredibly dangerous dependence on a nameless, faceless, incompetent and absent state who views you as just another entry on a database."*
>
> Mark Moss and Aleksandar Svetski, *The UnCommunist Manifesto*

Without family ties, without the authority, the structure, and the education that it entails, we are left dependent on these disembodied institutions, and just as badly, our peers for our maturation. Such environments make us susceptible to either equalitarian ideals and conformity, or they keep us immature well beyond our years, none of which are states in which we can reach or be vital.

"The family is the nucleus of the cell, in the body of humanity."

Mark Moss and Aleksandar Svetski, The UnCommunist Manifesto

Love of tribe is where I'd like to focus this section because tribalism gets such a bad rap in the modern world, even from pro-family types.

Tribalism is generally considered 'primitive', 'toxic', 'closed-minded' and 'non-inclusive.' I would argue first that these are part truths, and second that they are, in fact, positive attributes. Tribes are by definition non inclusive to out groups - but they are extremely inclusive internally. That's what makes such units strong and cohesive. This is not only for the anthropological reason of "survival", but for the psychological fact that you are more likely to care for those with whom you share space, territory, values or characteristics, and for the practical fact that you just cannot love or care for everyone in the same way. Time and energy are limited.

One result of such "tribalism", and I'd argue a key benefit, is actually **diversity**, especially of culture, on a macro scale. A greater number of tribes means that there is a broader and more varied tapestry of cultures and norms that make up the whole of humanity.

Without tribalism we'd have no diversity! There are many ways to skin a cat, and there are different environments in which to do so. Moral principles seem to converge to a small list, but there are definitely a host of different customs, methods and flavors in the service, display and practice of each.

So while there may be some enmity with out-groups, tribalism means that small groups of people can develop deeper bonds and greater internal cohesion, leading to a richer array of different groups that can then cooperate **or** compete. Both cooperation and competition are vital. This is why we have sports teams, and why smaller communities are more pleasant places to live. You can only get functional homogeneity up to a certain scale. Beyond that it is unnatural and forced. It becomes ugly. The Bitcoin community is a great example. As it's grown, it too has fractured. The natural limits to the size and scale of tribes and cultures are something I believe we'll see more of as the pendulum swings back and civilization starts to adapt to a hard money standard. It must optimize itself culturally and economically speaking.

Shared sacrifice

Sir Ernest Shackleton was a British explorer who led an expedition to Antarctica between 1914-1917. His story became one of the most famous survival stories of all time.

Shackleton and his crew of 27 men were stranded on the Antarctic ice after their ship, the Endurance, was trapped and eventually sank. He is remembered for his incredible leadership during this ordeal. Despite the circumstances, he always put the well-being of his crew first. He made sure they worked together to hunt food and build shelter, he organized games and activities to keep their minds sharp, and constantly lifted their spirits with his charisma and an indomitable will. If he wavered, he did so internally, and never showed his men. He was with them always, and remained steadfast at all times.

Shackleton and his men were able to survive *for over a year on the ice* through extreme cold, hunger, darkness, frostbite, scurvy, blizzards and desolation in an environment few on this earth could endure. This is not to mention the voyage he and a few men took across the frigid and wild Antarctic ocean, on a *lifeboat*, to get to the island of South Georgia where he assembled a rescue party to save the rest of the men.

Shackleton was the embodiment of courage and compassion, virtues that ultimately led to the survival of **all 27 members of the crew.**

2500 years earlier, in another barren environment, Alexander and his men crossed the scorching Gedrosian desert as they returned from the "ends of the world" as they knew it. The men and horses were suffering, their tongues swollen with thirst. Alexander himself was recovering from a punctured lung sustained during a recent siege, and despite his own pain, he pushed on, determined to lead his men home.

The column was strung out for miles, and at one point, a detachment of scouts came running back to the king. They had found a small spring and managed to fill a helmet up with water. They guarded this helmet in order to present it to Alexander intact, and when they did, all eyes turned to the king and commander, the man who had led them through countless battles.

Alexander thanked his scouts for bringing him this gift, took the helmet, and raised it toward the heavens, in what looked like an offering to the gods. Everyone held their breath in anticipation. Then, without tasting a drop he poured the entire contents of precious liquid into the sand.

Immediately, a great cheer rose from the ranks, rolling like thunder from one end of the column to the other. It is said that by spilling the water, he quenched the thirst of the entire army. The men believed that with such a king to lead them no force on earth could stand against them.

Alexander showed not through words, but sincere, genuine and severe **action** that he, the king, was willing to suffer **with** his men. He could easily have drunk. He was wounded, and not lightly. But he chose to suffer. This act inspired the army to endure and make it through the desert; which they did, with minimal losses.

There is a reason why Alexander became a living legend. There is a reason why men chose to fight with and die for him. Such a deep level of compassion implied not only courage, but extreme self control, responsibility, loyalty, honor and justice. All the virtues which make men great.

Other than Christ, there is perhaps no figure who exhibited this virtue more than Alexander - not just because of the deeds themselves - but because as king he needed not suffer or make sacrifice of himself. This is what makes his character and the story above so utterly powerful and memorable.

Selflessness

*"Courage is inseparable from love and leads to what may
arguably be the noblest of all warrior virtues: selflessness."*

Steven Pressfield, *The Warrior Ethos*

Selflessness is a form of compassion and a regard for others. It is related to respect and a recognition that there is something beyond you, whether a mission, a family, a tribe or virtues worth dying for. Selflessness works in the home, with the comrade at your side in war, your real friends, and to some degree, the community around you.

It's for the betterment of your own soul. You are selfless because it feels right, not because it looks good on Instagram. It must also be of your own volition, and something you would in fact do for what Ayn Rand argued are selfish reasons. Imposed selflessness always masks something more sinister. The "we are all in this together" of 2020 was a prime example of that.

Altruism is a modern interpretation of selflessness. Both Nietzsche and Rand were correct in their assessment that altruism is a scam masquerading as a virtue in an attempt to fleece you. This fake selflessness comes not from a place of love, compassion, or magnanimity, but from one of lack, envy, and deceit. It is always conjured up by the do-gooder and meddling classes who want to guilt-trip you into serving their agenda. And like in warfare, they seek to make you (their enemy) weak, while making themselves stronger.

Beware those who trumpet selflessness and then impose it as a virtue on others. Beware the professional "activists" out there using guilt as a tool to make you feel wrong about doing what's right for you and those closest to you. The deeper and more honest meaning of selflessness is devotion to someone or something that one chooses of their own accord. Any imposition on others to do the same is exactly where these modern 'social' ideologies go awry. People must choose to be selfless because they want to, and not because they 'have to' or because of a mandate by some faceless institution - especially when it's made up of members who embody none of the selflessness which they seek to impose.

This brings up one of the key dangers of compassion. Like justice, it also can be taken to the extreme. Take the nannyfication of the modern West as an example. Excessive compassion transformed a once strong and powerful culture into one full of "safe spaces" for adults, perpetual victimhood, indiscriminately open borders, flattening of hierarchies, and the cushioning of all adversity. This has all led to both a suffocation of truth - which can and often must be brutal - and an aversion to, or more accurately, an inversion of justice. Up is now down, black is now white, man is now woman, or worse, none of these exist, and everything is all the same. Compassion, selflessness and mercy unchecked, can lead to as many problems as their more honest and organic manifestations solve.

How can we protect against this? Is there a case to be made for *selfishness?*

Selfishness as a virtue?

Ayn Rand, author of *Atlas Shrugged*, one of the most prescient and insightful novels of the 20th century, also wrote a collection of essays known as "The Virtue of Selfishness." In it she argued that selfishness is in fact a virtue because it is honest, and furthermore, it is the only thing one should ever *expect* of others. In other words, it's a baseline of truth. To Rand, selfishness is necessary for the survival and flourishing of the individual, and it is therefore morally justifiable as long as it respects the rights and space of others.

What she's referring to is not the same as being cruel or uncaring, but rather to a rational and moral concern for one's own well-being and happiness. Her argument is based on the importance of individualism and the right to one's own life. She believed that individuals should be free to pursue their own goals and values, and that this is the only way for them to fully realize their potential and achieve happiness. In her view, the pursuit of one's own self-interest is morally justifiable because individuals who act in this way are the people who create value and contribute to society. Honest selfishness is a prerequisite for all kinds of achievement.

She tempered this by saying that individuals have a moral responsibility to respect the (property) rights of others, and that selfishness does **not** mean the right to violate said rights. She always maintained that it is possible to be both selfish *and* respect the rights of others.

I agree with this for two reasons. Being selfless does in fact feed some part of you, so you could almost call it "Spiritual Selfishness." But key here is the order of operation. Before you can really be selfless, you have to develop yourself. Self-development, self-education, self-direction, self-improvement, self-reliance. These are all forms of selfishness, necessary to make you competent and capable enough to actually help others. This applies in a warrior, corporate or general social context. If you are fat, lazy, and untrained, the man whom it's your duty to shield will be at greater risk. In fact the entire rank will be, if there is a weak link. If you're a hopeless dependent and a burden on society, you're not making things better. Before you go crusading to help the environment, migrants or the homeless, get your own house in order. "Clean your room" as Jordan Peterson would say. The most selfless thing you could do is therefore to acknowledge this order of operations, and develop the self. *"Put the mask on yourself first before you assist others"*, so to speak.

There is also a difference in the **context** of application. The degree to which you can be functionally selfless depends on your proximity and relationship to others. This is an extension of the order of operations. Your family comes before your community, which comes before your city, which comes before your country and so forth. The further out you go, the more selfish you should be. The closer to you and your tribe, the more selfless you can be.

Selflessness and sacrifice in a unit

When Plutarch asked, *"Why do the Spartans punish with a fine the warrior who loses his helmet or spear but punish with death the warrior who loses his shield?"*, the answer was: *"because helmet and spear are carried for the protection of the individual alone, but the shield protects every man in the line. The group comes before the individual."*

This tenet is central to the warrior ethos, and this kind of selflessness is critical to the cohesion of such a unit. This is not evident in a more mercantile, individualist context where the core unit is not a "band of brothers" but the individual.

I'm not referring here to the morality of one or the other, but rather pointing out that context matters. If you're mission oriented and your survival depends on working as a unit, selflessness must be embodied by all of the individuals in the unit. *"The group comes before the individual"* so that the individuals themselves can survive. These units are only as strong as their weakest link, and true leadership is less about showing off and more about drawing out of your unit the best they have to offer. The goal is to increase the *baseline*.

During Alexander's Bactrian campaigns, he chose to trek across the Hindu Kush - what is now the mountainous regions of Afghanistan, Tajikistan and even Pakistan - in the dead of winter. Many considered Alexander mad because he had a penchant for taking on the most difficult marching routes possible and sharing the ordeals with his men. Lesser men, let alone kings, would have made crossings with their entourage, in comfort. Not Alexander. He led men both on the battlefield and across the very rivers, valleys, mountains and deserts in order to gain the advantage on his enemy, and to inspire his men to greater heights (to raise the baseline).

It is said that once an old soldier, frozen and almost blind from a blizzard, stumbled into camp and was helped in by the troops. They gave him a seat by the fire and prepared hot broth to thaw him out. When the old soldier had recovered enough to comprehend his surroundings, he realized that the young man who had given him his seat by the fire was Alexander himself. The veteran leapt to his feet, apologizing for taking the king's place. Alexander is said to have set a hand on the man's shoulder, making him sit again and said "No, my friend, for you are also Alexander."

We will never know whether this is fact or legend, but we can infer by the distances traveled, the season they were traveled, their terrain and the kind of culture of the Macedonian army, that this quality of leadership had to have been present in order to inspire the men.

Does leadership like this exist anymore? Do men like this even exist anymore? I don't think so. I certainly do not claim to be one. I have done things I am not proud of. I've lied and cheated. I've faltered in the face of adversity. I've taken the easy road many times.

Alas - perhaps this is too high a degree of virtue to expect from modern man, or too impractical in an age where civilisation is so complex. Maybe the Alexander's of history are more of a beacon that lights the way, or an example for us to aspire toward. They exist to remind us that there is more in the world than the 'marketplace.' We can still give up a seat on the bus for the elderly, help the old woman cross the street, or carry her bags up the stairs. We can still build sanctuaries that have no "commercial value" but are full of meaning, sentiment and beauty. If you seek something more substantial, go build something grander. Become a producer and a provider so far beyond your own needs, that you can help an entire community or city. This is what great benefactors like the Medicis did, and why their legacy lives on centuries later.

If you aspire to do great things, become a benefactor who conducts themselves with greater virtue and compassion. The stories told on these pages, whether they're myths or factually true, are here to plant the seeds of greatness in you, and inspire you to show up as more, in your next encounter.

Bitcoin & Compassion

A wealthy, mature society can afford to be a more compassionate society. A broken one cannot. Wealthy, mature people can afford to be more compassionate. Broken ones cannot.

Bitcoin, by its very nature, encourages meritocracy and value creation through individual or cooperative effort and innovation. It fosters an environment devoid of artificial safety nets, or state-enforced wealth redistribution. This might appear harsh at first glance, however, it inadvertently nurtures a form of compassion that stems from individual choice rather than institutionalized mandate.

Compassion, when authentic, is a personal endeavor driven by the voluntary actions of individuals. The same goes for Mercy. The decision to forgive others, or to help them, to share wealth, or to invest in communal projects becomes a direct reflection of one's values and principles. It's something you want to do, not have to. Something like this can only occur in a wealthy society.

As Bitcoin continues to mature, and holders become more wealthy, they will be faced with a choice. Kindness and compassion do matter, and they'll have the ability to help and impact those around them, or that matter most to them.

It becomes real. A shift from state-driven to personally-driven compassion ensures that help and generosity are not abstracted away into faceless bureaucracy but can instead become tangible expressions of empathy and magnanimity.

In such a paradigm, compassion is not a policy; it is a personal choice.

Finally - the fixed supply and deflationary nature of Bitcoin prevent the insidious erosion of wealth through inflation, a phenomenon that disproportionately affects those furthest from the monetary spigot. By fixing the money, Bitcoin grants people greater control over their financial destiny, and makes it next to impossible for parasites to leech off society. What could be more truly compassionate than enabling individuals to rise, not through handouts, but through merit?

Honor
(meiyo)

Honor

"We make men without chests and expect from them virtue and enterprise. We laugh at honor and are shocked to find traitors in our midst."

C.S. Lewis, *The Abolition of Man*

Honor was one of the standout virtues in the feudal era. In a spiritual sense, I believe honor is a measure of true nobility; in a practical sense, I believe it is how order was maintained, and the moral ledger balanced, at an individual and local level throughout history. Today we call it by other names: someone's "reputation", their "word", or their "handshake".

Honor implies a vivid awareness and appreciation of personal dignity and individual worth. It is a reputation not only with others, but with yourself and your own standards. Inazo Nitobe calls it *"the immortal part of one's self."*

Gregory David Roberts, ex-fugitive and international gangster turned author of the world-renowned autobiography Shantaram, said that *"Virtue is concerned with what we do, while honor is concerned with how we do it."* I think this is a great way to frame it, which explains why gangsters can in many cases be honorable despite not being virtuous.

The Japanese word for "honor" is *meiyo*, which is made up of two kanji: 名誉.

The first kanji, 名 (*mei*), represents the concept of name or reputation. It is composed of two elements: the top part, 夕 (*yū*), originally depicted the evening or sunset, but in this context, it represents something distinguished or known. The bottom part, 口 (*kuchi*), means "mouth," signifying speech or what is spoken about. Together, 名 suggests the idea of a name or reputation as spoken of or recognized by others, highlighting the social aspect of one's standing.

The second kanji, 誉 (*yo*), is more to do with honor directly. It is composed of a combination of 言 (*gen*), meaning "word" or "speech," and 堯, an ancient Chinese emperor known for his virtue. This character originally signified the idea of speaking highly about someone, especially in recognition of their virtues or achievements. Over time, it has come to embody the concepts of honor, glory, and esteem.

Together, 名誉 (*meiyo*) combines one's name and reputation alongside one's word or virtue. I find this definition of honor very compelling. It not only emphasizes a behavior but an identity. ***Who you are matters.***

Once again, there is deep overlap with the etymology and history of the English word. Honor derives from the Anglo-French word *onur* which meant "glory, renown, fame earned." This in turn comes from the Latin *honor* which referred to "dignity or office" and most importantly, *reputation*. In fact, this too is where the word honest derives from. The Latin *honestus* is formed by adding the suffix "-estus" to "honus," indicating a quality of being full of honor. Thus, "honest" originally conveyed a sense of dignity, integrity and truthfulness with oneself - qualities associated with being worthy of honor.

In Middle English, honor also came to mean "splendor, beauty and excellence", virtues which sprang from or were seen as a measure of a person's worth and reputation. Honor is a reputation, an intangible value, earned and accrued to one's name. It can't be bought or sold - which is precisely what differentiated the true noble class, from the later "formal aristocratic" classes of the enlightenment. The latter were an outgrowth of the merchant class who sought to buy their way into nobility and the king's favor. They are the ones who ultimately sullied the notion of nobility (and also the ancient conception of the word aristocracy) and brought about the end of feudalism. We will discuss this further in the chapter on feudalism.

Honor still means the same thing today, despite not being as common in the modern world. It is in effect, not just doing *what* is right, but doing it in 'the right way' - even when you don't have to, even when nobody is watching, and even when you have the advantage, or could get away with doing the wrong or dishonorable thing.

Honor is an inner-righteousness that is displayed through **acts or deeds**, tied to one's identity. A couple of examples will help better illustrate the point, as words fall short.

In the time of the late crusades, during the ongoing battles for Tyre in 1187, the Great Saladin (Salah al-Din) captured William the Old, father of his enemy, Conrad of Montferrat - one of the most important military noblemen of the Third Crusade, and defender of the city. During the siege, Conrad is said to have refused to surrender as much as a stone of his walls to liberate his father, and while Saladin could've tested this claim by ransoming William, torturing him, or killing him, it was not the honorable thing to do.

When Saladin eventually withdrew his army from Tyre in 1188, William the Old was released unharmed. Not only did Saladin let the father of his enemy go, he showed him a degree of hospitality which took his enemies completely aback. This is part of why even the Christian Crusaders revered and respected Saladin to such a degree. He was not just a worthy adversary, which is what all courageous men seek; he was an *honorable one*. That was rare then. It is even rarer now.

Another even more ancient story is that of the aftermath of the battle of Granicus. Darius II, King of Kings in Persia, had fled, leaving behind his mother, wives, and almost the entire royal entourage, who were captured by Alexander. The Persians were certain that they would be maltreated, tortured, killed or sold into slavery.

Nothing of the kind happened. In fact, Alexander treated them all with such a degree of respect and reverence, that Darius's mother, Sisygambis, famously declared Alexander her "true son" and refused to leave his side until the end.

Alexander could've done whatever he wanted with them. He could have ransomed them and used them as bargaining chips for the conquest of Persia and the East - but honor calls upon the greater part of a man to do what is right. The greater the man, the greater the righteousness and acts of honor.

This was certainly the case with Saladin, Alexander and many of the great men of conquest who shaped history.

Shame and appeals to honor

> *""It will disgrace you," "Are you not ashamed?" were the last appeal to correct behavior on the part of a youthful delinquent. Such a recourse to his honor touched the most sensitive spot in the child's heart."*
>
> Inazo Nitobe, Bushido: The Soul of Japan

Appeals to honor are a call to do the right thing, even when more expedient or advantageous paths present themselves. The earlier examples I gave were proactive deeds of honor, but in life there are many more reactive deeds. In other words, an individual is compelled to correct course if their honor is called out. This helps to create moral symmetry by balancing the 'moral ledger' (as we spoke of earlier with duels), and to steer society and its norms away from utter perversion.

Those who did not heed the call, were often shamed. In fact, shame, which differs from guilt, is how warrior cultures helped to inculcate honor in their people.

> *"Shame is the soil of all virtue, of good manners and good morals."*
>
> Mencius

Shame is the other side of honor. In warrior cultures, honor is a man's most prized possession. Without it, life is not worth living. Honor is the basis for one's dignity, and is the measure of one's reputation.

Shame is the method of public feedback used by these cultures to both deter dishonorable behavior, and to make very clear who could be trusted under pressure or in the presence of vice, and who could not. Shame-based cultures are different to guilt-based cultures in that they impose their values from outside, through the opinion of the tribe or group. They enforce the code unto its members through shaming, ritual acts, or shunning and ostracism from the group.

> *"The Japanese warrior culture of Bushido is shame-based; it compels those it deems cowards or traitors to commit ritual suicide. The tribal cultures of Pashtunistan are shame-based. The Marine Corps is shame-based. So were the Romans, Alexander's Macedonians and the ancient Spartans."*
>
> Steven Pressfield, *The Warrior Ethos*

Another story tells us about an attempted mutiny by Alexander's men. They'd made it to India after years of constant, bloody campaigning through Turkey, Bactria, and the Hindu Kush; through deserts, mountains, and God knows what else. The men were worn out, and wanted to turn back. But Alexander, so close to what he believed was the "edge of the world", couldn't accept this symbolic defeat. Not yet. Not when he was so close.

It is said that he stepped before the army, stripped naked and proclaimed:

> *"These scars on my body were got for you, my brothers. Every wound, as you see, is in the front. Let that man stand forth from your ranks who has bled more than I, or endured more than I for your sake. Show him to me, and I will yield to your weariness and go home."*
>
> Steven Pressfield, *Virtues of War (Voice of Alexander)*

Through this act of physical, public demonstration, Alexander used shame to challenge the honor of his troops. Of course, not one man came forward. Instead the men begged their king's forgiveness, and rallied behind him for the next stage of their conquest. That is what you call leadership.

Warrior cultures—and their warrior leaders—were masters of enlisting shame, not only to counter fear and spark courage in their men, but more importantly, **to goad honor.**

> *"The warrior advancing into battle (or simply resolving to keep up the fight) is more afraid of disgrace in the eyes of his brothers than he is of the spears and lances of the enemy."*
>
> Steven Pressfield, *The Warrior Ethos*

Honor is so sacred, and the fear of shaming so damning that many moral codes are simply known as codes of honor. *Nang* in Pashto is honor; *nangwali* is the code of honor by which the Pashtun tribal warrior lives. Bushido is the "Way of the Samurai", implying a "how." The Chivalric code was known as a code of knightly honor. Even in modern cultures, such as the US Marine Corps, the most widely used phrase - often tattooed on a Marine's biceps - is the imperative: **"Death Before Dishonor".**

The most noble and powerful Samurai were also the most far-sighted, knowing that dishonoring themselves, even by a slight humiliation in their youth, would compromise their character. To them, "dishonor is like a scar on a tree, which time, instead of effacing, only helps to enlarge." To bear such a scar was shameful, akin to a metaphysical brand. The Samurai's conscience had to be pure and elevated, and honor was its measuring stick.

This is an area in which warrior cultures differ from Christianity for example, which is guilt-based. For Christians, the sense of shame comes from within because 'God is always watching.' The Chivalric code seemed to blend this internal guilt with external shame and this is part of what made it so powerful. Modern culture on the other hand, seems to have lost both, in its complete disregard for both God and the warrior ethos.

Our culture is sick. Beautiful, excellent and courageous people are made to feel guilty for the things they worked hard to build or display, while ugly, fat, resentful and distorted people are protected from shaming through hate-speech laws and an Overton Window that has moved so far to the left that centrists like Elon Musk are considered fascists. Schools reward participation instead of merit, HR departments and hate-speech laws censor both truth and fact, obscene displays of debauchery are actively encouraged all which contribute to a normalization of insanity. The cultural outgrowth of such a cancer is ugliness and extreme nihilism. The worst behaviors and the worst practices are on full display, while the best of what we have to produce, and display, is made out to be evil, and in some places, illegal.

This is why, while some will think it harsh, I believe shaming should be normalized once more. From a young age, all the way up to old age. Bullying in school, while not "nice" on the surface, evolved for a reason. It helped kids, when they were young, calibrate behavior. In fact, if you go back to the 80s, before society fully softened, movies like Karate Kid showed us how the kid being bullied was able to stand up and develop himself. The bully was a catalyst for personal growth! The key is not to remove the shaming and social pressure, but to have parents, teachers and mentors channel that pressure to help develop the characters of their children and students. The same goes for adults, whether in the workplace or more generally in society.

Shame is integral to honor: you cannot remove one without also doing away with the other. It is the opposite pole of the same fundamental substance. If you remove honor, as C.S. Lewis said, do not be surprised to find *traitors and those without heart in our midst*. Honor is the soil of virtue and it is the basis of a strong, beautiful and noble society.

> *"Weakness is in demand—why?… mostly because people*
> *cannot be anything else than weak. Weakening considered a*
> *duty: The weakening of the desires, of the feelings of pleasure*
> *and of pain, of the will to power, of the will to pride, to*
> *property and to more property; weakening in the form of*
> *humility; weakening in the form of a belief; weakening in the*
> *form of repugnance and shame in the presence of all that is*
> *natural—in the form of a denial of life, in the form of illness*
> *and chronic feebleness; weakening in the form of a refusal to*
> *take revenge, to offer resistance, to become an enemy, and to*
> *show anger."*

Friedrich Nietzsche, *The Will to Power*

Impatience and short temper

Much like justice and courage, honor can be taken to extremes—and in fact, often is, as social norms turned into dogma in the feudal societies of both East and West. In Japan, the deeply powerful practice of *harakiri*, also known as *seppuku*, was often mis-used in the later centuries.

> *"Life itself was thought cheap if honor and fame could be*
> *attained therewith: hence, whenever a cause presented itself*
> *which was considered dearer than life, with utmost serenity*
> *and celerity was life laid down."*

Inazo Nitobe, *Bushido: The Soul of Japan*

Many Samurai were so consumed by the fear of dishonor that it hung over them like the Sword of Damocles. This often led to extreme behavior in the name of preserving their honor. Deeds not justified by the code of Bushido were performed in order to preserve one's reputation. Some Samurai, known for their quick tempers, would react with violence at the slightest offense or even imagined insult. This rashness led to much unnecessary conflict and bloodshed.

This is why the code must include other virtues such as patience, respect and compassion. The balance between masculine virtues and the softer, more feminine virtues, helped ensure that the entirety of the code did not become a recipe for antisocial or self-destructive behavior. The challenge for Samurai to balance his desire for honor within this broader tapestry of virtues, is how real strength came to be measured: the ability to bear what you think you cannot bear. This was accomplished through a call to a greater degree of sophistication and nobility, to exercise more discernment regarding where, when, and to what degree to respond (and whether even to do so at all). As Mencius said:

"Anger at a petty offense is unworthy a superior man, but indignation for a great cause is righteous wrath."

Honor over money

The decision of character has always been of utmost import for the true warrior. Character comes before economics; honor, before money.

> *"Chivalry is uneconomical: it boasts of penury. It says with Ventidius that "ambition, the soldier's virtue, rather makes choice of loss, than gain which darkens him." Don Quixote takes more pride in his rusty spear and skin-and-bone horse than in gold and lands, and a Samurai is in hearty sympathy."*
>
> Inazo Nitobe, Bushido: The Soul of Japan

In 480 B.C, at Thermopylae, the Persian king Xerxes stood at the head of an army outnumbering the Spartans and their allies by at least fifty to one. He demanded of the Spartan king Leonidas that he and his 300 Spartans, along with the 4000 allied defenders lay down their arms. In return for doing so, Xerxes offered him rulership of all Greece, and with it money, riches, and material comforts beyond his wildest dreams.

Leonidas famously responded to Xerxes' demand with two words

ΜΟΛΩΝ ΛΑΒΕ (Molon labe)

Translated as: *Come and take them.*

This is what it means to place honor over money, and in fact, over life itself.

Not only did the 300 Spartans cover the retreat of the 4000 allied defenders, but they fought to the last man to defend the pass. They held it against insurmountable odds, and made the Persians pay dearly. Their stand may have lasted even longer had they not been betrayed by the Spartan turncoat, Ephialtes.

The memory of Leonidas and his brave 300 is enshrined in a monument containing only the two words: ΜΟΛΩΝ ΛΑΒΕ

Conversely, the Greek city states and generals who sold their people out are lost to the annals of history, the other king of Sparta is forgotten, and the name 'Ephialtes' is spat upon to this day. This is the eternal price of dishonor.

A century and a half later, Alexander rekindled this memory: Darius offered to buy him off on multiple occasions, but Alexander refused. He was called by something greater, compelled toward conquest and destiny. He was driven by *pothos*, an inner yearning not measurable in coin or material value. John Keegan in his book The Mask of Command says: *"He [Alexander] saw that the Persians for all their material superiority were vulnerable to the confrontation of a superior will, and of the strength of his will he had no doubt."* This is why the Macedonians conquered the East, and laid the foundations for the West. It was not for the love of gold, but for glory. The modern leftoid or bugman simply cannot comprehend this.

This same ideal was embedded into their very culture and social order of feudal Japan, shaped by the Samurai: there existed such a disdain for mercantilism that the merchant was near the bottom of the class structure.

It was Emperor first, followed by the Shogun, then Daimyos, Samurai, the artisans, then the peasants, and finally below them were the merchants. The only people below the merchants were the "Eta," known as the non-persons, or outcasts.

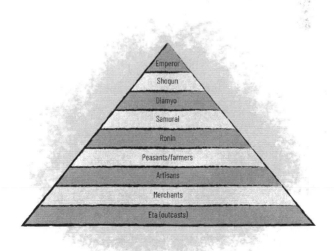

The Samurai, and warriors in most such cultures, viewed the merchant class as below them, as impure and untrustworthy, because they were more likely to trade their honor and dignity for money. There was a saying in Feudal Japan: *"the civilians loved money and the soldiers feared death."*

When the West ultimately came to subjugate Japan (at what cost and karma?), it was through mercantilist means, thus revealing the flaws of a strict social structure where the merchant was near the bottom. Still, there was an undeniable wisdom in that structure. Japan was known for its orderliness, decorum, respect, cleanliness and beauty. The society itself maintained a relationship with the sacred, while the West had begun to lay the foundations for the secularism and collectivism that it's now suffering from.

"If it makes dollars it makes sense."

Boxing manager played by 50 Cent/Curtis Jackson, Southpaw

Does such a quote not make you feel dirty when you read it?

The tendency toward excessive Randianism or Libertarianism risks trending toward empty materialism if it is not counterbalanced by something more sacred, like a faith or warrior ethic. The world is full of those who are all too ready to trade their reputation, compatriots or children's futures for not even a bag of silver, but an "account" with made up digits courtesy of some bureaucrats a thousand miles away.

Whether we're talking about cheap influencers peddling crypto scams, bankers selling out their own customers, neighbors snitching on neighbors, celebrities becoming political commentators, comedians being paid to push climate agendas, or overweight scientists pretending they know something about health - it's the same sickness.

In the absence of honor we find only echoes of Judas. To hell with truth or justice. Why is any of that important when morality is relative and when nobody is watching from above? And who cares who's watching from the crowd, because there are no standards anyway. Right?

We must reverse this, and understand that honor is tied to something deep within the spirit or psyche. For those who don't believe in this more spiritual element, think of it this way:

Honor is like a set of standards, which you first and foremost measure yourself with, then make public so that your peers, and those who you respect, can keep you accountable. Being dishonorable is akin to lying to yourself and such consistent lying creates a dissonance in your own psychology. So whether you believe in something more metaphysical or not, there is a clear and measurable *psychological* price to pay. The path of dishonor or selling yourself out leads ultimately to dissonance, which in turn often leads to emptiness and nihilism, unless you're clinically a psychopath.

Selling one's soul for the short-term material gain, and paying for it with a long-term sentence to spiritual or psychological purgatory is known as a Faustian bargain for a reason. Dostoevsky wrote an entire book about this with *Crime & Punishment*. Theologies from the beginning of time warned of such trades in a spiritual sense, and warrior codes since the ancient times guarded against this because they knew this "moral dimension to the universe" is not just imaginary. Whether you want to call its judge God, or conscience, the effect is the same. The point is to hold you to a standard beyond what's materially measurable.

"The present system of paying for every sort of service was not in vogue among the adherents of Bushido. It believed in a service which can be rendered only without money and without price. Spiritual service, be it of priest or teacher, was not to be repaid in gold or silver, not because it was valueless but because it was invaluable.

Here the non-arithmetical honor-instinct of Bushido taught a truer lesson than modern Political Economy; for wages and salaries can be paid only for services whose results are definite, tangible, and measurable, whereas the best service done in education—namely, in soul development (and this includes the services of a pastor), is not definite, tangible, or measurable. Being immeasurable, money, the ostensible measure of value, is of inadequate use."

Inazo Nitobe, Bushido: The Soul of Japan

Reputation

When nothing is sacred and nothing matters, status is no longer measured by the character of a man, but by the currency he has access to. It follows that in a world where currency is fraudulent, so too is status - in many cases at least. Without intangibles like honor and reputation, we find ourselves with an inversion of status, which leads to an inversion in order. Hence why we live in an age where the despicable and resentful rule.

To fix this, reputation needs to be revalued. Not repriced, in an economic sense, but re-*valued* in a social sense. Reputation can be thought of as the more practical aspect of honor. Like capital, it is something you acquire and build up over time. It's hard to earn, very easy to squander, but can open doors for you that money alone cannot. It acts like an intangible token for respect and trust that we recognize as real because we've used it in every culture since the beginning of time. Even moderns, generally poor in this currency, and who would rather pretend it does not exist, still act in such a way that proves it does.

We cannot put a price on reputation - at least not a monetary price. Those who are trying to tokenize reputation, and turn it into another material currency, don't seem to understand this. Reputation is neither fungible, nor should it be saleable. It operates on rules that are more culturally influenced, so there is no one version or measure. It's different to money which needs to be fungible because it works optimally as a singular language or measure. The whole point of reputation is that it is **not** something you can trade. While reputation can be viewed as a form of metaphysical currency, it's important to remember that it's *not* money, and be wary when the lines are being blurred.

Ultimately, reputation matters, and the only way to build it is with time, honesty and integrity. Nobody is perfect, mistakes will be made, but the solution remains the same: proof of work.

Bitcoin and Honor

Honour has to do with one's word and reputation. This has a number of things to do with Bitcoin. First of all, Bitcoin is a promise, or a set of promises. It's something you can "bank" on, which interestingly enough is not dependent on the word or honor of a person or group, but on a unique method of social and mathematical consensus. Through this process, Bitcoin is something which resembles the traditional meaning of honor, but goes about it in a novel way.

More important to our discussion is Bitcoin's impact on behavior. Reputation has and always will be important. It is an intangible form of capital, and as discussed earlier, opens doors that money alone cannot.

As the world becomes more digital and interconnected, reputation will become more important. Doing what's right, when it's right, in the right way, is honorable and separates the noble from the base.

This has always been the case, and is so today, though skewed because of how prevalent the money printer has become. Fake money is like a magnet that distorts the image on a screen. Honor is still important, but the monetary magnet draws attention and energy to places where it otherwise may not have gone.

On a Bitcoin standard, the virtue of honor will likely be re-evaluated.

Honesty / Integrity
(seijitsu)

Honesty / Integrity

誠
実

Honesty is related to honor and, as we saw in the previous chapter, both English words share a common Latin origin. To avoid repeating myself, I'll explore instead the etymology of the words which I believe echo the spirit of this virtue more than any others: integrity and sincerity.

The Japanese word for "Integrity" is Seijitsu, which is made up of two Kanji: "誠実"

The first Kanji, 誠 (Sei), which is also read as "Makoto," means "sincerity" or truthfulness. This is how this virtue is most commonly referenced in Japanese Bushido. The Kanji is in turn composed of two elements: 言 (gen), meaning "word" or "speech," and 成 (sei/naru), which means "to become" or "to accomplish." It originally expressed the idea of words becoming reality, or one's words being a true reflection of reality. As "Makoto," it emphasizes the purity and authenticity of one's heart and intentions, representing sincerity, honesty, and faithfulness not just in words but also in the authenticity of one's character.

The second Kanji, 実 (Jitsu), conveys the idea of reality or truth. It combines the elements 宀 (u), which is a roof or a house, and 木 (ki), meaning "tree." This character originally depicted a tree reaching its full potential under a roof, symbolizing growth, fruition, and reality. *Jitsu* has evolved to represent concepts like truth, reality, and the fulfillment of promises or potential. This is not to be confused with the word "Jiu Jitsu", a romanized version of "Jujutsu" or "Jujitsu", which is, in Japanese, composed of two Kanji: "柔" (Ju) and "術" (Jutsu).

Together, 誠実 (Seijitsu) combines the profound sincerity and truthfulness embodied in 誠 (Makoto) with the concept of reality and fulfillment in 実 (Jitsu). It conveys the idea of "Integrity" in Japanese, emphasizing not just honesty and sincerity in one's words and actions, but also the deep alignment of these actions with one's true intentions and the fulfillment of commitments.

In Japanese, the word honesty best translates to sincerity, and the Chinese Ideogram for sincerity is a combination of "Word" and "Perfect".

The etymology of "integrity" is fascinating. Through Old French *integrité*, which referred to "innocence, blamelessness, chastity, purity", it comes from Latin *integritas* ("soundness, wholeness, completeness"), and in turn from *integer*, meaning "intact, whole, complete" literally and "untainted, upright" figuratively. Indeed, *in-* ("not") and *tangere* ("to touch") combined mean "untouched" or "pure.".

As for sincerity, it derives from Old French sinceritie, which comes directly from the Latin *sinceritas* meaning "honesty, purity, soundness, wholeness," in turn from sincerus, "whole, clean, uninjured," or more figuratively that which is "sound, genuine, pure, true or candid".

Both sincerity and integrity share the common themes of untouched or unmarred completeness, so you can see why I've decided to combine them here. In practice, I believe that sincerity is the softer, more compassionate twin sister to the more masculine essence, raw and direct, of Integrity, which was more akin to "Veracity" in the context of the Samurai.

Sincerity in bushido

Confucius saw sincerity as having transcendental power, almost identifying it with the Divine: *"Sincerity is the end and the beginning of all things; without Sincerity there would be nothing."*

For the Samurai, sincerity was an earnestness that comes from deep inside. It came from a place of courage, while lying was deemed cowardly. Notice again how the different virtues are woven together.

> *"The bushi held that his high social position demanded a loftier standard of veracity [sincerity/integrity] than that of the tradesman and peasant. "Bushi no ichi-gon"—the word of a Samurai, or in exact German equivalent, Ritterwort—was sufficient guarantee for the truthfulness of an assertion.*
> *His word carried such weight with it that promises were generally made and fulfilled without a written pledge, which would have been deemed quite beneath his dignity.*
> *Many anecdotes were told of those who atoned by death for 'ni-gon;' a double tongue."*

Inazo Nitobe, Bushido: The Soul of Japan

In Samurai culture, unlike in the West, lying was not considered a "sin;" that concept did not exist. The Japanese have "tsumi" which translates roughly as "fault," "Jaku," or "Yowasa," conveying a weakness or fragility whether physical or moral, and the broader concept of "haji", which translates to "shame or dishonor." Lying, specifically, was denounced as weakness, and as such, it was considered highly dishonorable.

We saw above how powerful fear of dishonor and shame can be, as well as the importance of honor in Bushido. This is an interesting way of dealing with transgression: by framing it as weakness, and therefore shameful and dishonorable, the impetus to steer clear of such course of action was all the greater, especially for the warrior class who would put honor above life.

Perhaps this is why we live in the age of lies. The civilian populace no longer aspires toward virtues such as honor, while religious calls to "tell the truth" are seen as 'archaic' in secular, post-modern and post-truth world.

We've witnessed the rise of cowards who believe material wealth trumps spiritual or moral wealth. They will lie, cheat and steal, just to 'get ahead' economically - ultimately selling their own souls for paper. The Faustian bargain.

In my opinion, it's far better to die honestly than to live a lie. There is a wholesomeness to the former, despite the tragic overtones. There is an emptiness to the latter, which can only conjure up greater levels of nihilism. It is plain to see as the West continues its decay. Affluence gotten through lies, degenerating into blind hedonism and aimless pursuits of YOLO flavored pleasures. It's sad.

> *"The coward dies a thousand deaths, the soldier dies but once."*
>
> William Shakespeare, *Julius Caesar*, act 2, scene 2, lines 34-35.

These are the acts of a hero. To tell the truth in a world of lies. To inspire others to do the same.

The hero and the logos

In Inazo Nitobe's chapter on the virtue of sincerity, he draws a parallel to the Neoplatonic doctrine of 'The Logos'. You may be familiar with this concept thanks to the work of Jordan Peterson.

The Greek term *logos* means "word, speech, statement, discourse." The philosophical concept of the Logos is "the divine Word," it is Truth with a capital T, the "Golden Thread" and the essence of things. It is the "indivisible," another word for "whole" or *integer*. Notice the relationship?

The great Thomas Carlyle, in his book *On Heroes, Hero-Worship, and The Heroic in History* talks at length about the *"deep, great, genuine sincerity"* of the Hero. He writes that while most people can *"walk in a vain show,"* heroes cannot. Heroes cannot live except in the *"awful presence of Reality,"* especially when that reality is coated in falsehoods. This inability to buy into lies, or indulge in pretenses for social 'brownie points', is a core trait of The Hero.

The Hero is he who is unable to lead an insincere life, and therefore, he who embodies the Logos. He goes on a journey, faces down demons and monsters (i.e., lies), and prevails because he *walks with God* (i.e., truth). He returns from his journey renewed and complete, a living example of alignment with certain ideals or principles, for all others to emulate. He discovers truth and brings it back.

> *"The hero organizes the demands of social being and the responsibilities of his own soul into a coherent, hierarchically arranged unit."*

Jordan B. Peterson, 12 Rules for Life: An Antidote to Chaos

The Hero is belittled, dismissed, demonized and fought because he opposes the 'established order of lies', yet he continues onward (and upward). He seeks to instantiate an alternative 'mode of being', as John Vallis would say: *"grounded in a more coherent and high-fidelity perception of 'what is' — that is, one which is more truthful."*

The Hero cannot abide by views or decisions just because they are common, socially acceptable, or have the experts' approval. He rebels against the decreed (fiat) order of things. He resists the conditioning of society that seeks to place him in a box. The Hero discovers how to tap into a deeper, subtler truth: Instinct.

Jash Dholani reminds us that: *"Being heroic is not a conscious decision - it's a healthy instinct,"* and Carlyle writes of the heroic figure: *"His sincerity does not depend on himself; he cannot help being sincere!"*

The Hero has gone by many names throughout the ages. He was Achilles at Troy, Ulysses in the *Odyssey*, Prometheus with the Fire, Leonidas at Thermopylae, Alexander on his conquest of the East, Jesus as the Messiah, Thor or Odin of the Norse, King Arthur of Brittania, and Miyamoto Musashi in Japan.

In all of these cultures, the Hero was praised for his unwavering integrity and sincerity. In Japanese culture, Samurai mothers would teach their children to embody the virtues of Bushido through the example of heroic figures.

The hero has a deep appreciation for time and energy. He wastes none of it on illusions. His sincerity is the source of his greatness. His unrelenting grip on reality is why his actions have weight.

It's useful to understand this idea *via-negativa*: what not to do. Carlyle describes the opposite of a hero as someone who falls into skepticism and insincerity. Skeptics replace action with endless questioning, dilettantes replace commitment with permanent dabbling, and insincere people hide cowardice behind irony and sarcasm.

The Hero, the man of integrity and sincerity, is the man of action. The Hero is a man of radical responsibility, which I'll explore in the next chapter.

Bitcoin and Integrity

Integrity, much like honor, revolves around consistency of actions, principles, and values, regardless of external observation or pressure. The Bitcoin system is in itself an embodiment of integrity. It is "whole and complete" in the sense that we know its maximum supply and the full ruleset. It is a 'Truth-Machine', not unlike the Logos: it just is, in its glorious completeness.

As a transparent ledger, recorded and distributed worldwide, it is as honest a record of human action, value and money as we've ever had (and possibly ever will have). There is no papering over what's there. Bitcoin is an immutable record, an incorruptible source of truth.

It goes further. Bitcoin's consensus mechanism is the most elegant solution we've seen to ensure honest node operation in an adversarial environment. By combining monetary incentives, the real cost of energy, cryptography and the law of large numbers, Bitcoin orients validator behavior toward honesty, without the need for coercion, trusted collaboration, or trusted third parties: it solves the Byzantine Generals Problem. At the same time, it incentivizes individuals and collectives to cultivate integrity.

Bushido is a playbook for life on a Bitcoin Standard. I believe that in such a world integrity, like honor, will be valued more than guile and opportunism. The entrepreneur will earn more than the trader. The producer will be valued more than the consumer. The short-termism and nihilism will give way to a lower time preference and greater meaning.

Bitcoin not only embodies integrity at a systemic level, but demands it from individuals. Still, practicing this virtue is not easy: Bitcoin alone does not fix that. I believe it is our duty to cultivate this Logos within, and do it not "because Bitcoin", but because it makes for a more wholesome existence; first for ourselves, then radially outward.

These are the acts of a Hero: to tell the truth in a world of lies, and to inspire others to do the same.

Responsibility
(sekinin)

Responsibility

責
任

The root of a large number of the world's problems is the renunciation of responsibility. The same applies to individuals. Too much emphasis is placed on the value of freedom, and too little on the virtue that makes it possible: responsibility.

The Japanese word for "responsibility" is *sekinin*, which is made up of two Kanji: "責任"

The first Kanji, 責 (Se), conveys the idea of obligation or debt. It is composed of two parts: 貝 (kai), meaning "shell" or "money," and 尺 (shaku), representing a unit of measurement. Those familiar with Nick Szabo's *"shelling out"* might notice something here. Originally, this character symbolized the idea of holding someone accountable for something, as in measuring or weighing their actions against a standard. Over time, it has evolved to represent the concept of responsibility in the sense of being accountable or liable for something.

The second Kanji, 任 (Nin), means duty, and represents a man standing next to a king, by combining the elements 人 (*hito*), meaning "person" or "man" and 壬, which means either king, monarch or chief; or the 'best and strongest of its kind.' The traditional interpretation of 壬 is that the three horizontal strokes represent Heaven, Man, and Earth and the vertical stroke is the king: the one who connects them together. This is also relevant, for it is the king, or the 'best and strongest' who must bear the greatest weight: the burden and duty of responsibility.

Together, 責任 (Sekinin) combines the notions of accountability and the bearing of duties to convey the idea of "responsibility" in Japanese.

This term emphasizes not just the act of being accountable for one's actions, but also the strength necessary to bear the weight that comes with being responsible. This virtue, like all great virtues, is both a privilege and a burden. It encapsulates the sense of having a moral, social, or professional obligation to act correctly and take charge of the roles or tasks one is given. The etymology also relates very strongly to the deeper idea of money as an obligation or debt: the measurement of one's monetary obligations to the sovereign, for example. It's something like 'a man standing next to his king, ensuring that exactly what's owed is given to the other.' The fact that 'duty' itself is 'man next to king' is very feudal.

Once again, we find similarities in the origins of the English word. Responsibility, like response, comes from Latin *respondere*, in turn from the verb *spondere*, which means "to pledge," "to engage oneself" or "to promise." Its roots go back to Proto-Indo-European *spondeio*, meaning "to libate" or "to pledge," which also gave Greek *spendein*, "to make a drink offering."

Together these essentially mean "to answer to the original act", "to promise in return", or "the payment of consequence" - all which were ritual in nature.

As such, responsibility defines a *"Quality of being which promises to answer for the consequences of the actions taken in the original place"*. A virtue, etymologically reinforced here, of immense importance.

The absence of responsibility

Responsibility is not explicitly enumerated in Chivalric codes, Bushido, or even in the Christian Cardinals, all of which focus on other virtues more valor-like or spiritual. So why do I include it here?

For three reasons. The first is that responsibility is implied in each of these codes. If you look at the language used to describe the virtues of most warrior codes, the tone of responsibility is central, and the deeds emerging from the exercise of those virtues, often reflected as much. In Bushido for example, Samurai were willing to take responsibility for their actions and to restore their honor even at the cost of their own lives, through the ritual act of seppuku. No other culture backed their words with such a profound and symbolic deed.

Secondly, the scale of the civilizations who witnessed the emergence of such schools of thought was far more local. There didn't exist "grand cities" (at least not as they do today) in which people could hide, with widespread "welfare programs" funded by money expropriated from people, for 'public goods', or "Wall Street" via which banksters could create a never-ending array of financial products to suck up the excess liquidity from a central bank that is literally robbing everyone via inflation.

Yes - the Romans, the Chinese, the Japanese and the great European empires of the Enlightenment all developed sophisticated societies with administrative classes, bureaucracies and micro-versions of the statist abominations we live within today, but they were far smaller in scale and impact.

Finally, we are social species and naturally grow closer to those we are responsible for. The linkages of mutual responsibility, and the fulfillment of those responsibilities, are to a large extent the glue that holds society together. Prior cultures were tribal, communal and deeply connected, so responsibility was a part of their DNA. Today we live in a hyper-individualized world: people are more connected to their iPhones than they are to their families. Instead of being present at dinner, people are scrolling Instagram, hooked by dopamine hits their personalized social media feed literally *feeds* them. Instead of training together at the gym, everyone's walking around with headphones on, lost in their own personalized playlist. Ironically, most of these playlists and feeds are actually similar, which if anything, is a testament to our deeper desire for connectedness.

We are so extremely independent, that we are alone. We've become isolated from one another to such a degree that people, especially the younger generations, have lost touch with how to connect and communicate with other human beings. They literally text each other while sitting across from each other. Social experiments have been done on the street where an actor will snatch a bag from a woman right in front of a crowd of bystanders. Instead of doing something about it, people will watch the crime occur in front of them, they will cross the street or pretend to be on their phone to avoid doing anything about it. The 'brave' ones might record and post it on social media. In fact, it's gotten so bad that instead of being celebrated, the people who actually do take on responsibility in public places, and do something about a nuisance or a crime, are made an example of. Jordan Neely was one such case in 2023.

Extreme individualism is how you erode responsibility and are able to take someone's freedom or control them. A single branch is easy to break, but tie a bundle together and it's much stronger. All of the stupid rules and regulations imposed on us, the humiliation rituals of wearing masks and being x rayed and strip searched at the airport, are only possible because we're isolated and individual. The bureaucratic and parasitic classes **need** this. They actively look for the lone wolf and swoop. Imagine some petty mask enforcer trying their tactics on a group of deeply-connected, responsible strong men. It doesn't work. The petty tyrants lack the courage and the will, so they convince us all that individualism is the way, and then pluck us one by one.

The "renunciation of responsibility" has been baked into our very social, economic, political, physical and psychological existence. Modernity is one big game of **Responsibility Hot Potato.** It's even coded into the language we use and our cultural norms. You're no longer responsible for your own health, but somehow vaguely responsible for everyone else's. You're not responsible for your own home, but vaguely responsible for the entire global climate. You cannot defend yourself, but you must be a martyr for the poor refugees in other countries.

Such inversions and perversions cannot last, except to the detriment of the host, which is why I'm being explicit about this virtue for the Bushido of Bitcoin. Responsibility is fundamentally at the root of all the great virtues. In fact, you cannot truly practice courage, honor, duty, justice or love without it. It must be central to the life of anyone seeking to be a leader, and core to the spirit and DNA of any new civilization that we build from the ashes of the democratic welfare state.

Agency and NPCs

"There are three types of people in this world:
Those who make things happen,
Those who watch things happen,
Those who wonder wtf happened."

Unknown

Responsibility is being "answerable" for one's actions and accountable for their consequences.   It is a measure of maturity and strength. Responsibility and the ability to respond, are liveness tests. The difference between a living being with agency, and an NPC, is simply the virtue of responsibility. It differentiates the living from the zombies.

Humans are adaptation machines.   We observe, we ingest information, we calculate both consciously and unconsciously, we decide, then we act, after which we observe again, ingest, calculate, decide and act - and so forth, until the day we die. The distance between our actions and their consequences is a measure of how well we, and therefore our societies, can adapt and improve.

The OODA Loop was developed by US Air Force Colonel John Boyd. It's a decision-making framework which stands for Observe, Orient, Decide, Act.   It describes a continuous process of interaction with a dynamic environment: one observes the situation, orients oneself by analyzing the information and past experiences, decides upon a course of action, and then acts on that decision.

It was designed for application in a military context, but really, it's a description of agency and life.   It's about being aware of one's surroundings, orienting, making decisions, acting, then adapting as necessary. The key to it all is responsibility and being accountable for the results of the decisions you make and actions you take. Remove that and the loop breaks down.

Outcomes, results and consequences, like pain and pleasure are feedback mechanisms. They are central to an actor's ability to respond and adapt. Adaptation is how life 'finds its way'. In fact, if you cannot adapt, are you really even alive? I would argue no. You are inert. You don't move by your own volition, but by the inertia of an external force. You are passive. The unfortunate reality is many are like this. Some call it "going with the flow", while others simply remain oblivious to their environment and operate in a state of eternal unconsciousness. They are the herbivore equivalent of humans. Vessels for agents "in the Matrix".

When your entire society is full of such automatons, don't be surprised that totalitarian states arise, supported by mindless crowds eager to obey mindless mandates. Understand this: ***If you want to take away someone's freedoms, first relieve them of their responsibility.*** This is the trick, and this is the psyop! While everyone's been so focused on their "freedoms" and "rights" they've forgotten about the other side of the ledger, and slowly relinquished responsibility for all the things that matter in life, from their minds, their body, their families and their relationships. They've become dependants of the State, and wonder why they're no longer "free." The truth is, they no longer deserve it. They've behaved like cattle, and have come to be treated as such.

Oswald Spengler, in his book *Man and Technics*, differentiates between different life forms, with a kind of hierarchy. At the base lies inert matter, the non-living substrates of the world—rocks, water, and air. These are the fundamental building blocks, lacking agency or the ability to respond. They exist in a state of static equilibrium, subject only to external physical forces.

Above this, we find plants. While still anchored, they represent a leap in the hierarchy of life because they interact with their environment in a more dynamic way, absorbing nutrients, growing, and reproducing. However, they remain largely passive.

"It doesn't take much intelligence to sneak up on a leaf."

Larry Niven, *The Ringworld Engineers*

The next layer is the herbivore. These creatures introduce mobility and a degree of basic agency. Their lives are a constant search for food and avoidance of predators, driven by survival instincts rather than a conscious, vital, desire for life. They do not hunt - they gather and graze. Their physiology and physiognomy are designed for defense. Their eyes are on the side of their heads. They have impeccable smell and hearing, to warn them of danger, so they can run away from something. They are herd animals, similar to the Human NPC, whose physiognomy and life is reminiscent of such creatures. You see it in their eyes: that often empty, "deer-in-the-headlights" look. Their lifestyles are largely sedentary, spent either in an artificially-lit office cubicle, or a home office with Netflix and social media in hand while they graze on vegan snacks. This archetype prides themselves on not eating their cattle brethren, instead, choosing to ingest industrial sludge made of soy and chemical plant extracts, so long as it comes with an ethical "vegan and cruelty free" tick on the box. It's no wonder the same kinds of people line up to be injected with strange foreign toxins "for their safety." There's a reason we call them sheeple or cattle.

"What is the opposite of the soul of a lion? The soul of a cow."

Oswald Spengler, Man and Technics: A Contribution to a Philosophy of Life

Carnivores are the next stage of life. They are hunters. Their prey is not a plant that just sits there, but a herbivore which runs, and is often larger, heavier and can, at times, hit back. Furthermore, carnivores must hunt and outwit both their prey and other competitors. This requires a higher level of awareness and adaptability, a finer attunement to the environment, and the ability to make more complex decisions. Their physiognomy and physiology are once again designed for it. The eyes of the preying animal give it a target. A lion's eyes are in the front of his head, so he can triangulate and attack. While the herbivore runs *away* from something, *the carnivore runs toward it.* This direction is *everything* and once again describes humankind extremely well. Some people have "predator eyes." Their psyche & physiology are goal oriented. They choose something to focus on then run toward it. They are by definition leaders and rarely part of a great, massive herd, but a small, tribal pack. While herbivores have strength in numbers, carnivores have strength in soul.

> *"The animal of prey is the highest form of mobile life. It implies a maximum of freedom from others and for oneself, of self-responsibility, of independence, and an extreme of necessity where that self can hold its own only by fighting and winning and destroying. It imparts a high dignity to Man, as a type, that he is a beast of prey.*
> *A herbivore is by its destiny a prey, and it seeks to avoid this destiny by escaping without combat, but beasts of prey must get prey. The one type of life is of its innermost essence defensive, the other offensive, hard, cruel, destructive. The difference appears even in the tactics of movement — on the one hand the habit of retreating, fleetness, cutting of corners, evasion, concealment, and on the other the straight-line motion of the attack, the lion's spring, the eagle's swoop."*

Oswald Spengler, Man and Technics: A Contribution to a Philosophy of Life

Humans are the apex predator because we hunt the hunter. We transcend all other life forms because we are imbued with the highest agency. We are the animal of peak responsibility and adaptability. This is precisely why we have conquered the world and learned to literally transform matter and energy with our hands, our minds, and the mechanical appendages they've produced. What you're reading now and the very fact that you can read it, is proof of that. Alas, many have forgotten this. Nowadays, more humans are more herbivore than carnivore, and the carnivores among us have lost touch with this vital energy. We've been overcome by a sense of guilt about our greatness and in doing so have shirked our responsibility. By dropping the load, we've become weaker, and left the world without leadership and guidance. Like sheep without a sheepdog or shepherd.

The only cure is radical responsibility and ownership.

The psychology of responsibility

"He who blames others has a long way to go on his journey. He who blames himself is halfway there. He who blames no one, has arrived."

Chinese Proverb

Radical ownership is not a new idea. It is deeply ingrained in the psyche of the best of us, and remains a core tenet of high performing teams and leaders. This is evidenced by the popularity of personalities like Jocko Willink, retired Navy SEAL commander and author of *Extreme Ownership*, and Jordan Peterson whose core message in *12 Rules for Life* is about taking responsibility and ownership. Before them, it was Tony Robbins and the personal development crowd, with their emphasis on owning what happens in one's life and placing oneself 'at cause', not 'at effect'. Going back even further is Alfred Adler, the forgotten father of psychology, whose entire psychological philosophy centered on individual responsibility. For the great warrior cultures of the past, this was a way of life. It's always been there, and no matter how much modern society conspires to ignore it, it will always be there, because it's part of our DNA.

Alfred Adler held the individual responsible for his own mind and behavior, instead of "external events," arguing that it wasn't on-going therapy or etiological reasoning, but the courage and honesty to take personal responsibility which helped deal with psychological issues. According to this school of thought, known as "Individual Psychology," each person is an integrated whole striving toward an outcome: each feeling, each belief and action taken, while seemingly irrational, ultimately represents a *choice* made by the individual, not something *happening* to them.

Adler infamously didn't believe in trauma, which triggered his contemporaries and especially modern psychologists. He didn't deny the existence of traumatic events, of course, nor the mental and emotional scars they leave, but he emphasized that people have the capacity to choose and direct their behavior, and therefore their reaction to such events; yes, you may be traumatized, but that's not the end of the story: instead of placing yourself at the effect of trauma, powerless against it, you have agency to deal with it.

His work is largely glossed over in modern psychology, most likely because it negates the need for ongoing therapy, medication and the never-ending labeling of every emotion as a syndrome or disorder, not unlike how the Austrian School of Economics, which does away with the bureaucratic central banking apparatus, is conveniently ignored. Coincidentally, Adler too was Austrian; there was clearly something about that region and era.

The problem with most modern psychology and all kinds of therapy is that by dwelling on trauma we enable its effects, giving it both life and significance. Looking back over the last century, mental health issues, depression, and a plethora of syndromes and disorders have steadily increased, in lockstep with the rise of 'psychology' both as a discipline and as a well-funded institution.

We have come to ignore the body and the very things that make us alive. We've drugged the feelings which are otherwise signals to act, into oblivion and replaced them with numbness and docility. Through this modern psychology, we've separated the mind out, while trying to make everything safe, comfortable and **not your fault**. By abdicating responsibility in this way, we've made it okay to be a victim. **Remember this: victims are not free!** That is precisely because they are not responsible for their own circumstances or how they react to said circumstances. A victim is a slave, whether to circumstance or his own beliefs. If you're wondering why we're surrounded by compliance maximalists and the world has turned into one big game of Oppression Olympics, this is it. It's not the grand conspiracies we should be worried about, but the renunciation of responsibility, and the obsession with things you cannot change or influence.

This is the whole point of Adler's school of psychology. It is teleological, meaning that it is concerned with the present and the future, the things you can control or have influence over. Contrast this with essentially all modern schools of psychology which are etiological: they focus on how past events and biological factors impact psychology, that is, things you have very little influence over. One is goal oriented, the other is causation oriented.

In other words, you have more power and control over it than you'd like to admit. Which is ultimately another way of saying you're more responsible for it than the world would otherwise have you believe. *It's not what happens to you but what you do with it that matters.* The bro-psychologists were right again, as were the personal development gurus.

> *"No experience is in itself a cause of our success or failure. We do not suffer from the shock of our experiences—the so-called trauma—but instead we make out of them whatever suits our purposes. We are not determined by our experiences, but the meaning we give them is self-determining."*
>
> Alfred Adler, *What Life Could Mean to You*

For over fifteen years I've triggered my psychologist friends by calling depression an act or a behavior, not a syndrome or disease. You don't "get" depression, you "do" depression, by choosing to remain in that state. It's not just something that happens to you, or that you catch like the flu. It's a *choice* or at most, it's a temporary feeling. Of course, life knocks you down, and instead of feeling elevated, you occasionally feel **de**-pressed. That's normal, it happens to all of us - and it's your body's way of telling you to take stock and introspect for a minute. This ***feeling*** is a healthy signal from the nervous system to adjust your behavior, a warning that you are lacking focus or meaning in your life. Instead of using it as the catalyst for change, or riding it like the wave of emotion that it is, modern psychology short-circuits the natural process by teaching you to numb yourself into oblivion with drugs, or marry the feeling and label yourself "clinically depressed."

Unsurprisingly, behind the myth that depression is a "chemical imbalance" that needs to be "corrected" via the use of medicines or drugs, we find a multi-billion dollar SSRI industry. But it's a scam as blatant as the idea that printing money creates more wealth. A recent review published in the journal *Molecular Psychiatry*, which looked at studies involving thousands of people across decades of research - found no evidence that depression is even caused by serotonin abnormalities, nor by lower levels of reduced serotonin activity![1] Despite mounting evidence against this myth, and the common sense, first-principles approach of "bro-psychology", the trends toward more drug use for depression and less responsibility for choosing to don these labels both continue.

You are taught to feel powerless about whatever situation or circumstance you are in, and as a result, you abdicate your responsibility. Your 'trauma' and labels such as depression, bi-polar disorder, anxiety and the like are just enabling your choice to keep focusing on what's wrong, instead of doing something about it.

You are always choosing how to feel, think and behave, whether it's conscious or not. In the end, it serves a purpose. It is you and only you that can associate meaning to an event or a circumstance. Acknowledging this requires courage and honesty. You must resist the modern, medicated, feminized, therapy infused schools of psychology and instead choose responsibility. This approach will make you elite, in the true sense of the word - and it will forever be the case, because it is always easier to blame others for your feelings of inferiority. The hard and noble road, the road of radical ownership is for the few. For the responsible and the excellent.

---

1   Moncrieff et al. (2023), "The serotonin theory of depression: a systematic umbrella review of the evidence," *Molecular Psychiatry*, 28/8, pp. 3243-3256.
https://www.nature.com/articles/s41380-022-01661-0

"The one thing you can't take away from me is the way I choose to respond to what you do to me. The last of one's freedoms is to choose one's attitude in any given circumstance."

Viktor E. Frankl, *Man's Search for Meaning*

The energy of responsibility

Responsibility applies more to adults than to children or adolescents, and more to men than it does to women. Responsibility comes with maturity and it carries a masculine charge. This doesn't mean the latter cannot be responsible - but there is a spectrum and a charge.

Responsibility is a weight. It's something you carry, and men, both psychologically and physiologically are designed to lift and bear weight. It is why they are called to "carry frame" which essentially means to hold space, demarcate territory and assert standards. When a man does so, he brings order to the world around him, which frees the young and the feminine to explore, learn, nurture, play and love.

When a man doesn't take on this responsibility, he burdens those who depend on him. You see it with children who parent their parents, and with women who, because of the weakness of their men, have to pick up the frame. Both in time develop resentment toward their parents or partners because they cannot let go and be free.

"To be a man is to bear responsibility for all things."

Jerr, *The Wall Speaks*

Weight and responsibility age you, which for a man is more acceptable since we physiologically age later and remain fertile for longer. It's not the same for children and women. Ignoring this ignores the real cost. We're only children once, and exploration is critical for early development. Women are literally designed to bring life into the world, and it is a man's duty to create the frame and structure around her so she can do this safely and freely.

We have a saying in my household: "Everything is my fault." Wife is annoyed? My fault. Food didn't taste good? My fault. Traffic on the road on our way somewhere? My fault. I really mean *everything*. It may sound harsh, but it's true, and I wouldn't have it any other way, because it puts me in a position of ultimate responsibility. It means I can fulfill my instinctual role as a man and a husband, and more practically, that I can actually do something about it.

This energy extends beyond the household and through to society. The cycles of history can even be defined as the rise and fall of patriarchies. They grow and conquer, only to be run by weak men, who are easily corruptible and fail to maintain it. These weak men are then overrun by more vital invaders who are more patriarchal. We are living in the third innings: weak men behaving like women, and women, deceived with stories of independence and careerism, acting like tax-paying weak men. This not only lacks the strength of structure, but kills the charge between genders. Instead of the attraction that comes from polarity, we have the eternal friendzone: a place devoid of charge and life. Instead of building, being fertile and flourishing, society is engulfed in equality and sameness: where everyone is a copy of a copy of a copy.

This is all on men, who have abdicated their responsibility to lead and bear the weight. And the truth is, because there can be no vacuum of frame or leadership, the world currently operates from a feminine frame - one which does not carry the charge of responsibility or order. One which is not designed to bear weight, and is crumbling before our very eyes.

Feudalism and all warrior cultures were patriarchal. They were hierarchy and responsibility-based, because they were father-led. A matriarchal society is communal and egalitarian by nature. It works in the home but it doesn't work at scale. Civilisation demands excellence and differentiation. The world is not a womb, nor is it the warm embrace of the mother. The world is the wild, and it is a man's duty to build the structures that can withstand and protect. It is not a woman's duty or responsibility to bring order to society. Her energy brings life and vitality to the structure and order man constructs. It's about time we remembered this.

A man is designed to carry his responsibility, and the amount he can carry is the true measure of his strength. A strong man is responsible for his territory: he is the father who bears the responsibility for his family; the man who runs a company and thus bears responsibility for his employees; the man who mentors the young and thus bears responsibility for the development of their character. This is what it means to be *powerful*.

We all know that with great power comes great responsibility, but the inverse is also true. With great responsibility comes great power, and power is a good thing. For too long we've been told that "power is evil" that "power corrupts, and absolute power corrupts absolutely" but I've come to realize that this is a lie.

Power only corrupts the weak. Power, like technology, is agnostic. Put technology in the hands of a sadist, and they will use it to dominate those weaker, and to bring down those who are better. This is communism in action. It's why everything that comes from communism is ugly. It's anti-life. It's an attempt to make everything the same.

The man who bears the responsibility for his people or for an idea that changes the way the world works, the Nikola Teslas, Steve Jobs, and Alexander the Greats of the world. These men were the truly powerful.

Notice I did not say "Christine Lagarde," "Janet Yellen" or "Joe Biden." When I talk about strength or power, I am not talking about the man who steps on the ant and calls himself a hero. I am not speaking of the heads of central banks, petty politicians, and meddling bureaucrats who exist only to suck wealth out of the system. These people are too weak to actually build something, so they lie, cheat, and steal from others. They are the most dangerous kind: the weak with access to power. The envious and the ugly.

It is *our* job, as men of strength, to claim power, by first taking responsibility.

Freedom is NOT a virtue

"Freedom is in danger of degenerating into mere arbitrariness unless it is lived in terms of responsibleness. That is why I recommend that the Statue of Liberty on the East Coast be supplemented by a Statue of Responsibility on the West Coast"

Viktor E. Frankl, Man's Search for Meaning

The libertarians and freedom maximalists among you may have noted that freedom is not listed as one of the virtues. This is because it's not a virtue but a *value*. Values are something you desire while virtues are something you do. Freedom is a "state" we all seek, that can only truly come about as a result of *taking* responsibility. In fact, it is meaningless without responsibility. It's like flesh without bones. It's taken me two decades to come to terms with this. My younger self held it as the highest ideal - and a part of me still does - but freedom, like happiness, is a side-effect. We experience it individually and collectively, when we embody the virtues that make it possible.

Furthermore, it's not even freedom that you really want. What you actually want is agency and *autonomy*. Freedom is a nebulous term like spirituality, which devoid of a clearly defined frame doesn't mean anything: at that point, we are talking specifically about autonomy, the capacity to choose from a set of available options. Absolute freedom is absolute chaos, which doesn't really exist, or if it does, is unstable and unsuitable for life. Freedom maximalism quickly falls apart with one question: Where does your freedom end, considering it may be in conflict with mine? This conundrum proves that freedom is only meaningful if it exists within a framework of duties, responsibilities and boundaries (this is the definition of autonomy) - and if you really want to enhance your "freedom", you need to increase your responsibilities and the boundary of your domain (which requires power). You are not entitled to freedom, you can only earn it. When someone tries to take unjustly what you've earned you must fight to protect it, and you cannot do that without taking responsibility.

Consider the military dictum that 'rank hath its privileges'. Privileges can be understood as liberties or freedoms; and that they come along with rank is not accidental, because the privilege of rank implies the burden of responsibility.

> *"You have never tasted freedom, friend," Dienekes spoke, "or*
> *you would know it is purchased not with gold, but steel."*
>
> Steven Pressfield, Gates of Fire

By way of example, King Leonidas I, whom we encountered earlier, was the king of Sparta between 490 BC and his death at the Battle of Thermopylae in 480 BC. He was one of two kings at the time because the Spartan constitution established a diarchy—a system where two kings ruled simultaneously, each coming from different royal families: the Agiads and the Eurypontids. Leonidas hailed from the Agiad dynasty, a lineage believed to be descended from the demigod Heracles.

It was Leonidas who took the initiative to lead a small force of Greek allies, including his famous 300 Spartan warriors, in their heroic stand against the massive invading army of the Persian Empire.

Leonidas was a king. A man with wealth and power, who like many other city-state leaders of the time was *free* to side with the Persians in return for silver and gold. But he didn't. He knew the price for true freedom was a responsibility to his land, people and legacy. So he chose to fight, fully aware of the certain death that awaited. He led his men against all odds, not merely as a duty to Sparta, but for the future of Greek civilization, and what it represented. He chose freedom in death, over servitude in life. He chose to be an agent, not a subject. He took the **responsibility** to preserve what they valued most, while others 'freely' chose to do nothing. How many modern statesmen could compare with such a man? None, of course.

His leadership at Thermopylae and his decision to fight to the last man, inspired and galvanized Greece into a defense that changed the course of history. It also immortalized Leonidas and 2500 years later we still remember his sacrifice. The Eurypontid king, on the other hand, was entirely forgotten.

Rights and responsibilities

Most people who talk a big game about "freedom" and "rights" outsource responsibility for their thoughts, their actions, their health, wealth, families, psychology, safety, relationships, work and just about everything else of import in life. The state, HR department, the experts and the pharmaceutical companies now take care of all of these.

Feeling sad or depressed? It's not because of how you're living, what you're focusing on, the label you've adopted or your decision to blame someone else - it's just a lack of Prozac. Are you fat and unhealthy? That's not your fault, and certainly has nothing to do with what you're eating or your sedentary lifestyle. It's a syndrome and a lack of Ozempic. A few vials will fix you right up, along with a dose of body positivity! These people are the opposite of autonomous. They are *automatons.*

Know this: responsibility and rights are reciprocal. In the same way you cannot have freedom, without first taking responsibility for that which you want to claim dominion or freedom over. The former is the price paid for the latter. The only question is who's footing the bill? These are universal equations you cannot cheat: You cannot be responsible for something and not have the freedom to act on it; you cannot have the freedom to act without being responsible for your actions. It thus follows that without responsibility, there can be no rights, no freedom and no liberty. If freedom is one side of the coin, responsibility is the other.

The modern managerial state is an affront to this truth. It's like a giant condom suffocating society in a bid to make everything 'safe.' It denies people agency over their own lives and reduces their exposure to the consequences of their actions. This makes them stupid, weak and unable to adapt, and kicks off a vicious cycle. The bureaucratic apparatus needs more stupid people to substantiate its existence, and more stupid people need a larger bureaucratic apparatus to support them, resulting in a spiraling reduction in responsibility, whose outcome is akin to that of the condom it resembles: sterility. Sterility of ideas, sterility of culture, sterility of products and services and ultimately, as evidenced by the falling birth rates, *actual sterility.*

There must be a "Renaissance of Responsibility".

Maturity

Responsibility was and always will be the most mature and evolved of human attributes. You only transcend childhood and enter adulthood when you take responsibility.

> *"Masculinity is male maturity: a measure of how competently a man shoulders his age-appropriate responsibilities."*

> *Noah Revoy, on X.com*

We live in an age of infantilism where everything is being "dumbed down" so that the lowest common denominator of subhuman can 'understand'. It started gradually, decades ago, and is now at the 'suddenly' stage, where math is racist and honest use of language is banned for offending people. Can it get worse? I'm sure it can. Stupidity knows no bounds. But can it last forever? No. Stupidity is also self-defeating. Right now, the very thing keeping the show going is the fact that mature, productive people foot the bill for the overgrown children throwing the party. As soon as the money dries up, the party is over. This is actually another of my favorite attributes of Bitcoin. It offers a release valve, and an exit for anyone tired of paying for other people's mistakes. This is good because mature, sensible, responsible people can have more to do good things with, while the immature will either be forced, by economic necessity, to mature or just dissolve in their own squalor. Either way, it's a net positive for humanity.

In this sense, there is a lot to be optimistic about. The tumultuous period we're in is a sign of humanity in the throes of adolescence. As a species, we are on the verge of something greater and more profound. We are mid-rite-of-passage, and the infantile part of us is throwing a tantrum because it knows its time is up. But no matter the extent of the madness, this too shall pass.

With greater maturity comes greater agency, and only with agency does any real freedom exist. It's your time to choose. Will you be the main character or just another NPC? A victor or a victim? A carnivore or a herbivore?

Bitcoin & Responsibility

Bitcoin is the Renaissance of Responsibility.

The same powerful property rights that free you to do as you please with your wealth also place the onus on you to secure it against loss, theft and waste.

Responsibility is the cardinal virtue for Bitcoiners: you find it embedded at every step, from the radical custody and storage methods, the lack of "support line" or rewind button, to the importance of privacy and the weight of the decision to part with sats, due to Bitcoin's deflationary nature. I've coined the term Responsibility go Up Technology (RgU Tech) as a play on the "Number go Up Technology" meme in Bitcoin circles, and I find it far more compelling.

One-way functions with no "rewind button" force you to think twice about what you are doing. They come with added weight. Bitcoin forces you to grow up, to be an adult: as the absolute owner of your own wealth, you become the steward, the bearer and the guardian. This is real power, and responsibility, the social implications of which are nothing short of profound. Like nature, it is unforgiving: it's as real as it gets. You adapt to it, it does not adapt to you. Like life itself, it's up to you to decide how to direct your time, energy and attention.

If reality can be described as that which you cannot rewind or reverse, then Bitcoin is the realest money we've ever had.

The infantilization of individuals is a regression and de-sophistication of civilization. It is a sickness. **Responsible Money is the cure.** *A sound money standard will have a maturing influence on humanity....*

It will go a long way toward the obsolescence of the managerial state and the revival of agency. Through a relationship to responsible money we have a chance to become more free, and with greater freedom, we can look to the higher ideal of excellence and greatness.

Bitcoin makes the economic game fair and real. Nobody can win because of a money-printing monopoly. Such fancy methods of cheating become impotent. This cuts at the very heart of the parasitic and short sighted world we live in. It ensures consequence is localized and socialization of poor decisions is minimized. The onus is on the individual to climb and prosper, within the context of a fair economic game, made so through a radical ownership of one's wealth. Bitcoin rewards competence and responsibility, while stupidity and carelessness is more likely to be penalized.

There is already some evidence that Bitcoin inspires responsibility beyond finance: many Bitcoiners are reclaiming agency in domains such as nutrition and health, knowledge, self-defense and survival, family and the appropriate gender roles, and much more. It seems to transform people who come into contact with it: "You do not change Bitcoin, Bitcoin changes you.".

The truth underlying the "Bitcoin Fixes This" meme is precisely the localization of consequence for the actions taken by economic actors. So will Bitcoin itself be enough to revive civilization? Time will tell. We are now at the sink or swim stage, and the temptation to behave irresponsibly will only get stronger with more wealth. As we transition from the current paradigm to the new one, chaos will increase and scams and psy-ops multiply. But, as the saying goes, anything worth having is worth fighting for. These are the "interesting times," in which legends are forged. My prediction is that the responsible will come out on top.

Excellence
(yūshū)

Excellence

優
秀

"While in India and even in China men seem to differ chiefly in degree of energy or intelligence, in Japan they differ by originality of character as well. Now, individuality is the sign of superior races and of civilizations already developed. If we make use of an expression dear to Nietzsche, we might say that in Asia, to speak of humanity is to speak of its plains; in Japan as in Europe, one represents it above all by its mountains."

Inazo Nitobe, Bushido: The Soul of Japan

Character. Excellence. Mountains - These are the symbols of nobility and that which is most 'good.' Why? It will come to make more sense in the sections that follow.

The Japanese word which most closely translates to "Excellence" or "Greatness" is Yūshū, which is made up of two Kanji: 優秀.

The first kanji, 優 (Yū), conveys the idea of superiority and what for most seems counterintuitive: *gentleness*. To be superior does not imply that one is mean or brutish, but in fact comes with the inclination and duty to be kind and gentle. As noted in a prior chapter, "love" comes from a higher place and *condescends*. The kanji itself is composed of two parts: the phonetic component on the right 憂 (yōu), which alone means "to worry," and the radical 亻 (ren, indicating "person" or "human") on the left, is a simplified version of 人. The combination suggests a person of outstanding qualities, with an undertone of care and consideration. Over time, 優 evolved to represent the integrated concepts of excellence, superiority, and kindness both in terms of intellect and character.

The second Kanji, 秀 (Shū), represents the idea of standing out or excelling. It combines the elements 禾 (nogi), a symbol for cereal or grain, and 乃, which is an archaic possessive particle, meaning soft and clingy. The imagery in this character can be thought of as a grain stalk that stands out for being particularly tall or well-developed, symbolizing the idea of being outstanding or exceptional. It can also be interpreted as 'the ones who possess the grain' which would denote status and nobility in an agrarian society. Each of these interpretations imply "elite" - whose etymology we'll explore later.

Together, 優秀 (Yūshū) combines the notions of superiority and standing out to convey the idea of "Excellence" in Japanese. This term emphasizes not just achieving superior status or results, but qualities of distinction and the surpassing of ordinary standards in both ability and character.

In English, the word "excellence" comes from Latin *excellentia*, which means "superiority" or "eminence." It refers to the quality of being outstanding or exceptional at something. The word is made up of two parts: *ex* + *cellere*.

Ex is a word-forming element, which in English means "out of, from," but also "upwards, completely, without," and "former", and "out of, from within; from which time, since; according to; in regard to" in Latin. *Ex* itself comes from the PIE root *eghs* which means "out".

Cellere is Latin for "rise high, or raise, or tower," and its participle, *celsus*, means "high, lofty, great." They are related to Latin *collis* ("hill"), or *columna* ("projecting object"). Their PIE root is *Kel*, meaning "to be prominent", and also "hill." *Kel* is the basis for many words you'll recognise, both current and ancient: in modern English, colonel, colonnade, column, culminate; in Greek: kolōnos "hill," kolophōn "summit;" and in Baltic languages such as Lithuanian, kalnas "mountain," kalnelis "hill," kelti "raise;"

Tying it all together, we find that excellence is the virtue of *rising up and standing out*, emerging out of the ordinary, the commonplace and the expected. **Excellence is the virtue of distinction and significance.** Excellent is the man who climbs the mountain, and excellence **is** the mountain.

Participation awards, democracy & the death of excellence

> *"Set up standards of achievement open to all, to the least, to the most inept—and you stop the impetus to effort in all men, great or small. You stop all incentive to improvement, to excellence, to perfection."*

Ayn Rand, *Atlas Shrugged*

Both excellence and greatness refer to a form of superiority and distinction that reaches for the heights. They imply an earning, a raising or climbing, all of which are emergent in nature. Excellence does not come from above, but in fact leaves a trail to the summit where it is then admired and beheld.

In the modern world, unfortunately, it has almost become a derogatory term, as though 'being the best you can be' were some form of extremism. And perhaps it is in this context. I couldn't think of a more fitting viewpoint in a world that attempts to amplify lies, glorify laziness, applaud sloth, and praises "the average Joe".

Collectivist ideologies such as socialism, communism and of course, the most insidious, democracy, are all the politics of "average". They encourage people to trade excellence and personal potential for a 'share in a faceless whole' in which they are merely cogs.

A prime example of this 'cancer of average' that seeped into the minds of my generation are participation awards. That sort of idiocy would have been laughed at in prior ages. Today, these participation awards have metastasized into the celebration of nihilism and indolence. We have an almost complete inversion of virtue on our hands, where excellence is sneered at and perceived as evil, while victimhood, conformity, and disability are extolled.

In the physical realm it manifests as overweight mannequins, the vilification of health and fitness as "extremism" and the lunacy that going to the gym is somehow "bad for your health." We've seen the utter destruction of beauty pageants and swimsuit magazines, which used to appreciate beauty and hold it to a high standard, but now let anyone in, and worse, give the title to the objectively ugliest participants on account of some 'systemic' disadvantage.

In the emotional and psychological realms, if you are happy, driven, or confident, you are now seen as having a medical condition that needs to be looked at. You are likely labeled as toxic, overbearing, or too ambitious.

In fact, if you are a healthy human who experiences both emotional highs and lows, you are quickly labeled bipolar and doped up on drugs to 'stabilize' you into some median range where numbness becomes your center of gravity, and you lose the fuel that would otherwise have compelled you forward into potential excellence and greatness.

In the spiritual realm, we are no longer taught about distinction or quality, but about acceptance and 'oneness' - whatever that means. We are fed a steady diet of spiritual complacency where "nothing is your fault", "you are enough" the way you are, "there are no consequences", "we are all the same", "we're all in this together", and that if enough people in the world simultaneously ingest hallucinogenic substances, we will all be peaceful and happy.

Sounds like a Marxist dream to me.

The soul of man craves war, challenge and distinction. Peace is for recuperation and bliss is a reward, but if there's nothing to recuperate from or be rewarded for, what is a man's purpose?

Beware of unearned rest and reward. The price you pay is the vitality of your mind, body and soul. This is the path to decadence, the opposite of excellence: the pursuit of the common and easy, in place of a striving toward the rare and the great. It is the elevation of self indulgence over self discipline, the valuing of now at the expense of the future, the rising of time preference. Decadence mocks and denigrates all that is noble. It elevates sarcasm, materialism, apathy, and detachment, all of which ultimately lead to nihilism. Decadence is a demonstration of weakness, and passivity.

> *"Decadence is materialistic - it mocks idealism, the numinous, and the profound, and in place of the aesthetic of beauty, it champions the ugly and the banal. Decadence is, fundamentally, a manifestation of what is weak, shallow, pretentious and vain. It is the philosophy, and the aesthetics, of the coward."*

> *Chad Crowley on X.com*

The only antidote to this sickness is a striving for excellence and a commitment to bettering oneself.

Decadence decays.

Excellence elevates.

Excellence in a warrior context

A band of brothers in war are of 'one mind and one body'. They live and die for *each other*.

As Dyonekes said, "You fight for the man beside you." In such a context there is a dissolution of the individual into the group, from which springs the unit or männerbund (alliance of men). But don't get it twisted - this is **not** a 'democracy'. This is a small unit of elites, each of whom would die for the other in order to live forever in the hearts and minds of their comrades.

In times of war, such a cohesive instinct prevails. The rational, hesitant, self-preserving mind, anyone operating from that kind of individualist paradigm, is eliminated.

In warrior cultures, men are spurred onward and they drive each other upward by embodying and amplifying excellence. To be clear, this is not the narcissistic urge for self-aggrandizement, but the desire to earn the good opinion of their fellows, and benefit them. Men become great individually so that they may be great collectively. This is how the individual inspires his brethren and vice-versa.

> *"The strength of the pack is the wolf, and the strength of the wolf is the pack."*
>
> Rudyard Kipling, *The Jungle Book*

Note that mantras such as "we're all in this together" work in such a context, whereas they fail in a civilian or commercial context. Is it because they lack micro-unity, and a code of virtue to orient toward? Is it because they lack a war to unite them, and instead settle for a false peace that slowly turns their drives inward? Could the continued domestication of man cause him to slowly become resentful and bitter, like a caged animal unable to stretch itself out into the expanse of the wild. Is it better to be caged in safety or free in conflict? Is the ignorance of war, and the internalization of these drives something that makes us not only weaker, but also less likely to aspire toward virtue? *Could peace in fact, be an incentive for mediocrity?*

As is often the case, context and scale matter. Scale because you cannot have a band of brothers beyond a certain number. Deep bonds and relationships are by definition scarce and few. Large scale militaries have been defeated by smaller, tight-knit, mission oriented militaries for this very reason. Look no further than the late Persians against the Greeks, and later the Macedonians.

Average in a civilian context

The opposite of excellence is not 'bad', but average. This is one of the key distinctions that makes modern civilian and martial collectives so fundamentally different.

While the latter must be small coherent units - their very survival depends on it - the former are large conglomerations of people, masses whose survival is less dependent on the man beside them, and whose mortality is not a pressing daily factor. In time, at scale, and without a unifying mission with strong leadership, these civilian collectives can develop into political free-for-alls where the incentive is to be average, or worse, incapable so as to qualify for handouts. This is democracy in a nutshell. Without strong leadership and a cohesive code of virtues, these civilian collectives lose their moral compass, they devolve into a sea of needy victims demanding handouts. And those who have the capacity to provide and produce must do so not because they want to, not because they're going into battle together - but because some bureaucrat, who neither knows them, nor would bleed for them, said so. This is a toxic cocktail for a society and we've seen it administered in our modern day and age. It turns everyone into an enemy, and transforms all relationships into purely transactional ones.

When this happens, the only dimension in which modern, civilian man remains "together", is his collective compliance and a 'shared sense of average'. Being just another number, who neither rocks the boat nor rows too slow, while soul crushing, is at least safe. It's also perfect for the giant HR-apparatus of the modern state. The less excellence and variance you need to deal with, the more easily you can manage everything. In fact, the one-man-one-vote system of governance is quite useful for maintaining this status quo.

Under the guise of "equality and fraternity for all" these large civilian societies condition people to 'vote' themselves rights for, and receive benefits from, things that they have not produced but which they feel entitled to. Why? Because the 'average person' is just here to participate, and participation is enough. Attendance alone makes them deserving of stuff, because of course, in such a society, *"they are enough."* You deserve a say just because you were born. Beware this trap of entitlement.

There is a reason why the greats, whether Socrates, Aristotle, Alexander, Voltaire, Napoleon Carlyle, Nietzsche, Spengler, Sowell or Hoppe have been so critical of such ideas as democracy and equality. They identified them as the antitheses to greatness and excellence. Nietzsche saw and described it more clearly than most. He envisioned an age where everyone would feel permanently broken:

> *"Here everyone helps everyone else, here everyone is to a certain degree an invalid and everyone a nurse. This is then called virtue."*

> Friedrich Nietzsche, Twilight of the Idols

In such an environment, strength and excellence are frowned upon, while weakness and mere adequacy are glorified. In such an environment, humans devolve into crabs in a bucket; this is where we are now.

I believe we shall one day look back on this age with pity, but also with gratitude that there were some men willing to buck the trend of average and ignore the siren call of 'peace', 'ease', and 'average'. The warriors of the modern age.

I hope Bitcoin's brutal and unforgiving economic simplicity will smash both equality and average to pieces so that those who inherit what's left of civilization will orient themselves in such a way that virtue, in the deepest sense, becomes the North Star for themselves and those they influence. In fact, I hope that Bitcoin can orient society in such a way that we can engage in honest warfare and competition once more, where winning happens because you're better, not because you cheated.

There are few things more noble than becoming the best you can be, in your chosen vocation, your behavior, your etiquette, with your family, and in your community. To do so requires effort and the sacrifice of your most precious assets: time and energy. This is praiseworthy and the origin of the foundations we stand on.

The great man theory of history

The "great man theory of history" says that the course of history is shaped by the actions and influence of a small number of exceptional individuals. These "great men" are responsible for many of the major events and developments in history, because their decisions and actions have had such an outsized effect on the world.

I wholeheartedly believe this to be the case because humans are inspired to action in the presence of greatness. Sure, goblins and leftists behave the opposite, and sheeple are largely directed by whichever shepherd herds them, but this actually supports my position: when a great man rises, the goblins are defeated and the sheeple are led to the promised land.

It's been the case in every generation across all of recorded history. From Gilgamesh to Alexander, from Caesar to Christ, from Constantine to Charlemagne, from Medici to Da Vinci, from Ieyasu to Meiji, from Napoleon to Bismarck, from Jobs to Satoshi. It is the same in the greatest fictional stories too. Tolkien, Herbert, Rand and Simmons wrote of heroes, not of average men.

Greatness fundamentally gives direction. In the same way that the great rivers absorb and carry forth the many streams that make it so, greatness of character and spirit requires one to illuminate the direction which the many will follow. In this way, they shape history.

"You're just fine the way you are" and "be average" are the mantras of today's morally-bankrupt society, designed to discourage people from standing out. *"Don't you dare shame others through your success or by the achievement of a great feat"*.

Luckily for humanity though, the deep, inner desire for greatness cannot be quelled. It burns inside the best of us, like the infinite flame of the soul. In fact, it's during periods of mediocrity that greatness builds up inside of key men, gathering itself until it explodes on the scene.

> *"Great men, like great periods, are explosive materials in which an immense force is accumulated; it is always prerequisite for such men, historically and physiologically speaking, that for a long period there has been a collecting, a heaping up, an economizing, and a hoarding, with respect to them — that for a long time no explosion has taken place."*
>
> Friedrich Nietzsche, Twilight of the Idols

Excellence continues to drive the world forward, despite every social construct seeking to shut it down. May it once again take its rightful place as the North Star, as we transcend the era of equality. Let us once again wage war on average in the pursuit of excellence. Let us become elites in the true sense of the word.

Be elite

> *"The best choose progress toward one thing, a name forever honored by the gods, while others eat their way toward sleep like nameless oxen."*
>
> Heraclitus

In our pursuit of excellence, we must reclaim the word elite. Traditionally speaking, the elite were those who worked to improve their society. They were the leaders of men, leaders of industry and patrons of the art and beauty that fills the old towns strewn throughout Europe. Today's elites are not elite - but parasites who seek to undermine society. They spend their time leaching from the producers, bloating the government with a bureaucratic managerial class, revising history and filling the minds of the young with toxic ideology. Their goal is to weaken our culture with degeneracy and ugliness. To sully our history, and leave the world ugly, unsafe and uninhabitable while they retire to their opulent mansions behind private security.

As a result, the word elite is today erroneously conflated with parasite. This has to change. We must rediscover its root, and take it back. It comes from Latin *elitus*, which means "choice" or "selected," itself from *eligere*, "to choose" or "to select." The PIE root of the word "elite" is *leg*, which means "to collect" or "to gather."

To be elite is to be the 'selected'. The choicest or the selected means 'the best' and thus to be elite is to be the best in your field, to be the cream of the crop, to be distinguished and outstanding. *In short, to be **excellent.***

Most people suffer from anti-elite syndrome. And while I can sympathize, their misunderstanding of the true meaning of the word causes them to point their vitriol in the wrong direction. In fact, many are so brainwashed by narratives of the average man, that they've come to hate anybody who excels. This disease of average is prevalent even in the Bitcoin space. You hear it when people say stupid things like "we are all Satoshi", or celebrate being a "pleb". This also has to change.

We are **not** all Satoshi. Satoshi did something far greater than any of us probably ever will, and to lay claim to that is both arrogant and ignorant. Yes - I understand the reference to the whole Guy Fawkes thing - which is cute - but it's extremely inaccurate and disingenuous.

Aspire to be "like" Satoshi in grandeur and virtue, but do not claim you are him.

Furthemore, the pleb thing is not just cringe, it's hands down false, or will be soon enough. Just being in Bitcoin makes you part of tomorrow's economic "elite". Barring any mistake, you will wield significantly more financial and social power than someone who comes into Bitcoin a decade from now.

What will you do with that power? Of course, that is the focus of this book. It stands to reason that you must at some point come to terms with the fact that you are no longer a "pleb" but part of a small group of people who are *at the very least,* economically "elite." You should recognise this and begin to develop the attributes of a more holistic individual, working toward excellence in other areas of your life. You cannot hide forever behind the pleb moniker as an excuse for sloth or poor behavior.

Humility is important of course: "stay humble", but strive also to upgrade your behavior, enhance your vocabulary, deepen your knowledge, and become more cultured. With great power comes great responsibility. You don't want to be some rich turd in a Lambo, or the eternal Twitter troll. There's much more to life than that.

To operate on a higher energetic plane, we need a grander perspective. We must climb the mountain. We've been tricked into believing that "average" is ok, because it represents the little guy. But the truth is that there is nothing aspirational about being average. Average doesn't require courage, passion, drive, responsibility or self control. Average is a low energy state, and a small story designed to make you give up on your dreams—to trade all you could possibly be for what you're told you should be.

Pursuing excellence is one of the highest callings in life, as is the practice and cultivation of the virtues presented in this book. The world needs strong leaders - not trolls, plebs or parasites - there's plenty of that around. As a Bitcoiner, this duty rests with you.

> *"Equality belongs essentially to decline: the chasm between man & man, class & class, the multiplicity of types, the will to be oneself, to stand out – that which I call pathos of distance – characterizes every strong age."*
>
> Friedrich Nietzsche, *The Genealogy of Morals*

Bitcoin and Excellence

Bitcoin is a framework for excellence.

A lot of people think Bitcoin's greatest contribution will be to lift the masses up and "help the weak". While that will likely occur, it's my (unpopular) belief that Bitcoin's greatest impact on mankind will be to make the strongest stronger, the best better and the most powerful, more powerful.

This scares some people because they've erroneously come to believe things like "power corrupts" or that "absolute power corrupts absolutely". What they fail to realize is that power, like technology, is agnostic. Power is a measure of the rate at which work is done or energy is transferred, it is the capacity to channel energy. Power is a reflection of vitality and youth. These are not evil. On the contrary, what's evil is to be against life. What's evil is to convince everyone that the life-force inside of you, your 'Will to Power', is wrong.

*If you want a powerful, meritocratic society, you must encourage strong people to become powerful, by rewarding them for winning and for merit! Not for cheating, lying or stealing, not for quitting and not for just 'participating', but for **achieving.***

*Bitcoin encourages a life-affirming approach to living. It is a framework for excellence, and a bulwark against corruption. To win on a Bitcoin standard, you must be **better**. When the parasitic are starved and weak of character are no longer rewarded for losing, we can reward the best of us and inspire others to be better, stronger and more powerful....*

In such a civilization, we can develop the power and thumos to travel to the stars. Without it, we will wither away and recede into the dark ages.

Powerful individuals = powerful society
Energetic individuals = energetic society

*None of this implies the masses will or should be trampled. First of all, true strength seeks not to trample the weak, but to test itself against a worthy opponent. Second, a rising tide does and will continue to lift all boats. Instead, what I am talking about is our **collective focus**. You go where you look. If you're always looking down, that's where you will find yourself. If you focus on the masses, don't be surprised if you get more "average". On the contrary, if you can set your sights on excellence, you are more likely to find greatness. Groveling in the dirt comes from a different place in both the mind and the soul than does reaching for the stars. It's a different quality of energy. It's the difference between ascendant and descendant.*

Bitcoin is alive and ascendant. It aligns us toward excellence because it puts a real and accurate price on things. Like life itself, it is unforgiving. There is no rewind button. Those who waste and squander it must pay the price. Those who save, invest and deploy capital, will reap the rewards.

History is shaped by great men. With the dawn of a new age, what will you do, what seeds will you plant, what foundations will you establish, how will you show up, who will you raise, that might change the course of history and drive humanity to a higher energetic standard?

Respect
(sonkei)

Respect

尊
敬

"In its highest form, politeness almost approaches love."

Inazo Nitobe, Bushido: The Soul of Japan

There are five dimensions of respect, each which have a *direction*: respect for yourself, respect for others, respect for tradition, respect for authority (that which is above us), and respect for your enemy. We'll explore each in the coming sections, but before we do, let's look at the etymology of the Japanese word, which is exceptionally rich.

In Japanese, the word for "respect" is *sonkei*, which is made up of two kanji: 尊敬.

The first kanji, 尊 (son), means to revere or venerate someone that is noble, or something that is precious. It derives from Tibetan (btsun) meaning venerable and is also used to refer to something wonderful, glorious or marvelous. It is composed of three elements: the top resembles a wine vessel or an altar, which in ancient cultures symbolized reverence for a deity or for high nobility: the middle part, 寸 (sun), means "a small unit of measurement" which in this context conveys the meaning of something precious or valuable; the bottom, 廾, represents a pair of hands, which together means to 'set in place a valuable or precious cask.'

Together, 尊 represents valuing or holding something in high regard, carrying it with esteem, and placing it where it belongs.

The second kanji, 敬 (kei), expresses 'awe' and the act of devoting oneself or focusing attention on something. It is made up of two elements: on the left, 苟, which is sometimes interpreted as a sitting dog, symbolizing loyalty, watchfulness, attentiveness or deference, all qualities associated with respect; on the right is 攵 (pu), a radical denoting the act of striking, and the application of authority. Phonetically speaking, 耂, an ancient character representing an old man with long hair, (age or experience) is also embedded. The complete kanji signifies both deference towards someone with wisdom, authority or experience, and the act of concentrated devotion. Keep both in mind as we proceed.

Together, 尊敬 (sonkei) combines the ideas of esteem, reverence, devotion and awe, brought together to convey the notion of "respect" in Japanese, which underlies the social harmony characteristic of their culture.

For completeness, we must also include the virtue of rei (礼), which is more often referenced in traditional Bushido. Rei, most closely translated as "politeness," is about social etiquette and proper conduct, and therefore deeply related to respect. It is also a Confucian term for: *a system of various regulations.*

The kanji 礼 is a simplified version of the ancient 禮 which is a combination of 示 (shi), a radical indicating "altar" or "show," and 豆 (mame), which originally depicted a container for offerings, and referred to ceremony and performing rites at an altar. Historically, it symbolized rituals, formal conduct and ceremony; over time it evolved to represent manners, etiquette, and 'appropriate behavior' - all external manifestations of respect, or politeness. The modern form 礼 contains the simplified radical 乚, meaning: *'to hide; to cover; to shield'* - representing the care one takes with something precious. Altogether *rei* is about being intentional and expressing both respect and devotion through one's actions and behavior.

Both *rei* and *sonkei* are essential. They are also complementary. Together they contribute to a more holistic understanding of respect. While *rei* focuses on the outward expression of respect, *sonkei* emphasizes the internal aspect. I believe this is a big part of why Japanese culture is so rich in the dimension of respect.

The Western tradition in respect was similarly deep. In English, respect means *"to regard or notice with especial attention."* It derives from French *respecter*, to "look back", which comes from Latin *respectere*, the frequentative of *respicere*, "to look back at, regard, consider," which in turn is made up of *re-* "back" + *specere* "look at". The Latin form originates from the PIE root *spek*, "to observe". We see the use of *specere* in other words such as "introspect", from the the Latin *introspectus* or *introspicere*, which means to "look at, look into; examine, observe attentively," from *intro-* "inward" + *specere* "to look at." Also in "to speculate," a verb most maligned in modern times, yet essential to the entrepreneurial function.

There is a clear intention when it comes to respect, and central to it is an observation of that which 'came before' and that which is separate to you. Modern society has lost touch with what came before and as a result, turned itself into something more childish and petulant, demanding "rights" and "respect", but refusing to earn either.

Respect for oneself

Dignity is the highest ideal of the sophisticated and aristocratic man. You cannot have respect for others without first having respect for yourself. And like all kinds of respect it cannot be demanded or forced. It must be earned.

To develop self-respect, you must do something that demands your best. You must push yourself to, and at times, beyond, your limits. Nietzsche argued that the path to self-respect and dignity lies in the constant overcoming of oneself, in transcending the commonality that fetters the masses in mediocrity. You cannot merely exist within the confines of what has been deemed acceptable or comfortable; you must strive to push beyond these boundaries, to explore the reaches of your potential.

The word "dignity" has its roots in Latin, derived from "dignitas," which means "worthiness," and "dignus," meaning "worthy." It is not something bestowed by societal accolades or external validation. It is an intrinsic quality emanating from those who live according to their values and who dare to create themselves anew through the fires of trial and ambition. Such individuals do not seek respect; they command it through their actions. They understand that to have respect for oneself, one must be willing to suffer, if necessary, in order to grow, adapt and evolve. This is precisely what makes such people rich, and ultimately, noble in their bearing.

Ignorance of this fact is a large part of why the modern world is so poor. It's not only that infinitely printed money has hollowed out the capital base of civilization, but it's that people no longer have respect for themselves. It shows in the abominations we call "modern art" and the kinds of people in positions of influence and power; it shows in the hatred and envy these people have for the beautiful and the great which came before us. There is no more dignity in the mind, body or soul of the mindless masses. There is only emptiness. The NPC is real, and *it* is everywhere.

Case in point were the last few years. While adaptation may be humanity's greatest strength, it is also its greatest weakness. People either adapt to freedom by taking on more responsibility, or they adapt to slavery by renouncing it in exchange for what is often just the illusion or promise of safety. As mentioned earlier, the slow, consistent renunciation of responsibility leads inexorably to the erosion of freedom. It's very hard to notice early on because comfort and safety feel so nice. The movie *Wall E* comes to mind when I think about this, and is a caricature of the first few years of the 2020's.

Never in my life would I have expected a sane human to degrade themselves to the point of "showing their papers" and wearing a face diaper in order to drive a car, eat at a restaurant or go to work. If you'd told me that in 2019, I would've said "No way. Every restaurant will go bankrupt". Clearly I was wrong. The slavish, mindless masses donned their face diapers, injected themselves with experimental medication, got their paperwork and lined up 6 feet apart so they could buy groceries and eat food.

To lower oneself to such a level is to have no dignity and no pride. It's a clear example of a world filled with people who have adapted to slavery because they have slowly renounced individual responsibility. Society itself no longer has self-respect.

This is why a code of virtue is so important to have. Humans, as adaptation machines, will adjust to almost anything. We can and have adapted to a society devoid of beauty and dignity, across the board, because we've forgotten the virtue of respect. This is doubly important for men, considering they are the ultimate bearers of this responsibility, and the recipients of respect. For a man to earn it from outside, he must cultivate it from the inside. He must defend his name, his honor and his reputation. He must strive to reach his highest potential, to develop his mind, his body and his spirit, and finally, he must seek an honorable death. He owes himself this much, and by doing so, he pays it backward to his ancestors and forward to his descendants.

To fix society, we must fix the relationship we have with ourselves. To build real wealth again, we must become wealthy from the inside. We must develop dignity. We can and will adapt to something higher and more vital, if we choose to. But it cannot come from a place of desperation. Nobility is determined and driven, but it is never desperate. Holy Roman Emperor Charles V advised his son: *"Fortune hath somewhat of the nature of a woman, who, if she be too closely wooed, is commonly the further off."* When drive and determination become desperation, fortune backs off. You must behave with dignity and composure, even in the worst of times. This is the ultimate goal and the ultimate gift. It's not how much money you have - you can always make more of it later - but how much dignity you can build and maintain. This is the virtue of true wealth.

Respect for others

Samurai were expected to have respect for their master, their emperor, other Samurai, and even their enemies. There was a decorum in their behavior that signified their moral standing and therefore how they were viewed by both their adversaries and their followers.

Respect, much like courage, was taught from a young age. Customs such as bowing in the presence of others, or how to walk, sit, and speak, were taught and learned with utmost care. These customs extended beyond the home too. Thomas Cleary, in "Code of the Samurai" notes:

> *"Wherever you sleep, don't point your feet in the direction of your employer. Where you set up straw bundles for archery practice, don't let the arrows land in the vicinity of your employer, and when you set your spear and sword on their racks, don't point the tips toward him."*

This politeness toward others is something often mentioned by foreigners that have visited modern Japan. Their deference in hospitality is quite unlike anything else in the world. The following excerpt from Nitobe vividly illustrates this:

> *"You are out in the hot, glaring sun with no shade over you; a Japanese acquaintance passes by; you accost him, and instantly his hat is off.....all the while he talks with you his parasol is down and he stands in the glaring Sun."*

While a Westerner might assume this is foolish, Nitobe explains the Japanese custom and line of thought as follows:

> *"You are in the sun; I sympathize with you; I would willingly take you under my parasol if it were large enough, or if we were familiarly acquainted; as I cannot shade you, **I will share your discomforts.**"*

Do you recall what we explored earlier in compassion? Little acts of this kind are not mere gestures or conventionalities. They are the "bodying forth" of thoughtful feelings for the comfort of others. In Japanese culture, descendant from the virtues of respect and compassion inculcated in Bushido is the idea that we should weep with those that weep and rejoice with those that rejoice. This deep form of empathy is a remnant from a prior age that is still embedded in the DNA of Japanese culture.

An example which struck me as particularly interesting and profound is the approach to gift-giving in Japan. On the surface, it may seem a little strange in the West, but when you understand the reasoning, it makes sense.

In the West, when you give someone something, you sing its praises to the recipient; in Japan, they depreciate or slander the gift. The underlying idea is, to quote Nitobe, that in the West:

"This is a nice gift: if it were not nice I would not dare give it to you; for it will be an insult to give you anything but what is nice."

In contrast to this, the Japanese logic runs as follows:

"You are a nice person, and no gift is nice enough for you. You will not accept anything I can lay at your feet except as a token of my goodwill; so accept this, not for its intrinsic value, but as a token. It will be an insult to your worth to call the best gift good enough for you."

If you place the two ideas side by side, you'll find their essence is similar, but *"The American speaks of the material which makes the gift; the Japanese speaks of the spirit which prompts the gift."- Inazo Nitobe*

I believe such deep forms of respect and politeness are embedded in Japanese culture because of the enduring influence of Bushido, and the fact that it was the last major civilization on earth to dismantle feudalism.

The feudal social order gave pattern and structure to their culture. There was a reason why table manners grew to be a science, tea serving and drinking were raised to ceremony, and a man of education was expected to master all of these. Which brings us to the spiritual discipline of the 'respect for tradition', of which etiquette and ceremony were said to be the "outward garments".

Respect for tradition

"Tradition is not the past, but that which does not pass."

Dominique Venner

Julius Evola was an Italian philosopher of the mid-1900s who promoted the values and principles of a metaphysical and perennial tradition as a timeless unifying force. He was an advocate for spiritual and aristocratic hierarchies as antidotes to modern egalitarianism and materialism, and was a big inspiration for me, in coming to terms with this ideal.

I came to understand that *Tradition* does not mean a blind subservience to that which came before - as critics of conservative thought are often right to point out. For a true traditionalist, the value in preserving elements of the past is recognized, but it is **not** universally applicable. For example, there is very little in Communist traditions or institutions that merits conservation.

Traditionalism is more than caution, timidity, or conservatism. Rather, it's a commitment to **quality**. It is the careful application of judgment and discrimination. It's acknowledging that certain things are superior to others, and that striving for excellence across various domains - be it in physical fitness, entrepreneurship, martial skill, religious faith, or even homemaking - is worthwhile. Tradition is the belief in the significance of distinction, from the humblest personal projects to the loftiest economic and political achievements.

This is the genesis of etiquette. While tradition is inwardly experienced as a reverence to those whose shoulders we stand upon today, it is outwardly embodied in the practice of etiquette, which cultures such as Japan, Victorian England and much of pre-1900's Europe had in abundance.

Sure, some practices became more ornamental than functional, but their essence can be traced back to something more meaningful and useful than moderns can easily comprehend.

Inazo Nitobe spends almost the entire chapter on the virtue of politeness discussing etiquette as the most "princely" of virtues and one which has particularly deep roots in Japanese culture. A particular example is the tea ceremonies Japan is so well known for.

"To a novice it looks tedious. But one soon discovers that the way prescribed is, after all, the most saving of time and labor; in other words, the most economical use of force—hence, according to Spencer's dictum, the most graceful."

"Much less do I consider elaborate ceremony as altogether trivial; for it denotes the result of long observation as to the most appropriate method of achieving a certain result. If there is anything to do, there is certainly a best way to do it, and the best way is both the most economical and the most graceful."

This "grace" in behavior was the practical element associated with etiquette, but there was also more importantly a *"spiritual significance of social decorum"*. Etiquette came to be understood as moral training, involving a strict observance of propriety. By constant exercise in correct manners, one brings all the parts and faculties of his body into 'perfect order' and into such harmony with oneself and one's environment as to *"express the mastery of spirit over the flesh."* The famous Ogasawara school of etiquette in Japan summed it up in the following terms:

"The end of all etiquette is to so cultivate your mind that even when you are quietly seated, not the roughest ruffian can dare make onset on your person."

While etiquette, to the uninitiated, is just an 'elaborate ceremony' - to the cultured person, it is a reflection of spiritual strength, grounding and depth. The word *"gracefulness"* actually means an *"economy of force"*.

"Fine manners, therefore, mean power in repose."

Inazo Nitobe, Bushido: The Soul of Japan

The older I've gotten, the more I've come to respect these traditions. You realize that while change is necessary, it's arrogant to ignore or disregard ceremonies or traditions that have developed over long periods of time. Many are there for a reason, and have stood the test of time because of their qualitative value. Removing them can open the door to all kinds of disasters. One of the clearest examples is marriage and gender roles. The west is facing its greatest ever decline in birthrates, not by accident. An entire generation of millennial women in their thirties are having to come to terms with the fact that their pool of suitable male partners has shrunk by a factor of 10 overnight, because they were convinced to spend their best and most fertile years working for somebody else in an office - all so they could be a tax and wage slave. At the same time, an entire generation of millennial chose to remain adolescents well into their thirties and are now wondering why they're alone and have no family, children or social skills.

While many things have contributed to this and other social declines, two key factors are the over-indexing for "progress at all costs" and "equality." This progressive mindset, applied to everything, has led to the deconstruction of the very foundations that took millennia to build in the first place. The wisdom of those who came before us has been disregarded as archaic and irrelevant to the collective detriment of us all. It's been replaced with the clueless, shallow viewpoints most often adopted by midwits and immature, self-proclaimed revolutionaries who are quick to pull the rug from underneath their own feet, for some misguided notion of equality or progress.

Thankfully, there are glimmers of hope. I'm not sure if it's a function of my bubble, or if my generation is maturing, but there seems to be some real momentum back in this direction. People are slowly realizing that something is "rotten in the state of Denmark."

The idea that we're somehow better than those who came before us simply because we are more materially capable or politically democratic is not only full of hubris, but wrong. Perhaps the only dimension in which we can call ourselves "more advanced" is technology. In all else we have actually regressed. People are psychologically, physiologically and spiritually weaker than ever before, and thus poorer where it matters. Just because we found better and faster ways to manipulate materials, does not mean we can do the same with basic humanity, morality, and principles. Virtues, ethics, and principles are not materials - they are something more enduring.

This is why a respect for tradition is so critical. Life is not only about making material progress so that everyone can have a toilet and a fridge. This is a Marxist misconception. An enduring and meaningful philosophy of life observes that which came before it and pays its respects. Tradition is not about regressing to the past; it's about honoring the past. The goal isn't to rewind but to recognize and preserve the beautiful, the excellent and the timeless for future generations. *Tradition* in this sense becomes a spiritual and moral guide for the future.

Respect for authority

"Respect goes up, love comes down."

Elliot Hulse, Podcast: Principles of Biblical Masculinity

Respect applies not just to the past or to tradition, but to authority - another word most moderns have an allergic reaction to.

Respect and love are similar, except for their direction. Love condescends, while respect ascends. I think a lot about the quote above because it contains a profound truth.

As noted earlier, the Japanese language didn't have a word specifically for love, but there were virtues that came close to describing it: respect is one of them. To *"treat with deferential esteem, regard with some degree of reverence,"* was to respect your superiors.

The liberal, classical liberal, and modern libertarian movements, all have major juvenile tendencies, one of them being this disrespect for authority. In some cases, it is aimed at false, or fiat, authority, which is fine, but it often goes much further - to their own detriment.

Authority is necessary. Authority is sacred. When I talk of authority, I am referring to **earned** authority, because that is the only true form. When you've put 10,000 hours of blood, sweat and tears into a craft, you are an Authority, with a capital A. You are the master, and traditionally speaking, the apprentice comes to you to serve and to learn.

As a wise, moral and just authority, it's your duty to lead, to guide and to condescend your love onto those who come to you for advice, for guidance, and for leadership. That is the point of a good leader, and as a student, apprentice, or disciple, you pay for this first and foremost with **respect.**

The Authority does NOT respect the apprentice, in the same way as the parent does NOT respect the child. This is a complete inversion of the love <> respect relationship. Respect goes up, and love comes down. The master is *superior*, the apprentice is inferior.

This is the correct way in all functional hierarchies, and is a big part of the reason the French Revolution broke so much more than it fixed. It should be called the French Devolution, because it simply undermined *all* forms of authority, from the father in the household, all the way through to the father of the country, placing in their stead the Republic; that is, the State.

Sure, there was a lot of fiat, unearned authority present in the 1700's, and perhaps this lack of true authority is what allowed for the inversion to actually occur. Things had decayed to such a degree that change was inevitable. The king was no longer worthy of leading or sitting on the summit. Perhaps there was such a clamoring for one's own skin, that structure, respect, and order be damned - each layer of the hierarchy sought to invert the one above, until the entire social structure was upside down, or inside out.

Whatever the case, the net result was that respect was forced to flow the other way, and in the process "love" was replaced by spite, anger, and hate. This is what happens when you break order and inhibit the natural flow of things.

Napoleon brought order and hierarchy back for a time. His competence, particularly in warfare, helped cement his authority - but we all know what happened next. Unfortunately, the disease caught on, and the European decay truly set in.

The net result of these inversions was the opening of an equalitarian Pandora's Box that destroyed Europe and from which a never ending stream of new absurdities continues to emerge to this day.

In order to buck this trend and heal, in order to build a strong future, we must, as we move forward, do two things. We have to rediscover, reconnect with, and learn to respect the cultures and traditions of the past, and secondly, we must reconstruct hierarchies of competence. We must place authority where it belongs and orient ourselves around it.

Doing so may be the only way we can heal the divides and allow for love to flow once more.

Respect for your enemy

"It's better to be the enemy of a good person, than the friend of a bad one."

Japanese Proverb

We discussed elements of this in the honor and courage chapters but it bears repeating here. That felt for the enemy is perhaps the noblest of all forms of respect, because it's the hardest to do.

If the greatest life is lived by being the most vital, forthright, courageous, and honorable version of yourself, then it stands to reason that your greatest enemy will challenge and call upon the greatest parts of yourself. What greater gift could one ask for than a life fully lived?

Ancient warriors considered a "good death" at the hands of a "worthy adversary" one of the highest possible achievements, for it compelled them to greatness. As such, while they sought to defeat and kill their enemy, they took them on with profound respect. *They didn't see them as 'evil', but saw the better man as the victor.* This is such an important point.

This reminds me of Nietzsche's conceptualisation of good and bad, instead of good and evil.

The idea of 'evil' was conjured up by those who could not compete with 'good'.

The ancients and nobles did not concern themselves with such petty ideas, and you see it in the grandeur of their texts. In Homer's *Iliad*, for example, neither King Priam nor Hector were painted as either "evil" or pure "villains" even though the *Iliad* was written by the enemy of the Trojans. If anything, Homer emphasized the nobility of the Trojans, and the story is therefore one of a higher and greater struggle. I believe this is what makes it more truthful (factual is irrelevant), and is the reason it has stood the test of time.

Traditionally speaking, nobility never considered the lower types their enemy. They didn't even register them. The enemy was an opponent of similar vitality, and to win meant to defeat them on a level playing field, because you were genuinely better.

> "To become better, I must play a fair game, not some rigged stupidity where I "win" because the other guy had his hands tied behind his back. There is neither honor nor dignity in that. One does not get better nor advance by cheating. That's what the plutocrats and parasites do not understand, that's why they are inferior, and that's why they will forever be bitter and envious of the natural elite."

> Aleksandar Svetski, Remnant Part 4.

Samurai culture, and the entire saga from Nobunaga through Ieyasu and on to the ultimate unification of Japan under the Tokugawa Shogunate, is full of such deep, memorable struggles.

One that comes to mind is linked to the blood-stained ceilings of five serene temples in Kyoto Prefecture. These temples – Yogen-in,

Genkoan, Shoden-ji, Hosen-in, and Myoshinji - house ceilings made from the floorboards of the Fushimi Momyama Castle, where Ieyasu's feudal lord, Torii Mototada, and his 380 warriors held out for 11 days against a vastly superior force of 40,000 soldiers. When they were finally breached, instead of surrendering, Mototada and his men committed seppuku (ritualistic suicide), resulting in their blood soaking into the floorboards. These warriors were honored and became legend. Today they are remembered through the story of "The Bloody Ceilings of Kyoto."

The greatest contests, battles, and most valuable trials come from competing against that which could actually defeat you. And even if you are defeated, as Mototada or Leonidas and his men were, by staring death down, you honor life, and your name lives on forever. This is the gift of a worthy adversary.

To be truly honorable and worthy of remembrance, is to have respect, for yourself, for others, for tradition, for authority and and even for your enemy. This is key to a richer, deeper and more meaningful connection to life.

Bitcoin and Respect

Bitcoin is a unique blend of classical principles and modern technology.

Its relationship to respect is to do with hierarchy and authority. The framework for excellence we discussed in the prior chapter also establishes a hierarchy rooted in competence and merit. In other words: a natural order.

This is one of the unique things about Bitcoin. While it is a new technology, and a fundamental reinvention of money, it is simultaneously a nod to the life-affirming principles that have, and always will make humanity ascendant.

Every age of greatness is marked by an adherence to a set of virtues and principles. By creating a monetary network, which like life, has no rewind button, those same virtues once again become prevalent. In a more economically honest world, we begin to respect what works. We rekindle a respect for authority and tradition. We develop the maturity to respect one another, because we respect ourselves, as more sovereign individuals.

Bitcoin is the dignified individual's choice...

...not because it's going to help all the disadvantaged, but because it's fair and right. Bitcoin is not for altruistic virtue signaling, but for better, fairer competition. That's what counts, and it's only in such an environment that the best of us can emerge. It's our duty to plant the seeds for this.

As stated, all these forms of respect start with a respect for oneself. When dignity is lacking at the individual level, it makes for weak, poor people and a weak, poor society.

There is no dignity in working, building a business, and trading what you've produced for toilet paper money printed by a bunch of bureaucrats 10,000 miles away, especially when they can just print more of it for their own benefit, **at your expense.**

How can you claim that you are free and sovereign, when you work, expending real time and energy in exchange for that which another can literally conjure up out of thin air?

Would you go to work tomorrow and at the end of the week accept payment from your boss in the form of a high-five, or some sticks and stones? Of course not. So why would you demean yourself by trading your labor for literal Monopoly money? There is no dignity in this.

Bitcoin is about respecting oneself and having the dignity to know your worth, which then radiates outward.

A strong and vital society is one where people's labor, value, effort, and ingenuity are genuinely rewarded, while the parasites and "traders" are starved. One where, as Confucius said, **"the producers are many, and the consumers are few."**

This requires a re-evaluation of time preference, which at scale, is determined by the hardness of the money and the quality of the culture. A Bitcoin standard goes a very long way toward fixing this.

Duty / Loyalty
(chūgi)

Duty & Loyalty

忠

義

Duty and loyalty are often seen as separate virtues, but in Japanese Bushido they were combined as the broader and more holistic "Duty of Loyalty". I've thus chosen to combine them in a similar way here, because duty can be understood as the practical expression of the bond that is *loyalty*.

> *"The duty of loyalty, was seen as the keystone making feudal virtues a symmetrical arch."*

> Inazo Nitobe, Bushido: The Soul of Japan

Bushido and Chivalry share a number of virtues in common with other systems of ethics, and it is this one above all that is their most distinctive feature: a sense of loyalty to your comrade and a fealty to someone or something greater, whether to lord, king, country, God or glory.

The Japanese word for "loyalty" is *chūgi*, which is made up of two Kanji: 忠義.

The first kanji, 忠 (chū), represents the concept of loyalty, devotion and duty to someone or something higher. It is composed of two elements: the bottom radical, 心 (kokoro), meaning "heart", and the top radical, 中 (naka), meaning "middle" or "center." This symbolizes the idea of one's heart being centered or steadfast, conveying a sense of unwavering devotion and fidelity. A sense of connection to another, originating from deep within one's values and psyche.

The second kanji, 義 (gi), as we have seen with the Japanese word for "justice" (*seigi*), represents righteousness or justice. It combines 羊 (sheep), symbolizing a sacrificial animal in ancient rituals, and 我 (ga), meaning "self", thus conveying the idea of setting aside personal interests for higher principles, a promise, a moral duty, and a commitment to doing what is right.

Together, 忠義 (chūgi) combines the steadfastness of the heart with the commitment to a righteous promise. This term reflects both a duty and devotion to some higher cause, but a loyalty and fidelity grounded in ethical principles and a deep desire to follow through, regardless of the consequences.

It's worth noting briefly that the modern Japanese term for duty is 義務 (gimu), which encompasses the idea of obligations and responsibilities one has towards society, their family, or their personal roles, with 義 (gi) once again meaning "righteousness" or "justice," and 務 (mu) "task" or "service." For our purposes, I've chosen to focus on *chūgi* as the closest interpretation of this virtue.

Once again, we find similarities in the origins of the English word "loyalty." It comes from Old French word *loialte*, which means "fidelity" or "faithfulness", and is related to *leal* from the Latin *legalem*, from *lex* or "law", in reference to being *"faithful in carrying out legal obligations; or conformable to the laws of honor."*

The PIE root *leg- is fundamental in understanding this connection. It signifies "to collect" or "gather," and it forms the basis for a wide range of terms associated with law, legislation, and legal obligations across various Indo-European languages. The root reflects the process of collecting or gathering societal norms and codifying them into laws and regulations. This process is inherently linked to the concept of loyalty, as being loyal in this context implies a commitment to uphold, follow, and gather around the set of laws and ethical standards that a society establishes. *Fealty* also arises from this root.

In ancient societies, the law was not just a set of rules but a collection of the moral and ethical expectations of the community. To be loyal, in this sense, meant to adhere faithfully to these collected norms and to act in a manner that was in accordance with the collective wisdom and legal frameworks of one's community. Loyalty thus not only refers to a strong sense of commitment or devotion to someone or something, such as a person, group, cause, or principle, and a fidelity in carrying out one's obligations; it also entails a commitment to the law and its underlying principles of justice, honor, and communal welfare.

"Duty" comes from the Old French word *deu*, which means "owed" or "due." It refers to an obligation or responsibility that one must fulfill because of a social or moral code. Its Latin roots are found in *debere*, meaning "must" or to owe something, to be under obligation to and for something, or to be bound to do something; "I ought", "I must", "I should."

The PIE root *gʰabh- ("to give or receive") is closely related to "habere" (to have). This root encapsulates the exchange of goods, services, or promises, laying the groundwork for the concept of duty as an owed obligation: "I have to".

Note how energetically and practically speaking, duty and loyalty are both closely related to both honor and respect, and much like both, are virtues of nobility. To remain faithful, to keep your word, to carry out your obligations, to be bonded by your word, to pay your dues, to earn your stripes, and do what you said you were going to do - these are the traits and behavior of an elite individual, a gentleman, and of an aristocrat, in the traditional sense of the word.

Loyalty: beyond the individual

If love descends and respect ascends, loyalty goes both ways. It is the glue which bonds relationships that transcend mere commerce, proximity and even respect. One can trade with and have respect for a stranger, even an enemy - but one owes neither loyalty. This is a virtue reserved for the few.

The concept of loyalty to something beyond oneself, central to Samurai and other warrior cultures, is something lost in the world of the individualist. Coming to terms with this reality has been quite profound for me, especially having been so enamored with the modern, libertarian-like creeds of individualism. My prior book was even centered around the virtue of individuality! But I've come to realize that the Randian / Rothbardian / Anarcho-Capitalist creeds feel rather empty, cheap, and isolated in comparison to the richness and profundity found in warrior cultures.

Consider the depth of bond shared between warrior clans and band of brothers like Alexander and his Royal Companions, or the Sacred Band of Thebes, the Persian Immortals, the 300 Spartans, the Templar Knights, the 47 Ronin and other Samurai clans, or the Arthurian Knights of the Round Table. These sorts of 'männerbund' - a brotherhood of men, with shared values, rituals and loyalty to each other - literally transformed the world, and built the very foundations we stand upon today.

Similar bonds exist today, but they are fewer. And those at scale have metastasized into something shallower. You see it in street gangs for example. There is loyalty, but not of the same flavor because they are often driven by fear, money and Instagram-status. There might even be honor in these organizations, but they are missing the other virtues and a higher *raison d'être* for why they exist. But despite being only an echo of the männerbunds of old, there is something here for us to learn - and that's the fact that there is a yearning for brotherhood and loyalty among men. There is a desire to form a tribe, despite years of social conditioning that "tribalism is bad". Turns out it's not. Turns out it will always occur, and if not guided consciously and ritualized, it will become an ugly, violent version of itself.

The degree of 'asabiyyah' within a community determines whether it will rise or fall. Asabiyyah is an Arabic term referring to group consciousness, solidarity, and self-belief. It is not necessarily based on race, but on kinship and the loyalty that binds a group. Medieval Arabic historian, Ibn Khaldun, popularized the term as the chief ingredient in the rise and fall of civilizations.

We must recognize that while yes, the individual is the only 'real' unit in a society, it is the tribe that is most important. Humans are social and familial creatures. We do not, and cannot exist as individuals. We are biologically and psychologically designed to live and operate in groups, and the in-group, the tribe, is held together by loyalty. This metaphysical territory must come first: before economic reality, and before, in many cases, one's own life. When a tribe becomes an individual unit, it creates the kind of force-multiplier that can transform the world. In fact, it's the only way to establish tradition and culture, because these emerge from the tribe whom you are loyal to, build bonds and establish norms with. Loyalty is beyond immediate commercial concern - it is about low time preference and lineage. Loyalty to the tribe implies a loyalty to one's traditions and lineage, to one's ancestors and descendants. Once again, this is ever more important for men. We exist today because our ancestors fought and toiled. They invested their time, their energy and their life force into the creation of what has culminated into you and I. We each have a responsibility to continue this unbroken chain, to add our time, energy and life force to it, and to pass the baton to our descendants. As men of honor and loyalty, we bequeath unto our children, and thus their children, and their children's children, unto eternity, lessons, genes, ideas, capital, blood, and a story. It is your duty to make sure all of these elements are as vital and meaningful as possible.

Flattery is not loyalty

For a long time I believed that individuals are all that exist or that collectivism and just being a part of a group while losing one's own agency is the root of all evil. I even at times believed that loyalty was an outdated concept, that tribalism was brutish. The trouble with all such misguided beliefs is that there is a kernel of truth in them. To untangle what's true from stupidity requires understanding nuance, so allow me to establish what I do **not** mean by loyalty and duty.

Loyalty is often conflated with ass-kissing or flattery - especially in modern circles where material wealth has become the ultimate goal. You see this in the so-called "high classes" of today's social circles: the Hollywood or MTV types, or the crypto-bros wearing Louis Vuitton jumpsuits and Rolexes, showing off to their followers, surrounded by a close group of NPC yes-men with no agency of their own.

In warrior cultures, such sycophantic sucking up to the master or lord was scorned. They valued dignity and gave respect where it was due. Think about how the first leaders and kings must have come about. They were not entitled little brats as Netflix would have you believe. They had to prove themselves leaders of men. Over time, some of these lineages and cultures devolved into ass-kissing where natural authority was replaced by fake authority, but there was often some sort of violent 'cleansing' that rebalanced things and reformed a hierarchy worthy of fealty. This correction has always been necessary and is precisely where we find ourselves today. In order to build a new culture we must sacrifice the false gods and idols it holds up as beyond question.

> "A man who sacrificed his own conscience to the capricious will or freak or fancy of a sovereign was accorded a low place in the estimate of the Precepts. Such one was despised as *nei-shin*, a cringeling, who makes court by unscrupulous fawning, or as *chô-shin*, a favorite who steals his master's affections by means of servile compliance."

> Inazo Nitobe, Bushido: The Soul of Japan

The other nuance is to do with conformity. It's critical for a tribe to operate as a unit, and I've come to understand that sometimes, leadership has a better view or a grander plan which the team must follow - even if it means doing so blindly. But, once again, this doesn't imply lack of agency. The Samurai were some of the most fiercely loyal warriors in history, but if they saw their lord or leader dishonoring himself repeatedly, they would take action - even if it meant sacrificing themselves through a ritual act.

Keep these nuances in mind. When I speak of loyalty, I don't mean sycophantism, but a deeper bond between people. I'm not talking about blind obedience but cohesion and unity. Loyalty always comes from a place of dignity, love and respect - even though it is neither of the three.

Duty & love

I have already mentioned that feudal Japan had no direct translation of the word "love". The duty a wife had to her husband was a form of loyalty and respect, which combined to represent their conception of 'love'. More broadly speaking, and depending on the context, words like benevolence, compassion, politeness, and in fact, duty were used.

Duty can be understood as an expression of the loyalty you have to one another. It isn't unlike love, yet different. A Samurai had a duty to the man beside him and to his lord. He would be ready to give his life for both.

In Bushido, the chivalric codes of Christendom, and among ancients, dutiful respect had a reverent, ascendant charge, much like respect. It was upward flowing to that which was considered socially, hierarchically or spiritually above you. The children and mother to the father, the Samurai had a duty to his daimyo, the daimyo to the shogun or emperor, and the emperor to the gods, what we in the west might call, "the higher good".

On the flip side, was *noblesse oblige* - a French phrase meaning that the obligations of nobility extend beyond mere social or economic status. Noble status was understood to come with significant ethical responsibilities and duties to act generously and nobly toward those you protect, govern, lead and provide for. This is the kind of love the noble, the lord and the king has toward his people. He considers them "his people", much like the husband does his wife and children, or the master does his apprentice. This is the magnanimous kind of duty and love, condescending from above as compassion and benevolence.

This condescension, together with the ascendant, respectful duty subjects had to their superiors and the loyalty they each had to each other, made feudalism the basis for the most powerful cultures around the world and is why feudalism was so stable, contrary to popular belief. The average peasant had objectively less resources and material wealth than the average person does today, but he also worked only 2 out of 3 days, had a big family, and celebrated holidays. Compared to modern wage-slavery, loneliness, tax harvesting and theft via inflation, feudal life doesn't sound so bad.

Duty, love and respect are necessary in a functional society, and they pass through tiers from the little, through to God, and back. Children respect their mother and father, the wife, her husband, the husband, his lord or his mission, and so forth up the hierarchy to God or the gods, and back again as each tier condescends love, while providing and protecting. They each have a duty to each other.

Some of this thankfully still exists, and I've seen a renaissance in this sort of thinking that gives me hope. Behaving in such a way is a form of maturity and humility. But we need more, because the humility associated with duty has been eroded to the point where even people reading this might be correlating it with slavery or servitude. This is a childish viewpoint.

Think about it this way: Jesus considered himself a servant of men, despite being a leader. He embodied the most magnanimous kind of love and in return was revered by all. There is a quiet dignity in service, and the virtue of duty is the embodiment of dignity in the service of that which you love most. That's the essence of the term.

The greatest leaders throughout history were similar in their nature. They didn't demand loyalty or respect but earned it. They loved those they led and felt a duty of care toward them, while maintaining a duty to that which they aspired toward or fought for. Those who followed felt a duty toward both their leaders and the greater good, which formed the basis of their loyalty.

Contrast this with modern society, where loyalty and duty are sniggered at. There is an abundance of soft men and if we are to be the strong men of the next cycle who build structures that will absorb the worst of future weak-men cycles, we should ask ourselves today the following questions:

What is it that you have a loyalty toward, or are willing to pledge allegiance to? What is your duty or mission in life? Who and what do you love enough to go and fight for? What will you sacrifice when the time comes to pay the price for your beliefs?

Duty & sacrifice

Duty is the exercise of loyalty when it's hard or inconvenient to do so. This is why it requires courage, respect, selflessness, and most importantly **sacrifice.**

Moderns often view sacrifice as a superstitious relic of the past. This happens on both sides of the philosophical and theological aisle. Whether it's the soft Christians who read the Bible and make rationalizations about sacrifices being purely "metaphorical", or the historians and anthropologists whose scorn you can taste when they describe the 'barbarity' of the ancients and their methods. What they both fail to realize is that real sacrifice is deeply spiritual, symbolic, and righteous - and that's why it is both holy *and* meaningful. A sacrifice is the action or embodiment of true duty and loyalty in the service of that which you love and honor.

Ironically, despite this conceited air of superiority, symbolism and tea leaf-reading still run much of the world. We've removed the pain and sacrifice elements to make the symbols more palatable, but things haven't really changed much beneath the surface. Look no further than the top end of economics and finance. People hang on every word the Federal Reserve chairman says, trying to divine what they mean by this word or that gesture. Like voodoo on a grand scale, traders begin to draw pictures and patterns on charts while using magical "sentiment analysis" all in an attempt to decipher and predict what will happen next.

I say this not to discredit the importance of symbology, but to make clear that this is a deep part of our psyche. The symbology of sacrifice still moves us. It's found in the greatest stories, and is the substance of the most profound words we read or hear, and the bravest of acts we see. Just because we're not sacrificing goats anymore, doesn't mean we're any different from our ancestors. We've only changed the setting and the desired outcome - which is where the decay seems to lie. Instead of prophesying greatness and glory, we're prophesying how to get rich quick so we can acquire "creature comforts". Instead of real blood sacrifice, we're playing risk with video games and internet funny money.

Humans are profoundly symbolic creatures, and there is a depth of realization that comes with the act of sacrificing that cannot be described in words. Whether that's the sacrifice of an animal to a higher power - representing your sustenance - or the burning of the boats to take the island - representing your escape or chance for survival. A real, tangible sacrifice charges human beings in a way that fundamentally transcends the spoken word. It is ineffable.

Symbolism is the most powerful artform, and sacrificial acts are the greatest expression.

Modern equivalents are of course of a softer nature, but still important. Leaving a relationship, for example, in order to become the best version of yourself is an act of sacrifice. You may have to let someone you love and are comfortable with go, in order to truly become the person you need to be.

In order to build something of great value—a business, a book, a home—you may need to sacrifice time with your friends and family, your health, your free time, and your immediate enjoyment, but as the 20th century Dutch historian Johan Huizinga said: *"The height of heroism is reached in men who renounce the pleasures of life."* There is a reason why time preference is the ultimate marker for the health of a civilization.

Bitcoin is actually a great example here. To learn about Bitcoin and really appreciate it, many of us sacrificed bitcoin by losing it, gambling it away on shitcoins or selling when we were up 600% at $0.32. We spent thousands of hours "going down the rabbit hole" to really get it, and then

"HODL'ed" through ups and downs to earn the the appreciation of its purchasing power.

These are all rites of passage and leave marks on our psyche. Everything we do has a price, and I believe the ancients knew this at a far more visceral level than we do. They practiced it through rituals some might see as 'barbaric', but which were in fact deeply symbolic, and which moved men to action more than any words ever could. Furthermore, they were conscious and intentional about it.

Luckily, some of us are still building spiritual and psychological muscle away from mere strokes of the keyboard. Some of us are creating, developing and producing. It's you I'm talking to here. It's time to recognise the importance of symbolism again, and see how you can integrate it into your life and praxis. People want to feel something, and there is no better way to make them **feel**. For inspiration, let's look to feudal Japan.

The Samurai were the bravest and most radical of all when it came to the use of sacrifice in their display of loyalty and duty.

When a loyal Samurai had either shamed or dishonored himself, or when as a vassal, he believed that his lord was acting in error or might bring dishonor to the clan, he would make the point not by "talking at length", but through a sacrificial act. He would say his piece, often in the form of some last words or a death poem, and then proceed to take his own life through the painful act of *seppuku*.

Duty was so embedded within the culture that it called upon the truly courageous to give their lives in order to make a point to their superiors, whom they served.

Think about the level of courage, integrity and commitment that such an act requires. Seppuku was not just a quick suicide by slicing the throat. It was literal self-evisceration. A ritual suicide by disembowelment, made with a deep, horizontal cut across the abdomen. It is one of the most painful ways to die, and it was expected that the Samurai would show little to no emotion in the face, as any excessive contortion was seen as weakness.

Barbaric? I think not. This was a level of dignity, courage, honor, sacrifice and loyalty that few if any other cultures in history have ever displayed. Certainly no contemporary culture displays this level of commitment.

> *"When a subject differed from his master, the loyal path for him to pursue was to use every available means to persuade him of his error, as Kent did to King Lear. Failing in this, let the master deal with him as he wills. In cases of this kind, it was quite a usual course for the Samurai to make the last appeal to the intelligence and conscience of his lord by demonstrating the sincerity of his words with the shedding of his own blood."*

> Inazo Nitobe, Bushido: The Soul of Japan

A similar Western example I came across is the *Devotio*, or *Roman Blood Sacrifice*. The word itself is Latin for 'vow' and 'devote', which as the combination suggests is an act of duty and loyalty. It was considered a final attempt or ultimate act by a Roman devotee to sacrifice himself in exchange for his god's favor in triumph over an opponent. Chad Crowley, author and translator describes it as follows:

> *The religious ritual of the Devotio embodies the ancient Romans' fervent faith in divine intervention and valorous self-sacrifice. This hallowed ritual, a form of heroic suicide, symbolizes the ultimate act of devotion, where the shedding of one's own blood serves as the paramount offering to the gods. In this ultimate act of Votum—a vow made to a deity in anticipation of a request being fulfilled—Roman devotees, embroiled in the throes of battle, would willingly offer their lives to the chthonic gods, the deities of the underworld. In this mortal exchange steeped in blood and valor, the Roman who made the sacrifice sought Rome's triumph over an enemy opponent.*

As a leader and man of virtue, you should seek to embody such duty. I don't suggest that you commit *seppuku* should a family member buy Ethereum, or perform a final blood sacrifice if they identify as non-binary, but that it's your duty to guide those whom you love, care about and can influence toward better outcomes by leading from the front - and if necessary, sacrificing something of value in order to make a lesson more symbolic. Talk is cheap. Actions, especially sacrificial ones, count.

Bitcoin, Loyalty, and Duty

Loyal to your lineage

Other than a duty to yourself - the self respect we discussed in the prior chapter - Bitcoin comes with a duty and loyalty to your future self, your family, to your community or tribe, and for a select few, a duty to the world. These loyalties transcend Bitcoin. When you build wealth and become a person of power and influence, you are faced with the question of meaning and legacy. What is your life about, where will you find meaning and how will you be remembered?

If you've agreed with anything written in the book so far, then you will also believe that you have a duty to not only live by these principles, but to pay them forward. In fact, paying forward is an expression of your loyalty, to your friends and family, to your civilization, to your ancestors and ultimately to your descendants. This is the ultimate lowering of one's time preferences and perhaps the most fundamental utility of a sound money like Bitcoin.

Consider the structure of the Bitcoin network, with its indelible transaction record in the blockchain. It is profoundly "traditional" in the sense that it is one, unbroken string of recorded, mathematical history. It is law, and demands loyalty. What does economics look like when the blockchain is five thousand years old, and who will your descendants be?

Just because you can do something, doesn't mean you should.

To be a Bitcoiner comes with the duty to be an honorable person, because having freedom comes with the responsibility to do something with it. Life is more than just being able to do "anything you want." It's also about duty, sacrifice, compassion and justice. While Bitcoin is engineered to be largely impervious to bad actors and to function in an adversarial environment, a strong culture is made up of people loyal to each other, who live for more than their base-pleasures. People take on the duty of leading and providing, the responsibility of being a role model, and the courage to fight for that which has meaning.

While you are free to go and run an Only Fans pimp racket - should you? You could go out to pump and dump a shitcoin on retail, but should you? You could go out and peddle experimental medications, but should you? These decisions become more important in a world where loyalty, duty and therefore reputation mean something. And this day will come. When the ever-present desperation underlying a world with broken monetary properties is gone, there will no longer be an excuse. It will be time for us to construct lineages that last a thousand years, and these start with a loyalty and duty that transcend the individual.

Restraint / Self Control
(jisei)

Restraint / Self-Control

"For strength of character in the race as in the individual consists mainly in the power of sacrificing the present for the future, of disregarding the immediate temptations of ephemeral pleasure for more distant and lasting sources of satisfaction. The height of heroism is reached in men who renounce the pleasures of life and even life itself for the sake of winning for others, perhaps in distant ages, the blessings of freedom and truth."

Johan Huizinga, *Homo Ludens: A Study of the Play-Element in Culture*

I place this last because it is the virtue that ties all the others together. Other than courage, self-control (or *restraint*) is the quintessential warrior virtue. It is the virtue of maturity. Bitcoiners talk a lot about 'time preference.' **This** is where it comes from.

In Bushido, the Japanese word *jisei* most closely translates to "self-control", and is made up of two kanji: 自制

The first, 自 (*ji*), means self. It is a simple character, pictographically representing a nose, which was historically used as a symbol for the self.

The second kanji, 制 (*sei*), conveys the idea of rules or governance. It is composed of elements that include 刂 (a variant of "刀" meaning knife or blade), and "攵" (a variant of "攴,") which as seen earlier, represents the act of striking and relates to the idea of action or authority. It suggests the imposition of rules or restrictions, and can be read as either the law of the governing sword, or the law governing the sword.

自制 (*Jisei*) combines the self with the idea of control, authority and regulation. Together these kanjis emphasize the ability to govern one's own actions and impulses. This is reminiscent of the Chinese ideogram for warrior, 武, made up of the characters for weapon: 戈 and stop: ⼁. A true warrior has, ultimately, the ability to control oneself.

The English word "restraint" comes from Old French *restreinte*, which means "constraint, restraint, or limit." It comes in turn from Latin *restringere*, "to bind back, hold back, or restrain." *Restringere* is made up of *re-* "back" or "again," and *stringere* "to draw tight or bind."

Over time, the word "restraint" came to be used in English to refer to a variety of situations in which something is held back, controlled, or limited. It can refer to physical restraint, such as being tied up or confined, as well as more abstract notions, such as self-control, moderation, or limitation - the latter is what interests us.

Self-control as a broader concept is important here, and so is the etymology of both words. Self originates from Old English "self, sylf" (West Saxon), "seolf" (Anglian), meaning "one's own person, self; own, personal; same, identical." It derives from Proto-Germanic "*selbaz," found across many Germanic languages (e.g., Old Norse "sjalfr," Dutch "zelf," German "selbst"). The Proto-Germanic root "*selbaz" traces back to Proto-Indo-European (PIE) "*sel-bho," a suffixed form of the root "*s(w)e-," a third person and reflexive pronoun, also used to denote the speaker's social group, implying a sense of "(we our-)selves."

The word *control* emerged in the early 15th century as "countrollen," meaning "to check the accuracy of, verify; regulate." It comes from Anglo-French "contreroller," which means "to exert authority," and from Medieval Latin "contrarotulus" ("a counter, register"), combining Latin "contra" ("against") with "rotulus" (a diminutive of "rota," meaning "wheel"). The concept of "control" historically relates to the idea of checking or verifying accounts by a duplicate register, a method for maintaining accuracy and regulation.

Restraint and self-control, in the virtuous or ethical sense, thus refer to the ability to direct oneself and resist impulses that might lead to harmful or destructive behavior. It is the act of exercising personal authority or regulation over one's own actions, emotions, or desires. It is the application of an internal 'check' or governance over oneself, analogous to how external controls regulate the accuracy and order of a system or process. Self-control is in the deepest sense, the prerequisite to self-ownership, agency and ultimately, free will. Without self-control, you are at the behest or control of something else - be it circumstances, impulses or another person. Without self-control - if you recall our discussion on radical responsibility and agency earlier - you are a slave.

Self-control, self-ownership, self-sufficiency

"There is no true scholar who has not the instincts of a true soldier in his veins. To be able to command and to be able to obey in a proud fashion; to keep one's place in rank and file, and yet to be ready at any moment to lead; to prefer danger to comfort; not to weigh what is permitted and what is forbidden in a tradesman's balance; to be more hostile to pettiness, slyness, and parasitism than to wickedness. What is it that one learns in a hard school? To obey and to command."

Friedrich Nietzsche, The Will to Power

The slave is not virtuous; neither is the unhinged man. It is not virtuous to live as a dependant, or off the sweat of another, and there is certainly no virtue in imposing on others ideas you yourself do not live by. Central planners and bureaucrats are much like HR managers and airport security staff: they revel in the creation of arbitrary rules and decrees - almost as if it gives their life meaning. Their army of NPCs then spend their lives blindly enforcing these orders under the guise of whatever flavor of morality suits them at the time - all as if it was asked for - and worse, with other people's money and resources. There are few things in the world as vile as a self-proclaimed 'savior' that nobody wants. This is why we find the WEF types so repulsive, and all those who support and impose their fake order.

What most people truly desire is to follow great leaders, not because they have to, but because they **want** to. A great leader, a man of virtue, or a true hero, does not bestow himself that title, nor is it decreed by some fake globalist organization; it is freely given by others to the man who leads by example, from the front, demonstrates extreme self-control, and inspires through vitality and action.

> *"Being alive constitutes an aristocracy which there is no getting beyond. He who is most alive, intrinsically, is King, whether men admit it or not."*
>
> D.H. Lawrence, Essay: Aristocracy

Two great figures come to mind here: Christ and Alexander.

Christ is the ultimate image of restraint. By bearing his cross, he became a symbol of the ideal mean, and the son of God. He rejected the offer to turn stones into bread, despite fasting for forty days in the desert wilderness; he refused the kingdoms of the world the Devil presented him; and he refused to be crowned King of the Jews. He stood before Pontius Pilate, and his accusers, and he did not bend. The dignity with which he bore the cross changed the fabric of civilization, morality and behavior; the very course of human history.

Alexander is second only to the figure of Christ. He was the first man over the wall, he rode the lead horse in a cavalry charge, he would eat last and most sparsely at the banquet, all despite his position. He would sleep on the hard ground when he could sleep on a luxurious bed large enough for ten; he would abstain when he could've been with concubines in the harem; he would show incredible mercy and magnanimity when he could have been savage - as demonstrated by his treatment of Darius' family - and he took great care to know the names and stories of as many of his men as possible, visited them in the infirmary, while wounded himself, in order to inspire them to strength. All the great leaders who came after him followed this example - and the result was that men voluntarily *followed*.

Alexander was also known as the general who banned his men from looting after victory. After the battle of the Granicus, he declared that none of his soldiers would be allowed to sack the countryside. They were to come into the territory as liberators, not as thieves, which was rare in ancient warfare.

He carried this frame onward. At the battle of Issus, the rematch with Darius, the Macedonians once again pulled off an incredible victory against incredible odds (Diodorus and Arrian suggest the ratio may have been as high as 40:1, while modern historians place it closer to 5 or 10:1). On Alexander's return from pursuing Darius, he found the Macedonian army plundering the Persian camp, helping themselves to *"riches in such quantities as our men have never seen—horses and women, stacked arms, suits of mail, golden vases, bags of money meant as soldiers' pay"* (Pressfield, *Virtues of War*).

He was taken aback with despair, which became rage at this "defilement" of his army's good name and *raison d'être*. Alexander gathered his generals and commanded that they line the men up for drills - right after a bloody battle and an incredible victory! He's said to have drilled them long into the night as punishment for this behavior - against the protests of his generals.

Stephen Pressfield illustrates this powerfully in *The Virtues of War*, in a speech Alexander gives to his men:

> *"Brothers, I will suffer your crimes this day out of my love for you only. But hear me now and sear these words into your hearts: That man who disgraces this army again, I will not chastise as I do this night, as a father punishes his sons with care and concern for their character, but*

will banish that man from me and from this company forever."

"Ultimate responsibility for this debacle lies with me. I have not impressed sufficiently upon you, my officers, the code of chivalry by which I expect you and this army to conduct yourselves. Therefore I shall take nothing from the spoils. That portion that would have been mine will be distributed to our wounded and mutilated comrades and donated to raise memorials for our fallen."

The next morning, all of the loot, gold, vases, everything, had been laid out in front of Alexander's tent, but he remained unmoved. He refused to acknowledge them for another day until he was begged by his generals to respond. Ultimately, a soldier named Socrates the Redbeard, bandaged and beaten up, comes forward and says:

"Have we not been true to you, Alexander? Have we not bled for you, and died for you? Have we failed you ever, or served you with anything less than all our hearts? What more do you want of us?"

To which Alexander responds:

"I want you to be . . . magnificent."

The power of NO

"I teach the No to all that makes weak—that exhausts. I teach the Yes to all that strengthens, and stores up strength."

Friedrich Nietzsche, The Will to Power

Restraint and self-control are effectively the act of saying no. No is a standard: it is the setting of a boundary and the building of a wall. It is the separation of what's important and what's not. Hierarchies exist because of "no." Chaos comes from the never-ending yes.

Moderns live in a "yes-man" society, so it's no wonder they are so agreeable, so quick to jump onto the next trend, so inclined to conform and to obey arbitrary mandates. Most people have no staying power.

Their language and beliefs are all about inclusivity and open-mindedness, they lack gumption, the will to sacrifice and the fortitude to experience short-term pain for the potential or promise of long-term gain.

Since the Berlin wall was (rightfully) taken down, society has (wrongfully) decided that it's a good idea to tear down every other wall or structure that was meticulously built across the millennia. Unbeknownst to us, we tore down the very walls of the house we lived in and are now wondering why the roof is leaking and the squatters have settled in.

The ability to say no is a superpower. It means focus, it means staying on the path, and it is the basis of a low time preference. Without 'no', you cannot have a future. We've all heard about the marshmallow experiment: the ability to delay immediate gratification is the prerequisite for doing something greater and more meaningful later. This is true for health, for wealth, for relationships and for anything of value. You can't build wealth if you spend everything you make; you won't get healthy if you eat every time you're a little hungry. Compounded results cannot occur if you succumb to every urge.

Saying no to a temptation requires courage, strength and fortitude. Whether it be no to the drink, drug, hallucinogen, women, bribe, shitcoin, snooze button, fast food, seed oil, chocolate, or the elevator instead of the stairs. Refusing to take the easy path takes an act of will.

Furthermore, no is freedom! We've been conditioned to believe yes is the manifestation of freedom and choice, but no is in fact also a choice - and often a more powerful one. Slaves must say 'yes' to everything, but the master and sovereign individual is he who can say no. Alot of modern personal development and spiritualism has got this wrong. The incessant focus on "yes" has taught people to be overly agreeable and therefore helped undermine their fortitude. They're so open-minded that their brains have leaked out.

Saying no to one thing actually means saying yes to something else. This is how you prioritize and create a hierarchy. No helps you focus and do what's right and important, instead of being distracted by the noise and options. Elon Musk and Steve Jobs are famously men of no.

The eternal yes, and the inability to delay gratification has led us to an age of mass consumerism. The very economic indicators we use are built around consumptive measures. We are drowning in a never ending sea of stuff, content is everywhere, media is everywhere, cheap plastic products are everywhere. We are bombarded with inputs via all our senses, and as a result have become completely desensitized. We can no longer hear the subtle tones or taste the subtle flavors. It's all noise.

To counteract this, and to reclaim sanity, taste and beauty, we must learn to say no more often and to become more selective. We must exercise judgment: discern and discriminate, separating wheat from chaff. Furthermore, we must say no not only when it's easy to do so, but especially when it's hard to do so. For the no to truly mean something, you must say it when you think you cannot.

*The mantra must become **quality over quantity***. Recall the definition of excellence and elite! *The select*. **The choicest**. To make a choice, and to select, fundamentally means saying yes to one or a few things, at the explicit exclusion of all else. In other words, selection comes from more no, and less yes. And ultimately, by saying no to most things, you are giving proper weight to the things you say yes to: you state your respect and appreciation for them. This is what it truly means to value something.

The monster

Self-control is only a virtue if your unconstrained self is capable of causing damage. Only a dangerous man can truly be "nice." Only someone with the capacity to be a monster, and with the strength to keep it in check, can lay claim to this virtue. It's why Jordan Peterson says that the best men he knows are the most dangerous ones. It's also why women are instinctively attracted to the bad boy. This archetype of man is the real protector. The man who could crush her, is also the one who can most keep her safe.

"Nobody deserves to be praised for goodness unless he is strong enough to be bad, for any other goodness is usually merely inertia or lack of will-power."

Francois de La Rochefoucauld, Reflections: or Sentences and Moral Maxims

Self-control is the virtue of maturity, because it's not the man that can swing a hammer to crush an egg that is truly powerful, but he who can swing it and stop the hammer before the point of impact. "*Praus*" is an ancient Greek word that is often translated as "meek" or "gentle" in English;, however its classical meaning is much richer. One interpretation is that "*praus*" described the virtue of strength under repose, or power under control. It was used to describe a previously wild horse that was tamed and trained for war. Jordan Peterson and other Christian scholars often translate it as *"those who have swords, and know how to use them but choose to keep them sheathed"*. Whatever the exact definition, the idea of strength under repose is important. The best men are dangerous, because they have the **capacity** to inflict harm, but consciously decide not to. They check their inner monster. As I have repeatedly emphasized, ***it's not power that corrupts, but weakness***. It's the weak who run around crushing eggs with a hammer, and inflicting harm on those who cannot defend themselves; it's the yes-man who lacks the fortitude to say no; it's the conformist, that is most vile and ugly. He is not the progenitor of action, but the reagent. He is the slave who lacks courage and agency, the one outsourcing responsibility for his actions. He is inertia, devoid of life.

The man of virtue takes responsibility and has the courage to fight the greater foe. He takes on risk, he consciously unleashes his monster. He cultivates it. He knows that it's when you "can" do something, but do not, that you have real power and strength. Alexander, Caesar, Napoleon all embodied this. Instead of just doing what was obvious or easy, they chose to do what was at the very edge of possibility. They consciously directed their energy toward climbing higher, reaching farther, and making the unknown known.

Non-interventionism

"The essence of the interventionist policy is to take from one group to give to another. It is confiscation and distribution."

Ludwig Von Mises, Human Action

Non-interventionism is an expression of self-control. It is a character trait that powerful leaders exhibit (they do not micro-manage), that great societies have baked into their laws and norms (privacy, free speech, right to defend oneself), that great parents exhibit when they allow their children to explore - even if it means they can hurt themselves - and that intellectual heroes such as Mises, Menger, and Rothbard advocated, above all else.

Dystopian societies are built on micromanagement, interruption, interference and surveillance. They are built on the idea that the human beings who make them up are numbers on a spreadsheet, that can be mathematically manipulated as though they're all equal. This approach ironically makes the populace more docile and dependent on the nanny-state, slowly eroding not only freedom, but agency and the free will of the people under its yoke. Constant interventionism and surveillance come from a place of desperation and inner projection. The people who believe that society must operate like a modern HR department are often overweight, depressed, ugly and envious. They have no self-control, so they project this lack of virtue onto everyone else. They erroneously believe everybody else is as weak as they are, and if they are presented with any evidence to the contrary, someone who is better, stronger, smarter and more beautiful - they will do everything they can to tear them down.

"Of all tyrannies, a tyranny sincerely exercised for the good of its victims may be the most oppressive. It would be better to live under robber barons than under omnipotent moral busybodies. The robber baron's cruelty may sometimes sleep, his cupidity may at some point be satiated; but those who torment us for our own good will torment us without end for they do so with the approval of their own conscience. They may be more likely to go to Heaven yet at the same time likelier to make a Hell of earth. This very kindness stings with intolerable insult. To be "cured" against one's will and cured of states which we may not regard as disease is to be put on a level of those who have not yet reached the age of reason or those who never will; to be classed with infants, imbeciles, and domestic animals."

C.S. Lewis, God in the Dock: Essays on Theology (Making of Modern Theology)

For too long we've let the bureaucratic micro-managers of the world lord it over us. Proximity to the money-printing apparatus made that possible. There they found a place where they could hide and stealthily extract wealth from everybody else. They didn't have to produce or risk anything: we assumed that risk, while they funded themselves into positions of power and influence. From these positions, and in their infinite stupidity, they decided to then interfere with us, surveil us, humiliate us and make their petty presence known.

It's time we changed that, and the hour is now upon us. You can feel it in the air. In late 2023, a shot was fired that was heard all around the world: Javier Milei won the Argentinian presidency on the back of a non-interventionist message. He brought the Misesean message into the mainstream.

"Stop fiddling with things" is the maxim of the Austrian Economist. Until Milei, this position has mostly been relegated to obscurity, or falsely wielded to attract votes. Everything else in modernity has been about intervention taken to a degree of unhinged excess.

For a century now the Austrian credo has been non-interventionist, a call for fiscal and financial restraint and responsibility. Now with Bitcoin in hand, the time has come for an age where their sound, first-principles line of thinking shall not only be vindicated, but become the playbook for those who want to exceed and excel in life. Imagine a future in which books on success and personal development are those written by Hoppe, Sowell, Hazlit and Mises, instead of snake oil salesmen pushing more consumerism. That would be a true intellectual golden age.

Bitcoin is the first step, and leaders like Milei will continue to step up. But it's not enough. Bitcoin fixes the fundamental 'meddling with the money,' problem but it will take time - probably three generations - to really come out on top. And even when it does win, there will be opportunities to drive ourselves into excess in other areas of life, individually and collectively. This is where restraint becomes the 'sacred virtue.'

Temptation has such a powerful allure, and the ability to say "no" and walk away from it in favor of a higher calling, a greater commitment or because it could be detrimental in the long run, is truly a 'holy virtue.'

If courage is the peak virtue of the warrior, then self-control is the peak virtue of the leader. If he has self-control, he inspires others around him to be better, and therefore has no need to micromanage their lives. Contrary to the meddling middle managers, *a true leader turns the desire for control inward.*

He who has no self-control, loses the respect of those he leads, and thus reduces his influence. Ironically, any subsequent imposition of control over others has the opposite effect. Conversely, he who has supreme self-control inspires it in others, and thereby increases his influence.

Leading by example is the key. Nobody really respects or follows the fat personal trainer. Remember that.

As future socio-economic elites, the temptation to intervene will be strong. It will be your duty to abstain, and I hope this chapter serves as a catalyst to build that muscle. Draw inspiration from the examples of Christ, Alexander, Leonidas, and even Satoshi.

Satoshi's disappearance

Finally, considering this is the last chapter of the virtues section, I'd like to pay homage to Satoshi. Whoever he was, he displayed a level of self-control that very few since the ancient warriors I've examined in the book have.

He could've been the richest, most famous person in the world. But he had the foresight, strength, courage, and self-control to do what no man has done before: to fix the greatest social problem of all (the money) - *by disappearing.*

This is what separates Bitcoin from all the shitcoins. It's this initial sacrifice that makes it special. This is the immaculate conception of immaculate money.

Similar to Christ and Alexander, the exact facts of the story do not matter. What matters is that there is a fountainhead who performs an extraordinary feat, only to remain in spirit and in myth - but not in person.

The greatest movements are founded in this way.

Satoshi's disappearance was critical to the solution and without it, there would *not have been a solution.* If you stop to think about that, you may after a while come to appreciate the gravity of this move.

Its importance is only further highlighted when you see the character of the people who've come since then. Each of them have come not to solve a problem, but to enrich themselves at the explicit expense of others through fraudulent or stupid means. Whether Vitalik, Hoskinson, Heart, CSW, or Bankman-Fried, these people, if they serve any purpose at all, show us what it looks like to be completely incapable of self-control. They are all the exact opposite of Satoshi, and a perfect illustration of what happens in the absence of this virtue. That kind of contrast in itself is a gift, so in some perverse way, I guess we can thank each of these characters for that.

Bitcoin & Self Restraint

Bitcoin is restraint in action.

Up there with responsibility, Bitcoin is the literal and metaphorical embodiment of this virtue. Perfectly self-restrained by the consensus ruleset that defines it, Bitcoin is the first time we've engineered something that is so fundamentally valuable, while also perfectly finite.

- A restrained total supply of 21 million coins.

- A restrained block size creating demand for space.

- A difficulty adjustment which restrains block time.

- A network resistant to change (restrained rules) because coordination doesn't scale.

This fact has an incredible impact on people, which is to think twice before acting. By localizing the consequence of one's actions - as I've noted multiple times in the book - people learn to be more intentional with how they behave. When you can't just paper over a loss or get bailed out, you learn to value the future more. Lowering time preference is an exercise in self-control and intentional restraint. Maturity itself is the ability to know and be perfectly capable of doing something, but having the fortitude and self-ownership not to (if not doing so is the honorable thing).

The Immaculate Conception of Immaculate Money.

History shows that restraint is necessary to ensure the soundness of money. Satoshi, recognising this, engineered a money with particular in-built restraints, boot-strapped it long enough for a critical mass of nodes to be achieved, so that they actually restrain each other, then **disappeared** *so that it would grow to be outside the reach of even the most powerful governments and organizations.*

In doing so, he displayed a level of self-control out of the reach of most, save for the ancient warriors I have examined in this book. This primeval sacrifice, this immaculate conception, is what distinguishes Bitcoin from the shitcoins.

Satoshi launched Bitcoin toward the same realm that is forever out of our reach, but that we are also forever inspired by. Call it Physics. Call it Purity. Call it Perfection. Call it Harmony. Call it Beauty. Call it, dare I say, God-like.

I know that's a big claim, but Bitcoin seems to live here, and in doing so, relieves us of that which we cannot bear full responsibility for individually or by committee: maintaining the ledger of praxis and value. This frees us up to channel our willpower toward pursuits we can be held accountable for, while this 'ledger in the sky' continues to keep score, forever.

Bitcoin's example acts as a reminder to embody greater restraint in our own lives, and in the other pursuits, quests and adventures we find ourselves on.

Closing Out

A new socio-economic standard requires a new way of life. As institutionalized lying, cheating and stealing is made more difficult, the door opens for creating a new, more honest and ascendant culture. To build the kind of civilization we know in our blood is possible, we must start with virtue and behavior - and this is the playbook to make it happen.

It's no coincidence that the virtues we covered have come up repeatedly across all the cultures whose civilization are the foundations we stand on today. Their cross-cultural presence points to something very important: *virtues transcends beliefs*. Humanity had and will continue to have many differing beliefs, not only in different religions, but within the same religions (how many sects of Christianity or Islam exist, alone?). Virtues like excellence, courage, compassion and loyalty have and will remain valued by all of them, because they are fundamentally *exceptional*. They are the antithesis of average.

> *"Virtue has all the instincts of the average man against it: it is unprofitable, imprudent, it isolates; it is related to passion and not very accessible to reason; it spoils the character, the head, the mind — according to the standards of mediocre men; it rouses to enmity toward order, toward the lies that are concealed in every order, institution, actuality — it is the worst of vices, if one judges by its harmful effects on others."*

Friedrich Nietzsche, *The Will to Power*

A focus on virtue is also more useful than 'morality' because the former is more practical (behavior) while the latter is more theoretical (belief) and therefore simply ignored or used by immoral people to browbeat those who do care about morality. Of course, there are also virtue signalers everywhere these days, but they are easy to spot, because their *behavior* does not match their *words*. Like a fat person lecturing an athlete on health or fitness - something doesn't add up. Things like courage, integrity and responsibility are much easier to recognise. This is also why I laid out the etymology of the words which express these virtues, and gave examples of what they looked like in practice, *across cultures*.

Besides, people who spend all their time talking about "morality" usually have something to hide, and those who believe them are often led astray. This is why it's best to select for action, behavior and principles or, in other words, virtues. The greatest cultures throughout history understood this, and also knew that war and conflict are integral parts of life: *"si vis pacem, para bellum."* They were the most powerful, because they existed at the nexus of life and death.

I do not suggest we return to earlier times - we cannot - but we can recognise the principles themselves and begin to integrate them into something new. *"Nothing new under the sun"* and *"change is the only thing you can be certain of."* Both are true, and we must contend with this paradox. Somewhere between these two concepts lies the truth and the way forward.

PART III

Integration

Integration

How do we integrate these virtues into our modern society, and even more importantly, into a future, post-post-modern society? Is it even possible in the current paradigm or does there need to be a wholesale shift away from where we are now? Do we have to build something entirely new? And if so, what are the challenges we will face along the way?

This section will explore four key areas: culture, governance, wealth and cycles - and the history, make-up, challenges and opportunities related to each. We will grapple with and try to answers questions such as the following:

- How do we contend with the mismatch between civilian and warrior cultures?

- Was history shaped by the crowd, or great men?

- Was feudalism as bad or backward as we've been led to believe?

- How did democracy and an over-indexing on equality turn the west from ascendant and powerful, to weak and decaying?

- What really happened in Zimbabwe and what does that teach us about today?

- Does material affluence breed weakness and entitlement, and what can we do to limit the damage?

- Why money and power are necessary, for beauty, culture, civilization and legacy.

- How cycles and seasons shape everything from the smallest atomic and cellular process, up through the technological winds that shape society, and beyond.

- How technology and economics are related, and together bring both abundance and dependence.

Finally, we'll look at Bitcoin's impact and relationship to all of these. As I said at the outset, I won't focus on whether or how Bitcoin will prevail economically. That's the base assumption for the book, and I've also listed various resources at the end of the book which you can use to validate those claims. I'm more interested in whether or not humanity wins if Bitcoin wins, and if so, *what* does it win, in these four key domains.

What's undeniable is that the current socio-economic paradigm cannot continue, and we will certainly move into a new one. Bitcoin is simply in my opinion the leading candidate for becoming the new monetary and economic substrate.

Culture

The word "culture" derives from the Latin *cultura*, meaning to cultivate or 'care for' and stems from the Latin *colere*, which means to tend to the earth and to grow or nurture the soil. It wasn't until the 1500s that "culture" was more widely used to refer to human society, and came to mean something more like *learning and taste; the intellectual side of civilization*, and in the last couple centuries, *the collective customs, norms, ideas, and achievements of a people*.

Culture exists everywhere: from the petri dish and garden, to the home, school, football team, the company you work in, and the society you live in. Culture matters because it shapes and guides all of these. It is not only upstream of politics and governance, but of civilization, because the ideas, customs, and social behavior of the people who make up society, influence all three. People who are strong and vital, produce a culture with similar characteristics, which leads to the kind of governance that breeds more vital people, and so forth. The reverse is also true: weak people bring about bad or hard times, for this very reason.

Peter Drucker, the great management consultant, educator, and author famously said: *culture eats strategy for breakfast*, which means that no matter how great your business, marketing or product strategy is, it will fail without a company culture that encourages people to implement it. The same is true for your football team, society, the home, and every other domain I mentioned above. You can theorize all you want, but when the rubber meets the road, who is going to execute it? What do they believe, and how do they behave?

Culture is defined by many things. In the context of a society, it can include the period of time, the climate (is it always hot, like at the equator, or does the temperature vary significantly, as in temperate zones), the landscape and territory (flatland, mountains, deserts, ice caps, islands, etc), religion, race, history, and the biological predispositions of the people the size of the population, the food and diet, the gender split and roles, material affluence, music, the arts, scientific capacity, holidays, traditions, architecture and much more. As with all complex systems, it's not possible to know what has the most impact, because all parts influence each other. Trying to take one piece out and analyze it in isolation is a fool's errand and peak left-brain thinking. This is why leftists are always breaking things: they are blind to the gestalt, seeing only the part they are most concerned with - to the exclusion and detriment of all else.

Cultures are alive, and they are always changing. It's impossible for them to remain in stasis. This is a good thing, because life must continue to experiment. If it stops, it is no longer alive. But it comes with its own set of challenges, particularly when the change is somewhat artificial or imposed. Humans are unique in that sense, because we are both a part of the culture *and* can have an outsized influence on it, almost as if we're external to the system. This means we need to be careful. The upshot is that we can evolve very quickly, but we can also ruin the very culture we are a part of. Wisdom and experience thus suggest that we take care not to blindly deconstruct everything around us like children. Reinventing the wheel every generation is not so smart. This is the purpose of tradition(s): to maintain a tether to what's worked in the past and to maximize survivability into the future.

Cultures naturally form traditions as stabilizing mechanisms, because changing or destabilizing a culture is relatively easy. By forcing a big change in one dimension, many other things have to change for the system to find a new equilibrium. This is true of sourdough, of the local biosphere, and of social cultures - hence why immigration is such a big issue. A large number of people entering into a territory, who don't share the same values, beliefs, behaviors, or norms, will have a huge impact on the home culture. This is not a novel concept! Governments take great care to ensure you're not bringing fruits or vegetables that might carry foreign parasites into the country - but they conveniently ignore it when it comes to human biomass. They'll import everyone and anyone, then blame young men, capitalists, or Trump for all the problems they're experiencing.

Another method for changing culture is to 'nudge'. Humans are adaptable and we recalibrate as we go. If things change little by little, you slowly accept or tolerate more and more, inch by inch, until you wake up and find that the principles you lived by are no longer adhered to, the person you were is no longer the same and the culture you lived in no longer exists. This is akin to slowly boiling a frog in water. As with most things, the nudge works both ways: compounding and attrition. It's how we build great cathedrals, wealth, physical bodies, and cities, but also how we age, get fat, introduce participation awards, are overrun by other cultures, and slowly turn into leftists. The most "right-wing" of right-wingers today would have been considered leftists only a couple of centuries ago.

This is why a strong, unyielding minority matters. A vital culture needs both change and tradition. In fact, it's in the tension between them that we find the most optimal path - like the tension between the virtues. The intolerant minority keep us true to tradition, while the mavericks inspire us to change. This creates a charge. Those who guard the gates, and secure the territory might look and feel harsh, they might even act as an impediment to freedom, but they serve a greater purpose in the grand scheme of things. Just as freedom and responsibility combine to produce autonomy in an individual, the warrior culture is the necessary tether to tradition, order, and justice that makes possible for civilian culture to exist and flourish. They are the force that keeps us upright and resists attrition, so that other elements of civilization can produce and compound.

You need both, but modern society has all but discarded the noble shades of intolerance, replacing them with open-ended liberalism and a suffocating totalitarianism that is **not** warrior-esque, protective or inspiring, but instead feels like some blend of a nursing home and children's playpen. As much as we must fix the money, we must fix the culture.

Civilian & warrior cultures

"The civilians loved money and the soldiers feared death."

Feudal Japanese Proverb

What place does the warrior ethos have within a greater civilian society? Steven Pressfield, in *The Warrior Ethos*, tells us that *"Spartans and Romans and Macedonians, Persians and Mongols, Apache and Sioux, Masai and Samurai and Pashtun all share one advantage over Americans: They were (and are) warrior cultures embedded within warrior societies."*

The opposite is the case for all modern, developed nations, whether the United States, Australia, or Russia: modern militaries are warrior cultures embedded within civilian societies. For many this is a desirable structure, as Pressfield notes:

> *"A too-strong military, unfettered by civilian restraint, might be inclined to adventurism or worse. No citizen disputes this or wishes to set things up any other way. The joint chiefs answer to Congress and to the president—and ultimately to the American people. This is the state that the Constitution intended and that the Founding Fathers, who were rightly wary of unchecked concentrations of power, had in mind. But it is an interesting state—and one that produces curious effects."*

Steven Pressfield, The Warrior Ethos

The problem is, civilian and warrior cultures don't sync up very well. Warrior virtues and principles are not broadly shared by the civilian populace, and quite often, they diverge completely. Selfishness and selflessness as explored earlier in the book is a prime example. Let's look at three others: freedom/duty, pacifism/aggression, and comfort/adversity.

> *"Sacrifice, particularly shared sacrifice, is considered an opportunity for honor in a warrior culture. A civilian politician doesn't dare utter the word. Selflessness is a virtue in a warrior culture. Civilian society gives lip service to this, while frequently acting as selfishly as it possibly can."*

> Steven Pressfield, *The Warrior Ethos.*

Civilian societies prize individual freedom, while warrior cultures value cohesion, duty, and a responsibility to the unit. Soldiers, much like sailors, are a part of a unit. You cannot just "do what you want".

In 1786 the British Royal Navy vessel *HMS Bounty* was sent to Tahiti to acquire breadfruit. The voyage through the Atlantic and around to the Pacific was horrendous, and ultimately ended in a mutiny and series of events which inspired a number of stories and a motion picture two hundred years later. Before the mutiny, the *Bounty* first had to round Cape Horn. Despite most of the crew disagreeing with the captain's decision, they did it anyway and survived by a hair's breadth because they worked like a unit. Men in such an environment must operate this way. You are at war with the ocean, and there is no room for choice. You can't just "sit it out" due to some libertarian principle of self-determination. No. Instead, you **must** serve, you must perform your duty, you must put the practical reality over the theoretical idea - or you and everyone else will simply perish. Such high stakes environments are wholly incompatible with the civilian principles of extreme individuality, and self-determination.

A civilian society optimizes for peace and pacifism, while in warrior cultures, it is the exact opposite: aggression is deeply valued, cultivated, and channeled. In the civilian world, we are taught that aggression is anti-social, whether that is libertarians referencing the Non Aggression Principle, or how any form of violence or aggression is discouraged by civilian authorities. Of course, aggression is something that must be kept in check, but it cannot be "eliminated". A tension between the poles of aggression and peace is necessary. The trouble is, modern society has taken safety, peace, and pacifism to an extreme. From the never-ending messages of "for your safety" at the airport, the train, or the bus, to the computerization of the cars we drive that now "warn" you erratically about every movement you make, to the ridiculous 'safe spaces' for adults in the workplace. Everywhere you look, you see weakness coddled and encouraged, while strength and aggression are vilified.

Finally, adversity. Warrior cultures not only train for adversity, but they revel in it. To be hard, one must train hard and live hard. There is no shortcut. Civilian culture on the other hand is all about comfort, from the participation awards given out at school, to the convenient apps we use to get a cheap dopamine hit or food delivered to our door, to the beds we sleep on, to the "ergonomic keyboards" and cushioned office chairs that are sold to low-T office workers staring at screens, through to the endless cocktail of antidepressants and numbing agents people are fed by therapists and psychologists every time we feel a little uncomfortable. This is a warrior's idea of hell. Without adversity, how can one become strong? To build muscle, one must first tear it down. It is the same for the mind and spirit. Adversity for a warrior is not only the key to growth, it is a way of life. For civilians, luxury and ease are the goals while adversity is just a "problem to be solved".

"Adversity makes men, prosperity makes monsters."

Victor Hugo, Les Misérables

There is clearly something to be learned from warrior cultures, especially when you compare their character and competence to the mediocrity of modern man. The Japanese Samurai, the European knight, the Greek hoplite were held both in high esteem and to account. Instead of trying to emasculate men with seed oils, mundane office work, and safe spaces, we need to rethink their role in society. In Robert Heinlein's *Starship Troopers* the only true citizens with the right to vote were those with military service. Europe in its peak required sacrifice for suffrage. Men paid for their full charter of rights with blood, tears and pain. Switzerland's mandatory military service is an interesting modern example: a citizen warrior ethic embedded in a broader civilian culture that is neutral in war, but can fight if it needs to. Whatever the approach, there is a yearning and need for this warrior energy to be re-integrated into society.

Iron sharpens iron

A warrior class or culture is like the border enforcement mechanism, or the white blood cells of an organism. It keeps the boundaries intact and maintains the standards and integrity of what's inside. Traditions, enforced by this conservative, intolerant minority, develop strong virtues and guide future generations. Without them the safety the civilian center enjoys erodes or evaporates, and the entire culture collapses.

So how do we keep them sharp? *Conflict.* Anyone who tells you we will reach an age where conflict is transcended and we will live in perpetual peace is about as stupid as those who think we'll reach an age where money is no longer required. Both statements are naive and wrong.

We will *always* have conflict and we will always need money, because resources and energy are finite, time is irreversible, and we all have preferences. This is why we are biologically wired for territory and why private property is so fundamentally necessary. It's an extension of what works in nature, and gives us a mechanism to deal with the inevitable conflict that comes from real scarcity. At some point in your life, you will have to resort to violence in order to defend it. No matter how many books you've read by Mises, or how much you believe in the Non-Aggression Principle, some idiot is going to come into your house - that has neither read those books, nor believes in the NAP - and will try to take your shit. At this point, you are already playing defense. You are on the back foot. The capacity for violence is more important than the violence itself, but in the absence of the latter, the former begins to diminish. Western civilization is here now. We've sterilised everything to such a degree, that we are now too soft to even fight back, when we are actively being invaded, pillaged, robbed, and raped.

Ignoring the brutal facts of life and trying to theorycel your way out of them is a waste of everyone's time, so let's instead reframe conflict as: *a good thing that is central to life*; and violence too, by extension. If we appreciate that conflict is not only inevitable but *necessary*, that iron sharpens iron, and that only in the face of real danger can we discover what we're truly made of - then we might have a chance at turning this cultural decay around.

As it stands, we have leftoids and trust-the-science nerds trying to engineer conflict and aggression out of humans with implants or vaccinations in a misguided attempt to "hack" biology. Just like blocking out the sun to prevent climate change, this will surely end in disaster. The truth is, we will always have disagreements. That's what it means to be different and unique. That's what it means to be **alive.** Aggression emerged for this reason. It's extremely useful. Warrior cultures were successful because they learned to **direct** it. What we're lacking in the world today is not more weakness, but masculine strength and the innate capacity for violence.

If these people are successful in removing the aggression gene, or continue on with their experiments to lower testosterone, humanity will morph into a species of compliant pets. I'm sure this kind of domestication is useful for those who lack the agency necessary to live their own lives, and especially useful for the kinds of so-called 'leaders' that require putty, not people, in order to maintain their fake and weak hold over society. But only a fool would call this progress, and only a petty tyrant that wants a compliant, malleable mass of NPCs to direct, would think it a goal worth pursuing.

Real man has agency, and he can choose to be sophisticated or savage. He is unique because he is both rational and primal, both beast and saint. If you remove the beast from man, he becomes nothing but a slave or a pet. Likewise if man does not work to be sophisticated, he is nothing but a wild animal. So we must work towards both. That being said, it's better to be a wild animal, than a pet, as it is better to be a warrior in a garden, than a gardener in a war.

Ultimately, the existence of a warrior class is critical to the integrity, stability, and longevity of a civilisation. It strengthens its men, and provides structure and safety for its women and children.

The remnant

> "*Democracy basically means: of the people, for the people, by the people. But the people are retarded.*"
>
> *Rajneesh Osho*

I've always believed in the importance of excellence and, in recent years, I've also come to believe that it is most embodied by a natural one percent.

Those who are the best in their fields share a special intrinsic ingredient or set of characteristics that drives them to exceptionalism. They naturally exude excellence, which is by definition uncommon.

I call this kind of people "The Remnant" because they are a kind apart: non-conformists, who are not only unique in ability, but often eccentric in character. I first wrote about them in 2021, at the peak of the global flu and lockdown hysteria. I was struck by how utterly ridiculous the entire world had become when I walked into a store to buy water, in the jungle, and was refused service because I wasn't wearing a mask! I remember looking at the cashier and seeing a humanoid roomba vacuum cleaner telling me "I can't accept your money". The only few people I found with any pushback happened to be those who also had a disdain for ideas like democracy and equality, so I wrote an essay about them: the Remnant. I've found more recently that this persona also aligns quite closely with the warrior archetype, and they are naturally drawn to the virtues I've explored in this book.

Contrast this with the run of the mill "masses:" the kind of people who settle for average and are either unable to find the ambition and drive to do, build, or create something significant, or worse, who scorn, belittle or mock those that want to; those who conform and blindly do what they're told, despite clear evidence to the contrary. In my Remnant essays I offended many by saying that these people don't matter. I stand by this, not because I despise them or want the worst for them; to the contrary, I want the best for everyone. I mean it because the lives they lead and their opinions are mostly noise. At best they are irrelevant and at worst, they are obstacles or impediments to greater things.

> *"The masses resemble inertia. The dumb, deaf, blind default that will not change unless a new force is applied. They are the 80% of the Pareto distribution that make 20% of the difference."*
>
> Aleksandar Svetski, *The Remnant Essays*

Luckily for those of us with agency, and in fact humanity at large, inconvenient or contrarian *truths*, upheld by the few, always prevail in the end, despite mass obedience to falsity. It's the same old story, and is as true for destruction as it is for progress and opportunity. This is why all great civilisations are oriented toward excellence and beauty, and are superior to those built on participation awards and alms, which are weak, brittle, decadent and backward.

> *"Social evolution, in so far as it is other than biological, may be defined as the unintended result of the intentions of great men"; further, that historical progress is produced by a struggle "not among the community generally, to live, but a struggle amongst a small section of the community to lead, to direct, to employ, the majority in the best way."*

William Hurrel Mallock, Aristocracy and Evolution

If the remnant can be defined as those exceptional individuals with the highest agency, who consistently embody the warrior virtues, then it is they who will be leaders of the communities that make up new, more beautiful and vital civilizations.

The great stories

> *"In the most chivalrous days of Europe, knights formed numerically but a small fraction of the population, but, as Emerson says, 'In English literature half the drama and all the novels, from Sir Philip Sidney to Sir Walter Scott, paint this figure (gentleman).' Write in place of Sidney and Scott, Chikamatsu and Bakin, and you have in a nutshell the main features of the literary history of Japan."*

Inazo Nitobe, Bushido: The Soul of Japan

There is a reason why the greatest stories are those in which a hero faces off against insurmountable odds or sets off on an impossible quest. The oldest written epic is that of Gilgamesh, who not only confronted the gods but embarked on the search for immortality. The Bible is similar: it tells of central figures that had to do the impossible, such as Noah building the Ark and saving all of life on Earth, Moses escaping from Egypt, only to have to part and cross the Red Sea, and of course Christ, who not only overcame the greatest of temptations, but who ultimately prevailed over death itself.

It is for the same reason that Homer wrote of Odysseus, Achilles, and Hector, the bravest and most virtuous of all - and not of the forgotten soldiers. It's the same reason we today have zombie movies, in which the protagonist fights for survival against the mindless hordes running rampant through the streets. There is a reason why Morpheus was looking for Neo and not just any random person to unplug from "The Matrix."

> *"The Matrix is a system, Neo. That system is our enemy. But when you're inside, you look around. What do you see? Business people, teachers, lawyers, carpenters. The very minds of the people we are trying to save. But until we do, these people are still a part of that system, and that makes them our enemy. You have to understand, most of these people are not ready to be unplugged. And many of them are so inured, so hopelessly dependent on the system that they will fight to protect it."*
>
> *Morpheus, The Matrix*

Every great story requires a hero and his crew pitted against an anti-hero or a villain and their crew. The masses remain in the background. They are like a limited-animation canvas against which the main characters battle - but they are not players in the game. At best they don't really matter, and at worst they make up elements of the "construct" that can easily be used to impede progress or create further obstacles.

The great flatteners of modernity require these Non-Player Characters for the stable operation of their centrally planned models. The masses are ideal NPCs because they lack both nuance and vitality, making them easy to mold and direct. Excellence is in the way because it interrupts the 'program,' which is why weak, parasitic "world leaders" want to eradicate it, and any person exhibiting it, by equalizing us all.

Alas, such experiments always fail, even in the movies! The architect from *Matrix II*, explains as much to Neo. The first 'simulations' failed because they were too "perfect." They did not resemble reality, and were thus rejected. Mechanical perfection is not alive but dead. It cannot account for the anomaly that is the human spirit, or will to power - however you'd like to frame it.

This is an important lesson for future builders of society. The temptation and even social pressure to "manage" things will be great, but often the path to take will simply consist in leading by example and embodying the right virtues - *even if that leads to more unequal outcomes*.

You cannot sacrifice the excellent and the just for the equal and the nice. There is both a hierarchy of importance, and an order of operations. The only way to truly help those around you is to inspire others to rise, not to cut yourself down to their size. Help, yes, but do this by helping yourself first, and *by your example you will inspire others*. Modern equalitarianism is ignorant of this fact and it's a big part of why we're in this mess. We've built a society for automatons, and wonder why we have so many of them. Learn from these mistakes, and build for beauty and greatness instead. The rest will take care of itself.

Governance

"If you are not prepared to use force to defend civilization, then be prepared to accept barbarism."

Thomas Sowell, Knowledge and Decisions

The term governance originates from the Old French word *governer*, which means "to steer," which itself derives from Latin gubernare, also meaning "to steer" or "to direct." The Latin term was directly borrowed from the Ancient Greek word for steering or guiding, *kybernao*. The Greek root *kyber* relates to the act of steering or piloting a ship and over time, and evolved in usage from the specific act of steering a vessel to the more abstract concept of guiding or governing a political entity or organization.

Note that governance refers to the processes and systems of governing, while government refers to the specific institutions and entities that carry out the act of governing. This is important because if the governance model is rotten, broken, or corrupt, switching out the government will have little overall impact. You need to fix the governance problems first - which ironically may require a government or governor willing to sacrifice themselves for the cause.

Satoshi's development of Bitcoin is a profound example of governance reform in the economic domain. Governance, politics and society itself rest on an economic base, so economics is arguably the most important element. By establishing a governance model for money immune to centralized control and open to anyone, Satoshi was able to separate money from the state, and thereby fix the root cause of the thing which so often poisons the rest of the governing apparatus. As such Bitcoin opens the door for a truly new world where we can build better and more robust governance models.

There will always be a need for guidance and steering. The idea that society can somehow exist without governance is ridiculous - there needs to be some sort of steering mechanism. You don't build a car without a steering wheel or a navigation system of some sort, whether a human is driving it or not. What this implies is that there is a governor or -ment of some kind in charge that enforces the rules, or does the guidance. Whether that entity or mechanism is centralized or decentralized, large or small, bottom-up or top-down, human-driven or autonomous is up for debate. We all have our preferences, though some things clearly seem to work better than others. The key is to focus on good governance, and to make sure that if government does get corrupted, it can be removed before it poisons the chalice and ruins it for everyone else. There is no perfect solution, but strong virtues and principles, inspiring leadership, and of course sound money and economics are all essential ingredients.

Democracy and equalitarianism

> *"Nobody is more inferior than those who insist on being equal."*
>
> *Friedrich Nietzsche, Richard Marshall on 3:16am.co.uk*

Almost every government in the modern era is a democracy of some form or another, a situation which arises from the axiomatic belief that 'all men are created equal'. Taken to the extreme, this is the ideology of equalitarianism: the idea that there is no difference whatsoever between the capabilities of any two individuals or groups of humans. This century gave rise to the most radical levels of equalitarianism, making ideas such as 'democracy' and 'equality' sacred cows in the mind of modern man. These ideals represent the greatest psychological obstacles to the reintegration of the great virtues into modern culture.

Too many people are convinced that we've reached peak civilisational order, or in the words of Fukuyama "the end of history", thanks to the panacea that is democracy. As such all our efforts should be toward making every process "more democratic" and every structure more "equal". Unfortunately for them, and the rest of us, the truth is just the opposite. Democracy and equalitarian-like ideals are more likely the greatest threats to excellence, and therefore to the survival of the human race. The only peaks Fukuyama was right about were the democratic peak that is coming apart under the weight of its own stupidity, and perhaps the social and cultural peaks we reached in the nineties - that actually came as a result of inertia from prior decades and centuries of real progress and excellence, not 'democracy'. Since doubling down on these flawed ideals, we've managed to reverse a lot of our ancestral progress and begun to erode the very foundation of the West.

Humanity is now at greater risk of dissolving into the gray goo of average than it is of being defeated by any form of 1984-like totalitarianism. The latter at least calls upon the human spirit to rise up to a challenge. The former nullifies the need for spirit altogether and is more insidious. The greatest threat to excellence is not some great evil or tyranny, but mediocrity. Nietzsche warned us of this over a century ago, as did Hans Hermann Hoppe in his excellent book *Democracy: The God that Failed*, in which he summarizes democracy as sophisticated theft orchestrated by parasites and powered by the blind masses.

Democracy has many problems, but the most important issue is its equalitarian essence. This places it in the same class as communism and socialism. These are all "governments of mediocrity" and are dangerous for both economic and biological reasons. Their gradual erosion of private property and individual agency, and their replacement with a disembodied bureaucratic apparatus meant to be 'representative' of large swathes of people, simply turns into the tyranny of the lowest common denominator. Such forms of government - the "great flatteners" as we should call them - incentivise equality over quality, the ordinary over the extraordinary, the ugly over the beautiful, the disabled over the able, the stupid over the intelligent - all in the name of equality.

Governments of the mindless majority are oriented in such a way that their constituents are economically tied together en masse, each with a hand in another's pocket, while simultaneously spiritually and emotionally disconnected from each other because people cannot develop meaningful relationships and localized communities at nation-state scales.

They are the very worst of both worlds, and are only made possible by the existence of a mechanism for theft, whether by voting or through the more sophisticated method of printing money. These large homogenous regimes become bloated, wasteful, and top-heavy. They lack the dynamism and structural diversity necessary for adaptation. In time they run out of resources and competence, so they collapse or dissolve. The issue this century is that they've become larger than ever because of mass populations, mass migration, mass politics, and most importantly, money printing. This is why Bitcoin is such an important ingredient. It limits the possibility of such equalitarian structures to reach scale again by rendering them economically infeasible.

> "In the doctrine of socialism there is hidden, rather badly, a "will to negate life"; the human beings or races that think up such a doctrine must be bungled. Indeed, I should wish that a few great experiments might prove that in a socialist society life negates itself, cuts off its own roots. The earth is large enough and man still sufficiently unexhausted; hence such a practical instruction and demonstratio ad absurdum would not strike me as undesirable, even if it were gained and paid for with a tremendous expenditure of human lives."

> Friedrich Nietzsche, The Will to Power

There is something about democracy that simply breeds ugliness and envy. Nietzsche captured this anthropological element most accurately when he framed socialism as an illness and form of biological warfare that eats away at the human organism. To really drive this home, let's look at a real example of how this inherent resentment ruined one of the most prosperous, peaceful nations on earth.

"In the beginning, the Republic is ruled by great citizens with a strong sense of justice. Gradually, their sons start to chase status more than justice, and the means to measure character becomes money. The Republic then descends into a Plutocracy, where a few rich men exploit the citizens with schemes and debt. In response to this, the citizens form into a mob to defend themselves, so the Republic becomes a Democracy. Now, there exists a giant impulsive mob...

If one man is willing to promise them the world, he can have the Republic for himself. He announces he will save the mob from the Plutocrats and he will forgive all their debts...if only they grant him power. At this, the People cheer, and the final stage ensues...The Republic is passed out of the hands of the People and into the hands of a Tyrant..."

Uberboyo on X.com, summarizing book 8 of Plato's The Republic

Rhodesia and its affront to the equalitarian lie

Everyone knows that Zimbabwe is a failed state. People will point to Zimbabwe's multiple hyperinflations and hand out worthless trillion dollar Zimbabwean notes at Bitcoin conferences, as meme-like omens of the dangers of money-printing. Almost everyone, however, is completely ignorant of who and what Zimbabwe was before 1979. In fact, most won't even know the name of that lost country: Rhodesia.

Rhodesia was a British colony founded at the beginning of the twentieth century, with an economic model founded on large, modern plantations farming cash crops. Despite being lightly populated and landlocked, it was prosperous, industrializing, and known as the "Breadbasket of Africa" because it exported food to the rest of the continent. Its main difference with the other British Dominions – Canada, Australia, New Zealand – was that Rhodesia had a property-based voting system, which ensured that people with actual skin in the game had a greater say, thus ensuring more responsible governance. The country also had an extremely selective immigration system, with a strong preference for men of proven ability and character. As a result of these features, Rhodesia preserved a form of life more characteristic of the old British landed aristocracy, long after this had been largely abandoned elsewhere in the Anglosphere.

Despite Rhodesia's evident success, it found itself beset by nearly universal trade embargoes while battling communist terrorist militias trained and funded by the Soviet Union. Why did the West abandon Rhodesia, while it quietly supported its supposed enemy, the USSR, in its campaign to destroy a prosperous and peaceful land? The ostensible reason was that Rhodesia' property-based voting franchise prevented its black population from voting. Great Britain demanded majority rule as a condition for independence, which the Rhodesians balked at, for they knew that allowing everyone an equal say would destroy their country.

Rhodesia was not a "racist" country: there was no requirement that one be white to vote and there was no apartheid system, as in South Africa. Rhodesia had better white-black race relations than America, and no race-based slaughter like the Congo and other failing African states at the time. The charge that Rhodesia was "racist" was a mere excuse. The truth was that as one of the only stable, prosperous countries in Africa, Rhodesia showed that a propertied voting republic worked far better than "mass democracy." Its very existence showed that limiting political power to a natural, propertied elite led to a better government, a more orderly society, and a more prosperous economy than democracy. Rhodesia was a clear example contrary to the equalitarian agenda being pushed everywhere in the world.

The "collapse of Zimbabwe" was not caused solely by money printing, but by the replacement of Rhodesia with Zimbabwe. The forced removal of a functioning aristocratic political system that worked, and subsequently, the expropriation of the productive landed gentry, is what killed Rhodesia. Printing trillions of dollars of worthless money came later, as a symptom of the sickness that is equalitarianism, not the cause: the money printer was more like a way of scraping up the "last loot." Zimbabwe never recovered, and remains a broken, bankrupt state to this day. Will Tanner, of the American Tribune, explores this in much greater detail.

Feudalism

> *"So the light of chivalry [Bushido], which was a child of feudalism, still illuminates our moral path, surviving its mother institution."*
>
> Inazo Nitobe, Bushido: The Soul of Japan

If codes as powerful and profound as chivalry or Bushido came from feudalism, then what are we to make of the way it is framed within modern politics, as "bad" or "backwards"? If it was as evil, broken, corrupt, and dysfunctional as we've been led to believe, then why are we still drawn to the beautiful art, architecture, and literature produced during that age, centuries later? How could a backwards system produce such a beautiful culture?

The common claim is that "feudalism is bad" because "it was despotic." There's no doubt that there were periods in both the East and West in which despots rose to power under feudal systems, but how is that different, or worse, than what we've seen in the post-feudal democratic age? At least under feudalism, a despot's days were numbered by his life expectancy. Now, we are faced with a faceless hydra that sucks the life out of civilization, and there's little you can do about it but "vote harder" (which doesn't do anything).

People are quick to confuse duty with a lack of liberty. They conflate a devotion to something higher with mental or spiritual imprisonment, which is the viewpoint of an infant, a socialist, or a run of the mill libertarian. Duty, loyalty, and the responsibility they come with, are virtues. They are choices that lead to a strong, beautiful, and devoted cultural structure.

> *"Under the regime of feudalism, which could easily degenerate into militarism, it was to benevolence that we owed our deliverance from despotism of the worst kind. An utter surrender of "life and limb" on the part of the governed would have left nothing for the governing but self-will, and this has for its natural consequence the growth of that absolutism so often called "oriental despotism", as though there were no despots of occidental history!*
>
> *Let it be far from me to uphold despotism of any sort; but it is a mistake to identify feudalism with it.*
>
> *When Frederick the Great wrote that "Kings are the first servants of the State," jurists thought rightly that a new era was reached in the development of freedom. Strangely coinciding in time, in the backwoods of Northwestern Japan, Yozan of Yonézawa made exactly the same declaration, showing that feudalism was not all tyranny and oppression."*

> *Inazo Nitobe, Bushido: The Soul of Japan*

This gross misunderstanding of feudalism is somewhat expected considering what happened during the French Revolution. While the revolutionaries may not have been entirely successful at the time, the Pandora's box they unleashed in their eradication of feudal order and overthrow of the paternal order (both in the home and in society) led the world to the worst collectivist, despotic atrocities seen in the history of mankind. The monarchies that ran Europe before the 20th century, despite their bickering and feuds, were far more peaceful and noble than the communist blobs that emerged after the Bolsheviks took hold in

Russia, to say nothing of the soft tyranny of managerialism emerging in modern society.

> *"A feudal prince, although unmindful of owing reciprocal obligations to his vassals, felt a higher sense of responsibility to his ancestors and to Heaven. He was a father to his subjects, whom Heaven entrusted to his care."*

> Inazo Nitobe, Bushido: The Soul of Japan

Liberally-oriented moderns have developed an innate distaste for paternalism. There is a knee-jerk reaction to words such as "patriarchy" or "masculinity" as immediately evil or "toxic" and "big-brother" like. Ironically the same people who believe this often support arbitrary global mandates on health, weather, travel, speech, science, education, politics, food, biology, and media coverage.

These movements are full of dysgenic psychological infants with no life experience. The Jacobins, Bolsheviks, eco-terrorists, LGBTQ+++ activists, BLM supporters, and Antifa movements all share in common cohorts of these entitled brats and environments of unhinged liberalism, irresponsibility and chaos. It's as if they never had anyone to guide or raise them - which is actually often the case. In fact, the rise of these movements coincides with the decline of fathers in households, spanking and even bullying. Role models are key to the healthy development of any child, and their job is to maintain order with authority. We fail our kin when we fail to be the best adult versions of ourselves. The same applies at the grander social scale, and was a major part of the role a warrior class would play: the institution of a local paternal order. Children used to both fear and respect their elders, especially the warriors, and thus they learned manners.

> *"Bushido accepted and corroborated paternal government—paternal also as opposed to the less interested avuncular (young / youthful / liberal) government."*

Inazo Nitobe, Bushido: The Soul of Japan

There's a reason why backward political ideologies such as communism and democracy didn't exist while a strong warrior class and a feudal hierarchy did. The warriors had to fall for these stupidities to rise up. Imagine one of these purple-haired eco-terrorists gluing their hands to the Tokaido road in front of a procession of Samurai on horseback, or throwing oil on a painting in the halls of the regional daimyo. They couldn't. Not just because either act would be their last, but because youths grew up in an environment of respect, so the conditions for such behavior did not exist. It was not "oppression" as Marx would have you believe, but a respect for the order of things.

Modern leftists in particular are allergic to order, and caught up in fantasies of 'absolute liberty'. They begin to skew the meaning of words like freedom, power, man, woman, rights or revolution.

> *"Revolution in the primary sense doesn't mean subversion & revolt, but really even the opposite: return to a point of departure & ordinary motion around a center."*

Julius Evola, Essay: The Inversion of Symbols

Traditional societies understood revolution as a movement that kept the moral and social universe spinning in harmony. Think about the meaning of the word in physics. An object's revolution refers to its trajectory around the center or focal point, like a planet revolving around the sun. This revolution keeps the planet in a stable orbit, it does not undermine the orbit and change it because Jupiter was "mean" to Mars. Contrast that with how we've come to understand the word today. Revolution now means a movement away from stable centers, a destruction of regularity and an inversion of order. It's the complete opposite of the traditional meaning, and puts everything in a constant state of instability.

> *"Modern Revolution is like the unhinging of the door, the opposite of the traditional meaning of the term: the social & political forces loosen from their natural orbit, decline, know no longer nor center nor any order, other than a badly & temporarily stemmed disorder."*
>
> Julius Evola, Essay: *The Inversion of Symbols*

There is a biological and memetic recognition that a return to paternal leadership and traditional "revolutionary" stability are what's needed to correct our bent-out-of-shape society and inverted culture. For this, patriarchs of a new caliber must rise - mature and responsible men who both respect tradition and have the courage to venture forth and establish something new.

It was only after the fall of feudalism that we opened the door to true despotism and large-scale democide, worldwide. Democracy and mob rule lead to the fall of nations, peoples, and empires. Money printing comes after and helps it along.

Russia, Europe, China, Southeast Asia, Africa, and South America have all been mired in conflict of the worst kind since the overturning of the monarchic or feudal hierarchies that existed beforehand. The resultant power vacuums in each territory were filled by parasites and megalomaniacs from both sides of the aisle, who captured power by virtue of "the masses". The petty money changers and bureaucrats - whom the knights and Samurai of old would have struck down on general principle - managed to send entire generations of good, strong men to their slaughter for their own private, economic gain.

Most people seem to agree that fascism was bad, but far less vitriol has been aimed at communism, despite it having been objectively worse, killing in excess of 100 million people in the past century, and convincing another few billion that being lazy, entitled, compliant, and mediocre is the optimum way to live. Karl Marx's books are readily available, and his statues stand tall in many places around the world. Contrast that with authors like Julius Evola or Guillame Faye, whose books are almost impossible to find because they've been labeled fascist or right-wing - despite the contents being a compelling vision for an ascendant world of beauty, strength and tradition. There is something seriously rotten going on here.

Might makes right

"The Free Man is a Warrior. I do not believe in any Rights that are not supported by the power required to enforce them."

Friedrich Nietzsche, The Will to Power

There will always exist the need for governance, and the governor is often the one with the biggest stick. Force is the most fundamental form of communication, because it requires no common language, no shared values, no pre-defined concepts, and taken to its logical end, definitively settles any kind of dispute.

Underneath all the sophistry and fluff, *might ultimately makes right*.

This doesn't mean that the governor must rely solely or even primarily on the stick. Good governance comes from good leadership. By inspiring people and pulling them along you create more leaders who each have more autonomy. Ruling by fear and punishment is ineffective in the long run because it produces hatred towards you, and a class of dependent lemmings who can't think for themselves. Furthermore, using or resorting to force is risky, generally expensive, and mostly not very enjoyable. This is why humans have developed many different proxies for force, such as persuasion, deception, negotiation and money. While these do not directly rely on violence, they are all proxies for the same underlying asset: force. Good governance requires using these proxies first, but also having the ability to enforce order and punish transgressions with direct methods when needed.

Big sticks are also necessary for deterrence. Like all animals, we can smell weakness, and that stench attracts predators. If you are incapable of attacking, you are incapable of defending - and therefore, you are incapable of leading. This is why they say an armed society is a polite society. It's not just a fancy quote. The threat of violence and force must exist beneath the surface of civilized society. You must be able to prevent others from messing with you or your people, be that your family, your tribe, or your countrymen. The best way to avoid violence in the first place is by making it known you can be extremely violent, to make sure your big stick is visible and has marks on it. This is the point of being a warrior in a garden and not a gardener in war. Warriors were the pinnacle class because they were able to cut through all proxies when necessary. The best of them learned to channel and master violence, and found ways to embed it into their culture via their strongest men.

I am sorry to break it to my libertarian and Austrian Economics friends, but even the private property rights upon which you base your entire philosophy, hinge on the capacity to enforce those private property rights. When push comes to shove, the coalition with the biggest stick is the ultimate enforcer. The law of the jungle applies. **Might *does* make right.**

Even in mature societies, where the game theory of governance is increasingly influenced by either economics, religion, or morality instead of direct force, what's beneath it all is still the threat of violence and the ability to enforce it. Punishment is deeply entwined with all morality and religion, and it fundamentally sits behind every commercial contract too. So while I understand the Misesean and Libertarian arguments about means and ends, mutual benefits and cooperation, these things can only exist on the bedrock of private property and contract rights that can be enforced.

Finally, the very act of respecting private property and choosing to trade and cooperate, instead of stealing and pillaging, carries with it an implicit motivation. Economic prowess itself leads to better technology and if intelligently used, better weaponry (defensive or offensive) in order to deter aggression. Either way, you seek to strengthen yourself, or form a coalition for greater mutual benefit and power (a greater capacity for violence) which ultimately means that you can deter others with sticks that might currently be larger than yours.

Welcome to the world of contracts, strategy, and statecraft, which the West mastered before everyone else, explaining why it spread civilization across the globe.

Violence & localism

> *"All men have an instinct for conflict: at least, all healthy men."*

Hilaire Belloc, *The Silence of the Sea*

Most in the Bitcoin community, and the broader libertarian or AnCap world, are proponents of the Non-Aggression Principle (NAP) and believe that the use of force against another individual in the appropriation or confiscation of their private property is wrong and immoral. While this is the correct logical stance within a safe and stable civilian culture, it ignores the reality of what keeps the civilian safe in the first place and glosses over the fact that not everyone is a libertarian with 150 points of IQ. This is a mistake costing the West dearly today.

So long as we live in a world where intelligence, culture, status, and wealth differ, while time, resources, and energy remain scarce (which they always will), the use of force or violence to take something that is not yours will play a role in human relations. You may personally be able to keep this drive in check, but will others? And how will you deter them if not?

Even if the 'returns to violence' decrease in the digital age as Rees-Mogg & Davidson predicted in *The Sovereign Individual*, this doesn't mean that violence will disappear. A rich and robust civilisation (or world) that exhibits true diversity - not the woke kind, but something more like the complex ecology of a rainforest or the broad range of species in the plains of Africa - is made up of a variety of different cultures, each of which compete or cooperate. This implies a couple of things. First of all, conflict is going to occur. In fact, localism breeds conflict. Similar to a healthy biological system, the result of more localism is more inner amity and outer enmity. Individual life forms or territories are internally cooperative but externally competitive, which can and does lead to conflicts.

The second relationship between localism and violence has to do with size and scale. Because all growth comes with excess and waste, there must be some sort of mechanism for the failed experiments to be cleaned out on a regular basis. It's better that this corrective element triggers early, and more often; not when everything is tied together, entirely interdependent and therefore fragile. This is akin to how small, frequent fires are a more natural and holistic method of forest management. Compare it to the vain attempt (as in California) to 'avoid all fires', which only leads to an accumulation of dry underbrush that provides fuel for devastating infernos that burn everything down. These 'small fires' and 'frequent corrections' are the violent part of the necessary "creative destruction" any truly 'living system' goes through. It's not supposed to be clean, sterile, and uneventful. There is violence along the way, but it's kept in check.

Localism and healthy conflict have an impact on the size and scale of a society. The larger the population, the more advantage multi-polarity has over unity because not everybody gets along or sees things the same way. Unity works best locally. The modern statist paradigm has it inverted, sowing division at the local level via mass immigration and multiculturalism, while demanding "unity" at the highest level, and telling us we are "all in this together". This clearly doesn't work. When a system scales in size, it finds a point at which it can no longer operate effectively, so it fragments. This is why centralization beats decentralization at the scale of a small business and why startups don't require a board, while decentralization beats centralization when you look at larger organisms such as nature or society. The latter requires more frequent experiments with more frequent failure, and corrections to avoid having the entire structure break all at once.

This is why a political landscape with fewer "large states" and more internally homogeneous but externally heterogeneous micro-territories is a good thing: more frequent micro-conflict is a feature, not a bug. We need more localism and tribalism and less of this large scale, homogenous globalism that's being rammed down all of our throats.

Conscious classes

> "There needs but one wise man in a company, and all are wise, so rapid is the contagion."

> Ralph Waldo Emerson, Use of Great Men

Nitobe echoed Emerson's words when he said that *"No social class or caste can resist the diffusive power of moral influence."*

Virtues are contagious. This is the reason why all great civilisations were led by strong men who set the example. Unfortunately, the same is true of vices, and this is part of the reason that modern states are so broken. They are rotten from the head down. So-called leadership is not only visibly ugly and deformed, but they are unabashedly corrupt. They will steal, from right in front of you, and then gaslight you into thinking that they're doing you a favor.

The captain steers the ship. The leader leads the way. By setting the example, whether in the family, the company, or the community, and embodying the right virtues, the rest tend to follow. This is also why the most enduring and vital civilisations and "codes of life" have always come from warrior cultures: it is among warriors that the sharpest iron is found.

"What Japan was she owed to the Samurai. They were not only the flower of the nation, but its root as well. All the gracious gifts of Heaven flowed through them. Though they kept themselves socially aloof from the populace, they set a moral standard for them and guided them by their example."

Inazo Nitobe, Bushido: The Soul of Japan

So what can we take from the past that worked? Social classes are one example. They're something nobody wants to talk about, but they have always played a role in society and always will. Feudalism at least delineated them clearly and consciously. Today's democratic order merely obfuscates them.

In traditional feudalism, the workers worked, the farmers farmed, the warriors warred, the merchants did business, and the monarchy led. There was a clear separation of duties, and everything worked together well enough for them to build both civilization and lasting architectural beauty - despite the much lower technological sophistication of their time.

Clear social classes are useful because they let you know where you stand. Only with awareness and clarity can you do something about your lot. We will always have classes of people - you can try to wish it away all you want, but it's like wishing away gravity. It's better to be consciously aware of them, and to construct society in such a way that there is some sort of permeability for the anomalies, the standouts and productive to rise, while the liars, cheaters and the weak descend.

Wealth

With culture and governance covered, we need to address what sits at the base of all society and civilisation: wealth and economics. While some people are naive enough to call it "a made up construct", it's in fact a real and inescapable measure and evaluation of human action. Praxeology, the study of human action, pioneered by Ludwig Von Mises, and expanded upon by Murray Rothbard, Friedrich Hayek, Hans Hermann Hoppe and others into what is known as the "Austrian School of Economics", is the most useful and sensical study of this necessary component of life I've come across.

In this section, I will ask the tough questions about money, honor, and society, particularly in light of the fact that the modern world is over-indexed for pure materialism. Does wealth ultimately corrupt us? I believe there is wisdom in the separation of these different forms of value, and their measures - and ignoring either one has consequences. The great Japanese warrior culture was ultimately subdued by the richer and more affluent West. Culture, technology, capital, power - all rest on the foundation of economics, so you cannot throw the baby out with the bathwater: it's a balancing act. Too much obsession with and ignorance of the economic dimension lead to failure.

Economic ignorance is at the core of why feudalism in general failed, and to use Marx's phrase, why *The bourgeois burst from asunder*. Division of labor and trade determine how complex and therefore powerful a society can become. The largest empires may have been forged through military might, but they could only subsist on the real wealth generated by the markets they established. These empires finally ended when trade did too, often spectacularly as their final rulers went on to debase their currencies. Money is power and you must learn how to channel it. This is why Bitcoin is such a force of nature. We live in a material world and you ignore this at your own peril. Learn from those who failed in the past, despite their great virtue:

> *"Hence children were brought up with utter disregard of economy. It was considered bad taste to speak of it, and ignorance of the value of different coins was a token of good breeding. Knowledge of numbers was indispensable in the mustering of forces as well as in distribution of benefices and fiefs; but the counting of money was left to meaner hands."*
>
> Inazo Nitobe, Bushido: The Soul of Japan

The Samurai who lived by a non-commercial code came to regret being disdainful or ignorant of money, and while some families adapted, many were not equipped for the 'new world'. The resulting inversion of the Japanese hierarchy was similar to the end of feudalism in Europe, and saw the replacement of the warrior class with the merchants and the traders, and those who understood numbers. Many Samurai, whose honor could not be bought and who did not understand trade, were left in a position of great disadvantage commercially speaking. Their lands were taken from them in exchange for government bonds, which some attempted to enter business with, only to find that they were outcompeted both by the honest but capable merchant and especially by the shrewd trader whose moral flexibility did not care for things like honor, duty, or integrity. In fact the trader class sought vengeance on the Samurai class, so they would lie, cheat, and steal, just to take revenge. As such, the traders and merchants prospered with the modernisation of Japan, while many of the old warrior class suffered.

The lesson here is *not* that we should become lying and scheming traders, but that we must master money like we master the sword or the pen. The Samurai families who did this became extraordinarily powerful, particularly because the "unscrupulous trader" approach has a short lifespan. They brought bushido principles like honor and integrity into the Japanese commercial culture, not unlike other parts of the world where the nobles found their way into business, and compounded their wealth over time. Some of the oldest Japanese businesses can be traced back to Samurai families and founders.

That all being said, things are never as simple as "be virtuous" and "master money" and all will be fine. We live in the century of fiat, where the incentives are skewed to support the parasite, the psychopath and the scheming trader - especially since 1971 when the US dollar came off the gold standard. Since then, the global economic pendulum has swung hard in their favor. The allure of the money printer is too strong. The optimum orientation for economic actors is to align as much as possible with the central banks and money monopolists. Easy money is like a cancer in the body of economics, because it transforms everyone into a trader or gambler not only to win, but to just survive. At the top end of town, faceless corporations form up, that are either directly led or influenced by the traders and parasites of Wall Street. These soulless organizations care not for things like virtue, morality, or humanity, nor are they troubled by the damage their experiments can and continue to cause, because they're not concerned with providing services to real customers - *they are interested in their proximity to the monetary spigot.* Why would Big Pharma go to all the trouble of *serving* people when they get free money via the government or from central banks? Who is the real customer in this case? It's all very simple when you *follow the incentives.*

This absence of conscience and lack of substance is quite sickening to say the least, but it's no surprise that these parasitic classes of people are at the helm. We opened the door for them with the destruction of the warrior class, our betrayal of the nobility, and our adoption of stupid beliefs such as "power is evil" and "average is moral". We've been hypnotized into a trance, believing that money itself can be conjured up out of thin air by bureaucrats. Instead of abandoning the lie, we go on feeding the beast with our own blood, sweat, and tears, and promise it the blood, sweat and tears of future generations.

It's about time we woke up to this, and fixed it - and we can only do so if we successfully blend wealth of character with material wealth. You have to both adopt the virtues laid out in this book, and master the economic game. Money is power, and power is necessary - not evil. Power is your capacity to channel energy, and money is fundamentally just that: *energy.*

By becoming better, smarter, and more affluent, we will beat them at their own game. We can, like the Medici did during the Renaissance, build a beautiful world. The vision and sheer force of character of these warrior-explorer-merchant-nobles changed the world, not unlike Steve Jobs and Elon Musk have done more recently. To ultimately wrest control from the parasites, we need a new class of leader: warrior-merchant-philosopher-kings, like some blend of Alexander the Great and Steve Jobs. This new archetype is the most likely candidate for Nietzsche's Ubermensch, and we are seeing early signs of his arrival with the rise of great men like Bukele, who have both the strength to be a leader of men, and the economic acumen to go with it.

How far could we go, if more like him rise up, and we as a people, have the courage to both put our weight behind the movement and stay the course?

To the stars, and beyond.

Does wealth corrupt?

"For what shall it profit a man, if he shall gain the whole world, and lose his own soul?"

Jesus Christ, Mark 8:36 (KJV)

In late 2022, I had a Twitter exchange with author and teacher Will Knowland about whether or not wealth and morality were divergent. I defended the notion of wealth as moral, while he challenged it. Having thought about this further, it's not so clear cut.

Material wealth in particular, seems to have an erosive effect on the behavior of individuals, and by extension, the 'morality' of civilization itself. I know that might sound incongruent coming from someone who wrote *The UnCommunist Manifesto*, but bear with me.

Material wealth is a paradox of sorts. We seek and pursue it, and when we finally grasp it, we tend to abandon the character we developed in order to attain it. This seems to apply to both individuals and societies. You see it with rich people who become slothful, disgusting humans (we have our fair share of Louis Vuitton-wearing examples in crypto), and also in the falls into decadence of Rome, Constantinople, France, and today the US.

The Ancient Macedonians under Philip II and Alexander were hard, courageous mountain-men. They crossed the Granicus as a brotherhood of warriors, for glory and honor. They yearned for something higher than the pursuit of material wealth: they sought to reach the ends of the Earth, and to claim space. But something changed once they conquered Persia, if not among the core generals, then at least among the upper middle ranks of men, who became 'soft with riches'. These men had never seen such vast wealth, and it slowly corrupted them. Many of the customs that seeped into this new Persian-influenced Macedonian culture were materialistic.

There was certainly a kind of high culture and nobility that came with it, but it was a different, softer, more elegant form, for Persia itself had transformed in the three centuries since Cyrus the Great had defeated the Assyrians and built the then-largest empire on Earth. Persia went from being led by Cyrus the Great to being defeated thanks to Darius, "the one who flees". It is said that in the end the Persians defeated the Macedonians by softening them with material wealth, much like how the Mongols were absorbed into the vastness of China and its lavish courts. There is substance to this argument when looking at what happened after Alexander's passing. The generals who inherited the empire, while all powerful men in their own right, were not Alexander and could not fill the vacuum he left behind. They were born atop the mountain already and the only thing that could really have kept the empire together was a spirit that wanted to continue reaching and climbing the next mountain. Perhaps that was Alexander's greatest flaw. He was *too* great. Nobody could fill his shoes, so those who remained sought to consolidate and keep what they had. The infighting that ensued split the empire into four primary factions, which within a few generations, became weak and were ultimately defeated by a new breed of militant warrior: the Roman.

The Romans of the early Republic had a hunger and ruthlessness that nobody could match, and this energy is precisely what set the stage for their Empire. They had the will and desire to reach *beyond* what even Alexander could in his lifetime. Where he was one man, Rome was an institution with the same spirit of conquest and *pothos*. It was so powerful that it remains the basis of all Western Civilisation to this day.

> *"The early Romans fought not with gold, but with iron."*

> *Unknown*

But alas, in time, the same softening befell the Romans. The political class amassed material wealth, and despite the more robust structure of the Roman-state, their civilisation began to reflect its leadership and began to weaken. The Romans, in their twilight, started to fight with gold, and no longer with iron. It got to the point where they could not negotiate with their enemies any longer. The Huns, under Attila, almost wiped them off the map within a decade. Attila despised Rome for how weak it had become. The elite senatorial classes of Rome tried in vain to buy him out, while watching Rome burn. Attila used the money the Romans paid to him against them, before rounding each of them up and putting them to the sword. The only person who was able to halt Attila's advance was Flavius Aetius - a warrior-statesman who was considered the last of the "true Romans" - and he did so with the sword. He was the only man Attila would respect. Ironically, after saving Rome, the political elite had him assassinated, and within a couple of generations, Rome had fallen entirely. It was replaced by a Christo-Pagan infused proto-Germanic,

Frankish, Saxon, and Celtic western-man which established, using the tracks laid by the Romans, the Christian West and became the next great global power.

In the early days of Christianity, there was a militant asceticism in the practice and image of its leadership. It wasn't so much that "poverty is great" but more that the early Church and its leaders represented and lived by faith, courage, purity, and abstinence. They were militant in their beliefs, and it was precisely with this energy that they managed to take hold after the fall of Rome, and to establish a common substrate for the different European factions and cultures strewn across the continent. But, as the Church became an institutional center of economic power, it came to weaponize guilt to extract wealth from the people while they lived in luxurious monastic 'poverty'. A thousand years later, the Catholic Church suffered a fate somewhat similar to the Romans. Their moral decay and hypocrisy set the stage for the Reformation, which transformed Europe once again.

A few hundred years later, and somewhat connected, was the final chapter of the French Monarchy. What was the richest, most powerful state throughout most of the medieval European period, with roots in the strongest, most warlike and chivalric leaders of all (e.g., Charlemagne), had become a center of debauchery. Louis XVI was too afraid and effeminate to stand up to his people and take charge. Like Darius he chose to flee, and was ultimately beheaded by his own.

Japan was subdued by riches too. The Tokugawa Shogunate resisted foreign intrusion for centuries, but in the end was overcome by the allure of silver and a new class of merchant who came to guide the emperor in national affairs, rendering the Samurai impotent. One of the last great warrior cultures was replaced with a Western-inspired merchant and trader culture, creating in the process, a confused national identity. This new culture has remained a strange superposition on the country - like a suit that doesn't quite fit.

Today it is America and more broadly "the West" that is decaying. Affluence and wealth are to social parasites like sugar and honey are to ants. They make way for the entitled and weak, while attracting the decadent and depraved, thus often leading to an age of decay. This is what philosophers like Spengler and Nietzsche saw coming long ago.

> *"Luxury was thought the greatest menace to manhood and severest simplicity of living was required of the warrior class, sumptuary laws being enforced in many of the clans."*

Inazo Nitobe, Bushido: The Soul of Japan

We are now living in the late stages of this material corruption in the West. The eradication of the spirit that made it successful is in full swing, echoing all those that came before it. A new age of goblins and creatures - that we all thought belonged to fairy tales, but are proving to be real - has come. Blue-haired, multi-gendered, dysgenic deviants are all over social media, and being normalized across the board. The broader social order of the West is looking more and more like Germany's 1920s Weimar Republic. Gambling, YOLO, scamming, and fraud is being peddled by degenerates who are either too stupid to know the difference between what they're selling and what they're supposedly fighting (the case of many crypto people), or genuine scammers who know the game they're playing and looking to take full advantage.

LARPertarians will argue that it's "people's right to sell whatever they want if someone else wants to buy it", ignoring the fact that this very attitude is part of the problem. Just because you can, doesn't mean you should; just because the technology exists to neuter young children doesn't mean you should make it widely available. Just because someone wants to pay to be punched in the face, doesn't mean it should become part of the culture. Just because you can make money by conjuring worthless tokens, doesn't make it right. Not everything is material and not everything has a price. Dignity and honor are not measured in gold, fiat, or Bitcoin.

So can the modern world be redeemed? I think so, as long as redemption doesn't mean some reversion to the old, but an integration of the old, and a construction of something new. Wishing for a past that will never return, or watching it all just burn to the ground like the accelerationists would like, are both defeatist attitudes in my opinion. There is a middle path. There is a white pill - which requires the most courage to take. I call it contrarian optimism. The ability to see what is wrong with the world, and not conform to it, coupled with the courage to know it can be better and to work towards that. Remember that true courage is when the odds are against you, when all hope is lost, when it seems that the foe is unbeatable. At that moment, will you rise to the occasion? Or will you stand by and wait for another to do so? We're at that moment now. It seems impossible at times, and the chances of prevailing against such a corrupt and omnipresent system are slim. But these are the fights all true warriors seek. The worthy foe. The biggest dragon.

> *"If a man wishes to become a hero, then the serpent must first become a dragon: otherwise he lacks his proper enemy."*
>
> Friedrich Nietzsche, *Thus Spoke Zarathustra*

Some things, money can't buy

The Samurai were forbidden to become merchants. In fact, not only was it forbidden, but it was a profession they saw as below them. In their social hierarchy, merchants - and especially the trader class - were considered lower than peasants, for at least the peasants did honest work.

This was similar in other militant ancient cultures. Lycurgus, the quasi-legendary lawgiver of Sparta who established the military-oriented reformation of Spartan society, did so by mandating that iron be used as money, not gold so that storing any large amount of wealth was impossible without drawing attention. In fact, household economics was also delegated to the women in order to keep the men out of it. These decrees were made so that the military men were focused on war and conquest, which made Sparta the most feared and powerful of all ancient warrior societies.

Honor before money was central to all warrior cultures. It established an order that was resistant to corruption and extended the "strong man" period of the cycle. It gave warriors something greater than 'loot' to strive for, and for the rest of us remains key to maintaining meaning beyond the material. Pure materialism is a key factor in the progression to the "weak men" stage of the cycle, because a core tenet suggests that everything and anything can be bought or paid for with coin, including morality, virtue and reputation. This is why governance models that are purely economic and utilitarian (like libertarianism) are so susceptible to decay: truth and morality simply have a price. This is the definition of corruption.

> "The present system of paying for every sort of service was not in vogue among the adherents of Bushido. It believed in a service which can be rendered only without money and without price. Spiritual service, be it of priest or teacher, was not to be repaid in gold or silver, not because it was valueless but because it was invaluable."
>
> Inazo Nitobe, Bushido: The Soul of Japan

Materialism also leads to nihilism because it lacks a connection to the sacred. The Samurai, particularly those who practiced Bushido and sought to be *bushi* or warriors, knew this so they separated the currency of spirit (honor / reputation), from the currency of material for their own spiritual development (i.e., beyond just the need for social order and cohesion). In fact, they valued spiritual currency more than they valued material currency. Nitobe reinforces the prior statement with the following:

> *"Here the non-arithmetical honor-instinct of Bushido taught a truer lesson than modern Political Economy; for wages and salaries can be paid only for services whose results are definite, tangible, and measurable, whereas the best service done in education — namely, in soul development (and this includes the services of a pastor), is not definite, tangible, or measurable. Being immeasurable, money, the ostensible measure of value, is of inadequate use."*

Notice how well he understood money: ***"the ostensible measure of value."*** That definition is more accurate than what 99.99% of modern economists will tell you. Notice also the emphasis on separating money from the immeasurable and non-tangible. Not all value can be measured in money, and this is critical for maintaining a relationship to the 'moral' or sacred dimension of the universe. While material wealth is important, spiritual wealth remains something no amount of money, whether Federal Reserve Notes, gold bullion, or Bitcoin can buy. The pursuit of profit at the expense of virtue and character is as empty as the pursuit of winning on the battlefield at the expense of your honor and soul. These statements might not be 'rational', but they're *real*.

So what do we do with this knowledge? Can we reverse the spiritual decay that is set in motion these past few centuries, and made infinitely worse with a money printer? And more importantly, can we thread the needle between spiritual and material wealth? I believe so, but it requires two things. One, linking more tightly actions and consequences, through a sound money standard **and** two, recognising that there is another necessary measure for wealth: honor and reputation.

Money matters

While my goal has been to make you appreciate the often inverse relationship between material wealth and morality, I am NOT here to tell you that money or even the love of money is the root of all evil. Far from it. The problem is less with money itself, and more with people forgetting that there are things money cannot buy, and also the fact that those without honor or character amplify all that is broken in them when they come *into* money.

To channel Ayn Rand: money is not evil but a "token of honor." She classified two kinds of parasitic class. 'The moochers' were those who would "take your labor by tears". They beg for alms and use guilt to draw it from you because they lack the pride and competence to do anything of value themselves. While the 'looters' would cheat and use "force" (not their own, but that of the moochers) to extract wealth from the productive class because they also lack the character or competence to build something of value themselves.

Rand said that money embodies the idea that *"the common bond among men is not the exchange of suffering, but the exchange of goods."* I would augment her words to say *unnecessary* suffering, because some exchange of suffering is always going to occur, and shared suffering is critical for developing bonds with others that far transcend those that can be measured with money alone. That being said, what Rand is referring to is a Stalin-like figure, who simply sucks dry the lands, wealth, and lives of those more practical and productive than he. That sort of behavior is not a 'shared sacrifice' for something greater, nor even an exchange of sacrifice, as two warriors on the battlefield might have. It is just empty, immoral thuggery. I agree wholeheartedly with Rand that *"Money will not buy intelligence for the fool, or admiration for the coward, or respect for the incompetent."*

Money cannot tell you what to value or how to behave. Money is a **tool** to realize your values and achieve your purpose. Poor values or poor purpose? Money will help you achieve them both. We see this all around us - people getting rich through means that don't add value to society, but suck from it, whether that's shitcoins, OnlyFans pimping, porn, transgender surgery, ESG and climate initiatives, fake meat, the entire SSRI and psychological medication industry, child-trafficking, politics, medical experimentation, and the myriad other social engineering initiatives that make money, but don't make sense. Money earned via lies, deceit or compromise is self-defeating in the end. You're not being a "libertarian" by printing your own money (shitcoin) just because there is demand from stupid people. You're no better than the rest of those who profit from social debauchery. Our values are reflected back onto society by how we all live and behave.

> *"Did you get your money by pandering to men's vices or men's stupidity? By lowering your standards? By doing work you despise for purchasers you scorn? If so, then your money will not give you a moment's or a penny's worth of joy."*

> Ayn Rand, *Atlas Shrugged*

Yes, there are degrees of bad, but it comes from the *same* place. Like I said, just because you can do it, doesn't mean you *should*. There are infinite problems worth solving that will both create wealth and make the world a better place. These are worth your energy and effort more than selling your soul for silver - because whether there is a heaven or not, you only live once in this world. Dignity and legacy have a price you can't measure in money.

This remains my greatest concern for the new wealthy, which is why I asked the question at the outset: **who** do we become as we're catapulted into a higher socio-economic status? The only solution is to work on your values and develop key virtues along with working on your fortune. You have to do both at all times. Slaves and parasites sell their souls, their dignity, and their honor for money. The point of being sovereign is that you do not.

Wealth and the family unit

"Gold was an objective value, an equivalent of wealth produced. Paper is a mortgage on wealth that does not exist, backed by a gun aimed at those who are expected to produce it."

Ayn Rand, *Atlas Shrugged*

Bitcoin should help move individuals and the world in a better direction, because it's a common standard for the language of material value that nobody can change or issue. As such, humanity is freed up to focus on building real wealth and capital: blood, territory and legacy. There is more to life than *just* money, and the sooner we free ourselves from this narrow paradigm, the better.

Family is *real* wealth. It is a biological investment that compounds over generations. If guided well, it can become something powerful and grand; if guided poorly it can turn into something vile and weak. Both Nietzsche's Ubermensch and his Last Man are outcomes of poor or sound investments in family. Neither will randomly sprout from nowhere. They are long-term, intergenerational projects involving the compounding of conscious decision-making across multiple lifespans, in the case of an Ubermensch, or unconscious meandering in the case of the Last Man.

Compounding is the eighth wonder of the world, and family is its biological manifestation. Conscious mate selection, conscious living, careful nurturing of one's offspring, family rituals, religion, rites of passage, and the passing on of wealth from father to son, are all elements in the ancient process of cultivating one's lineage.

Some might ignorantly laugh at this and call you an elitist or a eugenicist just for talking about passing on "good genes". Do not let these bitter, brainwashed fools deter you from what your soul and DNA are calling you to do. Family is the most important unit, and is precisely what's been attacked by the globalist, communist, slave, and ghoul classes of the world because it is an institution of savings and compounding, not only of material wealth, but of biological, intellectual and spiritual wealth.

It's our job to pave the way, figuratively and literally speaking, for tomorrow's new leaders to come into and drive the world forward and upward again. This is a large part of why money is so important, and you cannot ignore it.

Philosophy aside, the practical reality is that savings are the cornerstone to a stable, sovereign life and civilization. You cannot plan for the future, you cannot have a family, you cannot build a community, you cannot think long-term, you cannot exchange goods or services with others, and you cannot build any form of beautiful or ascendant society, without first being able to save using a common medium that can also be exchanged.

People in religious and conservative circles rail against the destruction of the family unit. They (accurately) point out that women are working mindless jobs so they can be tax slaves, instead of staying at home, performing their most vital duty: bringing life into the world and raising it. They are becoming increasingly aware of the fact that it's almost impossible for a family to survive on a single income, and that because of this, many couples are remaining childless for longer so they can "save up" while others are giving up on it altogether because it's like running on a treadmill. The harder they work, the less they can save, and the more trapped they feel. Everyone knows there is something wrong, they can see all of the symptoms, but they are oblivious to the fact that it's a function of a very particular upstream problem.

It's not just Disney and Netflix destroying families, because propaganda alone doesn't work unless there is some evidence or "fault" to point at. If everything is fine, it's hard to cry wolf. But if the world around you is broken, it's very easy to identify a scapegoat and direct people's vitriol towards it. Global warming, evil capitalists, the patriarchy, the unvaccinated, Trump supporters, white people, gym bros, men, colonialism, or whoever else some mainstream midwit reporter wants to complain about. It's the classic magician's sleight of hand. The real trick is not so evident initially, but when you know where to look, it becomes so obvious.

If your money is increasingly becoming worthless, then both husband and wife need to work. If you're both working but you cannot save, then you put off children because you cannot create the economic buffer needed to take the necessary time off. You are then left with a choice to either "YOLO" and remain "DINKs" (dual income, no kids), or gamble, or live in relative poverty, month to month on a single income, or take on the stress to both raise children and work a job to help pay the bills - so the kids end up raised by the school and the state.

It's no wonder people are choosing to enjoy life and defer the family (until more often than not, it's too late, biologically speaking). It's no wonder their time preference is skewed toward shorter time horizons and, downstream, behavior adapts. They remain adolescents into their thirties because it's economically impossible to get ahead anyway, so why try? They see their friends take on extra jobs, only to pull their hair out trying to manage family, work, relationship and kids, so they ask: "why should I put myself through that?"

This is actually somewhat rational at a superficial level, but of course comes with the price of **not** having kids, of **not** passing on your genes, of **not** leaving a legacy and ultimately of ending your lineage, and making society weaker (through low birth rates). We are all human, and as much as we can tell ourselves abstract stories and rationalize all the things, we are **wired** to procreate. We desire, more than anything else, the ultimate act of creation: bringing life into the world. But because the economic system is so broken, we are trapped. Trapped between the future biological regret of extended adolescence and the current economic pressure of trying to start a family while consistently playing catch up.

There is a whole generation of childless 30-somethings who are beginning to feel the biological regret of their otherwise rational economic decisions. It's no wonder people are so angry. It's no wonder they're gambling on shitcoins, or fantasizing about living forever. It's no wonder porn, AI girlfriends, climate crusades, and superfluous social media stupidity are all so popular. These are all coping mechanisms.

Broken money breaks everything else downstream. It destroys the individual, the family, the community, and in time, it destroys the state itself, unless they have full, digital, panopticon control over it - which is why they want CBDCs so badly. They will distract you with fairy tales about AI, racism, and climate change, while the real threat is coming to a bank account near you.

Money is supposed to make possible an exchange of excellence between voluntary peers, but this exchange is worthless if the money is fake. It quickly becomes an exchange of degeneracy and desperation - which is evident today in the twilight of the West.

So if you have *any* interest in the importance of family, children, or legacy, then saving independent, incorruptible money (i.e., Bitcoin) must be the central part of your economic focus. It cannot be ignored. If you're conservative - in either the traditional or political sense - and you have not migrated onto a Bitcoin Standard, you are doing yourself, your family, your legacy, your community, and the world a **major** disservice. Every debauched civilization has at its core, a debauched money. When you come to realize this, everything else becomes clear. So wake up and stop supporting the enemy. Pull the umbilical cord connecting you to the Leviathan. Stop supporting the parasite and cease degrading yourself by trading your precious time, energy, and your family's future for some bureaucratically conjured-up token they can print out of thin air and control from their distant office. Have some self-respect and store your wealth in Bitcoin.

If you're a Bitcoiner, it's your duty to go have a family and build wealth beyond just the material and economic. That's why I wrote this book. "Number go up" is cool, but there is more to life than the amount of satoshis in your wallet. You have the opportunity to lay the foundation for a better future.

And if you're already doing both, then perhaps it's time to focus on building beyond just your family. We need leaders who can take on more responsibility and channel more power. We have to actively throw the parasites out and take back control of the ship.

Power and money

It's not only okay to be rich and powerful - it's necessary. It's the duty of those who have the will, desire, and capacity to leave their mark on the world. It's the duty of the father who seeks to provide for his family, the creator who wants to produce and solve problems, and the leader who seeks to govern and guide his people.

This is why, despite all his flaws, Trump is a greater leader than any other modern American politician could ever hope to be. He walked the walk before he talked the talk - and people know it. In fact, they don't even need to know his past, because they can feel it when he speaks. He's unique, quirky, and often crude, but he's authentically *himself* - which is rare.

Contrast him with career politicians who have never produced anything of value in the marketplace or worked a day in their lives. Not only are they actors, but they have a degree of detachment and insulation from the populace that makes them tone-deaf and ignorant to the reality and needs of the people they supposedly serve. These politicians, like parasites, are beneficiaries of wealth and resources they did not help build or create, and as such, they can't help but take it all for granted. They wield power and have money because the monetary system and the political system are interwoven, *not* because they are worthy of being called 'powerful individuals.'

Power and money are deeply **entwined**. Everyone knows that, but few can tell you why. Let's answer this question at a high level. Think about what each of them are. Money is a kind of "crystalised energy" representing an amount of value generated, that can be stored and transmitted across time and space. It represents resources and time. In physics, power is defined as the rate at which work is done or *energy is transferred* over time. So if money is a form of metaphysical energy, and power is the capacity to channel energy, there is a clear relationship, beyond just their surface level associations. You have potential power if you have money. Beyond that, your ability to move it and do with it as you please is a measure of how much actual, functional power you have.

> *"In this country, you gotta make the money first. Then when you get the money, you get the power. Then when you get the power, then you get the women."*

> Tony Montana, Scarface

What is politics? Politics originally referred to the affairs of the city and its governance. It comes from the Greek *politikos*, meaning "of, for, or relating to citizens." Today it carries a broader meaning, which I would sum up as "the game of social influence and power." There is a relationship between money, power, and politics. Traditionally speaking, if you were a major landowner, employer, or a benefactor of some sort, then you had influence and power, particularly over local resources and thus politics. This is natural and worked quite well when the "state" was small because the landowners who made the decisions had skin in the game. It was their land, lives and wealth on the line - so morally, functionally and practically speaking, their opinion mattered most. This was the reality for most of Western history, bar a few periods of excessive state growth, which always ultimately led to a fracturing, because the larger the territory, the harder it is to maintain influence and power (let alone absolute power).

Fast forward to today, and we find ourselves at a new fracturing point; only this time, it is far more exaggerated than ever. For the past two hundred years, we've seen a continued consolidation of political power into the hands of a larger and more distant "state" apparatus that no longer has **any** skin in the game. In fact, the level of dissociation from the *polis* (city/state) and the *politai* (citizenry) has never been so large - and that is due to multiple factors, the two primary being the abolition of landed/hereditary/royal family ruling class and their replacement with a 'democratic state', along with the creation of central banks and their sole-right to issue money and govern monetary policy. This transformation of the ruling class from visible families who owned the property, into an obfuscated apparatus that controls the property but doesn't directly own it, has turned the state into a hydra. In that scenario, we no longer have governance by the competent and naturally elite - we have instead one giant resource siphoning machine that attracts parasites like moths to a flame.

Those who wield political power today are not powerful individuals who built their own wealth and know how to channel it, but most often frauds who use the wealth of others to fill their own dead-end bags. There is no higher purpose or desire to create something beautiful, because none of what they have is theirs. In the same way you don't do improvements to, or for that matter even care about, the car you hired from Thrifty or Budget, today's ruling class cares nothing for the territory they temporarily 'rent' governance over. They use their position to get closer to the money printer and do their best to siphon as much as possible during their tenure. Their entire goal becomes: print more money, to amass more political power, so they can print more money to amass more political power. And all the while, you and I pay for it.

This makes the game unfair, and people know it: *"rules for thee, but not for me."* These fake elites have sullied what it means to be powerful and wealthy, and in the process convinced otherwise good and capable people that "power is evil", and that "power corrupts", all so as to create a vacuum they can fill. It's about time we changed that, and I believe that Bitcoin separating money from state is a critical step in that direction.

Money and culture

People are longing for a world that is good not only for the elite man, but also the common man. One where everyone has skin in the game. We all know it did one day exist, despite what we're taught in school, because when we visit Europe or old America, we see it.

We all know deep down that art is a reflection of the quality of a society, and if you compare what we have today, with what was created during the Medieval period, and you're honest with yourself, you cannot help but wonder if what we've been fed about that period and its noble families was all a lie. Sure, there was (and always will be) injustice, corruption, and stupidity, but was it really as dark, backward and brutal an age as we're led to believe?

I don't think so. It seems to me that only a society which cares about its common people would go to the effort of making the streets beautiful for them; only a society which valued beauty and valor would commission public art depicting it. On the other hand, only a society which values neither, and whose 'leaders' are detached from both the people and the property, would allow the streets to decay. In fact, they might even go so far as to tear down anything that can remind its inhabitants of prior beauty and greatness, lest their charade be uncovered.

Modern public art, modern copy/paste architecture, the defacing and destruction of antique art and the statues of the greats who forged our civilization, are all symptoms of the latter: an attempt to bury the past and induce social amnesia. But some of us are remembering, and some of us are waking up to realize that society is not faltering today because we lack the talent to produce things of beauty. No, on the contrary: the blood of great artists, sculptors, philosophers, and inventors flows through our veins too. We possess a blood memory that no amount of cognitive and cultural brainwashing can erase. And it's precisely this that we must latch onto. Society is faltering and becoming increasingly ugly because the best of us have abdicated our responsibility to be rich, powerful benefactors, and in doing so, have left a vacuum for the parasites to fill. We have forgotten who we are, and the truth is, we are descendants of the families who were successful enough to live, bleed, breed, and pass life down to us. It's about time we woke up and honored that gift by doing something great, producing things of value, and making the world more beautiful.

There are many ways to do this. Not all of us will have the talents of a Michelangelo or a Da Vinci, who come first to mind when thinking about Renaissance Italy. Their paintings of the Sistine Chapel and the Mona Lisa continue to captivate people centuries on. But those of us who have neither the talent or ability to produce the art directly can certainly become patrons and benefactors who make that kind of work possible. The glorious Renaissance artworks that people of all religions, backgrounds, and cultures continue to make pilgrimages to today were made possible by the patronage of the great families - who not only permitted, but encouraged their creation.

Chief among those patrons was the Medici family, and the greatest of them all was Cosimo de' Medici (1389-1464), also known as Cosimo the Elder. He was the ultimate patriarch and visionary founder of the Italian banking family and political dynasty that first consolidated power in the Republic of Florence during the first half of the 15th century.

While the effective founder of the family was Giovanni di Bicci de' Medici (1360–1429), who amassed great wealth in trade in the early 1400s, it was Cosimo that consolidated the family's power and established the so-called elder branch of the family that would go on to fuel the very Renaissance itself. The beautiful artworks, the Sistine Chapel, the Statue of David, the Uzzi Museum, the Duomo di Firenze - are all part of what makes Italy one of the most visited countries in the world today, five hundred years on! People are drawn to its ancient and classical beauty, in large part thanks to the **vision** and patronage of a single family and the **vision** of one great man.

> "The higher we soar, the smaller we appear to those who cannot fly."

> Friedrich Nietzsche, Thus Spoke Zarathustra

Meanwhile, the same people who enjoy the fruits of the labor funded by these former rich and powerful families, have come to believe that these people and their wealth and power are somehow evil. Make it make sense! This is brainwashing on a grand scale, and it's not only the modern democratic state that's to blame. Christianity in the West became its own worst enemy by teaching otherwise good people that poverty was virtuous, while power and riches were evil. This guilt and misplaced envy is precisely what the parasites picked up on and used to justify the creation of the modern state and convince great men to abdicate. Nietzsche picked up on it and warned us of what would happen if we went down this path. Instead of listening, unfortunately, everyone laughed at him. Otherwise good people chose poverty instead of building wealth and power, and justified it with religion. Many do the same today but use "the globalist government" as the excuse. In doing so, they make way for genuinely evil and corrupt people to fill the power vacuum. And this is how they've come to control modern culture.

Make no mistake about it. It's not that film, media, technology, advertising, medicine and publishing are evil, and it's not even that they are run by crooked people. The fault lies with all of us, with the good people who abdicated our responsibility to build, lead and create these things. Our choice to not be involved is where the problem stems from, and what we must first address.

Ask yourself this. What if just and virtuous people were in charge of these industries? What kind of beauty and grandeur might be produced or created? The Renaissance was but a glimpse of what's possible. Imagine what we could do with our modern technological prowess and the help of precision machines, AI, and software.

The Renaissance was a time when good people weren't afraid to be rich, and therefore powerful. They used that power and their vision to influence culture. They embedded the virtues they lived by into the public works and the art that we, centuries on, admire. It is time we found the courage to be like this again: to leave the world more beautiful than we found it.

Seasons and Cycles

The final of the four pillars is the one that ties everything together: the cyclical or seasonal nature of life, humanity, society and the universe itself. This is a concept so deeply woven into the fabric of our consciousness that it's embedded in the everyday language we use: *"What goes around, comes around," "There's nothing new under the Sun," "the cycle of life."*

This is because cycles are everywhere. They make up reality. There are micro and macro cycles, long cycles, short cycles, and super-cycles fractally composed of smaller and smaller cycles all the way down. They start with the very smallest of the small: the quantum fluctuations that make up the foam of the universe and the electrons orbiting a nucleus; then scale up and through biology with the metabolic cycles of the cell and the larger organism, including its hormonal cycles, reproductive cycles, sleep cycles, and it's very life cycle; biology extends into environmental cycles such as the hydrologic cycles that move water around the world through stages of evaporation, condensation, precipitation, run off and back again, and the climatic cycles which give us seasons and drive the migration cycles of herds of wildebeest in the Serengeti, flocks of snow geese in the Arctic, and schools of salmon in the Pacific, who after migrating to the ocean to grow and mature, return to their original freshwater birthplaces to spawn and die.

These cycles are all nested inside greater planetary, solar, and celestial cycles like the Earth's rotation, giving us night and day, or the Moon's orbital cycle around the Earth which literally attracts the ocean toward itself, producing tides and stabilizing the Earth's tilt. Zooming out we find Earth's orbital cycle around the Sun which gives rise to the year and the seasons that cycle within it, along with the orbital cycles of the other planets, and their moons, which protect us from asteroids and together gravitationally stabilize the Solar System. Solar cycles such as the eleven-year sunspot cycle, two of which make up the twenty-two year Hale cycle (or magnetic reversal cycle), influence the solar winds and the interplanetary magnetic field which forms an integral part of the delicate balance making life possible on Earth. These all flow into longer cycles, such as the 80,000-year Milankovitch cycles arising from the Earth's eccentricity (which drive Ice Ages) and the 26,000-year precessional cycle (the 'great year' of astrology, which leads to the changing from one astrological age to the next), on through the longest and largest time scales, such as the 30 million year cycle with which the Sun bobs up and down through the Galactic disk, and the 225-million-year 'Galactic Year' of the Sun's orbit around the Galactic Center.

Everything is clearly part of a cycle at some level, and when you zoom out and observe from this vantage point, you can't help but laugh at the globalists and bureaucrat archetypes who believe that "they know best" or that their policy is the right one. Particularly entertaining are the climate catastrophists convinced that they can predict the weather decades from now while being constantly wrong about next week's weather. They're certain that the Earth's climate is so heavily influenced by what we do here, but conveniently ignore that it has been changing for 4 billion years because of what happens 'out there'. That anyone can even know what "better" means in the context of such a complex system, or at such grand scales, is the height of hubris: the Fatal Conceit, to echo Hayek.

The early 2024 cloud-seeding activities and the subsequent floods and storms in Dubai are a perfect example of how meddling with complex systems can backfire. And this is a relatively small-scale experiment when it comes to environmental tampering. Some of the more stupid ideas, like "blocking out the Sun" to prevent further global warming could prove far more catastrophic for everyone, not just the residents of a single city.

The truth is that things change and when one season comes to an end, another one spawns. With each change, new opportunities and hardships arise and this is really how life finds its way. Understanding the stage or season you're in is more important than trying to change it. In the case of the climate, for instance, the world has its own climatic cycles linked to its relationship with the atmosphere, biosphere, the Sun, the Moon, and the rest of the planets in the solar system. These relationships are the real cause of global warming and cooling, phenomena which have and will continue to occur with or without humans in the equation. Thinking these changes are solely the result of the anthroposphere is ignorance or naiveté at best, malice at worst. Unsurprisingly, the people who couldn't predict that inflation would occur if they printed copious amounts of money, or who thought that shutting down the entire global economy over a flu variant was a good idea, are the same who think they can predict what's going to happen with the weather and climate decades from now.

These meddlers will gaslight you into believing that taxation and regulations on human activity will somehow defeat the celestial cycles that have been going on for unfathomable timespans, long before humanity existed. They want to put their fingers in everyone's pies because they cannot make one of their own. These are self-proclaimed saviors nobody asked for: false leaders, fake elites, and cheats whom nobody respects because they don't respect themselves enough to build their own wealth, so they must take it from someone else. We must discredit them at every turn and remove them from positions of power before they do more damage.

Life cycles

We zoomed out to the climate, the planets and the stars. Let us now zoom back into the human life-cycle and observe how it continues in a social, financial and civilisational context.

We are born into the world, helpless and entirely dependent on our mother. As we grow up, we learn, adapt, discover, become functional (some of us at least), reach adulthood, find our peak, we continue to mature further and then, slowly, we begin to lose the best of our faculties, we age, and ultimately, get to the point where we're once again helpless and dependant, before we die. This is the cycle of life, and within it there are "seasons." Each season comes with advantages and disadvantages, and when we finally complete our journey, and have experienced all the seasons, our time comes to pass on. Those who come after us then pick up this cyclical mantle of life and continue forth on their own journey through the seasons. This is inescapable.

The movie *Benjamin Button* is the story of a man whose seasons of youth and life are inverted. He starts old at birth, and dies young as a baby. Like all great fiction, it brings with it a number of deep messages. We cannot escape hardship, no matter what stage of life we're in, and even if we were to become more youthful as we chronologically aged, we can neither escape a beginning nor an end. What makes the beginning of life, and life itself for that matter, special, is that it has an end. What makes it transcendent is that one end signals a new beginning. One light goes out, another comes on, and the cycle continues.

There's a big lesson here for all the singularitarians who wish to live forever as brains in a vat. I used to think I'd live for at least 250 years. 500 was my 'goal'. The naivety of youth! I don't discount that we may increase our lifespans, and ideally extend our health spans too, but I no longer count on such fanciful ideas, nor do I buy into stupidities like "aging is a disease" that "we must defeat." Aging is a cycle, and it's beautiful. We can of course do things to mitigate the downsides (that are associated with weakness, not age), but there's a line between that and cyborgification, or the Peter Pan syndrome in which people like Bryan Johnson are trapped.

Johnson, if you've not heard of him yet, spends millions each year attempting to "defeat death", and while his mission may give us some useful data, I am not convinced it makes any sense. Not only because we're all so bio-individual that the data itself will not be all that useful but, more importantly, because spending the remainder of your life obsessed with trying to defeat aging - a battle you're just going to lose - is not practical. It's a bit like driving while staring at the rearview the whole time. Instead of experiencing and enjoying the fruits of life at **this** stage, you are constantly obsessed with clinging on to a past version of yourself.

In doing so, you miss out on the beauty of the season you're in - a bit like someone who remains inside with the A/C on all summer to 'stay out of the heat' but misses out on the sun, sand and beach.

There's an even more serious side-effect with these life-extension obsessions, namely the increased risk aversion and extended adolescence from actually succeeding in adding a few more decades to our lives. See boomers and Gen X as a light example. What impact will an extra decade have on people's maturity, or their desire to procreate? Could this make people even more safety-oriented (the opposite of courageous and alive), more comfortable, weaker and, ultimately, the opposite of vital (think sterile - like a hospital) while ironically having almost no influence in the grand scheme of things? Does an extra few decades really matter in the grand cosmic sweep? Perhaps, but not at the expense of a life of freedom, courage, risk and experimentation. Better to die courageously on the battlefield of life, than as a hospitalized neurotic in a prison of your own fear. Trying to defeat the seasons or cycles is not only naive and immature but fundamentally, *artificial*. Like lab-grown meat: it just doesn't really work, taste the same or do the job - I don't care how much money is spent "refining the science."

We'll see this interventionist issue coming up again and again in this chapter. Take close note, because there is an important lesson here.

Social and economic cycles

The human life-cycle gives rise to the most relevant cycles for our discussion: the abstracted social, cultural, political, technological and economic cycles that we create and contend with as an extension of our individual lives. While I disagree with many of his conclusions and his political stance, Ray Dalio, the billionaire hedge fund manager and founder of Bridgewater Associates, has done some great work documenting the economic and financial cycles humans both produce and experience. Most notably this includes the short- and long-term debt cycles, which frame and drive the economic paradigms we live in.

These cycles, like all cycles, are nested within each other. The short-term cycle, which typically lasts between 5 and 10 years and consists of periods of economic expansion and recession, exists within a longer-term debt cycle that spans 50-75 years and is characterized by periods of debt accumulation followed by a deleveraging phase.

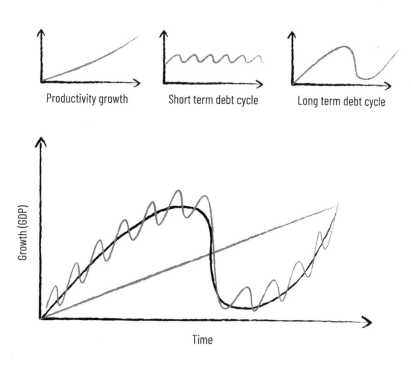

The long-term cycle begins with low levels of debt leading to increased borrowing, which fuels economic expansions. Eventually, debt levels become unsustainable, leading to a financial crisis. The deleveraging phase that follows involves debt reduction, austerity measures, and sometimes defaults or restructurings. It is closely associated with the political and social cycles he outlines, that shift between periods of peace and stability and periods of conflict and disruption. The beginning and end of these long-term debt cycles are connected to wealth gap cycles and what he calls the cycle of "Internal and External Order", in which regions cycle between periods of strong internal and external order and periods of disorder. In this case, internal order refers to domestic political stability, while external order refers to a country's international standing and influence.

If this all sounds familiar, it should. Recall **"Hard times create strong men, strong men create good times, good times create weak men, and weak men create hard times"**.

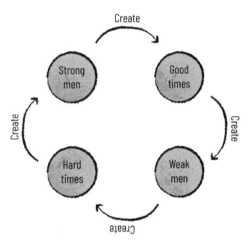

The quote is from a post-apocalyptic novel by the author G. Michael Hopf, called *Those Who Remain*. It's also discussed in detail as a theory of "generational seasons" in *The Fourth Turning* by Neil Howe and William Strausse.

Even if you've not heard of it before nor read any of these pieces, you will be intrinsically familiar with it because it is *archetypal*. It's buried in our collective unconscious. You see it in every great story, fact or fiction, all throughout **history.** Indeed, the greater the tale and grander the epic, the more of a seasonal or cyclical undertone it carries. Dalio's work puts a quantitative economic wrapper on this exact concept so it's more palatable to the sophisticated reader.

That being said, he is far from the first to discuss economic and political cycles. The Austrians had put all of this together in what's known as "The Business Cycle" well over a century ago. Ludwig von Mises, in his seminal work *The Theory of Money and Credit*, published in 1912, introduced the concept of economic cycles driven by monetary intervention. He showed that artificial manipulation of interest rates by central banks leads to misallocation of capital (malinvestments), which eventually necessitates a painful economic correction.

This is also best illustrated with a chart, where the boom periods are fueled by monetary or credit intervention, creating artificial growth, and are followed by a correction where rates increase, consumption decreases and recessions follow. The ironic thing is that a free market when left alone has a natural business cycle which follows the same pattern. The only thing that intervention does is exacerbate the boom-bust periods, making them more severe. Sound familiar?

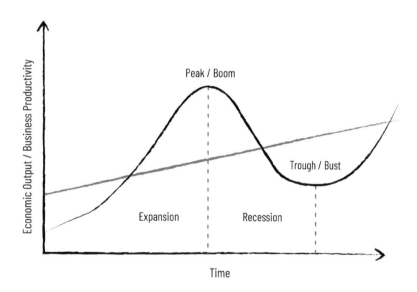

Both nested within and also adjacent to these economic and financial cycles (these things are complex and interrelated) are a whole range of technological cycles, each with their own fractals that swing from centralized to decentralized, aggregation to disaggregation, creation to destruction, innovation to iteration, stagnation to progress, obsolescence to advancement, and decline to resurgence. Nikolai Kondratiev, for example, studied the long-term cyclical movements in economies and the technologies they birth. The Kondratiev wave, or K-wave as it's now known, is a 40 - 60 year cycle that has periods of radical innovation which kick-start growth, followed by a period of incremental development and ultimately a phase of stagnation. Anecdotally, he also predicted that all fiat currencies have a life cycle, and ultimately trend to zero value.

Beyond K-waves, we find hype cycles, like Gartner's famous one depicting how the hype and interest around a particular technology or idea is over-emphasised in the short term, which, when expectations are not met, leads to a cratering in interest where nobody cares anymore, setting the stage for real, robust, long-term development to occur, driven by those who are really interested and working at the core of these technologies.

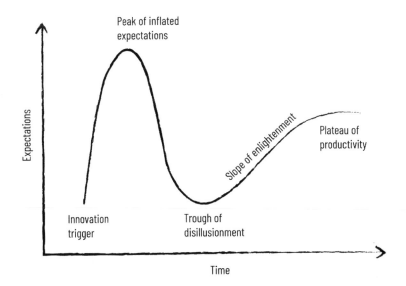

The S-curve cycle represents the adoption of new technologies, networks, products or services. These are particularly useful in showing how progress takes time to compound enough for either a network-effect or adoption and awareness to reach a tipping point - and when it does happen, growth is explosive. This is the "gradually, then suddenly" concept in action.

But, as with all such cycles, growth is not infinite. Once market saturation occurs, the growth tapers off - which opens the door to the next innovation, the next technology, the next trend and the next big idea.

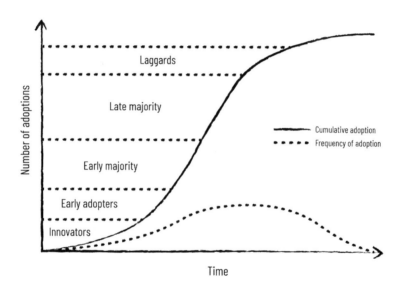

James Dale Davidson and Lord William Rees-Mogg, authors of *The Sovereign Individual*, introduced the concept of mega-political cycles, which are larger-scale patterns that contain within them the more immediate generational, technological, and financial cycles, but are characterized more by the "returns to violence" of a particular period. These civilisation-scale cycles span approximately 500 years each, and each one is marked by a transformative shift in social organization; for example, a large empire such as Rome disintegrates into the distributed fiefdoms of Medieval Europe. These cycles are driven by a blend of monetary transitions (easy/fiat to hard/sound money standards, and back), cultural transformations and technological advancements, particularly in the domain of weaponry (e.g., the discovery of gunpowder, or the development of armor). Davidson and Rees-Mogg argue that we're navigating the third of these monumental cycles in the AD period, where the emergence of digital technologies such as encryption and the Internet will challenge the dominance of the nation-state and, in its place, trigger the rise of the 'Sovereign Individual'. So far, their book has proved quite prescient. Despite being written almost 30 years ago, they managed to predict everything from Facebook or YouTube to Bitcoin, and even the recent travel restrictions. We are certainly in the throes of the paradigm clash between centralized globalism and decentralized localism. While both are accelerating - depending on the day and the news-source you subscribe to, either one could be considered to be 'winning' - I'm cautiously optimistic that the trend is in favor of the latter; if not for everyone, then at least for a new, natural elite.

The pendulum is swinging from centralized back to decentralized because the cost of defensive technology (economic, kinetic, and communications) is decreasing so quickly that it's creating a massive differential compared with the cost of attack and coercion. The returns on the kinds of aggregate violence the current cycle has been built on are no longer as tenable - and this is driving the current paradigm to reach a crescendo and, ultimately, sunset. The clash is part of the process, and will make way for something new, which will be the focus of the final part of this book.

A time and a place

This exploration of cycles would not be complete without including the work of the father of 'civilisational cycles' - Oswald Spengler. In his seminal book *The Decline of the West*, he developed the theory that civilizations are born, grow, mature, become senescent, and die according to a predictable pattern that he analogized to the life-cycle of a biological organism. Spengler believed each civilization has its own unique soul, which manifests in its culture, arts, science, architecture, mathematics, legal systems, religion, and societal structures. The life-cycle of each civilization follows the exploration of the 'world symbol' at the heart of each cultural soul. Over time, civilizations move from a culture phase (rural, vital, creative and organic) to a civilization phase (urban, mechanical, sterile and inorganic), culminating in their inevitable decay. Spengler cites Rome as an example of the civilization stage following the Classical Greek cultural stage, with Alexander the Great as the midpoint. The modern West, which Spengler calls the Faustian Civilization, echoes this with Medieval Europe representing the cultural stage, followed by the United States of America representing the civilisational stage (which we're now well into) and Napoleon, in this case, representing the midpoint, like Alexander before him. The point is that each stage has its genesis, peak, and twilight - the latter can happen either gracefully with a synthesis of old and new, or can be marked by decay, over-extension and debauchery. Either way, no matter how powerful the society, culture, or civilization, *the cycle remains inescapable.*

Spengler is often characterized as a pessimist because his work focused so much on the decline of the West, but I prefer to think of him as a realist. His point was not that *"it's all over and we should give up"*, but more that we need to understand and respect the stage of the cycle we're in. When a society, similar to a human being, matures, it will inevitably be less lively and expansive. Instead of trying to do what it did when it was younger, it should recognise and adapt. When you're 60, you probably can't deadlift the same weight you could at 30, and that's okay. The new season bears a different sort of fruit: we trade youth for wisdom, opportunity for experience. When you're older, you might not be able (or want) to work as hard as you used to, but you have wisdom that can be applied. In fact, if you remain vital, you can probably do more with a single phone call than you could have at twenty-five with a full 365 days of work.

This is the key to Spengler's philosophy, and ultimately to the point of this entire chapter. We should recognize that each stage of life has its own strengths and weaknesses, and try our best to act accordingly. The seasons will inevitably change and the stage will move on - trying to hang on in vain is a futile exercise. In the case of 'The West', not only are the circumstances which made the civilization great and powerful no longer there, but the next stage is going to require a cultural focus, and is thus incompatible with the current framework. Ironically, the more desperately some try to hang onto the current decaying civilization the more they will turn it into a totalitarian caricature of itself, fueling the actual reaction that drives the counterculture we're already experiencing today. Something new is birthing - an energy that will transform the current social paradigm.

So what does this all mean? Many things, but most importantly, that we need to ask better questions, such as:

- Given the cyclical nature of existence, can we even avoid these cycles?

- If not, can we short-circuit them?

- Should we even attempt to do either?

- If cycles represent life, what does an absence of a cycle represent?

- Is there another way?

- Can we dampen the cycles, or build structures to protect us when we're in the trough of the cycle or the winter of the season?

- Can Bitcoin help with the latter?

- Or is it too just another thing that will pass?

Finding answers to these questions matters more than just diagnosing clown-world and reminiscing on a past that will never return. Instead of blindly and ignorantly hanging onto what's dying, or trying to ignore the cycles and artificially change them, we need to figure out how to work with them. Tradition is necessary not because it is 'from the past', but because it is concerned with that which does not pass. We need both.

I wrote this book to challenge myself, and anyone reading it, to think *beyond* today. The pace of change is faster than it has ever been, and perhaps the greatest difference to prior civilizational shifts is that grand changes that took centuries to occur previously may take generations instead. Future leaders will have a whole new set of challenges to face and they must adapt accordingly. Recognising the stage of the cycle they're in, and leveraging the timeless virtues explored in this book, will be key to this adaptation and navigation.

With that, let us move onto the next chapter, and the big question.

Can Bitcoin Help?

"Fix the money, fix the world" - that's the promise many Bitcoiners rally religiously behind. But is it true? Could it really be that simple? Is Bitcoin a silver-bullet that fixes incentives enough for behavior to orient back to normality, and perhaps even excellence?

Maybe. I used to believe it fervently, but in the two years I spent writing this book, I've come to a different, more nuanced understanding. I now think of it less as a "silver-bullet", and more like a keystone to a bridge: without it, the bridge cannot be completed, but alone, there is no bridge.

> *Bitcoin Fixes This means: Fixing the money has positive downstream effects on culture and society, because action and consequence are more intimately entwined, and therefore localized, so good decisions are rewarded, while the socialization of poor decisions is limited.*

I'm still convinced Bitcoin will have profoundly positive long-term effects on society, but they will take generations to come about and require more effort on our part. Behavior and culture don't just change overnight. There is an inertia to overcome first, before any real turnaround, let alone positive motion can be had. We've just begun the pushback stage - to slow the decay - which is why it feels impossible at times. Our descendants will carry the responsibility of rounding the cape, and theirs will reap the rewards and push in a new direction. Our duty, like Sisyphus, is to keep pushing the boulder up the mountain. There is no time for black pills, and giving up certainly means losing. We have truth and beauty on our side - along with some other tools (like Bitcoin, Nostr & the Internet). We need to use everything at our disposal.

To close out part three of the book, I will explore the impact Bitcoin has on the four pillars of civilization we just discussed. Does its introduction into the life of the average individual help nudge them into the direction of greater virtue?

Could Bitcoin expose the equalitarian politics of the past century as the frauds they are, leading them to bankruptcy, and their ultimate demise? If so, could it lead to a world in which cultures become richer and, by force of economic reality, more unified locally, while more diverse at the macro or international level?

Could Bitcoin help establish a more robust "structure" that can better weather the weak-man stage of the civilisational cycle? Could this lead to material and moral wealth actually aligning in a way they've not done before?

I believe the answer to all of these is mostly yes - which is a big claim. So let's explore why before we proceed to part 4 of the book, the one that makes all the difference: *a praxis.*

Culture

Bitcoin impacts culture in various ways, though I'll focus on two here. One is the depth or richness of culture at the micro level (we'll start the discussion here) and the other is cultural variance or diversity at the macro level (which we'll examine afterwards).

Culture is upstream of politics and therefore civilization too. Society and the human cultures it contains are emergent phenomena influenced by many things: territory size and location, terrain (flat/mountains), climate (cold or hot, the presence of absence of strong seasonal variations), religion or beliefs, the behavior of leadership or key figures, rewards and punishments, shared values, family/blood ties, economic affluence, time preference, and more. It's the last two I'd like to focus on here.

Time preference in particular is a measure of maturity. The lower the time preference, the greater the ability to abstain or defer gratification.

In other words, the less you discount the future in relation to the present, and thus the more future-oriented you are. Saving and cooperation are generally signs of low time preference and economic maturity, whereas frivolous spending, blind consumerism and theft are signs of high time preference and immaturity.

This is where we find Bitcoin's first major influence on culture. By minimizing the ability to confiscate wealth, both at the individual and the institutional levels, Bitcoin is much harder to steal directly (theft) and indirectly (inflation) - one can imagine that in time, the incentive to thieve diminishes and the incentive for cooperation or competition increases. Put simply, you get less of that which is more expensive or hard to do. It's extremely easy for the government to take 40% of your paycheck before it lands in your bank account, or even to freeze your bank account for that matter. They are the arbiters and controllers of both the corporate and financial systems. With Bitcoin, on the other hand, it's not so trivial because they do not own the network and cannot influence its operation. At best they can scare people and try to suppress the price (both futile in the long term).

Economically speaking, cooperation and competition are better for both the producers and the consumers in a society, because they drive more effective and efficient use of capital (resources, time, energy). This is basically the essence of *capitalism*: using the resources, time and energy at your disposal in the most resourceful way possible (assuming you're rational).

All else being equal, having a form of money that is incorruptible and hard to confiscate should result in a shift away from thieving and toward cooperation, and a subsequent lowering of time preference. Insofar as time preference is related to maturity, this should also lead to a maturing of culture through grassroots means (mature people → mature culture) and to an increase in economic prosperity. This is not theoretical. Both first-principles reasoning and overwhelming empirical evidence (see early America, Australia, Canada or the West in general) show that division of labor, strong property rights and competition drove incredible prosperity - so strong indeed that despite decades of destruction via poor economic and political leadership, these regions are still the wealthiest on earth.

This chain of maturation becomes a positive feedback loop and actually gives the culture more **time**. With more time, man grows an interest for activities, such as play, art and philosophy. In other words, when we create wealth and therefore time, we create the possibility for higher culture. Unfortunately, this also comes with the risk of some using that time to conjure up socialist programs and equalitarian stupidities of all kinds. This is the double-edged sword of material prosperity we discussed at length earlier. The elite class in this period are often weaker men, prone to the corruption of the flesh and inclined to support such stupidities. It's important we remain most vigilant right when we are most wealthy (a lesson for people and cultures). Thankfully, Bitcoin may be of use here once again, as a kind of "economic circuit breaker" that triggers when weak men come into power and begin letting things slide. It's very hard to hide losses on a sound money standard, but very easy with money you can print. The equalitarian policies enforced by the weak descendants of earlier culture builders have always fallen apart, but not without significant collateral damage - like an invisible virus or cancer in the body, they destroy much more than what you see on the surface. The greatest damage occurs when these ideologies endure for extended periods of time, which can only really happen when the parasitic elite are able to mask the relationship between their policies and the consequences, through the debasement of money.

It's a trick as old as time. *Paper over real losses with fake money.* The only thing that's changed is its institutionalization. It's now like a polished magic trick. Slow enough that nobody realizes it's happening, subtle enough that it seems stable, and broad enough that little by little it creates massive wealth imbalances and distortions in the game before anybody can do anything about it. Like death from a thousand cuts, or slowly boiling a frog. This monetary debasement is *imperceptible theft* - like the Wesley Snipes and Jason Statham movie *Chaos*, where the bank robbers install a virus on the computer that, instead of stealing millions from accounts, steals less than a hundred from millions of accounts to avoid the sensors. They get away with it in the movie, like central bankers have been getting away with it for over a century. In an economy, we are the sensors, and inflation evades most people... until it doesn't, at which point they panic, and it becomes hyperinflation. If you want to understand how hyperinflation works, think of a person who can't really swim, standing in a pool with a rising water level. They're fine until the water reaches their neck. Soon they're on their tip-toes, trying to keep their mouth and head above water, but the water keeps imperceptibly rising. The panic doesn't really start until the level reaches the lower lip, and really kicks in when their entire head is submerged - but by then it's too late to learn to swim.

We're seeing this play out in real time around the world today. We're somewhere between inflation evading most people and the hyperinflation panic stages. The water is about chin level. It's evident in the growing sense of angst that everyone feels. People are angry and they *don't even know why*. They're clamoring for free healthcare and government stipends, and wondering why despite the handouts, they still can't get a break. Most people have no idea why the price of food, gas and housing has doubled, or tripled in barely three years. In fact, it's up by a factor or ten in less than five decades. So they blame *"the capitalists"*. The guys that *can* swim! Meanwhile, someone is pouring more water into the pool, drop by drop.

Bitcoin makes this whole game of monetary inflation and hidden theft much harder to play. In fact, it's impossible to issue new bitcoin, so if you adopt it, you're on that standard, and if you do not, in time the money you're using will trend to worthlessness against Bitcoin (soft money always loses, in time, to hard money). Therefore, like a force of nature or a physical law, we either choose to adapt to its reality, or pay the price of not doing so. This is the genesis of the saying: *"You don't change Bitcoin, Bitcoin changes you."*

This does not preclude insanity! Bitcoin is not a panacea for the human condition. Nothing is - that sort of thinking is utopian and shallow. Of course there will be derangement syndromes emerging in cultures where their affluence - on a Bitcoin standard - allows for stupid ideas, but the consequence of said ideas should in theory be more evident because it's harder to paper over the losses or fraudulently adjust the ledger. It's my hope that this will be enough to put the brakes on dumb behavior, or force the constituents of said culture to re-analyze and adapt before the decay or cancer of equalitarianism takes root.

Adaptation is necessary, and for it to be effective, the speed of feedback is critical. Money is a signaling mechanism. Prices transmit information. But, like any other network, when the cables through which messages are transmitted are broken, rusted, or damaged, the information necessary to make decisions is distorted. That's what the money printer does to a society and its economy. *Garbage in, garbage out.*

So, to recap: We have lower time preferences alongside better signaling and information flow through the economy. Together, they make the case for why Bitcoin, as sound, incorruptible and difficult-to-confiscate money, should lead to, or at least serve as a better foundation for, more long-term-oriented, responsible, and thus richer, deeper, and more mature cultures.

Which leads into the second point on culture: **macro variance and diversity.**

Governance

Bitcoin is **anti-equality technology,** and it will impact social and economic governance by making it more hierarchical, economically sound and multipolar.

First, good governance is hierarchical. Chains of command are necessary not only for delegation and separation of duties (focus), but also for speed of decision-making and accountability. Fiat governance models are subject to death by bureaucracy and the tragedy of the commons, where everyone and no one is responsible.

Equalitarian experiments will suggest that we're all unique, but conveniently ignore the inherent differences between people. The truth is that humans are **not** equal, precisely because we are all unique. Spoils naturally go to the winners, while the losers are left with feedback. Fair and functional games have winners *and* losers, and society - which is a form of game - needs to know who to reward and who to punish in order to prosper. If people are free to win, they must also be free to lose. In fact, freedom and equality are diametrically opposed. When you give people freedom, they naturally de-equalise themselves; and in order to equalize them, you must force them back into sameness by suffocating all natural variance and stripping them of their agency and *freedom*.

Second. Remember that while **good** governance is derived from leadership, inspiration, and maturity, what underlies **all** governance is ultimately the threat of violence, and in an environment where good governance is lacking, or made impossible because of cultural mismatch, no accountability and lack of order (hierarchy), things can get ugly.

Governance models don't often scale to very large numbers because people are naturally diverse in their thinking, beliefs, values, culture, behavior, intellect and levels of maturity. You can't just force them all to agree. Secondly, because territories vary in their climates, access to natural resources, local norms, history, size, soil, and heritage, they lend themselves to different forms of governance. Some are more hierarchical, some more tribal, others are more egalitarian and in some places, governance is entirely absent. This differentiation in approach causes many problems, and is a big part of why multiculturalism has never worked, and most often ends in either short-term violence to keep things in order, or long-term violence due to the decay that comes with open policies and disorder.

> *"Multiculturalism will destroy America. There is a danger that large numbers of Mexicans and others from South and Central America will continue to come to the US and spread their culture across the whole of the country. If they breed faster than the WASPs [White Anglo-Saxon Protestants] and are living with them, whose culture will prevail?... It would be sad for American culture to be changed even partially."*

Lee Kuan Yew, Visionary Founder of Modern Singapore

The large-scale, homogenous zombie-states resulting from the equalitarian experiments of the last hundred years are inorganic and fragile, and should've collapsed by now; but they're fed by the money printer, so they subsist on life support. Take the European Union as an example. It's both a parasite sucking the resources from the European people, and forcing the destruction of their cultures, and also a complete economic and political disaster. Within Europe alone, people live completely different lifestyles. Italians and Germans both have their own unique values and norms. People come to Italy for the food, the architecture, the leisure, history, weather and the Mediterranean Sea. They go to Germany for different reasons. Trying to blend everyone into one economic melting pot clearly doesn't work and creates an opportunity for these parasites to take advantage by printing more money, crusading against more Quixotic problems (while ignoring the real ones) and forcing "services" that nobody needs onto everyone (see electric car mandates, plastic bottle lids, vax passports). This is made a thousand times worse by importing people from countries and cultures that do not share the values. European countries, at the very least, have shared histories and religions. The people being imported most often do not, and it destroys what little integrity is left. Europe was much better off beforehand, as a patchwork of independent nations, each with their own decision-making power. Case in point, Hungary was recently fined €200m by the EU for protecting their own people and "not abiding by EU asylum rules." The same goes for the USA. The federal government is a bloated malignant cancer, leaching from its people and from the better managed states. Luckily for Americans, the Founding Fathers enshrined greater autonomy at the state level - and that's in my opinion why the US remains the best of a bad bunch.

In any case, what does this have to do with Bitcoin and money? Simple: ***fiscal responsibility and solvency.*** Without a hard limit on monetary expansion, I don't see why any government or governance structure *would ever* practice fiscal responsibility or satiate its desire for expansion. When someone else is paying for dinner you eat as much as you can, right? With such power at your fingertips, and a high degree of immunity from its consequence, why would you not continue to just spend and consume? Why would you not create larger and larger bureaucracies to maintain the status quo? The truth is, easy money necessitates that you keep growing the Leviathan, if for no other reason than to prove you have "checks and balances" - which of course, leads to more bureaucracy, and the bureaucratic death spiral continues.

Free money leads to a bloating of the government *far* beyond what would otherwise be economically feasible. Bureaucratic tentacles are fed by a constant flow of funds and find their way into every corner and crevice of the machine, until so many places and people depend on it or are entangled by it that it seizes up the entire contraption, and nobody can breathe. Then of course, something snaps. I don't believe we are far off from that breaking point in the West.

Consider the alternative. A money with not only a hard limit, but a verifiable one that becomes a common standard. What might that lead to?

Growth will require investment or deployment of ***real capital***. In other words, there better be a real return on that initiative. You cannot just grow for growth's sake. When you cannot thieve your way into more money, *when you have to pay for your own meal*, maybe, just *maybe*, you'll be less inclined to order everything on the menu. When it's real money on the line, you need to prioritize (think about how people play poker with real money on the line versus play money). The incentives change. To survive, you have to focus your energy and attention on efficiency, on greater productivity, on something actually useful. Furthermore, you are more inclined to mind your own business, instead of getting into everyone else's like some annoying activist. You might want to orient toward your strengths and trade with someone who is leaning into theirs (division of labor). Think about what this does on a social level. When you can't just print more money to pay for your ever-growing tentacles, they are much harder to expand, and you literally cannot create more dependents because you cannot pay for or feed them. Goodbye illegal immigration, goodbye welfare, hello stronger, tighter borders.

On a long enough time scale, Bitcoin's economic immutability will result in smaller governance structures that operate more effectively and efficiently. Couple that with variations in all of the other factors I mentioned (religion, territory, climate, culture, race, heritage, etc.) and you can imagine that we might ultimately develop variance in culture once again.

"Oh the horror!" The midwits might say. *"How will I live without a Starbucks on every corner, or without a McDonalds in Bali or that Burger King in Venice, Italy?!"*

My answer would be: ***"You can finally live authentically."***

As these more economically and territorially localized regions emerge, they will begin to find their own culture, their own style, their own flavor, and ultimately become stewards of their own destiny. What a colorful and truly diverse world *that* would be. And how much better than the gray goo of multiculturalism being forced down everyone's throats today!

In fact, this is not only more compelling, but also anthropologically sound. Robert Ardrey is a bit like the "Mises" of anthropology. In his book *The Territorial Imperative*, he argues that **territory** is at the root of cooperative species' biological drives, even more so than sex. He outlines how territorial species of all kinds develop "in-groups" and "out-groups" via instinctual territorial lines that delineate who is part of the group and who's not, or what is one's property and what is not. Humans do this in very sophisticated ways (property rights, walls, homes with doors and locks, cryptography, online communities, you name it). Every other species does it via more basic, biological methods.

Relevant to culture and governance is the fact that inside the territory, there is amity, while outside there is enmity, which result is **internal homogeneity** and **external heterogeneity.** We call this "tribalism", and it's often framed as a negative thing - but to the contrary, beyond the nuclear family, a healthy cohesive tribe is the most important unit for a strong and cohesive community and culture. Tribes are of course prone to come into conflict with one another, but as we established in the prior chapters, this is not necessarily a bad thing. Competition and conflict are necessary for growth. Iron sharpens iron, and so too does the marketplace.

I should also clarify that the existence of mature cultures, differentiated from another and therefore more diverse, does not imply some fantasy utopia where we 'transcend' conflict, competition or even warfare. That's childish thinking. If anything, we will likely have more frequent conflict in this kind of world, perhaps even more micro-warfare, and certainly more competition - all of which are *good things.* They keep the human race sharp. If we must struggle (and remember that struggle is essential to growth and life) then we should aim to have a better quality of struggle! Not the hopeless, dystopian, big-brother-like struggle. Let's actually **compete.** Culture on culture. Method against method. Warriors against warriors. Business against business. Athlete against athlete. School against school. Even warrior cultures against commercial ones, or in alliance with commercial cultures toward a common end. Greatness lies ahead if we grasp it. But we must cut the chains of fiat to reach it.

I believe Bitcoin will help transform culture for the better and force better governance. By standardizing and bounding the money, it changes the economic calculus for expansion, and increases the difficulty of artificially maintaining large scale monocultures. It makes room for a rich mosaic of smaller cultures, each of which can develop greater depth. This kind of environment may well foster the rise of new warrior cultures, or even the integration of the warrior ethos into different cultures around the world.

Wealth

"To love money is to know and love the fact that money is the creation of the best power within you - a passkey to trade your effort for the effort of the best among men."

Ayn Rand, Atlas Shrugged

There are two things to deal with in relation to Bitcoin and wealth. One is the general problem of "corruption by wealth" with which we opened the prior wealth chapter. The other is the large variance in holdings among Bitcoiners, to which I also briefly alluded a few pages back. Let us now explore this further, before we move onto the more important question of material corruption.

On a Bitcoin standard, we'll have large variations in wealth, similar to what we've always had. There are people who today stack satoshis at the same rate as Michael Saylor stacks full bitcoin. And in the future, people will work an entire week for a paycheck in sats, equivalent to what someone today has purchased for the price of a McDonald's happy meal.

You might think this "unfair" and yes, in some ways you might be right. It's also unfair that some people are born prematurely, some with a low IQ, some on a bad day, some in a certain era, some to bad parents, some five minutes before a bomb drops in Yemen, some in the slums of Africa, some to a central banker, and some to the richest man in the world (some of whom still want to commit suicide or disfigure their body). Remember: we cannot equalize things - we can only build better, fairer frameworks.

Bitcoin is such a framework, but we don't just go from where we are to a Bitcoin standard overnight. Who hears about it, when they hear about it, and what they do with it, has little to do with Bitcoin itself, and almost everything to do with the person and the environment in which Bitcoin is emerging. Therefore, it's what we all **do** with Bitcoin that ultimately counts. Finding a way to access it, taking the time to study it, and accepting the risk to buy and hold it will be a matter of luck, effort, will, time, energy, and desire. It is the same with all such paradigm shifts.

If you have a bone to pick, do so with the current system. It has far greater levels of wealth disparity than a Bitcoin standard ever will. There are central bankers who make in an hour what some people make in a lifetime, not because they're adding any value to society, but because they are closer to the monetary spigot. And worse, they can do so not just without adding value, but by actually *destroying* value, destroying lives, and destroying society!

That is truly unfair. When you can rig the game and continue to pay yourself at the expense of the other players in the game, you can't lose! You do not need real customers because the state apparatus can extract money from people through inflation or taxation and hand it to you. You don't really need to fight to win, because you win by decree. **By fiat.**

Ultimately, this game ends, because everyone gets poorer. The match-fixer keeps squandering his stolen wealth, because why not? There's more where that came from. Everyone else just gets robbed, and in the process loses the will to keep producing, or worse, chooses to partner with the match-fixer and distort the game even further, accelerating its demise.

That's where we are right now; and I can't think of a worse situation for humanity to be facing, economically or psychologically. It's no wonder the world is going to hell in a handbasket.

So while there will be a disparity in wealth on a Bitcoin standard, in time, the distribution will more closely and accurately reflect the very real differences across the populace. This is about as authentically fair as we'll ever get - and a hell of a lot fairer and just than what we have now. With that settled, let's now look at Bitcoin and corruption by wealth.

First of all, I don't believe this can ever be entirely "solved" because it's a cycle, and, as we discussed, cycles are forever. That being said, I do believe Bitcoin can have a positive impact because it can help manage or dampen corruption via **the threat of real, irretrievable loss.** What do I mean?

It's like the difference between real life and a video game. Lost or spent bitcoin cannot be reprinted. Corruption is cheap today because it's easy to hide with fake money. But when things have a real cost or, at the very least, are more accurately priced, corruption can become very expensive. When nobody can play "banker", and when indirect theft (traditionally the winning strategy) is made next to impossible, winning requires a new strategy. This leaves three main options: (1) direct theft - which comes with a host of dangers of its own; (2) cooperation; (3) competition. The latter two are the most practical for mature people, tribes and societies.

Sound money helps increase the proximity of consequence and action. In the absence of a means of replenishing your wealth through some obfuscated form of confiscation, one is less inclined to risk and squander it so easily, or gamble it away on fanciful ideas. Think of it this way: **if politicians had to pay for their welfare programs personally, you can be sure they wouldn't be campaigning for them.** When bad decisions actually cost you directly, you either adapt and make better decisions, or you are made obsolete, thus rendering your decisions and actions irrelevant in the future. Either way, problem solved.

The descent into the "weak men create bad times" stage of the cycle is accelerated by weak men getting access to the money printer, or the state apparatus, and **then** the money printer. In fact, it takes a weak man to conjure up the idea of a money printer in the first place, and the same archetype to want to continue it because they're too small to compete without a handicap. But no matter how many times society collapses due to the destruction of money before we return to a sound money standard, the cycle keeps repeating. The obvious question therefore is, how can I be so sure that Bitcoin is different, when all prior attempts have failed?

Well, at the risk of sounding like your average midwit: *this time it actually is different.* Bitcoin isn't about "going back". It's a zero-to-one techno-socio-economic breakthrough. It's not a physical object like gold, that requires storage and abstraction to scale. It's more like a decentralized digital constitution whose participants actually make up the network. It's a completely novel approach to money that results in something with an immutable set of promises. It uses human behavior, energy cost, and probabilities to ensure that nobody can change it. The incentives are finely tuned and balanced. It's not perfect (perfection doesn't exist), but it's by far the best shot we have at creating an incorruptible form of money, and it has critical economic mass (worth over $1T) - which is a key factor in succeeding.

What's stopping people from building their own versions and printing their own money? Creating your own money is clearly very lucrative. Well, not a lot these days. The average developer with a laptop can spin up a shitcoin and people buy it. It's happened 25,000 times already. But, like all frauds and scams, reality prevails in the end. Narratives built on lies are fragile: they can give the illusion of winning for a while but, in time, they shatter. Bitcoin is becoming an economic *mean*, and every deviation that occurs ultimately collapses back on itself. These corrections become economic lessons that our anthropic consciousness learns from. The weak are washed out, the strong consolidate, and the process repeats.

"But it can't be that easy!" I can almost hear you saying through the page. So hear me in return: I never said it was going to be *easy*. But just like losing weight, it *is that* simple. Stop eating so much, and you'll drop the pounds. Stop printing fake money and the economy will be less fake and corrupt. Rinse, repeat, and in time, the strong and productive rise to the top.

In the end, one of the most effective ways of dealing with the moral decay hastened by the allure of material wealth and corruption is with an incorruptible economic framework, like Bitcoin. The cycles will continue, the allure of easy money and corruption will always be there. All we can really do is build better economic structures that help us point things in the right direction.

Which brings me to my final point.

Cycles and games

Ignorance is not a winning strategy for life, and this certainly applies to the cycles of life. Anyone who thinks they can arbitrarily decree their elimination only creates a false continuity that has disastrous consequences when the veneer of stability shatters. The result is a correction that overshoots, well past the mean.

So, if cycles are inescapable, what can we do - especially when it comes to the destructive and ugly stage of the cycle? Is there a more holistic or mature approach? I think there is, and it revolves around building better structures. In a social sense, this means better, more antifragile cultures, and therefore stronger and more resilient people. In an economic sense, a mechanism to minimize fraud, theft, and corruption.

Let's 'build' on this structure metaphor. We build structures, like a house, to help us weather the elements: storms and, in particular, the bad seasons. If we know that winter is coming, we want to make sure we build it in such a way that we don't all freeze to death. If we know that earthquakes or hurricanes are frequent, then we must build accordingly. You see this reflected in architecture and building styles all around the world. When survivability is the name of the game, strong, antifragile structures with enough insulation are required. Not strictly rigid ones, made of glass, for example. A structure with a high degree of survivability must be both framed and adaptable.

To understand this fully, let's take a look at the games we play. What we call "society" and "civilisation" are simply a series of games played at a macro level, characterized by a whole array of roles, rules, and goals. Economics represents the resource allocation aspect of this game, while philosophy dictates our approach or the methodology of our play; culture is the style, and politics forms the decision-making structure governing power dynamics. Participants, acting as economic players, strategize to amass resources and control territory, with wealth serving as the scorecard. Competition, education and negotiation mirror strategic gameplay as players vie for advantages in political power, wealth and cultural influence.

The best games also have meta-goals, beyond just winning on the economic scoreboard. For example: to become a better person, to reach farther, to see the yet unseen, to find meaning, to leave a legacy, to create beauty, and to procreate life. Unfortunately, many of these have been forgotten as we've skewed so far toward the purely material. In fact, ignoring these meta-goals has led us to nihilism and despair. We no longer care "why" we're playing - all we are interested in is the tangible or visible points on the scoreboard, and we'll sell our souls for those points. This is obviously unhealthy for both the players and the games they play.

In all societies, there are different primary categories of players that vary based on the era, the period, the culture, and other factors. The modern world, the one we're living in right now, has four primary archetypes of players which I'd like to explore, to illustrate the point.

Player type one is the "state" and includes central bankers, politicians, big-tech/pharma/chem and anyone tied to or associated with the money printer. This player wins, no matter what they do or how they play. They're the banker in Monopoly, or some magical leprechaun who wins each round in poker, irrespective of the hand they play. This is the category most coveted by those who are hungry to win at all costs, whether that means lying, cheating or stealing, and is often characterized by those who lack the honor or integrity to win a game because they are actually better. You might call them the elite. I call them the parasitic elite, because they suck the life out of the game.

The second category of player is similar in their hunger or desire to win, and are cunning enough to understand the game, but are actually competent at their craft and can produce things. They might not end up with the finger directly on the money printer button, but they know how to make friends with those in the first category. They know how to partner with them, and oftentimes use them. The parasitic elite craves friends (because he doesn't have any), and he knows he needs to build alliances with men of true power and competence. If he's pragmatic enough, he will also acknowledge that he can't be the only one that wins, lest the game end too soon; so, he offers incentives (both implicit and explicit) for players to orient themselves around him. Second category players are the ones who get these offers, and some (not all), take them. Think of the poker game analogy again: now the best, most skillful players, instead of playing a good poker game, simply play a good "make friends with the leprechaun" game. This category of player may be found in Wall Street, Silicon Valley and other major financial centers.

We're left with two more categories. The third is the hard working player. This is the middle class and includes workers, craftsmen, artisans, most entrepreneurs, single- and even double-digit millionaires, and generally people who actually play because they want to become better, sensing that there is a deeper meaning to the game of life. This category of player keeps the game going. So long as they exist, and continue to believe in the game, the others can play. To a large extent, this is where most people are, and in a healthy society this 'middle class' is large and stable. But in a rigged game, this category becomes less of a place you remain and more of a transition point to either category two or four. In fact, the faster this third category erodes, the faster the game ends. *Hyperinflation happens when they give up.* People realize that they're carrying all the weight and, as they start to burn out, they decide either *"screw this, I'm going to join category two and get my share"*, or they opt for...

The fourth category is the end of the road. The nihilist, the hedonist, the forfeit, the dropout. Why play if the game is rigged? It's easier to just give up! There's many gradations to this category, from the homeless, to the welfare recipient, to the hippie, to the perpetual philosophy student, to the doomer or the basement-dwelling 40-year-old teenager. These people either lack the gumption, talent, skill, or luck to jump to category two, or they are deeply intuitive and feel how rigged it all is, so they throw in the towel and just drop out of the game altogether. Many more of course are born into category four, and taught to believe victimhood is moral. As such, like crabs in a bucket, they bring down anybody who tries to rise up from there, and because they are in proximity only to category three players, they try to bring them down too.

As the fake-game begins to break and the numbers on the scoreboard accrue to very few (especially those who clearly cheated), the third category dissolves. The second category, often composed of those more intelligent, may create new things to numb or distract the fallen (social media, VR, entertainment), while category one begins to loot the game for everything they can, while they still can. Because we ignored the more important meta-goals, the game has become meaningless. We are empty and nihilistic. Instead of playing the deeper and more functional game, we end up with a fake state of play and four categories of players that soon become just two. Category one and four become a pincer that crushes category 3, corrupts category 2, and ultimately leaves two remaining players: ultra-rich and slave-poors.

How does Bitcoin fix this? *Does* Bitcoin fix this? And what does it all have to do with structures and cycles? Two things: one, the game or rules of the game are a form of structure; two: the game itself goes through seasons or cycles.

First of all, Bitcoin as sound, incorruptible money helps by making the first category of player obsolete, or changes the very nature of category one into something more akin to a monarch with skin in the game. This in turn completely changes the economic calculus for category two players. Category three becomes less psychologically burdensome and more sustainable and category four, while likely to continue to exist, would (should?) become less enticing because the other styles of gameplay become more compelling and their rewards more achievable. Let's explore each (white pill alert).

Category one, option one: this player and their position is made obsolete. The parasites who otherwise would've been printing money or conjuring up ways to win by cheating will either be starved of oxygen and cease to exist, or if they do survive, will find new ways to scam, lie, cheat, and steal, but be forced to do so in smaller or more local dimensions; that way, they inevitably (a) do less damage, and (b) are more likely to answer for their behavior. *"Try that in a small town."*

Category one, option two: the nature of this player and this role completely transforms. It becomes some sort of CEO-King-Ubermensch that leads his nation, people and territory like an Alexander the Great-meets-Elon Musk. There is great power, but also great responsibility, and most important of all: skin in the game. Either outcome is superior to what we have today, and I would bet that we'll have a mixture of both. **The key is to eliminate the money printer.**

Next, the category two player: the entrepreneur, the mega-artist, the ruthless general, the hyper competitive, cunning, and adept players who were making friends with the leprechauns before, will now compete, produce, and create. The calculus for winning will no longer have anything to do with proximity to the monetary spigot, but to the efficacy of their "meta". Sure, there will be some bad eggs, most likely the psychopaths, but I would guess that this new kind of playing field will be good for the souls of such players because, like the greatest ancient warriors, they will have a worthy foe to compete against. They will get to play for excellence, glory and power. In such an environment, one could imagine a new elite that will either become the *new* category one player, or become the noble class around the CEO-King that keeps him accountable.

The most erudite of these category two players will recognise they need help from the middle class to gain alpha, so they might seek to inspire or lead them, knowing that more and better talent means more and better products, services, customers and power. You could imagine an upward spiral in such an environment. Category three players who may have previously been teetering on the edge of nihilism, hedonism, or hopelessness, may be more inclined to continue playing because there is actually a real chance of winning their micro games. *The situation is no longer hopeless.* In fact, knowing that you can win just might inspire more of these players to reach for the new elite categories, because they won't feel like they're selling out. What was once a burdensome and often hopeless category three could slowly become a broader, larger and more populous category where winners progress, losers receive feedback, and the game itself gets more interesting, useful, and worthwhile to play.

Finally, the bottom category. It's not something you can eliminate, in the same way as you can never eliminate evil, darkness, sadness, ugliness or depression. They will always exist, but if the other options are viable and compelling giving up might slowly lose its appeal. If the first step to climbing up out of the valley of despair is not as hard as it once was, some might choose to climb. And for those that stay, perhaps instead of being in a state of complete destructive nihilism, it becomes something else, like a place of rest, or a more innocent or innocuous kind of state.

This sort of structural change is a big deal and is, in my opinion, at the core of why Bitcoin helps with the seasons and cycles. Bitcoin helps create an economic environment, and therefore a socio-political one, in which weak men can do less damage! It's like building a shelter with a new material, so that when the winter comes around, as it inevitably will, we're warm and insulated, with well-stocked stores and won't freeze or starve to death if any idiots who have come of age decide to run amok and play with fire.

With Bitcoin, we have gone from a social structure made solely of twigs and thatch to one that incorporates wood, steel, concrete, glass, and other materials for structural integrity, strength, aesthetics, insulation, and connection to nature. It can protect us from the elements, shelter us from storms, keep us grounded and elevate us with its beauty, and - despite the inevitable damage done to the structure from the internal and external seasons - it can remain intact for the next generation of strong men to come of age. Even if the damage done by the weaklings and idiots is severe, the structure can endure. Instead of needing to rebuild again from scratch, the new generation of strong men can make the necessary repairs and build onwards to new heights.

This is how a Bitcoin standard may at the very least dampen the weak men/bad times part of the cycle, and allow humanity to better *conserve and compound* its progress. This is the key to real civilisational progress.

In closing

Finally, to bring this all back to Spengler: the goal is to grow old and wise, gracefully. When a civilization has passed its peak, it will continue to age until it dies, and something new will be born. Whether this death comes as a result of natural causes or from stupidity is the important factor. With Bitcoin we might extend the natural lifespan of a civilization, because its destruction does not occur every few centuries thanks to debauching the money. This civilizational life-extension may be what's necessary for us to reach for the stars, and at the risk of sounding even more hyperbolic, might be the key to seeding new civilisations across the galaxy. Compounding growth is the only way to get there, and time is the key factor in that equation.

Whatever the ultimate end, Bitcoin establishes a framework for a robust game with fair rules and more than just material goals, but access to higher meta-goals. I also view it as a resilient structure that can dampen the effects of bad seasons and down cycles, whether they are self-inflicted or the cause of bad luck and poor timing. Furthermore, by putting power back where it belongs (into the hands of those with skin in the game), it acts as a bulwark against democracy and equalitarianism - institutions and ideologies that have wrought nothing but destruction and poverty worldwide, particularly in places such as Rhodesia that were once the breadbasket of a continent. In the end, Bitcoin should lead to **better games, stronger structures, stronger people and less equality.** All net positives.

With that in mind, I'd like to finish this section with a call to *action*. Talking about virtue and morality is one thing, practicing them is another. Most people, including so-called Christians, Conservatives, Moralists, Libertarians, and Bitcoiners talk a big game online about what they believe, but are in reality as Netflix-obsessed, social media-addicted, antidepressant-addled and sludge-consuming as those they claim to oppose. There is little practical difference among them and the mid-wits they laugh at from their screens and keyboards.

The only valid expression of virtue is a practice or *"praxis." If you are just proclaiming your belief in something, and doing nothing in the form of a practice or discipline toward its attainment, then you are just LARPing.*

Everything I have discussed about culture, greatness and wealth thus far hinges on the fact that while Bitcoin's presence helps with the incentives and establishes a better framework, *the onus remains on the individual to **act.***

In order to win, grow, evolve, adapt or improve - whatever the game - you must act. That will never change, and you cannot shirk this responsibility. Thus my challenge to you is that you take what you will from this book, and then go do something about it!

Don't just read the words here. *Practice.*

PART IV

Praxis

Praxis

"Knowing is not enough, we must apply. Willing is not enough, we must do."

Bruce Lee, Tao of Jeet Kune Do

Knowing about the virtues discussed in Section 3 is one thing. It's a bit like having a map - a good first step but only meaningful if you're going to use it. Adopting these virtues is the next step, and can only come about through action and practice. If knowing them is the map, then developing them is like taking the journey itself. This is where true character is built.

"The first point to observe in knightly pedagogics was to build up character, leaving in the shade the subtler faculties of prudence, intelligence and dialectics."

Inazo Nitobe, Bushido: The Soul of Japan

Samurai and knights were men of character because they were first and foremost, men of action. Yes, some were also scholars, artists, lords, fathers, priests, and poets, but that all came second to their identity as men of war and action. Their morality was fundamentally expressed through what they *did* and not only by what they *said*.

In this chapter we will look at the role action, territory, training and rites of passage played in both classical and warrior cultures, then explore how these can inspire the training and development of a new elite class for a world on a new socio-economic standard. The future is what we make it. We may no longer be riding around on horses with swords at our hilts, but there are certainly new weapons to wield, and new territories to conquer. We need to carry this energy forward, along with the new tools at our disposal.

A Man of Action

"Think like a man of action, act like a man of thought."

Henri Bergson, Speech at Descartes Conference 1937

To understand Bushido meant to **act** in the way of Bushido. The virtues characterized the *behavior* and informed the actions of a Samurai who considered himself a *bushi*: a man of war. Recall that Bushido was an unwritten code, not some list of commandments drawn up on parchment and taught at an academy. It was a way of being, and could only be expressed in deeds. Thinking or reading about it was not enough.

"People whose minds were simply stored with information found no great admirers. Of the three services of studies that Bacon gives—for delight, ornament, and ability—Bushido had decided preference for the last."

Inazo Nitobe, Bushido: The Soul of Japan

Simple "book-knowledge" was insufficient to be considered a true Samurai or *bushi*. Wisdom and action were considered deeply entwined. Knowledge alone was at best an accessory. Comprehension is only the first step on the path. To truly understand is to act. Mastery occurs when the knowledge is in your body.

> *"The tripod which supported the framework of Bushido was said to be Chi, Jin, Yu, respectively, Wisdom, Benevolence, and Courage. A Samurai was essentially a man of action. [T]he word Chi, which was employed to denote intellectuality, meant wisdom in the first instance and gave knowledge only a very subordinate place."*

> *Inazo Nitobe, Bushido: The Soul of Japan*

This concept is more relevant in the modern age, as we drown in ever expanding oceans of information. Knowledge has become a cheap commodity, so much so that it is just noise. In fact, so too has the dissemination and synthesis of this knowledge. The rise of generative AI and tools like ChatGPT only serve to exacerbate the problem. It's now not only insufficient to be able to read a book, but also trivial to summarize it. Never has there been less value tied to mere knowledge or the ability to just intellectually grasp it. The classic teacher archetype who 'talks' but does not 'do' is in trouble, and even more so the midwit content creator who talks a lot but says very little, and does even less. These new tools will separate the doers from the talkers, so much so that only one's ability to act congruently will set one apart from the bots.

The Nietzschean Ubermensch is the man of action: the one who separates himself from the mediocrity of the average; the one who bends the universe to *his* will. In an environment of pure potential, he stands head and shoulders above the rest by being *kinetic*. By transforming potential knowledge into real action.

Such a man will hone his body and mind to be ready for any challenge that may arise, and do so in a way that they are one. This is why training is so important. Training is philosophy in action. The very word *"philo-sophia"* means the "love of wisdom," and before it was formalized as a distinct discipline in the ancient world, it was an action-oriented ideal. It was a 'learning by doing' and a 'gaining of wisdom' in the act of living - a very different concept to the modern, overly cerebral definition of Philosophy.

"To the ancient Greeks, philosophy embodied more than the pursuit of truth. It represented a way of life, a continuous journey towards self-discovery and personal growth. It was about the dynamic process of being and constantly becoming. The Greeks did not perceive philosophy as an abstract intellectual exercise, as it is commonly viewed in contemporary times. Instead, it was a way of being and becoming, influencing their actions, decisions, and the very course of life."

Chad Crowley on X.com

All great warrior cultures mirrored this. In feudal Japan, a Samurai's training consisted mainly of fencing, archery, jiu jitsu, horsemanship, the use of the spear and the sword, and tactics. Calligraphy, ethics, literature, history, and good writing were of concern insofar as they helped to **sharpen action.**

"Literature was pursued mainly as a pastime, and philosophy as a practical aid in the formation of character, if not for the exposition of some military or political problem. Religion and theology were relegated to the priests."

Inazo Nitobe, Bushido: The Soul of Japan

This is precisely my point for leaders of the future. The words on these pages should inspire you to **action** - not just to pick up another book. The mind and the body are inseparable. Physiognomy, physio-psychology, body language, mobility, action, character - they are all woven together, and they apply to women just as much as they do to men.

Modernity seeks to transform you into a brain in a vat, in part conspiratorially, and in part through its perpetual pursuit of ease. The result is that you succumb to comfort and are mastered by technology. True mastery lies in the realm beyond comfort, and requires you transcend technology, by becoming the protagonist of the story. You must use it, not the other way around. You are either the producer or the *product*. You are either master of your domain, or you are slave to circumstance. You either establish your own territory, or you are a guest (or a captive) in somebody else's.

Territory is fundamental: it's at the heart of evolution. And life, at its most basic level, is the struggle for ownership of space. From the primordial goo that gave rise to the earliest life-forms, through to the modern civilizations that sprawl across the globe - the essence of life has and always will be an impulse to claim, cultivate, and conquer territory - and we humans are its prime vessels.

This deep-seated instinct extends beyond land ownership or the desire to control resources. It is the *pothos* that drove Alexander to conquer the known world and to reach its end, and compelled Magellan to circumnavigate the Earth on a ship made of wood and cloth. It is a yearning to claim **space**, and, by extension, claim our destiny. Our destiny is a *destination*, or a *place*, or a **territory.**

Territory is not just physical, it is also metaphysical: it includes the body, the mind, and the spirit. It is psychological and emotional, starting with you and radiating outward. Your family is your territory. So is your business, your reputation, your land and your community. As a man, your wife and kids are *your* property, in the deepest sense of the term: it is your job to protect and provide for them. As a chieftain, captain, CEO or a leader of any kind, your tribe, crew and team are under your dominion and therefore protection: it is your job to lead and guide them.

The size of your territory is proportional to the quantity of life force that you can harness and channel. **This** is the true definition of *will to power*. And this is why your capacity to be dangerous is fundamental to your existence. *Your* territory is that which *you* can defend. All else is borrowed. Your territory is the terrain you can act on at will. This is why the man of action is king. Action separates the master from the apprentice and the autonomous from the automaton. The master knows the body is where action originates and thus where real mastery manifests. How to harness and command this, how to do, how to be and how to **act** are the subjects of the following chapters.

Training

The body must be trained: the mind is nothing without it. The separation of mind and body is a deeply erroneous construct. The mind evolved with the body - it didn't just appear one day, making the flesh suddenly animate and sentient. There is no mind without body, and there is no body without the mind; they are inseparable. Do not fall for these brain-in-a-vat fantasies from transhumanist nerds who lack physical vitality. They seek to bring everyone down to their level because they're too weak to raise themselves up.

The human mind evolved as an extension of the human hand - an appendage with such utility, dexterity and complexity that Spengler called it a "weapon unparalleled" in the history of *life* itself. The hand changed our relationship to the world around us, and in so doing altered our entire physiology. We became the apex predator because we stood tall on two legs, our eyes looked ahead, triangulating distances to home in on a target while our hands could create in reality that which we envisioned in our mind. No other organic appendage in the animal kingdom was or is able to create tools that enhance its own capabilities to control and manipulate *space*.

Combined with forward-facing eyes, we have the ultimate predatorial combination. The human eye observes, while the hand acts; the eye seeks out cause and effect, while the hand deals with means and ends. I'm not sure there is a deeper set of psycho-physiological truths than these.

This is why training is imperative, and all training must be action-oriented. Reading is a good place to start, but nobody won a race, conquered a territory or built a business by simply reading words on a page. *Action* was ultimately required.

"Words change nothing. They are at best signs of change."

Ernst Jünger, On Pain

Physio-psychology

"There is more wisdom in your body than in your deepest philosophy."

Friedrich Nietzsche, Thus Spoke Zarathustra

"Mind over matter" is bullshit. I don't care how much you "think" you can lift, it's only when you get under the barbell that you'll discover the truth. That's not to say that the mind doesn't count. It will help get you there, and might help push you that final couple of percent, but it's the body that does the work. The truth is you cannot separate mind from body, and true intelligence is both mental and physical. They reinforce each other. It's more like *body and mind over space and stuff* - although that doesn't roll off the tongue as well.

Nietzsche uses the term physio-psychology to describe this body-intelligence, and builds a large part of his philosophy on the following foundations: the mind and the body evolved together, there is no separation between them, and one cannot live without the other. This echoes Spengler's position on the human hand heavily influencing the development of the human mind.

The key take-away is that you are an *embodied* being, consisting of more than just eyeballs, fingertips, genitals and some gray matter trapped inside of a skull. While a disembodied brain in a vat may be Yuval Harari's erotic fantasy, it is thankfully not yet a description of reality, nor is it either viable or desirable.

Your thoughts and actions involve every part of your being. You literally **think** with the entirety of your body - not just with your mind. Your muscles, organs, brain, central nervous system, and the blood flowing through your veins are all involved, whether you are a scientist, athlete, artist, poet, or philosopher - your collective faculties come together in order to understand and create. This extends then beyond the physical and into the spiritual. The mind, body and spirit are all intertwined and work together to create a unified whole.

> *"A flabby body will produce flabby thought; weak arms will produce weak rhetoric. This is not mere analogy, it is biology. The entire tenor of your thinking is a complex product of hormonal cascades. Adipose tissue is estrogenic, it makes you think like a eunuch. Testosterone insufficiency will inflect your manner of thought, the topics you direct your attention to, the way you approach them, the conclusions you draw. You think that you are thinking with your brain, but in truth you are thinking with your belly-rolls; your brain is merely there to rationalize what your abdominal padding has already decided upon."*

> John Carter, Postcards from Barsoom: Just Fucking Lift Bro

"Virtual Man" is not progress. He is a dead end. Separating out the mind and placing it in a jar to somehow 'transcend' meatspace is nonsense. The marketing departments run by bugmen and bureaucrats seek to make you weak: they want to bring you down to their level so they develop convoluted ideas of singularities and trillion-dollar AGI tinmen, while spotlighting emaciated keyboard warriors in Time Magazine so that your mental imagery of success becomes a Sam Bankman-Fried, Sam Harris, or Vitalik Buterin.

They want you to think that the body doesn't matter, so they'll never tell you that Plato was a champion wrestler whose name actually means "broad-shouldered". They will ignore the fact that Miyamoto Musashi was a warrior first, and a philosopher second. They will call Saints like St. George 'myths' and pretend they did not achieve incredible physical feats in the defense of truth and God. They will call Alexander a 'brute,' a murderer, or a homosexual, while ignoring the fact that he was Aristotle's greatest student. They will forget that Thucydides was a general as well as a scholar, who 2500 years ago famously said that:

> "The Nation that makes a great distinction between its scholars and its warriors will have its thinking done by cowards and its fighting done by fools."

Perhaps these ridiculous ideas initially came from a place of naivete, because ease and comfort are sought-after when a society becomes wealthy and comfortable - but the false advertising has turned nefarious, and it's time you woke up and peered through the veil.

> "A well-built physique is a status symbol. It reflects you worked hard for it; no money can buy it. You cannot borrow it, you cannot inherit it, you cannot steal it. You cannot hold onto it without constant work. It shows discipline, it shows self-respect, it shows patience, work ethic, and passion. That is why I do what I do."
>
> Arnold Schwarzenegger, The New Encyclopedia of Modern Bodybuilding

A well-developed body and mastery of a movement is not just 'aesthetic'. It's a clearly visible symbol of status that money *cannot* buy. It puts on display virtues such as patience, courage, discipline, excellence, determination, respect, and devotion. It is "proof of work", and shows that the spirit of the individual that constructed that body and mastered the movement, is one that can make necessary sacrifices. It shows you can not only think, but feel and **do**.

> "To see is to be deceived, to hear is to be lied to, but to feel, is to believe."
>
> Bruce Lee

The bugmen and globalists are and have always been most afraid of a virile and vital populace. This is why they sought to trap us indoors for an indefinite two weeks: to weaken our spirits while they emaciated our minds and bodies with electronic comforts and seed oils. They know that the weak of body are weak of spirit, and easily ruled: it's not rocket science. But they failed, because some of us are just too stubborn. Bro-science and bro-psychology remain undefeated.

Anyone who has studied and observed body language or physiognomy intuitively understands this. Masters of their craft, like Tony Robbins and Derren Brown, are modern exemplars who have put this to use. Neuro-Linguistic Programming (NLP) studies the language of the mind and, unsurprisingly, one of its core principles tells us that more than half of all communication is non-verbal, body language. Whether these percentages are exact is beside the point. It's intuitively accurate and people know that while the mouth can lie, the body tells all. Even the tonality we use carries many times the weight of the words it comes with.

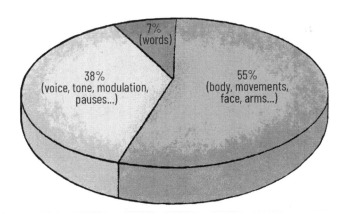

There are multiple layers of truth to this. For example, your physical level of fitness is a better indicator of your beliefs on health and fitness than what you say. If you're fat and sick, your opinion on health and wellness can be immediately discounted. There are also much deeper truths to this with respect to facial structure, posture, mannerisms, and the look in someone's eye. This is the bro-science of Physiognomy, about which Shopenhauer had a thing or two to say:

> *"There are some people whose faces bear the stamp of such artless vulgarity and baseness of character, such an animal limitation of intelligence, that one wonders how they can appear in public with such a countenance, instead of wearing a mask. There are faces, indeed, the very sight of which produces a feeling of pollution."*

People don't like to talk about physiognomy or weight because they're hard to hide and point to deeper truths. They prefer to talk about things they can easily wriggle out of, like spirituality, politics, or the news. And when you do bring up either, the guilty will hide behind meaningless tropes like "don't judge a book by its cover" (ignoring the fact that book covers influence buying behavior). Truth is brutal at times, but it exists to correct us.

> *"Manhood coerced into sensitivity is no manhood at all."*

> Camille Paglia, Sex, Art and American Culture: New Essays

Finally, none of what I'm saying implies that you ignore the development of your mental faculties or that you become a dumb brute. There are endeavors more cerebral in nature that require you to use your brain and to think. This is inescapable. But I am telling you that a strong body is critical, especially if you want to build and maintain a strong mind. Case in point, Steve Jobs was the greatest entrepreneur who ever lived. What more could he have done, had he taken a different path in how he treated his body? Had he better understood that the body needs more than just plants, or that movement and a strong frame are necessary for a vital disposition, might he have done more? We will never know. The point being: **do not ignore the body.** It is as much a part of the mind as the brain is. Work on it, develop it, grow it, strengthen it. *Become dangerous.* It will make your mind and spirit powerful.

Mastery

> *"Thinkers think & doers do. But until the thinkers do & the doers think, progress will be just another word in the already overburdened vocabulary by sense."*

> Francois de La Rochefoucauld, Reflections: or Sentences and Moral Maxims

Earlier in the book I said that mastery, in its essence, is a state of profound proficiency and authority in a particular field, marked by a lifelong discipline and the embodiment of duty, excellence, and respect. I defined it as "authority in the purest sense", and related it to competence and hierarchy. Here I'd like to build on this and the prior chapter, by giving you a physio-psychological framework for understanding how to develop mastery.

First of all, understand that true *mastery* is **physical**. It resides in the body. Understanding something intellectually is one thing, but knowing it viscerally is something entirely different.

Mastery is when action becomes instinct. A panther moving gracefully is intelligence of the deepest kind on display. No words, written or spoken, are necessary. Only pure instinct and action. It's one of the most beautiful things to witness.

Humans have both an advantage and disadvantage here. The power of our minds creates a separation from the body that can move us away from our instincts, making us clumsy and weak; but, if we direct the mind and unify it with the body, we can, through dedication and practice, achieve a level of mastery and accomplish things no other species can. We've built civilization on the basis of this capacity.

With that in mind, let's look at the four stages of attaining and achieving mastery.

Stage 1: You begin with unconscious incompetence (you don't know what you don't know),

Stage 2: You develop conscious incompetence (awareness of your shortcomings),

Stage 3: You move into conscious competence (you can, but must concentrate to execute)

Stage 4: You reach unconscious competence (you don't think, you just do). In other words, it's in your body, and you've achieved mastery.

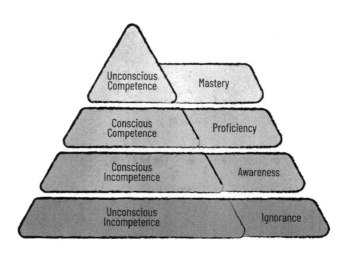

Few people ever reach the final stage, and this is why it's both so rare and valuable. Mastery is qualitative, not quantitative: it takes sacrifice, effort, and focus. Deep, deliberate practice over time literally enhances the fatty tissue in your brain that surrounds the neurons firing during your praxis. This intentional process physically embeds it deeper into your body and being.

This is the power of merging mind and body. When the act becomes second nature, or instinct; when you transcend doing, and actually start *being*.

Such mastery and instinct will set future leaders apart from the rest. The bravest of men, the progenitors of 'action', will be like lions among sheep. They will act, not only speak. They will have the capacity for war, and the self-control to direct it. They will understand the true meaning of freedom because they have the strength to carry the necessary responsibility. These will be the new "Masters" of the world, because they are in charge of their own destiny.

Pain

Pain and adversity are not villains, but compatriots on the journey of self-discovery. Jünger defined discipline as a "constant and voluntary contact with pain." Whether the goal is strength, endurance, courage, or self control, instead of trying to minimize pain all the time, we might seek instead to gradually increase how much pain we can bear. The goal being not an escape from pain, but a transcendence or integration of it.

> *"In our sensitive world, we try to marginalize pain and shelter life from it. In a heroic age though, the approach to pain is completely different. In a heroic age, "the point is to integrate pain and organize life in such a way that one is always armed against it."*
>
> Ernst Jünger, On Pain

This integration of pain into life, particularly as a marker of a heroic age, is a powerful point. It's reminiscent of the 'hard times build strong men' stage of the cycle. Jünger writes: *"Tell me your relation to pain, and I will tell you who you are!"* Pain, and his relationship to it, reveals a man's stature. It's a proxy for endurance, tenacity, courage, and self-control. "How much can you endure" is another way of asking: How strong are you?

Your character can also be measured through pain, because during such an experience, social pretenses slip away and what's left is what Jünger called *"man's innermost being."* Another way of saying "what's true."

So this begs the question: Have we lost touch with this truth in our technologically advanced age? Technology and material affluence are means by which we remove pain from life - an admirable pursuit - but it does have side effects, especially when we forget the greater role of technology: which is the extension of the Will to Power and the capacity to act. Over-indexing on pain removal comes with the removal of the signaling mechanisms that would otherwise cause us to act. It also removes an important scale by which we measure growth. Is there some way we can maintain the signal, while improving material conditions? Can we escape the "affluence trap"? It requires a broader view and approach. Bitcoin helps in an economic sense by localizing economic consequence, but it's not enough. We also need to train to build character and virtue. One way of doing this is learning to overcome (not escape) pain.

Our tolerance to pain improves when we lean into it. Experiencing intense agony can diminish the impact of minor pains, which positively affects your capacity to confront physical and cognitive distress. *"Pain is weakness leaving the body."* If you befriend it, it will sharpen you; if you fear it and avoid it, you will blunt yourself.

> *"A life of comfort has the opposite effect. It can decrease your capacity to withstand painful experiences, which can in turn lead to the avoidance of harsh truths and the seeking of solace in comforting lies and social conformity."*
>
> John Carter, Postcards from Barsoom, Truth Hurts

Have you not seen evidence of this lately? This is why becoming soft of body also makes you soft of mind and spirit. Your entire thought process is intricately entwined with your hormones. Excess estrogen will literally make you think like a woman or a eunuch. Your thoughts, the topics you focus on, the way you approach them, and the conclusions you come to are all affected by your hormones and your body fat percentage. You may think your brain is doing the work, but it's often your gut that's in charge. Your brain is just there to do the "logical close" on whatever your body was already sold on. Think about how this relates to the nerd's misguided attempts to develop "aggression vaccines" or to minimize testosterone in men. By changing the body, you also change the mind. They are entwined.

> *"Life has become entirely too safe, we are trapped in an eternal nursery that has become a prison, and it is corroding our very souls. Our lives in this luxuriously padded jail are largely denuded of physical peril, meaning we have few opportunities to develop physical courage."*
>
> John Carter, Postcards from Barsoom, Just Fucking Lift Bro

To turn this pathetic state of affairs around, we have to confront pain and face danger. Certainty is at the base of the hierarchy of needs for a reason. It's not something to aspire toward, but something to stand upon. Yes you need it, but it's not the goal. A life of constant safety is a prison sentence. A life of autonomy and freedom requires contending with both danger and uncertainty. Greatness is something you reach for *despite* great personal risk. By leaning into adversity and facing pain, you can rise above it.

By training physically, you grow and develop the kind of body that can carry your mind and spirit forward, and the best way to do this is alongside others who can push you, and via rituals and rites that force you to contend with pain (when necessary) and ordeals.

Rites of Passage

Q: How does one become a true leader, a warrior or Bitcoiner?
A: The same way you become a true anything: ***Time and ordeals.***

Rites of passage have existed since prehistory. They were present in tribes and cultures all over the world, irrespective of location or people, from as early as tribes themselves existed. They're yet another practice lost in the malaise of the modern materialist world - at least the conscious and intentional practice of a rite or ritual that is meant to symbolize the entry or exit from one period or paradigm into another. The world is still certainly full of rites which people perform unconsciously on a regular basis, that largely have no meaning or transcendent value. For example: participation in the public schooling system, the humiliation rituals at the airport or the four-year election cycle. Some might even have an echo of meaning: Steven Pressfield argues that the yearning to join the modern army, despite the low pay, the lack of respect and recognition and the absence of just cause, remains alluring because of its ancient roots. He may be right, but this too is disappearing as nihilism sets in, and people realize that the parasitic elite who want to send them to war are actually their real enemy.

> *"One answer may be that the young man or woman is seeking a rite of passage. One way to do that is to go to war. Young men have been undergoing that ordeal of initiation for ten thousand years. This passage is into and through what the great psychologist Carl Jung called "the Warrior Archetype."*

> *Steven Pressfield, The Warrior Ethos*

It's time we developed new, conscious and transcendent rites that draw from the old remaining current and relevant. The Bitcoin journey itself is a strange example, and one that emerged organically because of how wild of a proposition it is. Bitcoiners are a bunch of crazy people who not only agree that the world is in dire straits, but believe a better world is possible and that we have a practical and effective way forward! I call this contrarian optimism. *You're against the grain, but you have hope for the future.* The most famous meme in all of Bitcoin is HODL and, funnily enough, it implies endurance. Holding On for Dear Life through the ups and downs, and resisting all of the FUD (Fear, Uncertainty & Doubt) along the way, with everyone from your family to your spouse, teachers, favorite authors, the talking heads and others you may or may not admire calling you stupid, really takes a special kind of person.

While it's a good start, there's much more to do. We are all going to be tested, voluntarily and involuntarily. The hysteria of the first few years of this decade was an example of the latter. Those who held strong and didn't succumb to the propaganda, succeeded - at least for now. We must prepare ourselves for the next ordeal; and, in order to do so, to be better prepared for these involuntary, but inevitable, challenges of life, we need to both develop and undertake voluntary rites of passage. Social, economic, cultural, spiritual, psychological and physical. Like any form of training, it is a process of inoculation, and only in this way can you build real muscle.

Traditional rites of passage

We discussed sacrifice earlier, and we'll touch on it here too because it is central to all the male rites of passage throughout history. I will focus on these because I am a man, and female rites of passage are very different. Women bring life into the world, and in doing so experience their transcendence; men, on the other hand, experience transcendence when we stare death in the face. Nietzsche correctly pointed out that we are 'the barren sex'; as such, our roles, our drives and the rites that emerge from them differ significantly, as does our relationship to pain and suffering.

For men, pain leads to growth: exposure to pain is how we strengthen ourselves, physically, mentally, emotionally, and spiritually; it's how we prepare ourselves to perform our duties in life, whether that involves conquest, creation, providing for those we love or protecting them from the harsh realities of life. A man will shed blood for the duties that matter most, but in order to do so without breaking, he must be strong enough.

> *"Men nurture their societies by shedding their blood, their sweat, and their semen, by bringing home food for both child and mother, by producing children, and by dying if necessary in faraway places to provide a safe haven for their people."*

> *Professor David Gilmore, Manhood in the Making*

The word nurture sticks out here, because we think of nurturing as a feminine trait... which it is, but men nurture in a fundamentally different way from women: men nurture through sacrifice. The descent into hell is so prevalent in ancient literature and mythology because it's a metaphor for pain and suffering. To "climb out of Hell" is to defeat one's demons (flaws) and to learn of something higher and more beautiful (Heaven) in the process. It's part of an archetypal initiation and a 'facing of death' that all heroes - and for that matter, all males who become *men* - must undergo.

Rites of passage transform the boy into a man, and the man into a warrior. These often-hellish ordeals scar or alter the initiate in some way, so he emerges anew. They are acts that *transform* the actor. To be clear, I am not saying that "all suffering is good." *Conscious* suffering, suffering freely undertaken and endured, can produce these effects. Pointless suffering, for example the pain of a long illness, or the drudgery of life in a PoW camp, does not necessarily do so - although it *can*, if one is conscious about it and **uses** it. Recall our earlier discussion on Adler's psychology of responsibility: the key is agency. Preparation is the responsible person's antidote to life's unfair, but inevitable suffering. This is the underlying wisdom of the ancient rites.

Youths of the ancient Macedonian mountain tribes were only considered to have 'come of age' after killing their first boar. If you've seen a wild boar in real life, you'll know that's not something trivial. Their next great act, necessary for transformation into a soldier and leader of men, was to take the life of a man on the battlefield. Both were symbols meant to close the door to one chapter and open the door to the next, simultaneously teaching courage and establishing a new identity.

Another example was the footrace held each year among the boys of Sparta. They had to run ten miles, barefoot, carrying a mouthful of water and weren't allowed to swallow the water, but instead had to spit it out at the end of the race. This was a rite that entrained self-control and restraint above all else. There are many such examples which may, to the modern materialist, sound ridiculous. Why should I put myself or my offspring through such pain when I can have everything I want at the tap of a smartphone screen?

Therein lies the difference between a consooomer and a conqueror. The former feeds the belly while the latter feeds the soul. If courage maketh the man, then ordeals are not only desirable, but *necessary* for the proper formation of man. They are built into the very structure of the myths and narratives that shape history, knowledge, and even our very language.

Figures such as Beowulf would "travel deep into the woods" or "venture out across the seas to defeat the monsters," and likewise Christ himself would "descend into Hell to defeat Satan" or "rise up and conquer death." Contrast that with a "Jimmy went to therapy because he was feeling anxious" or "Greg couldn't say no to a bag of chips." It's about time we pushed ourselves again. If Beowulf could swim to the bottom of the swamp to wrestle Grendel's mother, surely you can lose a few pounds.

Rites of passage emphasize adversity, endurance, and self-sacrifice. They develop one's ability to handle fear and pain, and in doing so build tenacity. Strength could be described as your ability to be comfortable in uncomfortable circumstances. I don't know of any other way to stimulate and develop the quintessential virtues of man and warrior - courage and self-control. Life is the gymnasium for the soul, and ordeals or rites are the weights. To embody the great and noble virtues, we must earn them. St. Benedict's Rule says:

> *"Do not grant newcomers to the monastic life an easy entry, but, as the Apostle says, Test the spirits to see if they are from God. Therefore, if someone comes and keeps knocking at the door, and if at the end of four or five days he has shown himself patient in bearing harsh treatment and difficulty of entry, and has persisted in his request, then he should be allowed to enter."*

Courage is the backbone of morality, and its absence is why modern society is so morally weak. Without ordeals — without an opportunity to prove themselves, and actually **earn** something through real danger and struggle — men feel incomplete; instead of reaching the peak of their individual capacities, they live in a cocoon of quiet safety and ignorance, where things like courage are superfluous.

The color, flavor, and very energy of life are felt most keenly at the edge of death. This is why men are fundamentally drawn to extreme sports, why they are compelled to compete, why they fight, why they build. Men must **earn** the feeling of being alive. It's the price we pay to truly **feel**.

Movies like 'Fight Club' - nihilistic undertones aside - were successful because they touched on these primal truths and spoke precisely to the lack of fire and danger in the life of modern man. Tyler Durden was a manifestation of this suppressed masculine impulse. He was a modern Saint Benedict who rallied men that were disenfranchised, empty and longing for meaning. And like St Benedict, he tested initiates before they could join the Fight Club inner circle. They had to wait on his porch for three days while being insulted and told to leave:

"This is how Buddhist temples have tested applicants going back for bah-zillion years. You tell the applicant to go away, and if his resolve is so strong that he waits at the entrance without food or shelter encouragement for three days, then and only then can he enter and begin training."

Tyler Durden, Fight Club

It's no accident that this is a recurring theme. The warrior spirit is drawn to it like a moth to a flame. It yearns to grow, and knows the obstacle is the way, and pain is the price. Rites of passage are simply the gymnasium for the mind, emotions, and the soul. Enduring suffering prepares our mind and spirit as much as it does the body, which itself is conditioned through consistent and rigorous training - the topic of the next chapter.

The German soldier and philosopher Ernst Jünger wrote in his memoir *Storm of Steel* "*there is nothing to set against self-sacrifice that is not pale, insipid, and miserable.*" He describes pain as the truest experience of being *alive*. It's the only thing that is real, and now, but also transcends time and space. Pain uses the body as a portal to the deeper parts of our minds and spirit; learning to play with it or enduring it can prepare us for more in all dimensions of life. This is why we train. We transform the inner, by stressing the outer.

Modern rites of passage

In Sparta, boys of noble and warrior families stayed with their mothers until the age of seven, at which point they were taken and enrolled in the *agoge*, "The Upbringing." They were given one rough cloak to wear all year long and a sickle-like weapon called a xyele. They were allowed no beds and had to sleep outdoors in nests made of the reeds they gathered each night from the river. This training lasted until they were eighteen and could be officially enrolled in the Spartan army - at which point they were considered men and warriors.

Does this mean we send our children out, alone in the wild for a decade to fend for themselves? Of course not. This is an example meant to inspire you to ask what sort of *agoge* **you** can develop, within your family, or together with your tribe and community, such that your boys may turn into men. How can you create an environment of **useful** adversity that teaches the virtues listed in this book, while inflicting enough pain to inure and strengthen your son in preparation for the physical, psychological, and emotional challenges he will surely face in life?

Can we really adopt a new bushido or warrior ethos in the modern age? Time will of course tell. It's certainly less likely in a liberal or 'modern democratic' paradigm, for such frameworks are anti-excellence. I've also become less convinced that it's possible in a Libertarian culture over-indexed for freedom and liberty. We have to move onto something stronger.

To me, the answer lies in a culture of excellence. An Aretocracy, even more so than a Meritocracy, although they both go hand-in-hand. Only a civilization whose North Star is excellence, even more so that freedom, can be ascendant. This is ultimately the goal: to grow and ascend. It is the opposite to (and only cure for) decay. The development of such a society demands both agency and standards which, in turn, require the institution of conscious rites of passage.

Today's world is full of unconscious rites because we tried to ignore the reality of their existence, or we actively suppressed them, causing the impulse to manifest in other grotesque ways: like some Frankenstein-Streisand effect. The only thing we achieved was the replacement of traditional rituals and directed rites with strange, unnatural and completely unconscious ones such as getting blind-drunk when we hit 21, or spending 18 years in school for the 'privilege' of becoming a wage and debt slave with a pet or three, a sterile relationship, and more *month* at the end of the *money*. These are ordeals indeed, but more akin to a materialistic meat grinder squashing the soul of anyone and anything that runs through it.

It doesn't matter whether this was planned and intentional, or if it's an emergent outgrowth of ignorance and envy. What matters is that we fix it, and to do so, we must claim conscious control of the primal desire for rites. And by conscious I mean *intentionality*, not the ayahuasca-induced hippie kind of fluffy nonsense. I mean willfully tapping into the primordial instincts buried deep in our subconscious and into our collective archetypal supra-consciousness to extract wisdom, and couple it with the modern technologies we have at our disposal, to develop something new and powerful, that is also relevant to this age.

We are not "retvrning" back to some previous era. The only way forward is **through** because what lies ahead is not what's behind us. Yet neither can we ignore what came before like some progressive midwit. The thread to the past must remain tethered, like an eternal umbilical cord connecting each of us all the way back through time, to the earliest men of power that spawned us. Whatever we create *has to be new at the edges, and old at its core.*

New rites of passage must be crafted with this principle in mind. Their application and practice will happen first and foremost within the family unit, which will once again become central, and then extend outward to the race or community in which those values are shared.

This, along with the practice of said virtues in entrepreneurial pursuits, leadership in the community, the home, and in our own lives is how we will weave these rites into the fabric of a more beautiful age.

"Let us be, then, warriors of the heart, and enlist in our inner cause the virtues we have acquired through blood and sweat in the sphere of conflict—courage, patience, selflessness, loyalty, fidelity, self-command, respect for elders, love of our comrades (and of the enemy), perseverance, cheerfulness in adversity and a sense of humor, however terse or dark."

Steven Pressfield, *The Warrior Ethos*

By reinvigorating a respect for order, hierarchy, and traditions, we can set our sights on the next frontier. *Eyes must forward, shoulders back, chin is toward God - Jerr.* By doing so, we can rebuild the parts of our civilization that are broken, and reinforce the parts that currently bear all the weight. We have better materials and new tools to work with now, so we can do this - if we just **choose**.

Bitcoin is a beautiful example because it performs this repair and reinforcement quite uniquely in a social and economic sense. It is imperfectly perfect. It's a place in which entropy and order collide to form a sound heartbeat, every ten minutes. It's a modern solution with a classical ethic. It's simultaneously the oldest form of money; a transparent ledger, boring, hierarchical, and sound, and it is digitally alive; infused with energy and literally operating as *information*. It has transcended the limitations and shortcomings inherent in all forms of money to date, be they fiat, digital, or physical, while maintaining the very constraints that make money, **money**.

Such an elegant mix of these seemingly opposite concepts is both inspiration and proof that we can do something with our lot. It's up to us now to use it as a catalyst for other social, moral and psychological integrations. I've argued in the past that this synthesis could help lead toward a better integration of left brain and right brain, or the unification of matter (science) with 'what matters' (philosophy). It might foster greater cooperation between empirical/material progress and spiritual/religious constraint, and perhaps it can even lead us to develop the kind of character that can maintain a high degree of virtue and material affluence.

These are the opportunities that lie before us. The upshot of having gone through hell are the scars and experiences we've collected along the way. These give us a depth we did not previously possess. It's now up to us to use them for something new and more beautiful. Instead of outsourcing our future to politicians, priests or experts, we can claim the physical and spiritual vitality that is being stolen from us - or more accurately, that we've **allowed** to be stolen.

We can build beautiful families, cities, art and a beautiful future if we have the courage to fight for it. What's required is an *ascendant* energy. I can see this happening in the coming years and decades. Men are already coming together and forming brotherhoods, women are coming together and creating their own sacred spaces. Rituals are being formed. A new vitality and desire for excellence and beauty is being generated.

It's early days, and none of us are perfect. We have and will continue to make mistakes along the way, but if we can adapt and are willing to embrace the pain of the ordeal, we can learn and in the process become both smarter and stronger. If we continue to aim at something higher, as Thomas Carlyle would call "the heroic ideal," then we will infuse life with meaning again, irrespective of whether we reach this ideal or not.

> *"Carlyle argues that we shouldn't despair if the heroic ideal seems unattainable. A bricklayer can't lay a perfectly perpendicular wall, but the ideal of perpendicularity helps him lay an acceptable and strong wall. The ideal of the heroic plays the same function."*
>
> Jash Dholani on X.com

I'm excited by the prospects of such a future, heartened by what I have seen amongst the groups of people I am in touch with, and encourage you to do the same or to reach out. It's time we rebuilt our physical, emotional, spiritual and psychological muscles.

Slaying the inner dragons

Rites of passage mostly focus on the development of virtue, but there are also rites for helping the initiate deal with vice. In fact, while much of this book has centered around virtue, little has been said about dealing with vice which is, in many ways, just as important and, for some people, harder to deal with. I'd like to address this here.

Virtue is the North Star we orient toward, and vice is that which we must keep at bay while on the journey. Vice comes in many forms, and goes by many names. Symbolically and spiritually, it is Satan, and his demons; metaphorically speaking, it is the dragon you must face, or your own inner enemy; and practically or psychologically speaking, it is your bad behaviors, habits and tendencies. We all have them, and all people, cultures and societies have come up with ways to contend with them.

Christianity has one of the more sound models for understanding vice, via the seven deadly sins. Pride, greed, lust, envy, gluttony, wrath, and sloth represent the fundamental moral failings that derail a person from the path of virtue. Each sin, in its essence, reflects the corruption of something that, when properly directed, could otherwise lead to growth or good. For example, pride is a distortion of self-respect, and greed is an exaggeration of the desire for security. Christianity deals with these sins through confession to a trusted authority, repentance to a higher authority, and also quite powerfully, through community. People are encouraged to acknowledge their vices, seek forgiveness, and actively strive toward virtue. This framework was so useful that it helped pull the west through centuries of economic and technological development and establish one of the most powerful civilisations on earth. Atheism does the world a disservice by ignoring this - the results of which are clear.

The warrior ethos represents another way to deal with vice by framing it as an "inner enemy" that must be fought and subdued. In this paradigm, vice is recognised as an ever-present part of you, that you may never ultimately defeat but will forever contend with. This inner enemy is your eternal enemy, which is why they say that the biggest battles you will face are the ones within.

> "Here is the Warrior Ethos directed inward, employing the same virtues used to overcome external enemies—but enlisting these qualities now in the cause of the inner struggle for integrity, maturity and the honorable life."
>
> Steven Pressfield, The Warrior Ethos

In cultivating your capacity for war, you must also learn to direct it inward. Your inner dragons, be they doubt, anxiety, fear, cowardice or any of the sins mentioned above, are shadows of your ultimate inner enemy and hide the treasures that make you a man of virtue. Steven Pressfield calls this *"Directing the Warrior Ethos inward."*

The Indian warrior epic, the Bhagavad-Gita, references this inner battle in a story. The great *kshatriya* (warrior-noble) Arjuna receives spiritual instruction from his charioteer, who happens to be Krishna - God in human form. Krishna points across the battlefield to soldiers, archers and spearmen whom Arjuna knows personally, is related to in some cases and feels deep affection for — and commands him to kill them all. Arjuna is torn, but with Krishna by his side, he musters the courage to do what's necessary because, as Pressfield notes, the names of many of these enemy warriors, in Sanskrit, can also be translated as the names of key vices.

> *"Inner crimes or personal vices, such as greed, jealousy, selfishness, the capacity to play our friends false or to act without compassion toward those who love us. In other words, our warrior Arjuna is being instructed to slay the enemies inside himself."*
>
> Steven Pressfield, *The Ethos of War*

Many similar ancient fables teach and remind us that living a life of virtue requires we slay the foes which constitute our "weaker" selves, and wage war on the vices and inner demons that sabotage our path to becoming the best and highest versions of ourselves.

I'm reminded of the 1993 film *Dragon: The Bruce Lee Story*, with Jason Scott Lee. They did an incredible job showing how one of the strongest men of our age was plagued by demons all his life. We all have demons and we all must face them at some point. How do the great myths and stories instruct us to do this? Not by ignoring our baser instincts, for they are full of wisdom, but through the practice of self-discipline and the mastery over these drives and instincts. In other words, by the interior exercise of our otherwise externally directed warrior ethos.

We are each a living, breathing ball of drives and instincts, of habits and subconscious predispositions that we'll never fully understand. We must learn to be ok with that, or else it can drive us mad. Unhinged, or undirected, the drives themselves can and do cause unnecessary suffering, both in the internal and external worlds.

Some realize this and fall into nihilism. They feel that they are a slave or subject to their drives and that there is no point to any of it, so they give up on trying to direct them. Life becomes stripped of deeper meaning because "all meaning is just made up anyway". Others come to terms with this reality in other ways. Some detach themselves, becoming monks or ascetics: they believe the right path is the one which does not engage with these drives. Buddhism and Stoicism could be considered to be in this camp, and of a similar essence.

Other people, oblivious to this fact, wind up killing themselves. Their demons overcome them. Some spend their entire lives sabotaging themselves and the lives of those around them. Others yet become hedonists, pouring their energy, seed and vitality into whatever cup is placed before them.

There are those who, upon discovering the harshness of reality, find solace in alternate dimensions opened up by psychedelic substances like mushrooms or ayahuasca. I know many of them, and you quickly discover a pattern: they have trouble contending with the world and their drives in the absence of a 'ceremony' or more 'medicine' to 'heal' something. It's a slippery slope, if not done from a place of grounding in the harshness of reality.

The majority just remain oblivious NPCs, floating through life like a feather in the wind. Blown up, down and around in circles by the overwhelming consensus of the drives around them. They're like an iron filing, surrounded by magnets. No agency of their own, but a vessel that absorbs the drives of the crowd and environment around them. Not to be unkind here, because we all have that tendency - energy is infectious; but the reality is that some people are more prone to being mindless zombies than others.

There are of course people that are a blend of all of the above. In fact, many of us have at one point or another experienced one or more of these states, or learned to cope with reality and deal with inner demons through such means. Some of us grow up, while others remain trapped there forever like Peter Pan. Those who grow up, in my opinion, turn to God, to community, to brotherhood, virtue, or something else - but always, crucially, something higher. They seek to understand themselves, their traditions, their ancestors and the men or women of life and vitality who bent the arc of history. They are able to find inspiration, not escape, in such pursuits. They seek to order, govern and channel their inner drives and wage war on their lower selves. They inhale virtue, and exhale their vices. They seek to affirm life and inspire, before it is their time to expire.

I have found such inspiration myself in the likes of Christ, Nietzsche, Homer, Alexander, Attila, and Napoleon. The lives of such men have helped me find greater meaning in my own. In dark times, their stories, their words, and their characters have all helped inspire me to strength, and to face my own dragons. My goal with this book is to give you some inspiration to find your own, be they heroic examples, God, community or all three. Vice will forever be present, and the temptation to give in gets stronger with time. You must find ways to contend with it, which leads me to one of the most potent methods for men.

The männerbund

The männerbund, literally translated to "Alliance of Men", is the kind of association, group or brotherhood that all men seek to build, foster and operate within. It's a deep drive within us, and can manifest in both the most constructive and destructive ways.

Modern society has conspired to disband such associations with labels of toxicity and extremism. Having swung so far toward the individualist side of the spectrum (libertarianism is also to blame for this), any group of men working toward a common goal - whether of substance or not - is seen as suspicious. As a result, men either suppress this natural instinct and become isolated or, because they're just deemed evil by default, they lean into it, forming street gangs and the like. Society quickly discovers that you cannot eliminate the *männerbund*: all you can do is create an environment in which there are less incentives to be a strong, honorable, virtuous or heroic band of brothers. Where there were once prides of lions, there only remain lapdogs and packs of hyenas.

Technology amplifies things here again, and also transforms them. It has distanced us from each other while, paradoxically, simultaneously connects us to others at opposite ends of the world with like values. Couple that with a politics that has surrounded you with sheeple and mindless NPCs all too willing to comply while screeching at you for the act of breathing oxygen, and it's no wonder you feel isolated in your own physical domain, and go online to seek that connection.

Even the modern army is no refuge from this divide and conquer-like mind virus. You can see it both in the incredible drop in enlistment and in the kinds of people now enlisting. These organizations are merely the hired enforcers of a state apparatus which neither honors them, nor fights for honor anymore. The institutions of war have become devoid of all virtue and morality. Respect, honor, and duty come a distant second to blind compliance. If you are a part of one, I suggest you think deeply about what kind of world you want to see, and what you're doing to either make that a reality, or not. We're in a fight for the soul of man, and we need all the best men possible.

If you're not in that environment, and you find yourself alone, frustrated or perpetually online, then it's time to venture out and literally construct this in real life: get off Twitter and go to a Brazilian Jiu Jitsu dojo; go hunting or camping with a group of men and build a bond; take it upon yourselves to build an all-male bar, or an all-male fight gym; go build a business, or a house together. Get physical. Do something dangerous. Use technology where applicable to feed your mind and connect with like-valued men. These online connections **can** turn into offline tribes, but you *have* to move beyond the keyboard.

Find each other again, literally and metaphorically. Build an alliance of men to protect your women, your families and your tribe. Use this alliance to strengthen each other and hold each other accountable. Develop rites of passage together. Learn from the ancients once more:

> *"When they were boys, Alexander and his friends were forced to bathe in frigid rivers, run barefoot till their soles grew as thick as leather, ride all day without food or water and endure whippings and ritual humiliations. On the rare occasions when they got to rest, their trainers would remind them, 'While you lie here at ease, the sons of the Persians are training to defeat you in battle.'"*

> Steven Pressfield, *The Warrior Ethos*

Your band of brothers should be selected carefully. They are not merely those whom you've known the longest, and also not only those who are nice to you; in fact, beware of the latter, for a true friend will call you out when you're not living up to your potential. Your truest friends in that sense are those who might come off as assholes, because they're unwilling to waver or to watch you violate your own standards. Just being in their presence is like a rite of passage. They are your reminder to wage war on vice, as you are theirs.

> *"Those who want the best for you are by definition those who demand the best from you. These are your true friends. These are your community. These are the Remnant. In order to be among them, you must be the best and most honest version of yourself. There is no greater aspiration in life."*

> Aleksandar Svetski, *The Remnant Essays*

Your truest friends are the ones who would shed blood for you, and you for them; they are the ones whom you can train with, whose family you would guard and in whose care you would feel safe leaving your family should something happen to you; they are those you practice and sharpen your wits with.

Find them, and deepen your bonds. To do this, you must filter. You must create layers and levels. To become one of the brotherhood, initiates must endure ordeals; they must prove themselves and *work* for it. Recall my earlier comments about Saint Benedict and Fight Club. A brotherhood is a meritocracy and an *aretocracy*. For men to feel alive, they must earn their stripes. There are no participation awards in real life, and if you want excellence, you must build it into your micro-culture.

This is how you raise each other up, and I'm not sure there is anything more fierce or powerful in the world than a group of virtuous men with a common vision and the highest of standards. Like Alexander and his Royal Guard: a handful of men together on foot and on horseback reshaped half the known world in the span of a decade.

If this book serves only to inspire the formation of a few such groups, then my work here is half done. The other half will consist in meeting you out there in person.

The Bitcoiner's Arsenal

"Bushido made the sword its emblem of power and prowess. When Mahomet proclaimed that "the sword is the key of Heaven and of Hell," he only echoed a Japanese sentiment. Very early the Samurai boy learned to wield it."

Inazo Nitobe, Bushido: The Soul of Japan

Every warrior culture had their chosen weapon, be it the Arthurian Excalibur, Attila's "Scourge of God", Apollo's bow, Aries' lance, Alexander's helmet, the hoplites' *doru* or the Spartan shield. In Japan, the "Soul of the Samurai" was said to reside in their katana. These weapons became talismans.

Bitcoiners and the modern warrior must also wield weapons and tools that are both *symbolic* and *practical*. Like the Samurai's sword, they have to serve a purpose higher than just cutting your enemy down. Before we explore what those are, let us look at one of the most symbolic warrior-weapon symbioses in history.

The sword of the samurai

"It was a momentous occasion for him when at the age of five he was apparelled in the paraphernalia of Samurai costume, placed upon a go-board and initiated into the rights of the military profession, by having thrust into his girdle a real sword instead of the toy dirk with which he had been playing. After this first ceremony of adoptio per arma, he was no more to be seen outside his father's gates without this badge of his status, even though it was usually substituted for everyday wear by a gilded wooden dirk. Not many years pass before he wears constantly the genuine steel, though blunt, and then the sham arms are thrown aside and with enjoyment keener than his newly acquired blades, he marches out to try their edge on wood and stone. When he reaches man's estate, at the age of fifteen, being given independence of action, he can now pride himself upon the possession of arms sharp enough for any work."

Inazo Nitobe, *Bushido: The Soul of Japan*

Much of the Samurai's early life was a "rite of passage" and journey toward earning his sword. How it was forged, carried, treated, when and how it was used, and ultimately passed down - all were processes sacred, charged with meaning, and over the centuries came to be ritualized.

The sword was not just a physical weapon, but a symbol of the Samurai's commitment. It was seen as an extension of the Samurai himself, and its proper use and handling were of the utmost importance. This devotion to the weapon touches on something very important, and largely lacking in our age, namely *mastery*.

Mastery is the state of being highly skilled and proficient in a particular field or endeavor. It is the result of dedicated practice, discipline, and a constant striving for self-improvement. It is not just about achieving a certain level of skill, but about a *lifelong commitment* to learning and growing. It requires embodying virtues such as self-control, duty, excellence, and respect.

Mastery is not a destination, but an ongoing process of incremental improvement. To become masterful at anything you must have the humility necessary to subordinate yourself to authority, and the perseverance necessary to endure the journey. Mastery requires discipline, a desire for beauty, and the constant pursuit of perfection.

Mastery is *authority* in the purest sense, and as an apprentice or individual that seeks to attain it, you must understand that authority, like mastery and respect, must be **earned**. They each require the sacrifice of time, energy, and often pleasure and leisure in order to attain them.

The Samurai are in many ways the quintessential symbol of this devotion to mastery. They were deeply engrossed in the practice of their craft, be that the use of the sword, calligraphy, strategy, horsemanship, archery, etiquette and governance.

> *"He committed his soul and spirit into the forging and tempering of the steel."*
>
> Inazo Nitobe, Bushido: The Soul of Japan

They took their vocations on for life, starting out as apprentices with an upward flowing respect for their master, until one day they too became masters whose duty it was to lead and develop the next generation.

Recall our earlier discussion on excellence. People who are obsessed with anarchy or pure freedom or "masterlessness" and are always complaining about some "tyranny of authority" are not to be taken seriously. To be masterful is a thing of beauty. **True authority is earned reputation**. It accrues via the sacrifice of time, intent, and energy. Authority is *competence*. Without it we are left with an equalitarian orgy of mess, where up can be down down, black can be white, man can be woman, and right can be wrong.

Authority is necessary order, and righteous restraint. The master has the ability to abstain. He is the one who, having developed each of the initial virtues, integrates and keeps them all in check. Self-control is the virtue of maturity, mastery, strength and true power. If courage is the Alpha, self-control is the Omega.

> *"The question that concerns us most is, however, did Bushido justify the promiscuous use of the weapon? The answer is unequivocally, no! As it laid great stress on its proper use, so did it denounce and abhor its misuse. A dastard or a braggart was he who brandished his weapon on undeserved occasions. A self-possessed man knows the right time to use it, and such times come but rarely."*

Inazo Nitobe, Bushido: The Soul of Japan

A man with true authority and mastery has learned to channel his impulses. He understands that he is but a combination of drives, a furious array of primal energy seeking an outlet. He does not ignore these drives or try to suppress them. He acknowledges them and, like the captain of a ship, he directs them.

It's our job to 'Make Authority Great Again'. In a world of instant gratification, five minute abs, one day business turnarounds and teenage influencers masquerading as leaders, mastery is rare. This is precisely where the opportunity lies. The very word "master" is seen as a symbol of oppression and hate by the resentful equalitarians. Authority is shunned and disparaged. Self-control is almost entirely absent. Respect is framed as an entitlement instead of a virtue, and poor decision-making is socialized so people are unaware of the consequences of their actions. These outcomes and ideologies are only possible in the absence of hierarchy. They could never have taken hold in a culture of excellence and mastery, which is why you didn't see them in the age of the Samurai. The warrior class was the lynchpin that kept the hierarchy in place. It's about time we stopped complaining and started building new hierarchies of competence to move us back to quality and away from equality.

It's time to develop proficiency with a new kind of toolkit. A modern arsenal.

The strategic arsenal

The journey of a Bitcoiner is a rite of its own and, for the select few who choose to be defenders and advocates of the network, a devotion toward learning to use their chosen weapons should echo what I've described above about the Samurai. Hard work. Dedication. Humility. Curiosity.

Most people get into Bitcoin in a similar way. They generally start small, buying a little on an exchange or receiving it from a friend, or if you're really an OG, got it from a faucet in the early 2010s. From there, perhaps, your interest is triggered. You see things happening with the price, you might read a few articles, or even watch a couple of classic videos on YouTube by Andreas Antonopolous. This might lead you to Bitcoin Twitter, which has and continues to be quite an interesting Schelling point for Bitcoiners, despite the noise on there.

Along the way you may have heard things like "not your keys, not your coins", which have hopefully inspired you to explore self-custody. You may have even read or seen something by the likes of Michael Goldstein, with an emphasis on "running your own node".

Along this journey, there is an ever increasing call for greater proficiency in the use of these tools, which - make no mistake about it - will become weapons when the time comes to fight.

Let's review some of them now, and then dig into necessary skills beyond just those relating to Bitcoin, because it's not good just being a nerd that knows how to cut some code. You have to develop your other faculties too.

Tools & weapons

Keys

In Bitcoin, your keys are the centerpiece. They're akin to the sword of the Samurai. How you forge (derive), store, and treat these keys determines whether or not the bitcoin will remain in your custody. If you're to learn one single concept in Bitcoin, this is the one. Develop the skills necessary to manage and secure your keys properly. All else comes second.

Node

The node comes next. Only noblemen, warriors, knights, and Samurai rode horses, because they were first-class citizens. They were sovereign protectors of property, like node operators are the sovereign operators and custodians of Bitcoin's consensus rules. First-class Bitcoin citizens are the law, because they run the code.

Mining / Validating

The greater the hashrate, the stronger the network. The node and the keys are the two most important weapons to master in the Bitcoiner's arsenal, along with mining - which could be likened to the shield to extend the analogy.

Participating in mining, adding hashrate to the network and being rewarded for it make both you and Bitcoin stronger and more impenetrable. This industry will continue to grow as the Bitcoin network infuses itself with the global energy grid. Ultimately, it will form the backbone of the two largest markets on earth: money and energy. Don't sleep on it.

Bitcoin-Adjacent Protocols

There is significant technological progress being made with protocols that are related to, connected to, or adjacent to Bitcoin. One of the most promising is the Nostr protocol, which might form the basis for a new generation of applications that leverage a global, open social graph. Nostr is an incredible new identity-centric protocol whose topography makes way for rebuilding the social layer of the web in a way that is more censorship-resistant, private and deeply integrated with the Internet of money (Bitcoin). It's very early days, but there is a whole universe of products being built that leverage its social graph and digital primitives. Satlantis.io is but one example: a social network for "sovereign individuals" - which combines elements of Google Place, Meetup, TripAdvisory, Instagram, NomadList and alternative food directories like Seed Oil Scout - all with the express purpose of establishing parallel networks in the real world. There are many other products too. New public squares, new Patreon, Substack, YouTube and Spotify equivalents - all which leverage your social graph, and are accessible with the one key. This means you own your profile, your content and your follower/following list and by connecting to relays (servers, essentially) of your choice, you can better curate content and not be owned by an algorithm. Perhaps in time, as the protocol becomes more robust, giants like X and Instagram will be forced to build their applications as clients on Nostr, and re-engineer their architecture to adapt. I wouldn't sleep on this either.

Other protocols that are more directly Bitcoin-related include the Lightning Network, Fedi, Cashu and the Liquid Network. They are all what's called "second layer networks" on Bitcoin that enable cheaper, more private and faster transactions, higher network throughput, and really deliver on the promise digital cash without compromising on the core promises of the Bitcoin network, such as censorship resistance, decentralization, and immutability. While it is still early days, the Lightning Network's growth map is eerily reminiscent of the early Internet.

Identity & Reputation

Whether your identity is real, pseudonymous or anonymous, you will need to build *reputation*. This maps quite well to the concept of honor. Online reputations will become increasingly important in a world becoming more digital, full of AI-generated noise and midwit frenzies. The question is, who will own this reputation and this identity? And furthermore, how does one ensure the integrity of this identity in a world full of bots, spam and fake accounts? This is where tools like Nostr come into play once more. Most people will settle for a government-issued digital ID, which tracks and monitors everything they say and do; it will likely also be tied to a CBDC, which combined, are the noose around the neck. It's imperative you do not find yourself on these gallows. You must place similar importance on your digital identity, as you do with your money. Bitcoin is a bearer instrument, which you own by virtue of controlling the keys. Nostr is the same: because it is not issued by a central organization, but instead generated by math, you are able to spin up many identities. This allows you to build separate reputations, which could be extremely important both in cyberspace and meatspace. Many of the smartest people I know have done this, so they can speak the truth and avoid being silenced by the bureaucratic meat grinder. It's also important beyond just avoidance of political or societal risks. In the best case scenario, owning your identity on a protocol like Nostr is a bit like owning your email list in a csv file. It is *yours*, and no matter what happens to the app or platform you're using, or the algorithm they've decided to prioritize, your list and reputation all remain yours. Why would you build an online asset, whether audience, reputation or profile in any other way? Why would you allow someone else to own it? These tools are indispensable in the new world.

Skills

Skills are paramount: technical, social, psychological, spiritual, physical, emotional. The more you master, the more masterful you become. The following are some of the most important for now, and especially into the future.

Privacy

Master privacy. That should include financial privacy (through hygiene practices such as coin control and Coinjoin) and also your general online presence. You can think of privacy as armor. Learning pseudonymity and anonymity may save you one day, and at the very least gives you more power and control over your life, because it expands what you can say and limits your enemy's ability to attack you.

Many people in the Bitcoin circle call privacy a human right, and while I agree with their sentiment, I don't agree that it's a "right" necessarily. Privacy is a service, but an extremely necessary one if you want a society full of adults that have agency, autonomy and can practice free speech and wrestle with ideas. Without privacy, you infantilize civilization, turning everyone into a toddler at daycare, while the nanny keeps a watchful eye over everything you do.

Thus the key here is: if you agree with the broader sentiment of the book that in order to build a strong, beautiful and ascendant civilisation, we need men and women of agency and virtue, then privacy should be a **standard** we all expect from products and practice ourselves. Privacy demarcates territory, it establishes private property, and in the same way we build doors to our bedrooms and learn to close them so we can have our own space, we must build, support and use products and services that help to establish our own space. Having Big Brother or some bureaucratic, middle-managing nanny state surveilling over you all the time is for midwits, serfs and NPCs.

> *"Privacy is the power to selectively reveal oneself to the world."*
>
> Timothy C. May, Cypherpunk Manifesto

Communication: Spoken or Written

You must have something to say, and then know how to say it. Jordan Peterson reminds us that learning to write and speak are superpowers. These have and always will be some of the most important skills. Caesar was known for being a master of rhetoric, a master of strategy, and a man of action. Communication changes everything. If you can learn to clearly articulate ideas, positions, and concepts, you can be a leader in business, a leader of men, a leader in your community, and lead your family. You must of course support your words with action, else they are meaningless -

but the ultimate mix is a man of great vision, great words and great action: The Philosopher-Warrior-King.

Words and language have a huge influence on how we think, and therefore what we choose to do. A single social media post, or well-written article can lift the spirit of the reader and compel them to action. At scale, this can and does change the world.

Most of us will not be warriors in the old style, nor will we be in a position like that of the Samurai or knight, so we need to cultivate mastery in areas where the pen or word might be mightier than the sword.

Nietzsche was a prime example of this. He was a philosopher bookworm who brought vitality to the world through the art of writing. His writing was sharp, dense, full of sensory imagery and charged with big ideas. It's no accident his aphorisms are some of the most quoted in the world.

> *"It is my ambition to say in ten sentences what others say in a whole book."*
>
> Friedrich Nietzsche, *Twilight of the Idols*

There has been a significant amount of high-quality literature that's come from Bitcoiners, which is encouraging. My recent deep dive into other corners of Twitter have also revealed to me absolutely incredible thinkers, some of whom I've listed in the resources section of this book, and one in particular who helped me edit this book!

If you are interested in, or are already writing: keep at it. For most people who are not technical, this is an area they can lean into.

Networks & Community

Once you know how to speak or write, you need people to share these ideas with. The *männerbund* is the obvious example, but so too are women's circles, meetups, your gym, local food networks, the people you work with and more. This is a large reason why platforms like Satlantis.io exist and why protocols like Nostr are becoming increasingly important. They help you build networks online, which ideally you should then deepen *offline*.

This is why you need, and where you apply, *reputation*. Networks open doors and have always been a superpower, maybe even more so nowadays where people live next to and on top of each other in concrete boxes, without ever knowing the names of the people around them.

Notice I use the word "networks". That's because friendships are hard. They take a lifetime to build and require more than just common values, but time and shared experiences. The goal is to take the best of your networks and build deeper relationships (friendships), but you need both. It's almost like a funnel, and it is not something you can wait on or push for later. Deep relationships take time to build. There are no shortcuts.

The lone wolf theory is bullshit. I've had to learn that the hard way. The sooner you begin to build the necessary networks, the sooner you can deepen them - which in time may lead to true friendships. Perhaps not the kind that warriors like Leonidas had with his 300, or that Alexander had with his Royal Companions, but your own version nonetheless.

Modern, individualist culture has separated us - and the libertarians are very guilty of this sin. Every man for himself is a failed strategy. The tribe wins, and to build a functional, trustworthy tribe takes time and effort. Tribes and small collectives > the individual. It took me a long time to learn this one. The strongest unit in civilization is the männerbund. Once you've found these people, don't just talk over Telegram or Twitter, but go and spend time together and share experiences. Better yet, share ordeals. Go hunting, camping, fighting, get on the mats or in the ring, build a business. Push each other.

Finally, and very important: seek not just "like-minded" people but, more importantly, "like-valued". The most robust tribes are like-valued and multi-minded. This creates a powerful cross-section of skills, while ensuring everyone is on the same 'ship' or 'mission.' I cannot stress this enough. A powerful network and true friendships are the ultimate weapon.

Programming & Digital Product Skills

"Cypherpunks write code"

There's no way to escape it. We live in an increasingly digital world. Learning to master the tools of cyberspace will give you an edge. If you have a predisposition for math, language or logic, this is an area for you. You must of course balance this with movement, because it's easy to get lost behind a keyboard when you're getting dopamine from the screen - even if you're producing something.

I'll also place within this section anything essentially to do with computers: graphic design, UX, prompt engineering, video editing, data science, social media, online marketing; these are all digital skills relevant in a digital age. Pick that which fits you most, that which you enjoy and can be the best at, and add it to your arsenal. This will increase your ability to generate income and enhance your options.

Finally, in the age of AI, many are afraid that these skills will become obsolete. I do not think this is the case. In the short-term, language models and other AI tools are at best only able to produce average, middle-of-the-bell-curve results that, if anything, can replace the mid-wits and the content, code or designs they currently produce; hence why I call it "Midwit-Obsolescence-Technology". If your work is exceptional, you actually have an advantage and stand out even more. Medium to long-term, you should simply look to integrate these tools (which is all they are) into your workflow. Once again, as an artist, programmer and **creator** with *agency*, you will have the upper hand. This will always be the case.

Entrepreneurship

Beyond just programming and the associated digital skills, are the ever-necessary skills of the entrepreneur. The ability to notice a problem, to think up a solution, to communicate, to negotiate, to share a vision and inspire others toward it, to develop the fortitude necessary to see the vision through, and undertake this entire ordeal - despite the odds

- will never be made obsolete. No amount of AI or computation can ever produce *agency* - and this is above all else what the entrepreneur brings to the table.

Specialists are most likely to be replaced through automation in whatever form it comes. Entrepreneurs on the other hand, are hard to replace because they are generalists who choose to specialize in a particular problem space. The best entrepreneurs are not afraid to experiment and fail so they can learn something new. They can synthesize lessons from various life and business experiences, and bring a new perspective to the endeavor they've chosen to contend with. Their unique understanding of the world enables them to solve problems in a novel way, and fundamentally forge a new path.

The term "entrepreneur" originates from the French verb *entreprendre*, which means "to undertake." This verb itself derives from Latin *inter* (between) and *prendere* (to take or grasp), which itself traces back to the Proto-Indo-European root *preh*, meaning "to take." This is quite interesting, because in order to take, undertake or to grasp, you must have agency. The entrepreneur is an *agent* and, in my view, some blend of the merchant and warrior archetypes. He will go to war with a problem and profit by producing a solution. With this profit he will go to war with a new problem and continue building (think Elon Musk).

Entrepreneurship demands leadership and vision. The mix of skills it entails is something very few people have, and that the world genuinely needs. This is why it's the skill set that offers the greatest potential for monetary reward. If you can couple this with solving a meaningful problem, then it can also deliver a high degree of spiritual and psychological reward. It is like modern day warriorhood and, in many ways, the entrepreneur and creator is a blend of the warrior and merchant archetypes. The entrepreneur goes to war with a problem, serves his customers, and uses his wealth to forge an empire in line with his vision.

This is different to the trader archetype. Sitting in front of your computer deciphering tea leaves and charts is not a productive pursuit. Understanding markets and the macro environment might be a skill, but only insofar as it makes up a part of something entrepreneurially more holistic. Alone, it's far less fulfilling than building and creating something of value.

The digital age brings with it incredible new entrepreneurial opportunities. The atomic, one-person business is now a reality. The creator economy is worth hundreds of billions annually and it will continue to grow as we transcend the cubicle economy that preceded it. If you can write, teach, think, learn and solve problems, you can build an audience, create a product or service and develop a real business that adds value to the economy. In fact, coupled with the rise of Nostr and Bitcoin, you will for the first time ever be able to do all of this and get paid directly by your audience, without the constraints of legacy banking, walled-garden platforms and outdated jurisdictional frameworks.

The modern world is broken in many ways, but the technological undercurrent offers an opportunity to transform things for the better at an unprecedented scale. Bitcoin is a major catalyst for a whole slew of transformations that are together culminating in a paradigm shift of such magnitude and significance as has not occurred before. It's in these moments that the greatest opportunities lie.

Trial, Error and Thick Skin

Deeply related to entrepreneurship, but warranting its own section is the tenacity to try things and get back up after falling over, or 'coming back' after failing.

Everyone has to start somewhere, and failure is the most powerful teacher. Most people do not even make a start because they lack a mentor or teacher that will tell them this. They've been taught that pain, adversity or failure are bad, and that they should instead focus on feeling safe and comfortable, that participation alone is enough. This is false, as we've discovered throughout the book.

This is also not helped by purity commentators, whether on social media or in real life, who have a lot to say, but have done a whole lot of nothing when it comes to actually building a business. Ignore those people. Everyone has to start somewhere. You are NOT going to get it right the first time. In order to dig to the center of the earth you need to start from the surface. By definition the beginning will be superficial, and you yourself, when you look back on your early work, will also find it cringe and superficial. That is a good sign! That means you have grown, which is the whole point of life and the entrepreneurial fractal within it.

> *"It is not the critic who counts: not the man who points out how the strong man stumbles or where the doer of deeds could have done better. The credit belongs to the man who is actually in the arena, whose face is marred by dust and sweat and blood, who strives valiantly, who errs and comes up short again and again, because there is no effort without error or shortcoming, but who knows the great enthusiasms, the great devotions, who spends himself in a worthy cause; who, at the best, knows, in the end, the triumph of high achievement, and who, at the worst, if he fails, at least he fails while daring greatly, so that his place shall never be with those cold and timid souls who knew neither victory nor defeat."*
>
> *Theodore Roosevelt, Speech: Citizenship in a Republic*

It takes time to build something meaningful and beautiful. So pick something, and build a business. Make mistakes, learn from them, and then try again. I've made every mistake in the book - but what's kept me going *is that I kept going.* Almost a decade ago I decided to go on Shark Tank in Australia, young, stupid and naive, to raise money for our fledgling business. We had a fantastic idea, but it was my first real tech startup, and we were a bunch of kids who went from working in my lounge room for six months to actually raising some money and learning how to build a product and a business - on the job!

I look back on those days with fondness. We were all so innocent, and doing our best. I would slave away at the office for eighteen hours every day of the week. I was always first in and last out. Setting both the pace and the standard. We didn't succeed. It was an idea perhaps not before its time, but certainly under-capitalized and quite frankly, not executed very well. Had I known what I know today, perhaps we'd have had a chance. But this was the price we had to pay for a series of experiences that I'm sure each person on the team used as a prerequisite for any of their individual future successes.

Writing this makes me want to write a Bushido of Business too. There are certainly parallels to how the Samurai and noble classes of the west transformed themselves into some of the most economically powerful families in the world. In fact, some of the largest companies in Japan are run by descendants of Samurai families. The virtues are clearly applicable cross-contextually.

In any case, the skill of tenacity can be learned, and the only way to learn it is to be the man in the ring. You must be willing to try, experiment and fail - not for the sake of failing, but for the opportunity to succeed and prevail. And if you do not, the result of losing should be a lesson and thicker skin, so that you can go back and try again.

Cultivating self-control

Conscious abstinence is spiritual and psychological training.

Early Christians like Paul of Thebes and Anthony the Great would put themselves through physical and mental ordeals as a way to purify their souls. They became known as 'The Desert Fathers' and inspired the entire Christian monastic movement. Traditional Eastern philosophies and religions, from Zen to Buddhism to Hindu, have similar practices.

A feature of Samurai culture that was preserved far longer than other warrior cultures was their profound focus on the incremental improvement of an artform of their choice. Whether martial arts, literature, calligraphy, archery or swordsmanship, they would devote themselves to an awe-inspiring degree. This was productive self-control at its finest.

Fasting is another common example and widespread practice. Christian culture adopted it as a way to practice restraint by sacrificing the 'worldly pleasure' of eating, thereby appreciating food (sustenance) more, and experiencing a piece of what Christ might have in the wilderness (compassion). This is also central to Islam, with Ramadan. Fasting, in all traditional cultures, takes on a spiritual significance because it requires strength of spirit. *Willpower is a spiritual force.* If you've ever fasted for a significant period, you can attest to this. Your willpower grows, you appreciate the simple things more, and when you finally eat again, your senses are alive.

Fasting remains a powerful practice today. It is often sold as a health remedy in the West, which it can be when done right, but I believe the primary benefit is the inculcation and training of self-control. Having access to food in abundance, but being able to abstain from eating is a powerful practice.

Beyond fasting are practices of silence, meditation, or prayer. A powerful silence practice known as Vipassana can now be done as part of a professional retreat that involves a shorter 5-day period of silence, or the traditional and more deeply impactful 10-day practice. This might strike some people as crazy, but the impact on the mind, body and senses is staggering. You come out of it with a deep sense of stillness, and you can once again truly listen, taste, and see. It's like the taste of food after a long fast, but for the rest of your senses. You also don't need a retreat to do this. Book a cabin in the woods for a week, and practice silence.

Another practice is sexual abstinence, which in men's circles is known as "Semen Retention" or "No Fap". It might sound stupid to some of you, but again, the ability to voluntarily control your desires is of profound importance. Sexual energy is powerful, vital, and life-giving. If you learn to direct it, by first having the self-control to 'save it', you can experience its benefits in the form of greater creativity, higher testosterone, and increased energy. Some of the greatest thinkers, warriors, fighters and leaders all throughout history practiced periodic abstinence. They would do so before battle, or during writing and thus channel this energy into the pursuit at hand. Mike Tyson once said: *"I always read that the great fighters never had sex before fights and I was a young kid and I wanted to be the youngest heavyweight champion in the world, so I restrained myself from sex for around five years."*

Working with your hands

When the crowd zigs, it often pays to zag. If the more cerebral or communicative pursuits (or both) don't draw you, learn to work with your hands. Learn a trade. Most moderns can't use a screwdriver or a hammer. If you're able to construct things, fix things, produce things, grow things, cook things or heal people by using those magical appendages, then you set yourself apart from many of the people in this world who only know how to scroll, tap or type.

This doesn't have to be something that brings you income, nor even be your core mission. It could be as simple as tending a garden and growing food, or learning to cook; or something more complex, like building a table, a library cabinet, or what I think every man should do at some stage: be involved in building his home. One of my personal goals is to one day build a sauna with my own two hands.

You may even be able to couple this skill with some sort of digital component, and pass on your knowledge to others who are interested. There is huge potential as the creator economy becomes the medium for all future learning.

Hunting is another, which I was not sure where to categorize. It's not just shooting, and it's not supposed to be some degenerate or flagrant taking of life. There is a deeper relationship to be found between predator and prey. There is an entire ritual to be observed in the taking of a life and the subsequent treatment and work that needs to be done to for example turn that life into sustenance. This is another entire rabbit hole, which I suggest you explore.

Movement

You must learn to move, and then continue to move, and refine your movement. The body and the mind are linked. If your body decays, your mind does too. Move for strength, move for fitness, move for utility, learn to move with grace; learn to defend yourself, and also how to attack if and when necessary. Remember: *"it's better to be a warrior in a garden, than a gardener in a war."*

Movement was a core part of the Samurai's training, and should be central to the training of everyone reading this, man or woman. The Samurai trained in *jiujitsu, kenjutsu* (which later developed into *kendo*: way of the sword) and other forms of martial arts. You can do many of the same today. There is more available than just lifting weights at the gym.

> *"Jiujutsu may be briefly defined as an application of anatomical knowledge to the purpose of offense or defense."*
>
> Inazo Nitobe, Bushido: The Soul of Japan

Building physical confidence and mastery has an incredibly positive impact on your emotions and your psychology. When you develop a relationship with your body, you enhance your vitality and transform your relationship with the world: you become more confident, and *powerful*. Sacrifice your health and ignore this dimension at your own peril.

Self-defense

Deeply related to movement, but also important enough to stand on its own, is self-defense. Health and aesthetics are incredibly important. Feeling and looking good is beautiful and beauty is godly; but being able to use your body is such a way that you can defend yourself gives you a deep-seated confidence that aesthetics alone cannot.

Self-defense also extends beyond what you can do with your body to what you can do with a weapon, and with your mind. Shooting a gun, for example, requires not only motor skills, but knowledge of how to use the weapon itself and a psychology of calm, alertness and self-control. You should also learn to use other physical weapons: a knife, a sword, a stick; not to go out and beat up random people - that's what a two-year-old does - but so that if some muppet comes at you or threatens that which you love, you will not cower away.

"In combat, you do not rise to the occasion. You sink to the level of your training."

Dave Grossman, On Combat

There are many avenues for these practices, and some of my favorites are BJJ, MMA and of course marksmanship.

Rituals

"Rituals are to time what home is to space: they render time habitable."

Byung-Chul Han, The Disappearance of Rituals

The Art of Ritual

To deepen networks you need to develop rituals and experiences. There is an entire set of skills required to put together an experience and lead people through it. You need a blend of deep domain knowledge, great communication skills and the ability to guide. You need to be able to tell a story, to listen and observe, to intuit, and know when to push, or when to ease up, to know when to start, when to escalate and when to finish.

Study and practice rituals of all kinds. Religious rituals are incredibly powerful. Baptism, Christmas and Easter in the Christian faith, Ramadan in Islam. Find yours. You can also look into ancient gender-specific festivals. The Thesmophoria, for example, was celebrated by women in Athens to honor the goddess Demeter and involved rituals and ceremonies related to fertility and agricultural abundance. Men were prohibited from participating or witnessing such rituals, in the same way that women were not allowed to be a part of male ones.

Gender-specific rituals are particularly important because they allow both men and women to develop bonds within an environment geared to their biology, physiology, psychology and temperament. It helps to make men more masculine and women more feminine - something modernity is sorely lacking, and a necessary tool in both the development of virtue and the management of vice.

Rituals of Time

Beyond the art of ritual, are actual rituals themselves. Time is something we are all subject to, and each have a unique relationship with. We've come to define and demarcate the progression of time via measures such as minutes, hours, days and years - but there is so much more to this phenomenon than what we measure. When cultures were more connected to the natural flow of life and the cyclicality of seasons, they developed simple rituals more aligned with these natural arcs, whether it was the daily rising and setting of the sun, the monthly full moon cycle, the summer or winter solstice, new year celebrations, and even significant holidays (holy days).

Rituals associated with these cycles can be incredibly simple and require no investment, so there is no excuse not to start today. Get up with the sunrise and sun gaze, or develop a wind-down practice that begins at sunset, respecting your circadian rhythm. Turn off your phone at night, have a set time for family dinner, create your own 'Sabbath' and spend Sundays off of technology, do a 24-hour water fast every new moon, or plan a new weekend adventure every other month. The options are plenty.

Give some real time and attention to your native holidays. Go above and beyond what you've normally done to make these days a special time with friends or family. Set intentions, share moments together, connect more deeply. Spend a day or two each quarter reconnecting to your vision for life, your goals, and reflecting on what you've accomplished. You'd be amazed at what zooming out can do for your sense of gratitude and your relationship to time. Finally, learn to relax. I say this more for myself than anyone else, as my mind is always on. I believe that cats have this right: they know how to relax, but they also know how to take intense action when needed. Most of us in the modern world would benefit from learning how to relax better (it's about quality), and annual festivals, celebrations or other special occasions are a great chance to do that.

Psycho-Spiritual Rituals

Rituals are disciplines that train and condition the mind, body and spirit. The modern world is full of schizophrenia, anxiety, confusion and doubt, in part because there is a lack of psycho-spiritual scaffolding in place to keep at bay the ocean of unconscious noise and detritus we've filled it with. We used to have a lack of information - now we are starving for signal.

The problems here stem from a mix of scientism around psychology on the one hand, and unrestrained hippie approaches on the other. Psychology is, in my opinion, more art than science. By trying to turn it into a hard science, and ignoring the spiritual component, we've made the mind, and the people it animates, more machine than human. This is why psychiatry and therapy are so dry and dead. Worse, this approach has created an entire pharmacological industry that preys on people's weaknesses, conjuring up a new label to "treat" every few months. The other side of the coin is not much better. You have people that think they "broke out of the matrix" because they had some form of psychedelic experience. Their default mode networks are disrupted and they see the world through a new light for a moment, but when they come back to reality, there is a disconnect, so they long for the experience once more. A rare few with good grounding and a strong enough constitution might integrate the experience and become more, but often these experiences open the door for people to go on journeys they're not equipped for. "Psychonauts," or "Neuropharmacologists" - which is just a fancy way of saying psychedelic junkie - tell themselves they're doing it "in the right setting" and "for the right reasons" but in reality are just dependent on those states to feel whole or certain. It's why so many go back to the jungle, everytime they feel a little anxiety... until they fry their brains.

I recognise that there are powerful tools that, if used by very few, select people, can lead to incredible insights and breakthroughs - but their wide use and appeal are a net negative for society. These substances fundamentally uproot and open the subject. I think we have more than enough of that in the world today. What we need is a little more closed borders, closed-mindedness and grounding. We need deeper roots, and more strength. The very fact that they're called plant-medicines implies that the people taking them are weak, broken or sick: not a great foundation to build from, and also not how the ancients used these substances. They were part of greater, more profound rites in which strong men, leaders or initiates under guidance were challenged. The Ancient Greek 'Eleusinian Mysteries', for example, involved exclusive invitations, a pilgrimage to the location, a series of ritual practices and drinking the 'kykeon'. The invitations were reserved for the warriors and the wise, and the experiences were less about "healing" and more about "insight" or "access" which had to be earned, and could only be done by the strong, wise or committed. This is something your run-of-the-mill psychonaut knows nothing of. So the question then is, what kinds of psycho-social rituals can lead to more strength, grounding, fortitude and wisdom?

Once again, there are many that require neither money nor resources. Prayer and meditation are two obvious examples. Meditation more for clarity, focus and calm. Prayer more for intention, guidance, gratitude and access to higher wisdom. Some people might write these off as fluff or woo-woo, but do so to their own detriment.

There are more intense and esoteric options that are probably not for everyone. Ancient cultures, particularly among Native American tribes, performed 'vision quests'. These rituals involved extended periods of isolation in nature, often with no food or water, and used these moments of intense vulnerability and exposure to the elements to find clarity and guidance from a higher power. Yes, often these were combined with some form of psychedelic substance; but notice it was not for "healing your childhood trauma" - but more for visions and access to something greater.

Another is active dreaming or active imagination. Carl Jung viewed the mind as a complex interplay of conscious and unconscious forces; rather than seeing it purely as a calculator or learning machine, Jung believed the unconscious held vast reservoirs of archetypal wisdom. Active Imagination involves intentionally engaging with the unconscious and using dreams or the imagination to teach, guide and reveal. Astral projection, somewhat related to this, is like a more advanced and ancient version of active dreaming in which the subject attempts to create an out-of-body experience and direct it in the dream state. The CIA experimented with this and other more wacky ideas. I'm not personally sure what's true and what's fiction, but Jung's approach is certainly worth considering, especially for creatives.

Finally, I'd point to writing as another method. It forces you to order the mind, and really think things through. Journaling is incredibly powerful and often far more effective than therapy for people dealing with stress or problems. The greatest of the great, all throughout history, turned to the pen when they were not using the sword.

Purification Rituals

All rituals are somewhat forms of purification - whether of the mind, spirit or body. *Misogi* is a specific Japanese concept involving an intense but brief challenge, or purification ritual aimed at cleansing oneself. Traditionally it involved things like standing under cold and intense waterfalls, embarking on a strenuous or dangerous climb, or meditation in a painful posture or location (e.g., multi-hour horse stances or meditation in the snow). Either way, the point is to use pain or danger to bring you into the present and thus purify the body and mind.

Modern variants of Misogi have started to gain traction - clearly because men have this yearning inside of them. People are now developing and undertaking challenges outside of their domains of work or personal interest, with the goal of self-improvement, or breaking beyond one's current limits. Wim Hof and the entire ice-bath / cold exposure movement is a civilian example. Hell Week is a modern military example: a grueling weeklong initiation into the US Navy Seals which people like David Goggins brought into mainstream consciousness. There are also more traditional examples still practiced, like the 'marathon monks' of Mount Hiei who run around 1000 marathons in 1000 days in search of enlightenment.

The point here isn't to spend the next three years running marathons daily, or to try and become the next David Goggins. Purification rituals are less about the challenge itself and more about the transformation that comes from undertaking and overcoming such an ordeal. The goal is to emerge from the experience with a clearer mind, free of the noise of past or future. The best ones are designed to bring you into the present and strengthen your fortitude. Overcoming these ordeals is symbolic and, like any ritual or rite of passage, you come out of it having shed either limitations or doubt, or you've gained a new insight and, often, rediscovered a sense of clarity and purpose that might have been previously lacking.

Settling Disputes

Less of a ritual, but relevant here as an addendum is dueling. Its removal from society has simultaneously separated behavior from consequence and outsourced the application of said consequence (or moral symmetry) to some flaccid, uninterested bureaucratic appendage of the state. This has had some significant unintended consequences on how society functions and its level of maturity, restraint and respect.

Yes, there were valid reasons for its abolition at the time. The advent of more sophisticated weaponry came with the almost guaranteed waste of a young life, over what might have been a trifling matter; even more serious matters would in many cases not warrant someone's death. However, by removing dueling we also over-feminised the world. State policing and democracy slowly made all acts of male aggression illegal, whether necessary or unnecessary. Men are no longer able to fight or settle disputes directly, so instead they resort to other more political, indirect, and effeminate ways to deal with anger or injustice. This causes them to turn inward, becoming envious, resentful and, worst of all, acting without honor.

Can we learn from the past and bring back localized violence but be more sensible about the approach? Maybe. In December 2019, two Brazilian politicians settled a long dispute over a waterpark conservation project by fighting each other in the cage, during a 3-round MMA fight. "Alaric the Barbarian" (on X.com) noted:

> *"At the very least, men should be able to choose to fistfight without interference. Those Brazilian politicians stepping into an octagon over some zoning dispute — that is civilization, and far more honest than typical politics."*

Contrary to popular belief, there must be some way to settle disputes that does not boil down to social gaming or indirect scheming. The necessary substrate for a culture with honor is the very real threat of violence. Dueling is the ritualization of violence for this very reason. The mutual agreement to combat creates an environment where the consequences for poor behavior are more directly felt, and served by the party being infringed upon. It also forces men to learn how to back their word up with action, resulting in a stronger society.

This is the only truly civilized way to settle conflicts!

In Closing

As the battle for the soul of humanity rages on, Bitcoiners, being the most likely group to ascend economically speaking, have a duty to become better people, and men in particular must lead. Learning and mastering these skills, tools and rituals along the way is critical.

This is obviously not an exhaustive list, but a teaser. It's *your* job to dig further and find *your* chosen sword or vocation. You also don't have to do or master all of it: the best archers were not always the best swordsmen; the best writers may not be not the best fighters. My emphasis on entrepreneurialism doesn't mean you *have* to be an entrepreneur. In fact, most people are not wired that way, and that's fine. Some of you are more suited to being excellent operators or managers. There are a few savants able to achieve mastery across many of these dimensions, but those people are the exception; if you are one of them, then power to you: be the one who inspires the rest of us! If not, that's fine. Focus on your strengths and do your best to round things out between practices that involve your body on the one hand, and mind on the other.

For those of you who are thinking "but it's not so easy."

Yes, correct - *it's not supposed to be easy*. Learning something new never is. Earning something takes time, patience and dedication. You'll have to endure failure and participate in things you don't like. Welcome to life. It's not always sunshine and rainbows.

A common example of this is people with a reticence toward learning how to use Bitcoin. Their derision usually amounts to: "*I don't want to learn how to secure my keys, run a node or learn how to use a wallet, because it's hard.*" The truth is not that they can't, or that it's necessarily hard, but that they can't be bothered. They say this is a problem with Bitcoin's UX, but in reality the problem is in their (un)willingness to learn.

If that's been you, wake up. You learned how to use a smartphone to scroll on Instagram. I'm sure you can learn to back up a seed phrase and send a transaction. What we end up with is often a reflection of our willingness to adapt. You may not like it, but I'm sorry - this is **fair.** Reality doesn't care about your feelings.

Learning the skills and the use of the tools listed above is also going to help you develop the virtues discussed in this book. How, you ask? Through *practice*. Virtues are not innate qualities or inherent traits, but behaviors developed through repeated action. Aristotle argued that virtue is not something that can be taught through lectures or theory, but rather something that must be learned through practice and habituation. This view has important implications for moral education and character development: rather than simply teaching moral principles or rules, we should focus on cultivating virtuous habits through practices like the ones listed above. Practices that require you to act out the virtues you want to teach!

Not sure where to start? Go find a Bitcoin conference. Search for a skills retreat. Join a martial arts gym. Subscribe to a newsletter. Watch a podcast. Meet some people and put yourself out there. Go face your fears, get punched in the face, approach that girl you're afraid will reject you, start that business, quit that shitty job, add that extra plate to the barbell, and whether you fail or succeed, *keep going*. If you fall over, learn why, then get up again. All of this builds your character and, in the end, that's what counts.

If you're up for the challenge, take it up a notch and hold yourself accountable with some key metrics. Go hunt your own meal, squat twice your bodyweight, make your first dollar online, do a three-day water-only fast, learn to submit someone in BJJ, run a six-minute mile, spend an entire week offline, give a 20-minute presentation, or learn how to fix and splint a broken arm. All of these milestones, while arbitrary, require a deep process of learning and embodiment that will force you to be disciplined, master some skills and become a more capable badass.

And finally, if you're still not sure where to start, or you have started and want to join a brotherhood of men doing similar things, feel free to reach out to me directly and I'll point you in the right direction. My direct messages are open across all platforms.

PART V

What the Future Holds

What the Future Holds

I spent a lot of time beating up the modern world in this book, and for good reason. We are living in a broken simulacrum, with clown world running on repeat. That being said - I want to make clear that it's not all bad. Despite the madness and moral debauchery there is not only hope, but a lot of good, and much to look forward to. I still believe this is the greatest time to be alive. In this final section, I want to light a fire in your soul. I want to encourage you to think and feel, so you're inspired to **build** the future.

So long as the smallest blade of grass protrudes from the concrete or the weakest rays of light pierce the darkness, the opportunity for beauty remains. It is up to our generation to turn things around. This is our cross to bear, and we shall prevail, because life and vitality are both on our side. What comes next will draw from the best of what came before, and will manifest in a new, greater and higher form.

Our civilization is the most powerful since Rome - but it rose from Rome's ashes. The modern world, powered largely by shared, western, Christian values has reached its zenith and is now in decline. It too will be replaced by something new and more powerful that will rise from its ashes. This is our time.

Pressure is necessary for transformation, and not all transformation is equal, even under equal pressure. One substance is crushed, while another turns to diamond: the same is true with people. Clown-world will turn most people into Nietzsche's Last Man. The consooomer archetype, plugged into VR goggles, with soy and bug juice injected right into their veins. It will also awaken lions: it will turn them into leaders, men and women of vitality, of aligned thinking and action, beautiful and pulsating with energy. Project that difference out a few generations and you'll get a sense for what is on the horizon. A new strong and noble class, separate from a weak, base class.

This is nothing to be afraid of. It is the natural way of things. We all reap what we sow, and it magnifies across generations. We're at the bifurcation point now. Modern technology, combined with Bitcoin, Nostr, the Internet, online learning, communities and digital public squares like X, will transform the world faster than anyone can possibly imagine.

It's already happening. What we know today about health, strength training, food, sunlight and supplementation alone can help build superhumans. Add to that our technological prowess and access to an ever-greater quantum of energy, along with a global, interconnected economy built on an incorruptible monetary base and communications network - and you have the makings for an extraordinarily bright future. We just need the courage to claim it. It's on us now.

The earth has become small, and on it hops the Last Man, who makes everything small. His species is ineradicable as the flea; the Last Man lives longest.

"We have discovered happiness" – say the Last Men, and they blink.

They have left the regions where it is hard to live; for they need warmth. One still loves one's neighbor and rubs against him; for one needs warmth.

Turning ill and being distrustful, they consider sinful: they walk warily. He is a fool who still stumbles over stones or men!

A little poison now and then: that makes for pleasant dreams. And much poison at the end for a pleasant death.

One still works, for work is a pastime. But one is careful lest the pastime should hurt one.

One no longer becomes poor or rich; both are too burdensome. Who still wants to rule? Who still wants to obey? Both are too burdensome.

No shepherd, and one herd! Everyone wants the same; everyone is the same: he who feels differently goes voluntarily into the madhouse.

"Formerly all the world was insane," – say the subtlest of them, and they blink.

They are clever and know all that has happened: so there is no end to their derision. People still quarrel, but are soon reconciled – otherwise it upsets their stomachs.

They have their little pleasures for the day, and their little pleasures for the night, but they have a regard for health.

"We have discovered happiness," – say the Last Men, and they blink.

Friedrich Nietzsche, Thus Spoke Zarathustra: The Last Men

Visions of the Future

"Vision without action is merely a dream. Action without vision just passes the time. Vision with action can change the world."

Joel Barker, *Future Edge: Discovering the New Paradigms of Success*

A state and a government are two different things but they are often conflated. A government is the specific body in charge of the direction and governance of a territory or a people; a state includes the government, along with the economic apparatus, the military, internal security such as the police, the intelligence services, the regulatory apparatus and the civil service. It is the complete tool or structure that orders, demarcates, and governs a territory.

There are many kinds of state models. Rome was a multiracial state in its twilight and so too is the modern USA. There were aristocratic states like the medieval monarchies, which have no real analogue today outside of perhaps Rhodesia in the 60s and 70s, although it was a "landed republic" not a monarchy. There are also city-states as were characteristic of Ancient Greece, and which places like Singapore resemble most closely today.

The most common modern state is the nation-state, which became the standard after the Treaty of Westphalia which ended the Thirty Years War. The nation-state traditionally centered on a racial group, although most modern ones have morphed quite a bit in the last half century, thanks to mass migration. The word "nation" originates from the Latin word *natio*, which itself comes from the verb *nasci*, meaning "to be born." *Natio* originally referred to a group of people connected by common birth or origin, and was used to describe tribes or ethnic groups with shared ancestry. Thus the word "nation" means "of shared birth" and, technically speaking, the nation-state was a structure established to help govern a population of people who are culturally and ethnically related.

Unfortunately for the anarchists out there, there will never be a full dissolution of the state. It has always, and will always exist in some form. Only the name and style will change. As such, the more important question to address is what will future states look like? I have a number of ideas on this, all which point to a move away from democracies and large-scale, equalitarian states, in large part thanks to a changing monetary paradigm. As outlined in section three, economically non-viable territories and regions will find it impossible to persist without collapsing or intentionally splitting into smaller units that are more coherent and functional. I believe this will lead to a patchwork of state and governance models that vary based on territorial factors like the local climate, altitude, size, geographic location, locally available resources, along with social factors like ethnicity, culture, religion, and history.

In *The UnCommunist Manifesto*, Mark Moss and I argued that on a Bitcoin Standard we will see the rise of meritocracies. These are societies oriented around merit and will likely lead to more hierarchy, because people apply themselves to different things in different ways, all to varying degrees. Think of how a good business functions and who gets promoted versus who gets fired.

"We propose a transformation and reorganization of society not by decree, but by the natural, emergent force of competence and liberty.

One of dynamic inequality, where classes continue to exist (they always will), but are permeable. Where the opportunity to rise up is available to all, and so too is everyone subject to the risk of failure and falling down the hierarchy. Upward motion becomes a function of work, competence, skill, talent, perseverance, desire, will and of course, luck. Downward motion a function of waste, poor calculation, mistakes, bad judgement, immoral behaviour, incompetence, laziness and of course, bad luck."

Mark Moss and Aleksandar Svetski, The UnCommunist Manifesto

Visually, this could look like the figure below. Notice how there are still classes but, because they're permeable, you ideally create a population structure that is thicker in the middle, and more like a circle - which is probably what America looked more like in its heyday. A larger and healthier middle class, fewer poor people and an elite who by definition are a smaller fraction of the total.

→ Free market: Dynamic, social mobility

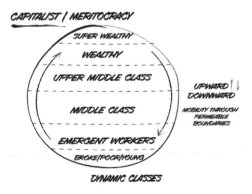

I'd like to take the idea further and suggest that there will most likely be many variants of meritocracy. The one that I think will be most prevalent, because of operational efficiency and the effectiveness of great leadership, is Meritocratic Feudalism. Imagine "CEO Kings" who lead for many decades, treat their territory like their home, their citizens as their family and have the commercial and economic acumen of a Jeff Bezos or Elon Musk. This is what I described earlier in the book: *an archetype that is some blend of Alexander the Great and Steve Jobs.* People like this already exist. President Nayib Bukele of El Salvador is a prime example, as was Lee Kwan Yew of Singapore. LKW made Singapore the economic powerhouse of Asia within a few decades, with minimal land, no natural resources, and a tiny population. Bukele has completely transformed El Salvador within one term, making it the safest state in the entirety of the Americas - which is a remarkable feat when you realize it was the **unsafest** when his tenure as president commenced. It's no wonder he has the highest approval rating of any leader in the modern world. Beyond this format, I'm sure we will also see Meritocratic Republicanism, and even Meritocratic Democracy, where your ability to vote is based on what you "bring to the table," economically or socially speaking.

I can also imagine Holocracies, with governance models that replace bureaucrats with mystics. Think "Sol Brah" as the head of a new micro-state's health ministry and Joe Rogan as the voice of the nation. Aretocracies are another idea: modern warrior societies built around excellence, like "Neo-Spartas", with highly advanced military orders and strict warrior cultures. Bioregionalism is also interesting: this idea recognises that cultural, political and economic systems can be more sustainable if they are organized around naturally-defined ecosystems and environmental features. It expands beyond arbitrary nation-state boundaries and ties its people directly to a territory, ecosystem and local knowledge. Examples of different bioregions might include wetlands, deserts, prairies, forests, jungles, marshlands and even the arctic.

Another approach is some sort of non-localised or "distributed state" model, similar to the Jewish diaspora. The Jews are a borderless state unto themselves sharing a common culture and religion and, to a large degree, DNA. A future version of this might be "Digital Nomad States" where participation requires certain meritocratic markers, economic capacity, or standards of aptitude and biological excellence. This is not unlike clubs and associations (secret or not) which many of us are familiar with, and have clearly worked since the beginning of time. This also leads to another few potential variants. Religion-based states, or DNA/ethnicity-based states. Both of these could actually transcend borders and territory, and we have prototypes of each today. Utah for example is practically a Mormon state. I can also imagine a Catholic state, where citizens are far greater in number, and obviously not confined to the Vatican territory. Likewise, DNA or ethnic states, which also exist today in some form (you hold a passport from a particular nation); but, instead of it being migration based, it is blood-based, similar to how the UAE works: almost anyone can become a resident of the UAE, yet only Emiratis can be citizens. This model also extends beyond borders, and can include a hub or a home like what the UAE territory fundamentally represents.

Some might say this is not possible in places like Europe for example, but I'd argue that it is! Norway, with all its oil wealth, could literally be the Abu Dhabi or Dubai of Europe. Instead, it's become a sterile, feminized country with low energy, more interested in celebrating pride month and importing immigrants who clearly do not fit in. They make their own people feel guilty, while invaders are welcomed who then cause trouble in the streets. I speak from first hand experience, when I was there last. Little hoodlums selling drugs and riding around on scooters with the stands down so they can scrape the concrete and be a public nuisance. Oslo is such a beautiful city, and the country itself has so much potential. The people are clearly intelligent, but you can feel the despair. They know they're being invaded, but it would be "mean" or "wrong" to point it out. Contrast that with how Dubai treats their own people, how they treat guests & tourists and how they treat immigrants. If Europeans, and Westerners more broadly speaking, drop their guilt and embrace both their own people and cultures, the kind of transformation that occurred in Dubai, Singapore and El Salvador is also possible there.

There are many other models to explore, but I will cover them all in depth in a subsequent book. For now, instead of me *telling* you more, allow me to *show* you a vision of the future.

The Sovereign Cross

An Executive Alliance Story.

Block 4,025,430: Morning, November 11th, 2084

The gray sky of the Old World hung like a stained blanket over the dilapidated concrete structures. No guards patrolled these streets — only the rheumy eyes of a surveillance state long past its peak. A cool wind carried the scent of rotting garbage. Flickering security cameras strained to stay functional. The jittering hum of malfunctioning drones patrolling the streets added to the cacophony of a dying city. From inside the perimeter of UN Zone-12, remnants of civilization limped along, shadowed by crumbling towers that once boasted grandeur.

The familiar stink of fried circuits burnt in the air, and beneath the constant hum of neglected machines, corruption thrived, as it always has. In these zones, black market trade occurred between smugglers and functionaries. This was where Thane did his business, exploiting the chaotic fringes of a regime that was too underfunded to fully monitor itself.

Beyond this decayed perimeter zone lay the cold heart of New Brussels, the largest UN City in West Europa. It was stark and clean, with brutalist megastructures rising in geometric silhouette against the pale sky. The sterile streets of the inner sanctum were lined with steel and concrete, devoid of color or life. Automated transports glided along pre-set tracks, and perfectly calibrated drones swept the streets, vigilant for any disturbance. Inside the spires, the elites—gene-tweaked bureaucrats engineered for precision—lived out their carefully managed lives, isolated from the decay on the fringes. A world was as lifeless as the machines that ran it, Thane reflected.

He turned back to Functionary Kline, who was standing across from him in the ramshackle office, eyes cold and glassy. Their skin had the sheen of artificiality, like an AI-generated image brought to life. Kline was an androgynous, low-level bureaucrat, their sharp, angular features a product of the UN's sterile laboratories, literally engineered to serve the Secretariats of the UN.

The functionary's gaze locked onto Thane's as he settled into the chair. "The Deputy Director sends her regards," Kline began, voice clipped and flat. "She asks when you will be returning to the UN? This... smuggling business of yours is becoming dangerous. Straddling two worlds is going to catch up to you sooner or later." Thane shrugged, leaning back in his chair, his gaze drifting momentarily to the long-dead cameras hanging impotently from the ceiling. "Since when did the UN care about the wellbeing of people like me? As long as you get your toys, your Secretary General and her friends are happy, right?" He kept his tone casual, but his eyes were sharp.

The functionary's lip curled in distaste, but they held their composure. "We don't approve of UN citizens living in the Executive States." Their voice dripped with heavy contempt. "Those so-called bastions of freedom." They made the phrase sound like a curse. "Free Markets and capitalism, but only for the rich. No regulations, no morals, no humanity."

Thane smirked. "It's not so bad" he said, nonchalantly. "And I don't make waves." He thought how much more humane NeoAlexandria actually was, compared to this shithole. But there was no point explaining that to this creature - they would never understand.

The functionary snorted softly. "Of course, they'd let in a smuggler like you without blinking, but God forbid any of our people want to enter. *Only Sovereign IDs accepted.* Ridiculous. They'll close their borders to our citizens but sell us their technology when it suits them."

The elites of the UN couldn't stand the Executive States, not just because they embodied everything the UN opposed — capitalism, free-markets, individual freedom — but because they were a closed society. The UN was always pushing for assimilation and globalism. *"One people, one world,"* as their slogan went. When the Great Remigration of the forties and fifties failed, the world split. On the one hand were regions like NeoAlexandria, Bayernland, Salvador, Formosa, the Vredeburg Republic, and the Free State of Texas - whose people came to be known as New-Worlders. On the other were the 'Old-Worlders' of the UN mega-states like West Europa, Eurabia, China, Australand, and the American Democratic Union.

Thane shifted the conversation back to business. "What they do with their land is their problem. It just means I can bring the tech you need over here for you and your pals. So let's skip the politics and get this done."

The functionary's eyes narrowed. "You're right. You wouldn't understand anyway." Their tone was sharp, dismissive. Then, almost without pause, the functionary's gaze shifted to the slim case in Thane's hand. "Did you bring the latest model?"

Thane opened the case, revealing fourteen sleek, black, high-bandwidth brain-computer interface chips, the kind that could connect directly to any networked system.

Thane locked eyes with Kline. "Not the latest, but you couldn't afford the latest."

The functionary's lips twisted into a tight line, their synthetic features betraying their frustration. "Things shouldn't be about price," they muttered, their voice dropping into the low, rehearsed tone of propaganda. "Goods should be traded based on need, for the benefit of the many, not the greed of the few."

"You can believe what you want," said Thane. "All I know is, these are genuine Neuralinks, not the shitty Microsoft Synapse you people are still using. If you want them, you have to pay for them. Simple as that."

The functionary's eyes flicked back to the chips. These weren't just tech — they were power. Their expression tightened, but they said nothing. Officially, the UN denounced all trade with the Executive States, labeling them anarchist states, and in many cases refusing to formally acknowledge their sovereignty, but in reality, they needed them.

The truth was as obvious as it was embarrassing: without black-market trade, the elites of the UN City would lose control of their sterile world. The commodities Thane brought—mostly luxury goods, high-end electronics, and even things like free range beef and butter—were critical for both the way of life the UN elites were used to, and for their grip on power.

"They'll do," the functionary muttered, trying to feign nonchalance. "How much?"

"Two point four million Sats," Thane stated flatly, and quickly added; "Which is a *fraction* of what they're worth to your boss."

The functionary broke into a mild sweat. "That's more than I have authority to pay you." Regaining their composure they quickly added, "But I do have UN credits I can transfer to make up the difference."

Thane pulled back the case. "Bitcoin only. That's non-negotiable." UN credits were not only in a constant state of inflation, but everything was traced and tied to his UN identity and social credit score. There was no way he could explain that kind of income without it either being frozen, confiscated, or taxed 80% - which was basically the same as being confiscated.

The functionary's face tightened, their composure faltering just for a moment. "But it's impossible! The Deputy Director has given me strict instructions and a strict budg-"

Thane cut Kline off. "I'm not risking *my* life for *your* boss. If you can't afford it all, go find another vendor, and don't waste my time." Thane knew he was being a little overly aggressive, but he'd been here before, and knew others who had compromised, only to end up in jail, or have their mobility privileges suspended for unexplained income. No chance he was taking that risk.

Kline stared at him with those cold eyes, then, face once again expressionless, said flatly, "Here is your two point four million." And added, with a voice suddenly colder. "You'd do well not to get too comfortable. The world might tolerate people like you for now, but straddling both sides won't work forever. You are vulnerable alone."

Two point four million received, his AI assistant Selene informed him a moment later through his own Hyperion-Grade NeuraLink. ***Moving the sats to a mixer now.*** Mixers erased all traces of Bitcoin transfers, before being consolidated with other unspent transaction outputs and deposited into cold storage.

"I'm not alone," Thane shrugged. "And nothing is forever."

He picked up his briefcase, turned and left the dim office. The functionary's gaze clung to him like a shadow, making the spot between his shoulders itch.

Outside, the wind carried that familiar border zone stench, and as he stepped back into the decaying sprawl of Zone-12, he couldn't help but think about the gap between the old and the new worlds — and how his life was a series of action scenes from right in the middle of it. He also couldn't get the functionary's final comment out of his mind. *You are vulnerable alone.* Was that a threat? Should he be worried?

No time to dwell on it. Cleo was back home in NeoAlex, probably worrying - as usual - about his latest mission. He'd almost forgotten that their last conversation was a bit heated. *Babe you have to stop crossing over so often. Something's going to go wrong one of these days... and I don't want to even think about what I would do if I lost you.*

Cleo. Please. I've got this under control. I've almost saved up enough to buy lifetime residencies for both of us. Once we've got permanent Sovereign IDs, I'll be done with that UN shithole

You've been saying that for years now! Why do we need lifetime residencies? Why can't you just get a job here and do it the normal way?

Cleo ... I'm not having this conversation again! You see the Capitol building out there? You see the AeroDome? You think that was built by people who settled for normal? No. It was built by people with vision, power, and money. I've got plans. For you, for me, for your mom and dad. For all of us. We'll have more than we ever dreamed of.

But what if you get caught?

I'm not getting caught! Fuck!

Ah, women. Beautiful, emotional, and irrational. He couldn't wait to see her again. **Selene, let's get the hell out of here. Get me a new Iris Lens printed. I'm taking the tube.**

I'm spinning one up now, Selene replied. **This ID has enough social scoring to get you into the city and back out to Zone 9.**

Great, thought Thane. Deal is done. Time to go home.

Would you like me to upgrade your Sovereign ID's to permanent status? Asked Selene

Twenty million each right?

Yes, replied Selene matter-of-factly,

And everything else is in order too?

Yes, Selene said again.

Thane met all the genetic requirements, his ideological and cultural alignment scores were all in the top one percentile, as were his health and fitness scores. His record was clean, and his IQ, EQ and aptitude scores were well above standard. It was just the payment remaining.

Well... it's what we've been saving up for. Do it.

He'd run dozens of these missions in the last few years. The money from this deal, along with what he'd saved up over almost a decade of smuggling, would give him enough to upgrade both his and Cleo's Sovereign ID memberships to permanent, and leave some to start his TransitDrone fleet. *Once that's done,* he thought to himself, *I'll do a ritual burning of my UN passport and start really making some money.* No more border crossings, no more smuggling... Well, at least it wouldn't be him personally doing the smuggling anymore.

Block 4,025,436

Thane picked up his pace, heading for the local tube station that connected the outskirts to the city center. The iris scanners at the entry were one of the few things still functional in Zone-12, along with the sentry drones on the carriages. It was the only way to keep the dregs of society from overrunning the inner city.

By the time Thane had entered the terminal, the *PolyCell Forge* in his briefcase had produced a new Iris Lens to Selene's specifications. He pressed his thumb on a particular section near the corner, which upon scanning his thumbprint, silently slid out a small compartment revealing two perfectly circular, translucent disks. The Iris Lenses contained a full UN-identity. **Alright Selene,** he thought as he entered the terminal, **Who am I?**

You're an accountant from the lower east side of Zone 12. Your name is Marshall, you have 3 pet Chihuahuas, and you're dating James from Zone 9, who is also an accountant.

Wait, what? You picked a gay guy with 3 dogs?

You're too well dressed to be straight, and it's a little more believable coming from this side of town, at this time.

Thane sighed audibly. **Yeah I guess you're right. Here goes.**

He lined up behind what looked like a stressed out lawyer, who was hurriedly pulling electronics from his briefcase, hands shaking as he fumbled through the security gate. It was a pathetic display, and Thane knew the routine well — just another part of the charade. The gate was deliberately placed before the iris scanner, forcing anyone without enough social credits to endure the humiliating pretense of security theater, only to be denied access to the tube afterward.

When it was Thane's turn, he stepped up to the scanner, his face a blank mask. He was nervous every time he did one of these imitation scans. If it didn't work, or if Selene ever made an error - which was highly unlikely - he'd be fucked. **Fear is the mind killer,** Selene whispered inside his head, sensing the increase in his heart rate and half jokingly referencing one of his favorite books.

Right.

The blue light flashed, cutting straight into his eyes. He winced internally, forcing himself to keep still. *I hate these fucking scanners. It's like they're designed to blind you, little by little.*

The door ground open, and Thane placed his briefcase on the security tray. The briefcase was designed with reflective surfaces that tricked scanners into showing innocuous images of paperwork or mundane cargo. The deception was seamless.

Block 4,025,439

The tube ride wasn't long. The sprawling border zones were connected to one another, and to New Brussels, by a tube network laid out like a hub with spokes. It allowed for rapid travel between the zones and the inner city, but getting from one zone to another required either multiple tubes — which drained mobility credits — or the use of an autonomous vehicle, a luxury that few could afford.

As he sat there, Thane thought about the hypocrisy of this place. The Secretary-General, the Deputy Director and her inner circle lived lavishly, propped up by the same contraband that smugglers like him risked their lives to deliver, all while their subjects starved. This was the equality they bragged of. He used to feel a little guilty about his role in it all, but not anymore. Not since he realized that people here actually *enjoyed* their slavery. They voted for the UN, they voted for multiculturalism, they voted for NeoCommunism. The masses here didn't want freedom — they wanted comfort, the kind that would make them sick, fat, and docile. *They chose this life.*

Thane hadn't.

His parents had been different. They were alive when the world shattered, the countries split and nations dissolved. They understood the truth, saw it with their own eyes, but they never had the means to escape. Instead, they moved to the fringes, to the outskirts, which at the time were not so bad. They grew their own food — real food — while they could, before the bans. Thane's childhood was marked by the smell of roasting meat, fresh milk, eggs, and the warmth of a self-sufficient life that now only existed in the Executive States. It was that diet that made him stand out. He grew strong, muscular, vibrant — everything his peers were not.

The other children in his school looked pale and weak by comparison. Malnourished, even. And that difference didn't go unnoticed. The school board reported his family to the Department of Sustainable Consumption. Their enforcement arm, the Nutritional Equity Council, showed up at his home one night. When the agents discovered his parents had been purchasing "excessive" animal products through underground markets, their social credit score was nuked.

He remembered the day it happened — his father being escorted out of the house by men in gray uniforms, his mother standing frozen in the doorway. Their status destroyed, their bank accounts erased, they had become pariahs overnight. Forbidden from owning property, stripped of their mobility rights, they were sentenced to a life of obscurity in the border zones.

That day lit the fire inside of Thane. He knew he couldn't live in a world where every aspect of life was measured and dictated by faceless bureaucrats. He wouldn't be reduced to a number on a social credit ledger like his parents. That's what led him to escape into NeoAlexandria, and run the risks he ran now.

Block 4,025,444

Thank you, mom and dad. Thane said a little prayer for them, and stepped off the carriage at Central Station to the familiar crush of bodies and the low hum of announcements in the air. He blended into the crowd, but not well enough. The people around him were pale, hunched, and malnourished. Thane's broad frame marked him as an outsider. He felt the stares almost immediately.

The guards stationed at the entrance to the next tube platform exchanged glances, their eyes lingering on him a bit too long. Not because they knew who he was — he hoped — but because someone like him didn't belong here. He was too healthy, too well-fed, and unlike the local elites, who often had a similar stature, he had a tan. His skin was all too *human*.

They don't like the look of you, Selene piped up cheekily.

No shit, he replied.

But it seems they're looking *for* you, Selene continued a moment later in a more serious tone. **A facial recognition alert has been triggered. You've got about sixty seconds before the guards find out.**

He cursed silently. His instinct was right. Not so much about being watched, but about that slimy functionary's tone and final words. The bureaucrat must've sent his details to the authorities so they could trap him here. *There's no fucking way I'm getting trapped here.*

Selene, find and fabricate a new Iris Lens. Something that'll get me through the next checkpoint. The old lens was linked to his face now. A new one was the only shot. If it fooled the scanners, he could get through the next checkpoint and on the next tube.

Already on it. Twelve more seconds.

The seconds ticked by like hours as Thane maneuvered through the station. He kept his eyes forward, pretending not to feel the growing tension. Ahead of him, the checkpoint loomed, the next obstacle between him and home. Fully automated, reliant on iris scans — in this case, the weak point in the UN's obsessive surveillance network.

Ready! Selene chirped proudly. Thane's fingers quickly slid over that familiar corner of his briefcase. He popped the old lens out and slipped the new one in with a smooth motion that looked like nothing more than rubbing his eye. His vision blurred momentarily, then snapped back into focus just as he neared the checkpoint.

Alright, he thought, trying in vain to calm his nerves. **Let's hope this works.**

Of course it's going to work. When have I ever let you down?

He stepped up to the scanner, staring straight ahead as the blue light swept across his eyes. It blinked once, paused, and then turned green.

Verified.

Thane exhaled, and picked up the pace as he stepped beyond the gate.

Selene, has that alert escalated?

Not yet, but once they match your face to the gate they'll know you're going to Zone 9. They'll also link the lens you used, so we can assume this one is burned.

OK ... so plan B... *"Agghhh."*

Thane had barely turned the corner when every muscle in his body spasmed and everything went black. No sound, no warning — just a sudden jolt of electric fire coursing through his nerves. Two SentryBots had hit him with pinpoint taser shots. He dropped to the floor, unconscious before he even registered the attack.

Block 4,025,475

Thane came to slowly, his senses returning in fragments. His limbs felt heavy, almost like he was in a high gravity chamber. He tried to move, but nothing responded. His arms were locked into place by metal cuffs that ran from his wrists half way up to his elbows, and his legs were the same, although he couldn't look down because his head was also in some sort of brace. Before he put it all together, he heard Selene's voice whisper to him. **Thane. I'm sorry. I didn't see them coming in the terminal. I've been unable to get a proper read on the room because your eyes were shut the entire time, but judging by your vitals, the room temperature and the coordinates, they have you in an interrogation cell.**

Thane had heard of these cells before. Smugglers, regime dissidents, and people unlucky enough to have gotten their hands on some Bitcoin but too clueless to properly mix it were brought here and tortured until they gave up access to their funds - and in many cases, they were lobotomized. **It's OK. It wasn't your fault. Can you transmit?**

No. It seems this head brace is also a signal blocker of some sort-

"Mr Drakos," a familiar voice came from the darkness. "How good to see you again so soon."

Kline, thought Thane as a fury rose up in his solar plexus. "I thought our deal was concluded? What's all the fuss about?"

"Mr Drakos. The deal was never concluded. It was merely ... *delayed*." Kline's voice carried an air of an animal toying with its prey.

"What do you mean delayed?" responded Thane with in ice his voice

I could fucking strangle this little lizard if I could get my hands on him, Thane said to Selene.

Not to worr-

Kline cut in with a venomous tone, *"You* didn't think you could just take the equivalent of four hundred million UN Credits and just leave, did you?"

"Take? I sold you fourteen NeuraLinks!!"

"This is the UN Mr Drakos. We neither use nor recognise NeuraLinks or StarLinks or any other corrupt capitalist technologies."

Thane remained silent, trying to gather his thoughts. **Don't worry,** said Selene again, this time managing to add, **I managed to send a sig-**

"You were arrested for illegally transporting contraband, and defrauding a public officer of the UN for a sum of four hundred million UN Credits."

"Fucking wha- *ARGHH!*" Thane's scream tore through the room as a surge of electricity ripped through his body. The cuffs around his arms and legs glowed faintly, as they delivered targeted shocks. His muscles spasmed uncontrollably, his vision blurring with the intensity of the pain. The interrogation chair was sophisticated, designed to send shocks directly to his nervous system, bypassing the skin. His heart pounded in his chest, his entire body trembling as the charge subsided, leaving him gasping for breath, drenched in cold sweat.

"You will hold your tongue Mr Drakos. Every time you interrupt me, my assistant, Mr Flloyd, will gladly remind you that you are in our custody."

"Yeah, and we don't take kindly to criminals in this country," added the assistant, stupidly.

Thane glared back at the functionary with a gaze that could pierce him. Kline looked away, unsettled by those cold blue eyes and continued, with some uncertainty in his voice, "you have one chance at being released, and that is to return the money. You will still be charged with smuggling, but I am sure the Deputy Director will see to it that any sentence is lenient."

"And If I can't?" Asked Thane, with a slight smirk, that defied his pain and exhaustion.

"Then we will *make* you," replied Kline with a cold finality.

After all these years, thought Thane, *these people still don't understand how Bitcoin works.*

"You do realize that Bitcoin transactions are irreversible right? This isn't some UN credit system or CBDC. Once it's spent it's spent."

"Spare me the lecture on finance Mr Drakos. Just have your fancy BCI chip transfer the money back to-"

Before the functionary could finish his sentence, the wall behind him lit up and exploded. Thane felt the heat of the blast and winced as small debris flew toward him and struck him in the face. Through the smoke he could make out four dark silhouettes. **Hyperion Hoplites!** said Selene, sounding extremely pleased with herself. Thane watched as four black-armored Hoplites stepped into the room, quickly and efficiently neutralizing Kline, his assistant, and three guards who Thane hadn't even noticed until they sprung into action.

One of the Hoplites approached Thane with a plasma cutter, its blade flickering with bright blue energy as it sliced through his restraints. Behind him a swarm of UN SentryBots flew into the room. The other Hoplites were waiting for them, and dropped the drones out of the air with quick Micro-EMPs bursts before they could get within range.

"Mr Drakos," said the Hoplite that had just cut Thane free. "My name is Commander Dios. We are here to extract, and bring you back to NeoAlexandria. Are you injured?"

Thane was still half in a daze, no longer from having been knocked out earlier in the day, but from watching the show in front of him, and wondering if he was dreaming.

"Mr Drakos, are you injured?"

"No ... no ... I'm ok. But, how did you-?"

I was trying to tell you, said Selene sheepishly.

"We'll explain on the ride home. Right now, we need you to come with us."

Did you organize this? Asked Thane

Yes. One of the relatively obscure benefits of top tier Sovereign ID membership, is access to an extraction team, said Selene triumphantly.

Block 4,025,511

On board the Sovereign Cross TransitDrone, Thane leaned back and exhaled. The adrenaline had worn off, leaving a dull ache in his joints, head and muscles. But it was ok. Thane was on the way back to NeoAlexandria.

How much did that just cost? he asked Selene, knowing the answer wouldn't be pleasant.

Six hundred thousand, Selene replied sheepishly.

Thane let out a short, dry laugh. *Of course it did.* **That's more than I made on this job.** He shook his head at the absurdity of it. *Busted my ass for this deal, only to piss it away on the same day,* thought Thane, then added to Selene, **I'm surprised I even had that much.**

Well … you didn't, not exactly, Selene admitted. **After paying for the two Sovereign IDs, you had some left over for the deposit on your next TransitDrone. Instead of paying for that, I opted for the extraction insurance which you were now eligible for. Given Kline's tone earlier, I ran some probabilities and figured you'd need it. And I was right,** she concluded smugly.

Thane stared out the drone's window, and then looked back over at the Hoplites. He couldn't even be mad. Selene had once again saved his ass, but the irony of it all stung his ego. **Thank you Selene,** Thane said sincerely. **I guess yours and Cleo's intuition was right this time.**

Women are like that, replied Selene, in a cheeky tone

At that moment, one of the Hoplites walked over, his face obscured by the sleek exo-helmet.

"Mr. Drakos, you were fortunate today. We were already in the Neutral Zone when we received the extraction order, and the coordinates from your assistant. Had we been farther away, it might have taken longer."

"I guess I am pretty lucky," replied Thane, straining to hide a smirk.

"There's some standard identity verification and clearance to do back at the AeroDome, but your assistant can begin handling the details now.

You have a direct uplink via the Drone's Beacon. For now, just sit back and enjoy the ride."

I'll take care of the docs, said Selene. **You just relax.**

The TransitDrone soared over the Southern Europa/NeoAlexandrian Neutral Zone. These were fully autonomous buffer and trade zones that were owned and operated by Amazon Industries: the robotics & automation arm of Amazon Global, Inc. No one lived there. From up here, the grid of blue-gray warehouses and connective tracks almost looked like a giant circuit board, etched into the earth.

Block 4,025,535

As they crossed into NeoAlexandrian airspace, the scenery shifted dramatically. Below, the industrial grid gave way to the natural beauty of green rolling hills, their contours softened by a network of glistening silver tributaries that all fed into the great River Thumos - which hadn't existed half a century ago, until the visionary founder of NeoAlexandria led its construction. From this height, the river shimmered like a vital artery, flowing from the towering mountains in the north down into the heart of NeoAlexandria, a city whose towering steel columns and glistening glass domes resurrected the ancient spirits of a grandeur once thought forgotten.

Within fifteen minutes, the outline of the city came into view. The hills met the gleaming skyline where sleek, silver towers rose out of the landscape, interspersed with lush green parks. Thane couldn't quite make it out from this height, but he imagined the park across from his apartment near the Elysian boulevard.

It was such a contrast to where he had just been. While the UN outskirt zones were drab, gray and suffocating, and their city center was as sterile as a hospital ward, NeoAlexandria was alive and vibrant. It seemed to literally breathe. Thane remembered the first time he came to the city. The blend of the natural world and modern technology was striking. Organic beauty combined with the refined, engineered elegance of modern architecture, where reflective glass and steel structures shot upwards, adorned with NeoGothic arches and intricate facades.

As they entered the city perimeter, Thane caught a distant glimpse of the AeroDome, and the swarm of TradeDrones surrounding it, flying in and out with goods from all the members of the Executive Alliance. This trade is what made the city prosperous, and he was a part of it. Thane smiled as the drone descended toward the AeroDome, which was flanked by the great stone and bronze statue of Alexander the Great. It was a fitting symbol for this place: a city built on vision, courage, and the will to achieve the impossible. The moment they touched down, Thane felt a weight lift from his shoulders. He was home.

"Welcome home Mr Drakos," said one of the Hoplites.

"It's good to be back," replied Thane.

"You'll need to head over to the Members Gate for re-entry procedures," the Hoplite added, pointing toward the sleek terminal building.

Don't worry, whispered Selene, **All the docs are completed. You just need to scan and sign.**

I guess this is what it feels like to have a full Sovereign ID eh?

The re-entry process was smooth. NeoAlexandria prided itself on how members were treated. The service was almost as good as the departure lounges in the main terminal, only minus the entertainment and relaxation chambers.

As Thane approached the Members Gate, he was greeted by a NeoAlexandrian border officer. "Welcome home Mr. Drakos," said the officer.

"I've probably said this like ten times now, but seriously ... it's good to be home."

"I'm sure it is. I can see here you've had a rough day."

"It could've been much worse had your boys not arrived in time."

"It's our pleasure to serve," said the officer. "The Sovereign Cross division is one of our city's finest, and they specialize in operations like these."

"They really are," replied Thane, and added, "Not cheap, but worth every Sat."

"Indeed. Everything seems to be in order with the documentation. I can see here that it was all submitted by your assistant. Your extraction was covered by insurance, and your membership is active, so just a quick scan to sign off the contracts, and you're good to go."

Thane leaned forward for the retinal scan. A brief beep signaled his clearance.

"You're all set Mr Drakos. Everything's been sent to your assistant. Enjoy your time back home."

"Thank you," said Thane as he walked through the Member's Gate, down the hall and on into the great arrivals terminal of the AeroDome.

The AeroDome was connected to Tempus—the underground magnetic transport system engineered by the Boring Company half a century ago. Instead of going straight home, Thane took a brief walk through the terminal to pick up a gift for Cleo, who would not be expecting him so soon. The atmosphere was vibrant, a stark contrast to the tube terminals in the UN. Here, people were full of energy, chatting, laughing, and engaging with each other. It was the sound of humanity. The air was clean. The colors were alive. The terminal was a seamless fusion of nature and technology with translucent walls and high ceilings flooding the space with warm, natural light. Vertical gardens, lush with greenery, lined the walls, purifying the air and creating a living, breathing structure. Towering NeoGothic arches framed the sky embodying the city's philosophy of progress, beauty and harmony.

Block 4,025,545

Thane stopped by a boutique and asked the attendant for the finest flowers, chocolates, and wine they had. "Make sure it's the best — price doesn't matter." The attendant smiled and quickly assembled the items into a stunning little gift bag which came out to 1650 Sats. A fortune back in the UN, and a decent sum here in NeoAlexandria. Thane didn't hesitate.

The money he earned from this job would more than set them up for the future. He zapped the attendant 2000.

Thane turned to leave, his mind already anticipating the evening ahead. Cleo wouldn't be expecting him, and that would make the surprise even sweeter. But just as he was about to exit the boutique, he stopped short. There she was. Standing at the entrance, arms crossed. Her bright eyes caught his immediately. She looked both furious, and relieved.

Selene... did you—?

Maybe. The AI sounded smug again. He made a mental note to check her personality settings.

Before he could react, Cleo had walked over and slapped him, the sound sharp and surprising.

"Promise me you'll never do that again!"

Thane rubbed his cheek. He couldn't help but laugh. "Ha! There's my girl." Without missing a beat, he picked her up, ignoring the curious glances of passersby. "I promise."

Cleo grinned and wrapped her arms around him. For a moment, the world outside faded away. The familiar scent of her hair flooded his senses, grounding him in the present.

Thane leaned his head in, and gently kissed her. Cleo kissed him back. The kiss was slow, warm, and filled with the unspoken relief of having made it back.

A New Heroic Age

"Enough of the squalor of democratic humanity. Time to recognize the aristocracy of the Sun. There will form a new aristocracy, irrespective of nationality, of men who have reached the Sun. In the coming era they will rule the world."

D.H. Lawrence, *The Sun Worship*

The path we're on is exactly the one we, as a species, *had* to take. Mingled in with the stupidity is much potential, and if we can find a way to weave the principles of this book together with our profound technological power, Bitcoin, the Internet and our understanding of the mind and consciousness, we will build a civilisation unlike anything that came before it.

My parents would never have understood the nuances around things like seed oils, blue light, relationship polarity, sound digital money or digital creator skills, let alone the myriad of other refined concepts you can find on the internet today. They did what they could with the tools they had, and with the comfort level they were conditioned for. The tools we have at our disposal are so much more powerful, and those who harness them effectively will lay the foundation for their children to truly become supermen and superwomen.

This period of human history will not only herald the largest wealth transfer in human history, but I'd go so far as to call it a speciation event. Those who cut through the noise and find the signal will build significant wealth, networks, and power: they will plant the seeds for dynasties that will one day go to the stars; their descendants will be powerful, strong, noble, and ascendant. At the same time, and in stark contrast, the growing horde of NPCs will become ever-more dependent on a broken state apparatus that needs to continually suck them dry and surveil their every move in order to maintain its fickle grasp of power, and the thinly veiled illusion of safety.

These diametrically opposed trends will set the stage for a true bifurcation. On the one hand, a love of life and a desire to reproduce, build and create will lead to population, power and wealth. On the other, envy and spite, fueled by beliefs such as "women don't need a man" or that there are "37 genders" will lead those who hold them to their own end as failed experiments, or withered branches of their family trees: the first of their line who failed at finding a good partner and raising a family; total biological and social failures, who did nothing but score an own goal to spite their own team.

But... this is nature's way of healing. It has a way of organically removing failed experiments from the gene pool. Beauty and life always win in the end, and this is why I believe that *we had to go through this*. We are the marble, and we are sculpting something new.

> *"Man cannot remake himself without suffering, for he is both the marble and the sculptor."*
>
> Alexis Carrel, Man: The Unknown.

The spirit of greatness most manifest in the "Western Man" has been dormant for too long, like a lion at rest, or a bear in hibernation. The parasites and hyenas have become overly confident and arrogant, thinking they can nip at our heels, torment our families and tear down everything beautiful around us, as if we won't notice. They've confused our tolerance and slumber for weakness. But we are neither weak nor entirely ignorant. We've been asleep and overly courteous, tranquilized by a society we helped construct. Now we are coming awake, and getting angry - which is precisely what the bureaucratic class is most afraid of. They know deep down, as we do, that there has never been a time when the hordes of goblins and trolls were able to stamp out the flame of beauty and virtue. Each era has its heroes, and this one is no different, bar the magnitude of our potential.

This is our moment, and to claim it requires a new code, and a new playbook. While Bitcoin is a measure of wealth, real wealth comes from the virtues we live by. If all we do is create Bitcoin, but continue on living poorly, we have failed. If we allow civilization to devolve into one giant dumpster fire, we have lost. It's time to wake up. We must build, create, construct, and live lives of virtue and meaning.

Confucius said *"Virtue is the root. Wealth is the result."* He might have also said: *It's not that Bitcoin fixes everything - but our choice to use Bitcoin, and to live by ascendant virtues - that really fixes the world.*

The truth is, while Bitcoin's existence might encourage better, more virtuous living, that does not make a virtuous life a given. This is something we must work at. This will require a new playbook and new alliances, formed among those of us who are life-affirming, whether you call yourself a Bitcoiner, AnCap, Libertarian, Christian, Muslim, Pagan, Nietzschean, Faustian, White, European, American, Westerner, Randian, Conservative or whatever. If you're on the side of life, you're with me.

> "History belongs above all to the man of deeds and power, to him who fights a great fight, who needs models, teachers, comforters and cannot find them among his contemporaries."

Friedrich Nietzsche, On the Use and Abuse of History for Life

This 'bushido' is not a new religion, nor does it take the place of your religion. It is a playbook and set of virtues we can all align on. We don't even need to be friends! Just an alliance, of the kind of men who, even though they're not of the same tribe, can have respect for each other. Like the leagues which made up Ancient Greece, Alexander's army or the Crusaders. There's no reason why we cannot be mature enough to ally around virtue. The hardcore Nietzschean Vitalist, Randian Objectivist and Christian Absolutist have far more in common than they have in opposition - and they all for damn sure share a common enemy in the form of the meddling bureaucratic parasite class.

This is how you fight and defeat a larger enemy. You develop the kind of respect that I can only describe as what you feel when "fighting a worthy adversary." The kind when you can look at your opponent and nod at him, and in the nod is everything. Without words, you're saying: *"I know who you are - where you've been. I get it.* **Yes."** And he nods back, because he knows too. This precise energy will keep such an alliance together and lead us to victory. The creeds, religions and tribal cult differences all come second to being men of honor, worthy of respect.

This is why I wrote this book. I'm not here to tell you what to believe, that's up to you to decide. This is a book about the virtues we cannot ignore if our goal is to build an ascendant civilization. Who we become is determined by **how** we behave. The fiat apparatus is completely captured, and there is no return. It will only become more sterile, barren and grotesque, and like an ever-receding piece of land in a flood, there will be less and less available for those who choose to remain. For the rest of us, a new land awaits.

> *"For believe me! — the secret for harvesting from existence the greatest fruitfulness and the greatest enjoyment is: to live dangerously! Build your cities on the slopes of Vesuvius! Send your ships into uncharted seas! Live at war with your peers and yourselves!"*

> *Friedrich Nietzsche, The Gay Science*

There is more than enough room and we can do so much more and so much better with the resources we have on this Earth - to say nothing of the solar system and the galaxy which await. Like Julian Simon, the great 20th century economist, said: *"we can never run out of molecules, only ingenuity."* There is **ALWAYS** more space to claim and energy to harness. Life abhors both a vacuum and a defeatist.

So go forth, and reach for the stars. Feel the burn of conviction, and bend the arc of eternity towards you. Become dangerous. Become... inevitable.

"I know of no better life purpose than to perish in attempting the great and the impossible."

Friedrich Nietzsche, *The Will to Power*

Afterword

In 2022 I took a hiatus from business to travel a little, get married and do some writing. During that time, I binge-listened to more than ten thousand hours of history podcasts and both history and historical fiction on Audible. I think my Audible listening average, alone, for 2022 was 92 hours per week, *alone*. There were moments I got so absorbed in the stories that I forgot what year I was living in.

I took notes during moments of inspiration, but generally just spent that time absorbing ideas and concepts. Your brain is wired to learn more from stories than from abstract philosophy, which is why experience counts so much: it's a *lived* story. Which makes sense considering that narrative is how we've learned since the beginning of time. **History** is a collection of stories about where we came from, and the men and women who bled, suffered, laughed and played, in order to create the civilisation we stand on today. As such it's become a subject very dear to me - and I guess for most men too (we're always thinking of Rome).

When it came time to do the actual writing, what I'd absorbed over that time, and all my life in fact, seemed to come "through me". I put the core of the first major draft together in the course of December 2022, from an Airbnb in Sao Paulo. I'd wake up at 5AM each morning to weave together ideas from notes strewn all over the place. It was all coming together quite nicely until... I started reading Nietzsche's work in January of 2023, and in particular Lise Van Boxel's *Warspeak*. In it I found a kindred spirit that I wish I'd discovered earlier.

Nietzsche was a special mind. Sure, he lost the plot in the end and died alone - but the line between genius and madness is very fine. How many people thought Christ was mad? Was he not also framed as a criminal?

How about Alexander? Caesar? Napoleon? Cortez? Jefferson? How about the more modern great men: Tesla, Ford, Jobs, Musk and Satoshi? The greatest men are also the most prone to insanity because they see reality differently. Oftentimes, what they actually see is the future, and many who were thought crazy at the time were vindicated posthumously. If the modern world tells us anything at all, it's that Nietzsche was one of these prophetic men. The sign of a true visionary is when their work not only remains, but becomes more relevant after their death.

My discovery of Nietzsche's work sent me down a number of rabbit holes which inspired me to write a new draft, much expanded from the first. As the concepts and ideas I had grappled with in the past, but not so clearly articulated, all of a sudden started to unlock, I wrote a second and third draft, each building on the prior. Around the same time, I discovered a brilliant writer on Substack who went by the name of "John Carter." I began reading his work and was immediately captured: not only was it sharp and witty but extremely aligned with my message. My appreciation of his work led me to reach out and enquire if he'd like to edit my book, since I had a disagreement with the original publisher. Looking back now, the extra year that went into the book was the best thing that could've happened. John challenged my half-baked ideas, and encouraged me to elaborate on the better ones.

I went on to write a fifth and sixth draft, at which point the book took on a new energy. Compared to the early drafts (which I may one day publish) there was an ascendant tone in my words. There was a sense of power coming through the pages. The earlier drafts focused a lot on what was wrong with the modern world, and how the warrior past was morally superior, while the new drafts took hold of the lessons from these great men and, like a shield and sword, thrust them into the belly of the nihilistic present and made way for a grand vision of the future. This transformation brought the book to life and increased its quality tenfold.

In the six months that followed, we moved into heavy editing, which produced a seventh and, in the final days of September of 2024, an eighth draft which is the book you're reading now. I'm sure he and I could've gone on for another year, refining it, adding sections, elaborating and cleaning, but we had to draw a line somewhere. In fact, the book had ballooned to 150,000+ words, which we had to cut by 20%. This, my young friend Louis Pomaret described aptly: *"haha writing is the easy part, editing is harsh like cold water on the heated blade. That's where greatness is."*

I believe we found greatness, and in fact, also an opportunity to continue. Some content we cut, because it didn't do the book justice - but some was so good that, quite honestly, warranted its own book. There was an entire "Part 6" in the seventh draft, titled: *"The Metaphysics of War & Beauty."* There was also the beginnings of a much longer *"Visions of the Future"* chapter. The former was entirely extracted and will make up the core content for Book 2 of the Bushido of Bitcoin series of books - which I aim to publish in 2025. The latter was condensed and, as you know if you've read this far, made way for a story to show you what the future might look like, instead of explaining it to you in abstract terms. These "visions of the future" will also form the basis for future Bushido-related books, both fiction and non-fiction.

I look forward to the future. Writing the book changed me. I was in a place of relative darkness and disillusionment when I wrote the first three drafts. My wife would continually tell me *"You live in another world"* and *"you were born in the wrong century."* And she was right - I felt that. But as the book transformed from a 'dark red-pill' into a white pill, and ultimately became a clear pill, so did my outlook on life, my hope for the future and my determination to not only talk about it, but to go on and build.

In the end, that's my hope for you, in reading this book. Ross Stevens very kindly called it a modern day *Declaration of Independence*, which is very humbling. While I'm not sure I deserve such a comparison, I do hope that it inspires modern young men, in the same way the words written by the Founding Fathers of America inspired the young men of their time. The duty sits with you, to make the future better. Life is not going to be all sunshine and rainbows. As Rocky Balboa said: *"it's a mean and nasty place, and it will beat you to your knees permanently if you let it."* The key is that you do not let it, the key is that you get up, and keep moving forward. One foot in front of the other. The future can only be what we make it. So make it beautiful, glorious and ascendant. Leave the bugmen behind.

One final note...

A bunch of people will be offended by different parts of the book, whether it's my sharp views on democracy, equality or the future, my elevation of feudalism or my ideas on Bitcoin as a framework for excellence, as opposed to a panacea for the poor; but the truth can often hurt, and I hope offense gives way to a new understanding of the world. I'm also aware that others will be mad at my weaving together of Christian and Nietzschean principles, calling it blasphemy or hypocrisy. To you, I would like to say this: those who are on the side of life, beauty and goodness must find an alliance. Christians, Nietzscheans, Bitcoiners and Austrians have far more in common with each other than not. Bringing together these worlds and finding common ground is what I hoped to achieve with this book.

Can you imagine what might come of a Christo-Nietzsche-Hoppean worldview, built atop a Bitcoin standard? In my opinion: *the new West.*

So whatever you may think about the compatibility, or lack thereof, of these ideas, I hope that they've inspired or moved you in some way. If you're a Nietzschean, I hope I've brought you closer to Christ, and if you're a Christian, I hope I've brought you closer to Nietzsche. If you're none of these, then perhaps I've revealed new rabbit holes for you to go down. And if I've just pissed you off, that's fine too. As John Lydgate said: *"You can please some of the people all of the time, you can please all of the people some of the time, but you can't please all of the people all of the time."*

Such is life, and such is the exploration of ideas at the edge. This is where I choose to live, and I accept the consequences. Thank you for reading book one of the **Bushido of Bitcoin.**

Aleksandar Svetski
September, 2024

Thankyou

I want to close out by saying thank you for reading this and supporting my work. I hope it was either genuinely eye, mind or soul opening (perhaps all three).

If you'd like to follow me or my other work, you can do so by following me here:

- @SvetskiWrites on X, Instagram and Substack

- @Svetski on Nostr (all of you should be on Nostr)

Or just go to: Linktree.com/Svetski

You can also check out the UnCommunist Manifesto & The Bitcoin Times (both on Amazon), which I co-wrote with many great authors from across the Bitcoin space.

Subscribe to my "Remnant Chronicles" Substack. This is where I will elaborate and workshop the ideas discussed in the book. Keep an eye out for opportunities to go deeper into this work with a community of fellow warriors, and if you would like to reach out to me directly, do so via any of my socials, or email me at: BushidoOfBitcoin@gmail.com

Finally, if you'd like to experience the power of Bitcoin, you can tip me via Lightning or On-Chain below.

Final Ask

The visibility and reach of this book, at least on Amazon, will be influenced by how much and how well it is rated. If you found value in the book, I would sincerely appreciate you leaving a review on Amazon. You can also share free chapters of the book with people by sending them to BushidoOfBitcoin.com.

Thankyou in advance for doing that.

Each share and review goes a long way.

Aleksandar Svetski

Appendix

If you found value in the book, and would like to go deeper, the following are the most valuable resources which I referenced, and I hope come in handy on your journey.

Resources and References

In 2020 I came across a book written by James Clavell, known as Shogun. This incredible piece of historical fiction had a deep impact on my life and really sparked my appreciation for feudal Japanese culture. It reignited my love for history, and spurred me down the rabbit holes which culminated into this book. Shogun has now been turned into a show, which thanks to the inclusion of Hiroyuki Sanada as the main character, did the book justice.

I highly recommend reading it, and the entire saga that follows. Beyond that, I have a full list of books below which I read, in whole or part, listened to and dissected during my deep dive. Below that are some notable substacks and blogs worth subscribing to. The lists are not exhaustive, but I have tried to order each one by influence.

Books

This list contains books which I read during the time I was writing *The Bushido of Bitcoin*:

- Bushido, The Soul of Japan: Inazo Nitobe

- Shogun: James Clavell

- Virtues of War: Steve Pressfield

- Man and Technics: Oswald Spengler

- Warspeak: Lise Van Boxel

- Warrior Ethos: Steven Pressfield

- Alexander the Great and the Macedonian Empire: Kenneth H Harl

- Thus spoke Zarathustra: Friedrich Nietzsche

- The Courtney Series, Books 1 - 13: Wilbur Smith

- The Gay Science: Friedrich Nietzsche

- Decline of the West: Oswald Spengler

- Gates of Hell: Steven Pressfield

- The Moon is a Harsh Mistress: Robert Heinlein

- The Afghan Campaign: Steven Pressfield

- Medieval Europe: Chris Wickham

- Endurance: Alfred Lansing

- A Short History of Man: Progress and Decline: Hans Hermann Hoppe

- The Book of 5 Rings: Miyamoto Musashi

- The Art of War: Sun Tzu

- Man's search for Meaning: Viktor Frankl

- Atlas Shrugged: Ayn Rand

- Attila "The Scourge of God" (full series): William Napier

- Maps of Meaning: Jordan B Peterson

- Killing Rommel: Steven Pressfield

- Metaphysics of War: Julius Evola

- The handbook of Traditional living: Raido

- On pain: Ernst Yünger

- Hagakure: Yamamoto Tsunemoto, William Scott Wilson (Translator)

The following books, while not directly quoted or referenced in the book, I know have influenced my thinking in some way.

- The UnCommunist Manifesto: Aleksandar Svetski & Mark Moss

- Musashi: Eiji Yoshikawa

- The End is Always Near: Dan Carlin

- The Bitcoin Standard: Saifedean Ammous

- The Era of the Crusades: Kenneth H Harl

- Hyperion (The full saga): Dan Simmons

- The Late Middle Ages by Philip Daileader

- Democracy: The God that Failed: Hans Hermann Hoppe

- For a New Liberty: Murray Rothbard

- Starship Troopers: Robert Heinlein

- Modern Man in Search of a Soul: Carl Jung

- Dune: Frank Herbert

- The History of Ancient Rome: Garret G Fagan

- The Madness of Crowds: Douglas Murray

- Rise and Fall of the Third Reich: William L Shirer

- The Wall Speaks: Jerr Rrej

- Training of the Samurai Mind: Thomas Cleary

I'm sure I could continue, but to try and list all of the books, podcasts and essays I've consumed would add another chapter to the book. All I know is that their information is embedded somewhere in my subconscious and it's come out as what you've read here.

Substacks and blogs worth subscribing to

The Remnant Chronicles: https://remnantchronicles.substack.com/
Social 2.0: https://futuresocial.substack.com/
Postcards from Barsoom: https://barsoom.substack.com
The Cat was Never Found: https://markbisone.substack.com
Old Books Club: https://oldbooksguy.substack.com
The American Tribue: https://www.theamericantribune.news
Becoming Noble: https://becomingnoble.substack.com
Born on the Fourth of July: https://williamhunterduncan.substack.com/
Locklin on Science: https://scottlocklin.wordpress.com/

About the Author

I wasn't sure what to write or how to describe myself in this bio. Most people know me for my writing. Whether it's the UnCommunist Manifesto I co-authored with Mark Moss in 2021, or the Bitcoin Times publication, which at the time of this writing has six editions published, alongside 30 world-class authors, or the two million plus words I've written online, via my personal blogs, Zerohedge and Bitcoin Magazine.

So… Am I a writer? An author? What about a content creator? Maybe a Bitcoiner? Or a "right wing Bitcoiner" ? Problem is, that doesn't do my main vocation justice. I've been building businesses for longer than I've been writing.

I came to realize that I have three distinct, but interrelated lives and associated identities, so at the risk of sounding self-important, I've listed them below, in no particular order.

1. Writer/Author.

I love writing. There is something special about exploring and refining one's ideas by splattering them on a page and grappling with their meaning, flow and style. I intend to publish at least another 10 books before my time on this Earth is up, maybe more.

I will also continue to write regularly on my Substack and Nostr via The Remnant Chronicles publication. If you're interested in ideas related to what I covered in this book, and want to get previews for up-coming books, that's the place to go.

2. Entrepreneur.

This was my first vocation, beginning at 13 with trading Pokemon cards and wrestling collectibles. I left University to pursue riches in the business world and along the way made every mistake, broke every rule, earned a fortune and lost it all on multiple occasions - stories I will share one day in writing.

In 2017 I founded the world's first Bitcoin-only savings app: Amber.app, and in 2024, my team and I open sourced the first Bitcoin-centric large language model: *The Spirit of Satoshi*.

Since discovering that much of the AI space is fraught with hype and solutions looking for problems, we found our way into developing a new kind of social platform. Satlantis is a niche social network for nomads, communities, parallel economies, frequent travelers, remote workers, geo-arbiters and sovereign individuals.

I believe I found my personal Ikigai and I intend to dedicate the next decade of my life to this project, so alongside writing about the future in books like this, I'm also actually **building** it. If you'd like to follow that journey, search for the "Social 2.0" publication on Substack or Nostr.

3. Personal/Family.

Last but not least, is my personal life. This is my private enclave, which I share only with my wife and closest of friends. I try to live a unique life full of "magic moments", because once it's all said and done, memories are all you're left with, and legacy is all you can truly leave behind.

If you'd like to discover more, you can do so via any of the following links and social media platforms:

Linktree:
Linktree.com/Svetski

Satlantis & Nostr: @Svetski

Instagram, X and Substack:
@SvetskiWrites

Book 2: The Metaphysics of War and Beauty

The following is a half-chapter from The Metaphysics of War and Beauty, book two of The Bushido of Bitcoin series. As mentioned earlier, I had a lot more to include in this book, but it was getting excessively long. I decided instead to give some of these ideas the time they deserve, in a dedicated follow up to the first book.

This excerpt is from what was one of my favorite original chapters. It is just a teaser, but I hope it whets your appetite for the second book.

Beauty Will Save the World

"If you crush a cockroach, you're a hero. If you crush a butterfly, you're a villain. Morals have aesthetic standards."

Friedrich Nietzsche: Work cited

Of Nietszche's many profound aphorisms, this is one of my favorites because it cuts right to a deep, visceral truth that few want to admit to intellectually, despite agreeing with intuitively.

The beauty of his statement (pun intended) is that the rationalist will argue with it, the equalitarian and democrat will be offended, the moralist will tell you that it's unethical, the theologian will say it's wrong, the hippie will tell you it's cruel and the materialist or atheist will disagree on subjectivist grounds. All of your modern, sensible, 'civilized' conditioning will try to tell you it is unfair... but when push comes to shove, you will step on the cockroach and praise the person who does, while you are very unlikely to do the same to a butterfly - and if you did see someone do it, you would be immediately, intuitively enraged by it. You might not say anything, but you will **feel** the anger, *and this is precisely why it matters.*

Visceral reactions like this reveal the deepest truths. They go beyond the intellect and our rational psyche. They are physio-psychologically true and reside deep in our subconscious. These are instincts, developed over thousands of years of human experience. The lessons learned and heuristics developed across generations become the intuition we store in our blood, bodies and DNA - none of which can lie.

Beauty transcends dimension. It is found in the material and the metaphysical, the poor and the rich, the small and the large, the young and the very old, the perfect and the imperfect.

Beauty is simultaneously objective and subjective. It's the only thing we know of with this paradoxical quality, other than the divine (which says a lot about what beauty really is). Beauty is everlasting and fleeting, powerful and fragile, dangerous and nurturing, all at the same time. Beauty can be found both in war and peace, conflict and cooperation, violence and love.

> *"Music is liquid architecture, architecture is frozen music".*

> *Johann Wolfgang von Goethe*

Few things are as beautiful (or violent) as a thunderstorm crackling across the sky, a lion hunting, or a volcano erupting. Few things are as beautiful (or peaceful) as the calm and stillness of the mountains or a tranquil cove in the Mediterranean Sea. There is beauty in the cold, barren, Antarctic ice caps, and in the hot rolling desert sand dunes of Arabia. There is beauty in the smooth contours of a woman's body, and the jagged edges of a sheer rock cliff face. There is beauty in the creation of life and the explosion of an orgasm. In a cavalry charge and in the march of a phalanx. Beauty is found in both deed and object. In both the uncharted, wild ocean of the Atlantic, and in its historic crossing. It is both natural and man made. There is beauty in the precision of a Swiss-made watch and in the chaos of the Amazonian jungle. There is beauty in the creative destruction of deep work and in the leisure of stillness. The combustion engine and the jet airline cutting through the sky are both marvels of engineering and beautiful in their own right. Likewise there is deep and profound beauty in the sword which has, throughout the centuries, shed the blood of many foes.

Beauty is beyond rational, but we can also rationalize it. It is beyond measurement, but we can in fact measure it, because it's found in the fractals that make up life: the Fibonacci sequence, the golden ratio, musical octaves, geometry, mathematics and numbers themselves. These patterns are not only beautiful, they underpin the structure and melody of the universe (uni-verse: one-song). Great artists can hear this song, and when they do, they draw the beauty out for the rest of us to appreciate. Men like Newton, Tesla, and other great thinkers of the world can see these patterns in their mind's eye, and with it, they can engineer the beautiful structures, motors, and engines that power the world. We are all in some way connected to this 'source', and when we tap into it, we produce the most beautiful things.

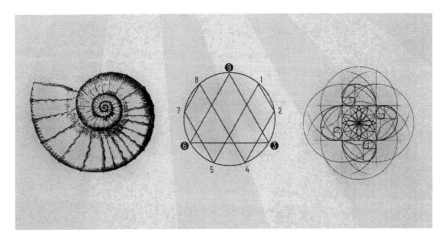

Beauty is the right thing at the right time. There is a time for war, and there is a time for peace. There is a time for life, to violently create, grow and expand. There is a time for it to slow down and take a moment of respite.

"To every thing there is a season, and a time to every purpose under the heaven:
A time to be born, and a time to die; a time to plant, and a time to pluck up that which is planted;
A time to kill, and a time to heal; a time to break down, and a time to build up;
A time to weep, and a time to laugh; a time to mourn, and a time to dance;
A time to cast away stones, and a time to gather stones together; a time to embrace, and a time to refrain from embracing;
A time to get, and a time to lose; a time to keep, and a time to cast away;
A time to rend, and a time to sew; a time to keep silence, and a time to speak;
A time to love, and a time to hate; a time of war, and a time of peace."

The Bible, KJV, Ecclesiastes 3:1-8,

Beauty, like truth, cannot be decreed - it can only be recognised. Beauty is something we feel, not something we think. Rationalization comes after the fact. You cannot be told a thing is beautiful; you just know it. The sunrise, the mountains, a beautiful face, a Van Gogh piece, an Aston Martin or the elegant curves of a beautiful woman. We might experience these in unique ways, but we all recognise their beauty intuitively because they ignite a feeling of some sort in us, be that awe, admiration, desire, love, appreciation, or even envy.

"Beauty is a form of Genius — is higher, indeed, than Genius, as it needs no explanation. It is of the great facts of the world, like sunlight, or spring-time, or the reflection in dark waters of that silver shell we call the moon".

Oscar Wild, Picture of Dorian Gray

The opposite of beauty, ugliness, has the same visceral characteristics. You know it when you see it. It has a repulsive effect. Compare for instance a Dylan Mulvaney to a Monica Belucci. Unless you have some sort of mental derangement or psychological deformity, you intuitively know (whether you're man or woman, gay or straight) that Monica Belucci is beautiful while Mulvaney is ugly. In fact, a good test for whether or not someone is psychologically sound, is their answer to this question.

This specific example tells us a lot about the practical role beauty plays in life and the universe. It acts like a magnet - it is literally an attractor - drawing or compelling us toward that which is life-affirming. Belucci is an example of a woman that represents fertility and life, while Mulvaney represents the end of the line, or a failed experiment. You don't need to rationalize any of it. You instinctively know the truth. We are biologically wired to value such beauty because it's a signal for health and vitality (evidenced by the multi-trillion dollar health and beauty industries).

"Beauty is the splendor of truth."

Plato

Truth is another key word here. If the highest good were the peak of a mountain, truth would be one slope while beauty was the other. They are deeply entwined and beyond their metaphysical relationship, serve the similarly practical purpose of helping us predict the future. The more true something is, the more likely it is to result in accurate decision-making, thus decreasing uncertainty and increasing survivability. Similarly, organic beauty which often represents something Lindy (time-tested), well-formed and healthy, increases the probabilities of survival and continuation.

This brings up another key point of confusion. *Beauty is organic.* In the same way you cannot decree it, you cannot fake it - at least not for long. The beauty industry, despite all the money and effort that goes toward creating artificial beauty, still falls short of natural beauty which can only be developed over generations through organic means: intentional breeding, healthy upbringing, adherence to natural, timeless principles. Biohacking, shortcuts, make-up and plastic surgery will only deceive you. The same goes for the food industry, and the myriad products developed to try and emulate what looks naturally beautiful and appetizing. Billions are spent each year on artificial colors and flavors in order to pass things off as appealing (beautiful), but ultimately make you sick and desensitize your natural taste buds - to say nothing of abominations such as fake meat, dairy alternatives and seed oils.

It's no coincidence that truth and beauty are the most co-opted qualities of all, and even more-so in a broken society. They are fundamentally critical for life. But in the same way that artificial truths (lies) have a short life, artificial beauty does too. This is why the evil witch loses in the end. She covets beauty because she doesn't truly possess it herself. She tries to take that which is not hers, and cannot appreciate the inevitability of the cycle.

Here we find another paradox of beauty: it is both within reach and out of reach. It is both eternal and ephemeral. While its highest manifestation (God) is out of our reach, it acts as a North Star and an intuitive guide to life. While beauty is timeless, you're not supposed to be beautiful forever. This is a feature, not a bug. When people say: *"oh but beauty fades"* in an attempt to discredit its importance, they actually reinforce it. Yes! Beauty DOES fade, but it does so for a reason: so that we are compelled to continue! Beauty is not stagnant. The entire point of it is that while you may get close to it, and some may even reach it, neither you, nor I, can ever hold onto it. Those who touch, taste, smell and experience it, do so for a fleeting moment, before it manifests elsewhere and shines brighter - once again, compelling the next generation to pursue, discover, express and create.

Realizing this forces us to face and come to terms with the fact that our time in the limelight is limited and we will die. And when we do, the only questions remaining are how, when and why. There is no living forever. Peter Pan is a fantasy for a reason and no amount of science, pill popping nonsense or Bryan Johnson caricatures will change that. We are not supposed to remain young forever. Life, like everything else which exists, is made up of seasons as cycles....

See you, in the second book of The Bushido of Bitcoin.

Made in the USA
Middletown, DE
11 November 2024

64343375R00314